Diversity and Inclusion Research

Series Editor
Thomas Köllen
Institute of Organization and HRM
University of Bern
Bern, Switzerland

The book series 'Diversity and Inclusion Research' examines the facets of diversity in a variety of contexts, as well as approaches to and perspectives on diversity and inclusion. It presents organizational research on workforce diversity, and covers diversity and inclusion-related issues within communities, cities, regions, nations, and societies.

The series welcomes functional and intersectional perspectives on diversity, as well as constructivist perspectives on processes of "doing" or "performing" diversity. In terms of inclusion, it welcomes research on broader initiatives (such as generalized diversity management approaches), as well as on practices of inclusion that focus on specific dimensions of diversity; these can include age, appearance, ethnicity, disability, gender, gender identity, nationality, race, religion, sexual orientation, sex, or any other characteristic or demographic in which persons can differ from each other, or, conversely, which they share.

The series publishes research from the broad range of academic disciplines within the social sciences (e.g. economics and business administration, linguistics, political science, history, law, psychology, sociology, geography, and education) and humanities (e.g. philosophy and religion). It strongly encourages interdisciplinary and transdisciplinary research, as well as critical perspectives on diversity and inclusion-related issues. By welcoming research from a variety of sectoral, national, and cultural contexts, the series will make an essential contribution to shaping the academic discourse on diversity and inclusion.

Despoina Anagnostopoulou
Editor

European Identities, Inclusion and Equality

Social Exclusion of Vulnerable Groups in the European Union

Springer

Editor
Despoina Anagnostopoulou
International and European Studies
University of Macedonia
Thessaloniki, Greece

ISSN 2662-5997 ISSN 2662-6004 (electronic)
Diversity and Inclusion Research
ISBN 978-3-031-90601-5 ISBN 978-3-031-90602-2 (eBook)
https://doi.org/10.1007/978-3-031-90602-2

This Springer imprint is published by the registered company Springer Nature Switzerland AG
The registered company address is: Gewerbestrasse 11, 6330 Cham, Switzerland

In collaboration with the Centre of International and European Economic Law (Thessaloniki, Greece)

and the UNESCO Chair of Intercultural Policy for an Active Citizenship and Solidarity, University of Macedonia (Thessaloniki, Greece)

Co-funded by the Erasmus+ Programme of the European Union

About the Jean Monnet Project EUVadis at the University of Macedonia, Greece

This contributed volume presents the research outcomes of the Jean Monnet Project "*Policy Discourses on Intercultural Dialogue, EU Values, and Diversity*" (known with the acronym *EUVadis*), conducted at the Department of International and European Studies of the University of Macedonia, Greece, and co-funded by the European Commission (EACEA), ERASMUS+ Jean Monnet Action Program.

The book encapsulates the findings of research and discussion undertaken within the framework of the Project's Research Axis Two, titled "*European Identities, Inclusion, and Equality,*" coordinated by Professor Despoina Anagnostopoulou. The research axis' events included: (a) a roundtable discussion on "*The Status and Image of Non-Europeans in European Societies*" in collaboration with the UNESCO Chair of Intercultural Policy for an Active Citizenship and Solidarity at the University of Macedonia; and (b) a 2-day online conference on "*Social Exclusion, Vulnerable Groups, and the New EU Social Rights Pillar*", co-organized with the Center of International and European Economic Law, in Thessaloniki.

The Jean Monnet Project EUVadis was awarded to the University of Macedonia in July 2018, following its selection for co-funding by the ERASMUS+ Jean Monnet Action Program. The Project EUVadis started in September 2018, halted its progress during the COVID-19 pandemic period, and was concluded at the end of 2022.

Its purpose was to stimulate research, reflection, and dialogue in the field of European integration studies, as well as promote debate, the flow of knowledge, and the provision of new research insights, with a particular emphasis on EU values, diversity, and intercultural dialogue from a multidisciplinary perspective.

Research under the Jean Monnet Project was conducted across four key thematic axes, which included the organization of roundtable discussions, conferences, and research:

- Axis One: Fundamental Rights, Values, and Diversity
- Axis Two: European Identities, Inclusion, and Equality
- Axis Three: Citizenship, Security, and External Relations
- Axis Four: EU Security Watchspot.

The EU Security Watchspot included the EU Security Database, and a series of relevant Guest Lectures. It was designed to report, discuss, and analyze current EU security affairs, collect commentaries on security, EU legislation, and case law on terrorism by the EU Court of Justice and the European Court of Human Rights. Axis Four was coordinated by Associate Professor Fotini Bellou, University of Macedonia, Head of the EU Security Watchspot.

In addition to the four research axes, two seminars were organized, titled "*The Challenges for European Societies*" and "*Intercultural Dialogue as a European Project.*" The research was further enriched by study visits of the Project's researchers to universities and research institutes in the United States (New York) and Canada (Quebec).

This ambitious initiative would not have been possible without the co-funding provided by the ERASMUS+ / Jean Monnet Action, which significantly enhanced the research capabilities and outreach of the researchers at the University of Macedonia.

Additional information, along with manuals and working papers, is uploaded on the official website of the Jean Monnet Project EUVadis at jmpeuvadis.uom.gr, a webpage designed and managed by Ms Angeliki-Aliki Hapsanidou-Vidaki, graduate of the Department of International and European Studies, University of Macedonia.

The Editor

Despoina Anagnostopoulou
Academic Coordinator of the Jean Monnet Project

Acknowledgments

As the Editor of the present contributed volume and the Academic Coordinator of the Jean Monnet Project "*Policy Discourses on Intercultural Dialogue, EU Values, and Diversity,*" I would like to thank all the distinguished speakers and contributors in this volume, each and every one individually, and all those who supported the Jean Monnet Project EUVadis in organizing all the conferences and events.

I am thankful to Professor Christina Deligianni (Jean Monnet Chair, Aristotle University of Thessaloniki, Director of the Centre of International and European Economic Law in Thessaloniki), for co-organizing and participating in our joint international e-conference, titled "*Social Exclusion, Vulnerable Groups, and the New EU Social Rights Pillar*" on March 5–6, 2021.

I would also like to thank the team of the UNESCO Chair "Intercultural Policy for an Active Citizenship and Solidarity of the University of Macedonia," who helped co-organize the conference "The Status and Image of Non-Europeans in European Societies," on December 5, 2019.

The project would not have been possible without Dr. Nikolaos Gaitenidis, Adjunct Lecturer at the Department of Political Sciences, Aristotle University of Thessaloniki, and Adjunct Lecturer in the Master's Program titled "EU Policies on Youth, Education, Entrepreneurship and Culture" at the University of Macedonia. He organized organized the submission of the successful Jean Monnet application and served as one of the principal researchers of the Project. His valuable support has always been welcome since 2012.

I am also grateful to Ms Antonia Koumpoti, LLM in International Studies, University of Macedonia, MA, Democritus University of Thrace, Konrad Adenauer Scholar, who has been selected as the Research and Project Management Assistant of the Jean Monnet Project EUVadis in 2019–2020. She has provided professional work in preparing the events and activities of the Jean Monnet Project and, in particular, the roundtable discussion on "*The Status and Image of Non-Europeans in European Societies*". She also contributed in coordinating the authors' submission and the relevant transcript procedure as well as in editing in the early preparation stages of this collective volume.

I would like to warmly thank Ms Maria Brokou, MA in European Youth Policies, University of Macedonia, former Accredited Parliamentary Assistant at the European Parliament during the 2014–2019 term, and researcher at the Jean Monnet Project. She has helped me organize, inter alia, the 2-day e-conference "*Social*

Exclusion, Vulnerable Groups, and the New EU Social Rights Pillar". She also contributed in drafting the publication proposal and she conducted the initial review of the chapters submitted.

Furthermore, I would like to express my appreciation to the interns of the Jean Monnet Project EUVadis for their excellent voluntary work. They assisted in the administrative support during the conferences, in ensuring the uniformity of the referencing system used in the early submitted book chapters, and in reviewing the use of English language. It is with great pleasure that I acknowledge them individually, grouped as follows: (a) the students of the University of Macedonia: Anastasia Chatzifotiou (February 2020–June 2021), Mary Chalyvopoulou (October 2019–March 2020), Georgia Tsalgini (January–March 2020), and Angeliki-Aliki Hapsanidou-Vidaki (October 2019–March 2020); (b) the graduates of the Department of English Language of Aristotle University of Thessaloniki: Ms Elisavet Sidiropoulou (February 2020–January 2021), Christos Natskos (February–March 2020), and Fotini Karagianni (February–March 2020); and (c) the students at the Law School of the Aristotle University of Thessaloniki: Vasiliki Liaskou, Nikoleta Stavroula Tsakaleri, and Theodora Zarkada (January–March 2020).

My sincere acknowledgments are addressed to Mrs Korina Asteriou and Mrs Malvina Kontou, PdD candidates, University of Macedonia, as well as Ms Olympia Toufexi, UNESCO Chair trainee and undergraduate student at the Department of International and European Studies, University of Macedonia, who undertook the final review of the use of the referencing system and confirmed authors' bibliographical sources and legal referencing.

Special thanks are due to Mr Jordan Nordenhaug, a sociologist and graduate student in Human Rights and Migration Studies Master's Programme at the University of Macedonia, a native speaker of the English language. He volunteered to provide professional-level English language revision and manuscript copy editing assistance for certain chapters of this contributed volume.

Finally, I would like to express my gratitude to the Jean Monnet Team in EACEA and, most of all, to the project officer Ms Olga Martin-Gonzalez, for her valuable advice and support during all the activities of the Jean Monnet Project EUVadis. My warm thanks go to Springer publications, and in particular Mr Niko Chtouris and Professor Thomas Köllen, for accepting this book as part of the publication series "Diversity and Inclusion Research" and the Production Editor, Mr Parthiban Gujilan Kannan.

None of this would have been possible without the Erasmus+/Jean Monnet Action co-funding, which contributed significantly to the outwardness and cross-fertilization of our research.

Disclaimer

The European Commission's support for the production of this publication does not constitute endorsement of the contents, which reflects the views only of the authors, and the Commission cannot be held responsible for any use which may be made of the information contained therein.

Contents

Part III The Role of the European Union and National Policies in Fighting Social Exclusion Based on Racial Origin and Other Characteristics

Part IV Contemporary Challenges and Solutions Proposed

Contributors

Sofia Adam Department of Social Policy, Democritus University of Thrace, Komotini, Greece

Tawhida Ahmed City Law School, University of London, London, UK

Despoina Anagnostopoulou Department of International and European Studies, University of Macedonia, Thessaloniki, Greece

Kalliopi Chainoglou Department of International and European Studies, University of Macedonia, Thessaloniki, Greece

Stella Christoforidou Dr. Juris, Post-doc Researcher, Law School of the Aristotle University of Thessaloniki, Thessaloniki, Greece

Nuno Ferreira School of Law, Politics and Sociology, University of Sussex, Sussex, UK

Delia Ferri Maynooth University School of Law and Criminology, Maynooth, Ireland

Christos A. Frangonikolopoulos School of Journalism and Mass Communications, Jean Monnet Chair on European Union Public Diplomacy, Aristotle University of Thessaloniki, Thessaloniki, Greece

Athanasios Grammenos Council for International Relations, Athens, Greece

Sophia Kaitatzi-Whitlock School of Journalism and Mass Communications, Aristotle University of Thessaloniki, Thessaloniki, Greece

Marianthi Karatsiori Department of Educational and Social Policy, University of Macedonia, Thessaloniki, Greece

Anna Korneeva Department of History and Ethnology, Democritus University of Thrace, Komotini, Greece

Dimitrios I. Koukiadis School of Law, University of Nicosia, Nicosia, Cyprus

Alexandros Kyriakidis Department of Political Sciences, Aristotle University of Macedonia, Thessaloniki, Greece

Kalliopi Lykovardi Deputy Ombusperson, Athens, Greece

Tina Magazzini Czech Academy of Sciences, Institute of Ethnology, Prague, Czechia

Ioannis Papadopoulos Department of International and European Studies, Center for Research on Democracy and Law, University of Macedonia, Thessaloniki, Greece

Anastasia Poulou Administrative Court of First Instance, Athens, Greece

School of Law, National and Kapodistrian University of Athens, Athens, Greece

Eleni Siapikoudi Department for Balkan, Slavic and Oriental Studies, University of Macedonia, Thessaloniki, Greece

Eleni Sideri Department of Balkan, Slavic and Oriental Studies, University of Macedonia, Thessaloniki, Greece

George N. Theodosis Department of Law, Democritus University of Thrace, Komotini, Greece

European Committee of Social Rights, Strasbourg Cedex, France

Vlasis Vlasidis Department for Balkan, Slavic and Oriental Studies, University of Macedonia, Thessaloniki, Greece

Philippa Watson City Law School, City St George's, University of London, London, UK

Barrister, Essex Court Chambers, London, UK

List of Figures

Zillennials Versus Millennials: Attitudes Toward Gender, Culture, and Migration

List of Tables

Zillennials Versus Millennials: Attitudes Toward Gender, Culture, and Migration

Introduction

Despoina Anagnostopoulou

Abstract

The aim of this contributed volume is to discuss the effectiveness of EU legal tools, as well as equality and social policies, in addressing discrimination and social exclusion at both EU and national levels. Through robust theoretical analyses and case studies, it explores their interplay with identities, stereotypes, diversity, and inclusion of vulnerable groups, offering a comprehensive interdisciplinary review of the way legal principles and policies translate into societal progress and inclusion.

The book consists of four parts. The *first part* emphasizes the role of identity politics and persisting stereotypes in social exclusion. The dilemma "enemy or victim," media portrayal, intergenerational attitudes and revisionism are some of the topics discussed. The *second part* is based on a social rights/policy approach. It discusses the significance of the European Social Charter and the EU Charter of Fundamental Rights, as well as the impact of decision-making methods on the effective governance of the European Pillar of Social Rights. The *third part* evaluates the EU and national equality law and policies and the degree they confront structural discrimination against vulnerable groups, such as Romani people, persons with disabilities, intersex and non-binary persons. The *fourth part* presents state and society initiatives against poverty and marginalization, focusing on the 2010–2018 Greek socio-economic crisis and on the digitalization trend, as well as the importance of judicial review to protect individual and social rights in times of austerity.

D. Anagnostopoulou (✉)
Department of International and European Studies, University of Macedonia, Thessaloniki, Greece
e-mail: danag@uom.edu.gr

D. Anagnostopoulou (ed.), *European Identities, Inclusion and Equality*, Diversity and Inclusion Research, https://doi.org/10.1007/978-3-031-90602-2_1

Introduction to the Topics Covered in the Book

The present book *European Identities, Diversity, and Inclusion - Social Exclusion of Vulnerable Groups in the European Union* employs an interdisciplinary and intersectional approach to present recent trends related to social exclusion of vulnerable groups. The topics covered include stereotypes for vulnerable groups and identity representation in media and policy-making; efficacy of social rights protection and EU social policy; confronting structural discrimination with non-discrimination legislation and equality policies; and the promotion of inclusion policies by the EU and member states, especially in times of austerity and digitalization. The central concept of the book revolves around the themes of social exclusion and discrimination. Social exclusion:

> *"involves the lack or denial of resources, rights, goods, and services and the inability to participate in the normal relationships and activities, available to the majority of people in society, whether in economic, social, cultural, or political arenas."* (Levitas et al., 2007, pp. 9 and 25).

Non-discrimination and equality are *sine qua non* prerequisites to fight the multidimensional phenomenon of social exclusion. The principle of non-discrimination, recognized as *jus cogens* at the international level, serves as a cornerstone for ensuring the enjoyment of human rights by all human beings. It prohibits states from treating individuals in similar situations differently without an objective and reasonable justification. The non-discrimination principle is enshrined in numerous international conventions and covenants under the auspices of the United Nations, such as Articles 2 and 26 of the International Covenant on Civil and Political Rights (1966).

At the regional level, the principle of non-discrimination is enshrined in Article 14 of the European Convention on Human Rights (1950) and articulated in the case law of the European Court of Human Rights (see, for example, European Court of Human Rights, 2024). Specifically, at the EU level, the prohibition of discrimination on grounds of nationality and equal pay for men and women were proclaimed since 1958 (Articles 7, 48 and 112 of the EEC Treaty). The Treaty of Amsterdam (1999) provided a legal basis for EU legislation prohibiting discrimination on many grounds (Article 13 of the Treaty of the European Community (TEC), now Article 19 of the Treaty on the Functioning of the European Union (TFEU)). The Lisbon Treaty (2009) mainstreamed the principle of non-discrimination in EU policies, and guaranteed equality as an EU value (Articles 8 and 10 TFEU and Articles 2 and 3 of the Treaty on European Union (TEU)). The EU Charter of Fundamental Rights (2000 and 2009) enhanced the EU commitment, explicitly prohibiting discrimination on grounds of "*sex, race, colour, ethnic or social origin, genetic features, language, religion or belief, political or any other opinion, membership of a national minority, property, birth, disability, age or sexual orientation*" (Article 21 EUCFR). Its dedicated chapter on "Equality" affirms additional rights for children and elderly as well as respect for cultural, religious or linguistic diversity. The Court of Justice of the European Union has played a crucial role in upholding the principle of non-discrimination (European Union Agency for Fundamental Rights, 2018). All these provisions demonstrate a robust EU commitment to embedding diversity, equality, and inclusion into all EU policies.

Combating social exclusion has been expressly included as an objective of EU social policy since 1999, with the Treaty of Amsterdam (Articles 117–118 TEC). Since 2009, it is embedded in the Treaty on the European Union and the Treaty on the Functioning of the European Union (as a societal value of a pluralist and tolerant society in Article 2 TEU, as a goal in Article 3 para. 3 TEU and as a policy aim in Article 153 TFEU). The EU Charter of Fundamental Rights promotes the fight against social exclusion, stating that:

> "*In order to combat social exclusion and poverty, the Union recognises and respects the right to social and housing assistance so as to ensure a decent existence for all those who lack sufficient resources, in accordance with the rules laid down by Union law and national laws and practices*" (Article 34 para. 3 EUCFR).

In 2020, the European Commission President, *Ursula von der Leyen*, proclaimed "a Union of Equality" as one of the European Commission's priorities. She also announced a 5-year anti-racism action plan for the EU in order to tackle the root causes of structural racism through legislative measures complemented by specific action plans (European Commission, 2020). The EU has long funded anti-discrimination initiatives and programs, including "Daphne" (since 1997), "Progress" (since 2007), "Fundamental Rights and Citizenship" (2007–2013), and "Rights, Equality and Citizenship" (2014–2020). In 2021, the EU intensified its efforts: It launched the program "Citizens, Equality, Rights and Values" (2021–2027) and also established the "European Social Fund Plus" (ESF+), which co-funds actions aimed at fighting poverty and exclusion, combating discrimination and facilitating access to the labor market (Regulation (EU) 2021/1057, 2021).

However, stereotypes, discrimination and social exclusion are still present in our societies, as confirmed by European Parliament Resolutions on antisemitism and antigypsyism (e.g. European Parliament Resolution, 2017; European Parliament Resolution, 2019) and European Commission strategies against social exclusion (e.g. European Commission, 2010). Why, then, does social exclusion continue to persist in Europe despite the existing legal tools and the social inclusion policies at both national and EU levels? This contributed volume aims to contribute to the discussion of whether the EU and its member states, with their multilevel legal and policy tools, adequately take into account all parameters that lead to the social exclusion of vulnerable groups.

The Structure of the Book

The book consists of four parts. The *first part* of the book pertains to identity politics, stereotypes and the eternal question of "Us" against the "Other." The first chapter by *Assistant Professor Eleni Sideri* (University of Macedonia) analyzes the role of stereotypes in simplifying identities, reducing diversity, stigmatizing the "Other," reinforcing social inequalities and constructing collective identities. Based on a strong theoretical background, integrating narratives and examples, Professor Sideri explains the structure, function and practice of stereotypes in distinguishing the boundaries of the Self and the Other, organizing the latter into categories. Following a historic trajectory of the development of European supremacy stereotypes from the Enlightenment up to the current refugee crisis, she uses the example of the complexity of modern Greek identity. She highlights the adaptation and persistence of stereotypes in contemporary society and everyday communication and emphasizes the importance of uncovering the actors systematically employing stereotypical images of others.

The European media's portrayal of the refugees and its implications for human rights or political manipulation are explored by *Professor Christos Frangonikolopoulos* (Aristotle University of Thessaloniki). He explains that there are two dominating frames in European media coverage: the refugee as a "threat" to national security or cultural identity that should be excluded from "our" community to the benefit of right-wing movements; and the refugee as a "victim" figure, towards whom Europeans have moral responsibility and should show solidarity with humanitarian aid. By addressing media myths and giving examples of effective media practices, the author emphasizes the need for a new communication strategy that allows migrants to speak for themselves. Such strategy could contribute in promoting their self-representation and in fostering a more inclusive and constructive public discourse, favoring the development of an image of immigrants and refugees as people with their own story and identity. He believes that "through the transformation of the migrant from *object* – of our compassion, our collective fear, our discrimination, tolerance, or integration – to an *active subject*, public communication will be able to produce alternative discourses." He also calls for peace journalism which provides comprehensive coverage of conflicts' roots, long-term consequences, and possible solutions, thus fostering constructive societal debate and promoting inclusion.

Professor Emerita Sophia Kaitatzi-Whitlock (Aristotle University of Thessaloniki) critically examines "Turkey's instrumentalization of refugees" to the detriment of Greece and the European Union as well as refugee rights. This instrumentalization is facilitated by the uniform, generalized identity often assigned to the refugees by officials, media, and NGO workers, disregarding the rich diversity of their cultural, religious, and political backgrounds. Refugees are depicted as either helpless victims or unwelcome trespassers, with no control over their lives. The author meticulously documents Turkey's evolving role as a host state to millions of refugees and its strategic exploitation of this position to negotiate with powerful international actors, contrasting these actions with international law, including the Geneva Convention of 1951. She focuses on the February 2020 incident at the Greek-Turkish border at Evros-Alexandroupolis that was used to portray Europeans as cruel and inhumane for denying entry to migrants. In her conclusion, the author underscores the urgent need for a cohesive and proactive EU refugee policy to address these challenges and counteract policy inertia.

The factors that influence intergenerational perceptions and attitudes towards diversity in comparison with social stereotypes adopted by undergraduate university students are discussed in the fourth chapter titled "Zillennials versus Millennials: Attitudes toward Gender, Culture, and Migration." Based on a strong theoretical background and a survey-based methodology, *Dr Marianthi Karatsiori* (University of Macedonia) analyzes the data collected through an online questionnaire which was distributed among students of two different generations and from diverse academic disciplines. Discussion of data is made with the use of established theoretical frameworks, including Bennett's Developmental Model of Intercultural Sensitivity and Byram's Model of Intercultural Communicative Competence, to evaluate participants' intercultural skills and attitudes. As the first research of its kind conducted at a Greek university, the author emphasizes the evolving perspectives of younger generations in Greece who seem to reject traditional stereotypes and demonstrate high intercultural awareness. The author highlights the importance of fostering intercultural competences in academic settings and adopting University strategies enhancing students' abilities to contribute to increasingly diverse societies.

Identity politics at the national level and the issue of creation and evolution of a national identity are analyzed in the chapter written by *Professor Vlasis Vlasidis* (University of Macedonia), *Dr. Athanasios Grammenos* (Council of International Relations), *Eleni Siapikoudi* (University of Macedonia), and *Anna Korneeva* (Democritus University of Thrace). They examine the sociopolitical development of a collective cultural and historical identity, focusing on the "Macedonian Issue" and the impact of the Prespa Agreement (2018). They analyze identity politics in the broader historical disputes of the Balkans, and the clash of the national identity of North Macedonia with the national identities in Greece and Bulgaria. The study explains that a specific collective identity can be acknowledged in different ways, using language, history, religion, and cultural heritage, so that it could be identified not only by the members of a certain state but also by other states in order to differentiate itself from the "others." The authors conclude that a national identity is a dynamic construct shaped by historical, cultural, and political factors. The collective understanding of the community, the cultural and historical representations of the past, and the public discourses are rooted in a society and its way of thinking, and need time and willingness to change.

The second part of the book discusses the role and enforceability of social rights in promoting social inclusion in the framework of the European Social Charter of the Council of Europe, the EU Charter of Fundamental Rights, and the European Pillar of Social Rights.

In his chapter *Assistant Professor George N. Theodosis* (Democritus University of Thrace) analyzes the interplay between two Charters protecting social rights in Europe: The first one is the European Social Charter (ESC) of the Council of Europe, adopted in 1961 and amended in 1996, which features an "*à la carte*" system that results in a non-uniform social protection across its member states. The second one is the EU Charter of Fundamental Rights (CFREU), adopted in 2000 and given legally binding force in 2009, which recognizes only limited social rights-and primarily as "principles" rather than "enforceable rights." Professor Theodosis highlights the challenges and limitations in the implementation and enforcement of social rights under these two Charters, particularly in light of successive crises in Europe, caused by austerity measures and by the Ukraine war. He evaluates the ESC's significance on EU social law and vice versa by examining the two Charters' content similarities and disparities and their seemingly reduced mutual influence. He then focuses on the justiciability of social rights enshrined in the two Charters and the effectiveness of their protection mechanisms. He also examines national and CJEU case law on the horizontal direct effect of certain social rights, expressing optimism for the enhancement of social rights protection in Europe.

Dr Alexandros Kyriakidis (Aristotle University of Thessaloniki) and *Professor Ioannis Papadopoulos* (University of Macedonia) explore the impact of the EU governance method selected on the effective implementation of the 2017-introduced European Pillar of Social Rights (EPSR) at the EU social policy multilevel system. Based on a theoretical analysis, the authors evaluate benefits and challenges for EPSR, derived by the use of the Open Method of Coordination (OMC) as a network-based flexible governance in comparison with the Community Method (CM) resulting in binding and enforceable legal provisions. Following an examination of EPSR trajectory and principles in the context of EU social policy, the main position adopted by the authors is that EPSR integrates OMC principles (e.g. benchmarking and peer learning) with CM mechanisms (e.g. legislative measures). Thus, the authors advocate for a hybrid governance model, combining OMC's flexibility with CM's binding force, to maximize the EPSR's effectiveness.

The *third part* of the book pertains to the implementation of the prohibition of discrimination in the European Union. Its purpose is to answer the question of whether the EU and its member states, with its legal tools and policies on equality, can efficiently address structural discrimination and social exclusion using case studies from Greece, Italy and Spain.

This part opens with two chapters focusing on the Roma(ni) people as the most deprived minority in Europe. In the first chapter, *Professors Tawhida Ahmed* (City, University of London) and *Nuno Ferreira* (University of Sussex) document the (in) efficiency of EU legislation enforcing formal equality and soft policy measures aimed at supporting Romani people, concluding that structural antigypsyism in EU member states is the key negative factor. Then they examine *Amartya Sen*'s "capabilities theory" as a potential alternative framework to empower Romani individuals beyond mere access to resources. In assessing the relevant EU law and policy through the lens of the capabilities approach, the authors identify systemic failures in protecting Romani rights, including the lack of legally binding measures against antigypsyism, ineffective enforcement of anti-discrimination laws, inadequate institutional support and limited participation of Romani communities in policymaking. They suggest that the EU should adopt a multipronged strategy, which could include the use of Article 7 TEU procedure, the adoption of Romani-specific hard-law measures, and the establishment of a Romani Truth and Reconciliation Commission. The authors argue that without substantial reforms, the EU's efforts will continue to fall short of achieving meaningful and sustainable inclusion.

Roma "misrecognition" and "misrepresentation" as well as the institutional barriers and gaps in the formation and implementation of National Roma Integration

Strategies in Italy and Spain are examined by *Dr Tina Magazzini* (Czech Academy of Sciences). Applying the theory of *Nancy Fraser* and acknowledging her critique on identity politics, the author highlights the issue of "misrecognition," where Roma identities are oversimplified—often reduced to poverty or marginality—ignoring their internal diversity and intersectionality. The author critiques integration policies that rely solely on legal prohibitions and affirmative action measures, arguing that they reinforce existing hierarchies rather than addressing systemic inequality in the status quo and the mechanisms that produce the injustices in the first place. By incorporating interviews reflecting the views, concerns and reactions of Roma individuals, she calls for a shift towards more transformative and participatory approaches that move beyond symbolic top-down representation to genuinely empower Roma communities and shift from a structure that constrains those struggling for recognition into a "victimhood competition."

Another vulnerable group, persons with disabilities, faces disproportionate social exclusion, due to limited access to economic, social, and cultural opportunities. In her chapter, *Professor Delia Ferri* (University of Maynooth) highlights accessibility as a crucial factor in removing societal barriers and enabling full participation. She explores the complex EU accessibility legislation in relation to the UN Convention on the Rights of Persons with Disabilities (CRPD), ratified by the EU in 2010, signaling a policy shift from soft law measures to binding requirements. The author examines Article 9 of the CRPD and its implementation by integrating accessibility into EU rules on transport, procurement, and audiovisual media, covering areas such as physical infrastructure, digital communication, and public services. In this context, two significant EU legislative measures are examined and compared to CRPD: the Web Accessibility Directive (WAD) of 2016, which mandates accessibility for public sector websites and apps; and the European Accessibility Act (EAA) of 2019, which extends accessibility requirements to essential products and services, including banking, software, as well as payment and ticketing machines. The COVID-19 pandemic has further demonstrated the critical need for digital accessibility, reinforcing the relevance of WAD and EAA in ensuring inclusive digital services and highlighting the growing social dimension of market integration in the EU.

The invisibility and systemic and intersectional discrimination against intersex, non-binary or gender-diverse persons is criticized by *Associate Professor Kalliopi Chainoglou* (University of Macedonia). She critically examines the binary legal, medical, cultural and societal frameworks discriminating against intersex, non-binary or gender-diverse persons across Europe, which fail to accommodate their identities, resulting in their exclusion from healthcare, education, and employment. The author discusses the relevant policies of international and regional organizations, i.e. the UN, the Council of Europe and the EU, which have developed soft law standards and adopted various documents and reports to promote rights and inclusion of these vulnerable persons. She points out the EU's LGBTIQ+ Equality Strategy (2020–2025), which advocates an intersectional approach and reveals significant gaps in national implementation. In addition, Professor Chainoglou analyzes the importance of case law at the national and regional levels for the protection of their rights, including recent judgments on *M v France and Y v France* (European

Court of Human Rights, 2022; European Court of Human Rights, 2023) and *Mirin* (Court of Justice of the European Union, 2024), which underscore the need for non-binary recognition. The author advocates for various measures, such as the inclusion of non-binary identities in legal and social systems in order to dismantle structural barriers and combat social exclusion and marginalization.

The legal basis and the criteria for evaluating positive discrimination measures are examined by *Professor Philippa Watson* (City, University of London). She explains that the concept of positive discrimination has been embedded in EU employment law for nearly five decades, originating from Directive 76/207/EEC on equal treatment between men and women, and progressively obtaining a larger scope and diffusion to legislation prohibiting discrimination on more grounds. She explains the purpose of positive discrimination, which is to rectify historically ingrained patterns of discrimination that cannot be addressed by anti-discrimination legislation alone. She reviews the specific provisions within the Directive 2000/78/EC on the scope and implementation of positive discrimination measures as well as other alternative provisions serving the same purpose. She then proceeds with a careful analysis of the criteria used by the case law of the Court of Justice of the European Union (CJEU), which has played a crucial role in shaping the interpretation and application of positive discrimination. She concludes by stating that certain limitations to the application of positive discrimination measures ensure they do not undermine the core principle of equality.

The mandate of national equality bodies in the EU and Greece for promoting substantive equality beyond legal frameworks, challenging stereotypes and promoting diversity is analyzed by *Kalliopi Lykovardi*, Deputy Ombudsperson for Equal Treatment in Greece. Following a brief trajectory of EU legislation, she first analyzes the role of equality bodies in the EU member states, explicating their powers and their collaboration within the European Network of Equality Bodies. She then analyzes EU Directives 2024/1499 and 2024/1500, which establish minimum common standards for organizational and functional independence of national equality bodies. She continues with the analysis of the legal framework for combating discrimination in Greece, focusing on Laws 3304/2005, 4443/2016 and their subsequent amendments, which expanded the list of protected grounds of discrimination. Furthermore, she systematically illustrates how the Greek Ombudsman applies the principle of substantive equality in practice. By summarizing specific interventions addressing structural discrimination in Greek society, she highlights emerging trends, gaps, and persistent challenges across all grounds of discrimination. She concludes that the incorporation of EU Directives 2024/1499 and 2024/1500 into Greek legislation will further enhance the Ombudsman's capacity to effectively fulfill its mandate as a national equality body.

The *fourth part* presents the implementation of social inclusion goals in practice starting with the presentation of state and society initiatives against poverty, focusing on the Greek socio-economic crisis, which started in 2010. The Minimum Guaranteed Income (MGI) Scheme in Greece and the Social Solidarity Economy (SSE) initiatives, and in particular the Social Cooperative Enterprises (SCEs) are examples used to protect society from poverty during that crisis. In addition, the role of the courts has been very important to protect social rights from austerity measures. This part ends with future challenges in the digital era, since the digital divide can marginalize people even more.

Dr Stella Christoforidou (Aristotle University of Thessaloniki) explores the effectiveness of the Minimum Guaranteed Income (MGI) Scheme implemented during the last decade in Greece, using the 2019 provision of the Greek Constitution and the broader ECHR and EU legal context. She first describes the legal background of the adoption of the above constitutional amendment introducing MGI. Then, she clarifies the content and the interrelation between certain key legal concepts such as MGI, real and effective standard of decent living, human dignity, poverty threshold and minimum wage. Her main argument is that current legislation could potentially reinforce unjust marginalization, thereby compromising the constitutional goal of preserving human dignity. The author is also skeptical of the supposedly panacean virtues of MGI schemes in terms of the financial crisis repercussions, as the deterioration of living standards and breaches of social rights remain largely unaddressed. Specific legislative actions are also examined, including the minimum wage law (Greek Law 4172/2013). The cases of asylum seekers and refugees are also analyzed regarding their respective entitlements, highlighting simultaneously the precarious transitional phase between these two legal statuses.

Dr Anastasia Poulou (Administrative Court of First Instance in Athens) examines the impact of the Eurozone crisis on the EU social acquis and the response of the courts. She analyzes the gradual change of the case law of the Court of Justice of the EU (CJEU) and of national courts in Greece that were called to assess the *locus standi*, as well as the legality and the justification of austerity-driven restrictions on social and economic rights. Dr. Poulou frames social rights adjudication as a legitimacy issue, suggesting that a procedural model of social rights adjudication would mitigate the tension between decision-making over social welfare decisions and the protection of particular social rights. She argues that courts largely deferred to lawmakers rather than challenged conditionality-driven policies. The chapter also highlights criticism from international and regional institutions, linking this to broader democratic legitimacy concerns. Ultimately, she portrays Greece's financial assistance framework as lacking adequate representation for vulnerable populations.

The underrepresentation of socially excluded groups in Greece's Social Solidarity Economy (SSE) initiatives, particularly Social Cooperative Enterprises (SCEs) is emphasized by *Assistant Professor Sofia Adam* (Democritus University of Thrace). The author attributes this discrepancy to the relative underdevelopment of vibrant social movements on behalf of social services' users, which could potentially allow for the active engagement of socially vulnerable groups in grass-roots initiatives. She initially revisits debates on social exclusion, exploring its framing within three discourses—moral underclass, social integration, and redistribution. Additionally, she presents the main findings of relevant empirical studies on SSE initiatives and certain descriptive data about the development course of social cooperative enterprises for social inclusion, emerging in response to Greece's socio-economic crisis, which demonstrated significant political aspirations (e.g. anti-austerity and solidarity-based political projects). Professor Adam makes useful policy and research suggestions based on the development of inclusive welfare policies, the strengthening of user-driven social movements and finally the embedding of empowerment strategies within SSE initiatives to ensure active participation and representation of marginalized groups in decision-making or management roles.

The last chapter pertains to the risk of digital exclusion. *Assistant Professor Dimitrios I. Koukiadis* (University of Nicosia) examines the intersection of digital exclusion, social exclusion, and the workplace digital divide, highlighting the legal and societal challenges of digital transformation. Based mostly on French case law, he claims that access to the internet should be recognized as a fundamental right or as a derivative of the right to freedom of expression, essential for democratic participation. The author explores legal recognition of internet access in the EU and the challenges of ensuring affordable and non-discriminatory connectivity. He then proceeds to discuss the concept of the "net neutrality" principle as a constituent of the digital inclusion/digital exclusion discourse using UN and Council of Europe reports as well as EU legislation. The author continues with the risks of digital exclusion, arguing that the digital divide is presented as a barrier to social and economic participation. The author uses *Jan van Dijk's* "resources and appropriation" theory to illustrate how unequal access reinforces existing inequalities. He also discusses the measures that the EU has taken to confront the digital divide, e.g. the EU's *Digital Compass 2030* initiative, which aims to bridge the gap through broadband expansion, digital skills development, and inclusive services. Moreover, the author focuses on the digital divide and digital transformation of work, particularly in the platform economy and in remote work, identifying risks, such as disparities in digital literacy, algorithmic management, and employee surveillance. The author proposes a three-pillar framework to address these issues and calls for proactive measures to prevent the enhancement of social inequalities.

Concluding Reflection

The analyses presented by the authors in this volume reveal several interrelated factors that may help answer our initial question regarding the persistence of social exclusion experienced by vulnerable groups. A central theme that emerges across many of the chapters in this volume is the persistent invisibility of vulnerable groups and the obscure and simplified collective identities assigned to them through stereotypes that systematically erase the individual identity of persons belonging to vulnerable groups. Another important factor is insufficient democratic representation and a lack of responsiveness to internal group diversity that further entrenches their marginalization. Against this background, legal rules on non-discrimination and positive discrimination measures are significant but have proven inadequate in addressing the structural challenges faced by these groups. In addition, weaknesses in the justiciability of social rights reduce the trust of vulnerable groups to the legal system. Moreover, soft policy approaches and mere coordination of national implementation strategies have limited effectiveness since prevailing societal frameworks often fail to recognize or accommodate the complex identities of vulnerable individuals. The role of the media is shown to be pivotal: it can either perpetuate simplified portrayals of vulnerable groups as either enemies or victims—or, alternatively, serve as a platform that empowers them to articulate their own voices, thereby enhancing their representation in society and informing inclusive and efficient policy-making. Empowerment of vulnerable groups transcends mere access to resources and legal rules – it requires their voice to be heard and be understood as well as their meaningful representation within the social, legal, and political spheres. These considerations on stereotypes and lack of representation have been and should also continue to be the foundation for the work of international and regional organizations and states on promoting equality. Most of all, the European Union with its multifaceted mechanisms and policies could step up its efforts using multidisciplinary tools and dialogue in order to accomplish equality and inclusion in "a society in which pluralism, non-discrimination, tolerance, justice, solidarity and equality between women and men prevail" (Article 2 TEU).

References

Court of Justice of the European Union. (2024). Case C-4/23, Mirin, 4 October 2024, ECLI:EU:C:2024:845.

European Commission. (2010). Communication from the Commission. Europe 2020 Strategy, COM (2010) 2020. https://eur-lex.europa.eu/legal-content/EN/TXT/?uri=CELEX:52010DC2020

European Commission. (2020). Communication from the Commission. *A Union of equality: EU anti-racism action plan* 2020-2025, COM (2020) 565 final. https://migrant-integration.ec.europa.eu/sites/default/files/2020-09/a_union_of_equality_eu_action_plan_against_racism_2020_-2025_en.pdf

European Court of Human Rights (2022). *M v France, Application* Application No. 42821/18, 19.05.2022

European Court of Human Rights (2023). *Y v France, Application* No. 76888/17, 31.01.2023

European Court of Human Rights. (2024). *Thematic factsheet–Roma and travellers.* https://www.echr.coe.int/documents/d/echr/FS_Roma_ENG

European Parliament Resolution. (2017). *Combating antisemitism*, (2017/2692(RSP)). https://www.europarl.europa.eu/doceo/document/TA-8-2017-0243_EN.html

European Parliament Resolution. (2019). *On the need for a strengthened post-2020 strategic EU framework for National Roma Inclusion Strategies and stepping up the fight against anti-Gypsyism* (2019/2509(RSP)). https://www.europarl.europa.eu/doceo/document/TA-8-2019-0075_EN.html

European Union Agency of Fundamental Rights. (2018). *Handbook on European non-discrimination law, 2018 edition.* https://fra.europa.eu/sites/default/files/fra_uploads/fra-2018-handbook-non-discrimination-law-2018_en.pdf

Levitas, R., Pantazis, C., Fahmy, E., Gordon, D., Lloyd, E., & Patsios. (2007). *The multi-dimensional analysis of social exclusion*. Department of Sociology and School for Social Policy, The Townsend Centre for the International Study of Poverty and The Bristol Institute for Public Affairs, University of Bristol.

Regulation (EU) 2021/1057 of the European Parliament and of the Council of 24 June 2021 establishing the European Social Fund Plus (ESF+) and repealing Regulation (EU) No 1296/2013, OJ L 231, (2021). pp. 21–59. https://eur-lex.europa.eu/legal-content/EN/TXT/?uri=CELEX%3A32021R1057&qid=1634212132188

Part I

Identities in Europe: The Perception of the "Other"

The Two Sides of the Mirror: Stereotypes of and from People on the Move in Europe

Eleni Sideri

Abstract

This chapter examines the role of stereotypes, especially ethnic stereotypes, in the European and Greek contexts. Stereotypes as categories of meaning and as communicative currency are studied. A brief historical account of the European Others and how they were contextualized in the Greek context is explored with emphasis on the Enlightenment period and the formation of the Greek state, the Cold War and Greek Diasporas from the Black Sea and the former socialist countries and the current refugee crisis.

The Story

My family was poor back home. We worked our land in the village where everyone knew each other. When the war began, we left everything behind. We did not have time to say goodbye to friends and neighbors. Mom had left the key in the door. Our granny was left behind. She couldn't walk.

I still remember her lips on my forehead when we said goodbye. We arrived in Lesvos soaked but alive. No, I don't remember the sea. I remember the cries. I remember a sea of cries and tears.

"This is our new home", mom said, when we reached the shore.

I could see no familiar houses, no trees or gardens. Nothing was the same. Nothing but the sun. The sun was burning me. The salt became my skin. Salty skin. Burning skin. "Sun is hope and hope is God's promise for a new day" my

E. Sideri (✉)
Department of Balkan, Slavic & Oriental Studies, University of Macedonia, Thessaloniki, Greece
e-mail: elasideri@uom.edu.gr

D. Anagnostopoulou (ed.), *European Identities, Inclusion and Equality*, Diversity and Inclusion Research, https://doi.org/10.1007/978-3-031-90602-2_2

grandmother used to say. We had nothing but the sun and hopes. And we had plenty of them.

My grandmother related the story from times past with a low and firm voice, as if another girl had made it to that shore. She fixed her eyes somewhere out there, between that shore and her garden back home. She was here but she wasn't. She was there but she wasn't.

The Question

The story above is not very different from the "refugee stories" we have gotten used to hearing in the last decades. Similar stories have been recorded and disseminated by media, academics and NGO workers. Images of refugees arriving at the shores of the Aegean islands have turned into trivial news. Refugee bodies, 'weak', 'needy', 'hopeless' or 'hopeful', became part of the narrative of everyday life. Who pays attention to their stories? Who would spare some moments to find out who that girl in the aforementioned story was? What happened to her after her arrival?

In the 1970s, Heinz Kohut (1971) argued that stereotypes were a cognitive process which helped human beings build an idea of a Self (see also Katz & Kenneth, 1933; Gilman, 1991; Dyer, 1977). In detail, Kohut argued that in the first 5 months of the infant's life, the gradual formation of individuality was linked to the separation of the infant's Self from the rest of the world. Taking a distance from the world meant perceiving reality and representing it in a different and distinct way from the Self. Mental mapping of the world is the space where stereotypes rise. "Stereotypes are a crude set of mental representations of the world. They are palimpsests on which the initial bipolar representations are still vaguely legible" (Gilman, 1991, p. 12).

Stereotypes sketch the boundaries of the Self and the world, organizing the latter into categories. However, stereotypes are not fixed. They change by moving the boundary of the Self and the Other in different contexts but not the distance between the two, because, in a different case, the Self would be threatened. These approaches underlined the significance of stereotypes as mental maps, and they considered them as something natural, an idiom of human development and nature. However, identifying stereotypes as natural overlooked the question of power. Stereotypes do not simply categorize the word and provide an assessment. Black and white are not only colours; they hide semantic connotations culturally defined and historically shaped.

Eduardo Galeano, in his *Mirrors* (Galeano, 2009, p. 92), portrayed how Arab scientists before the European Renaissance came up with mathematical theorems that were important for the work of Copernicus. Nevertheless, nowadays, the name of the German scientist is remembered and celebrated, but nobody remembers the Arab scholars. As Galeano stated, "Europe looked in the mirror and saw the world. Beyond that lay nothing". The short story is indicative of the way the European Enlightenment and colonialism produced an all-encompassing idea of the world, representing the latter through European eyes. One of Galleano's stories is entitled

"Euroeverything" in order to draw attention to the way the boundary between Europe and the rest of the world was fixed. The political and ideological construction of stereotypes became a dominant and hegemonic worldview.

Focusing on the European context, how was the formation of the European borders shaped vis-à-vis the construction of the Others in terms of cultural and ideological hierarchies? Which are the significant turning points in European history? From the Greco-Roman Mediterranean region and the Medieval Christendom to the rise of the colonial West, the formation of the European borders was framed within grand narratives of cultural supremacy, which intended to have an exemplary and self-fashioning impact on the Others. White Christianity was gradually fused with scientific positivism, which, through strict taxonomies, generated bounded territorial and cultural categories. Linear and evolutionary ideas about history and cultures stemmed out from the Enlightenment project, erasing, as Galeano's story postulated, memories of different mobilities, encounters and cross fertilization that challenge European supremacy. European ideas were exported together with economic and political colonization. Centuries of rural communal life turned into a void space, into empty lands of opportunity, where enrichment and progress (expectations that every generation of refugees or immigrants fosters in their journey) would be transferred from the European metropoles. Colonization meant that the inclusion of other peoples' history started the moment a European soldier set his foot on these colonies.

As Edward Said (1994) put it, the conceptual category of East was constructed in the western thought or even in the western imagination as a counterweight to the category of the "West" mainly in conjunction with the mental framework created by colonialism, imperialism and their intellectual ambitions, Euro-centrism. A number of evaluative positions on primitivism, underdevelopment, regression, irrationality, sexual promiscuity and, most importantly, the perception of the East and its societies as having a static and monolithic nature were all gradually shaped. These perceptions were taken to their final form and were consolidated in the nineteenth century, with the progressive colonization of different regions of the world. At the same time, economic and military colonization was combined with another project, that of ideological justification, which shaped another 'great narrative' about the cultural superiority of the western culture and the need for this culture to act as a model—even by force—at a global level (Gazi, 1999, p. 238).[1]

In the Greek context, on the one hand, the formation of the Greek state had to address the questions and the expectations of the European philhellenes, where Greece was projected as the birthplace of civilization. This tradition is identified with the category Hellene. On the other hand, Greece had to hide the 'embarrassment' of the Ottoman past, which is tied to the idea of Romios (Rum was the attribute given to the Christian Orthodox communities of the Ottoman Empire). In order to address this double take of the Greek past and how it influenced the Greek modern identity, Michael Herzfeld (1987) launched the concept of disemia in order to

[1] West and East are considered only as categories pointing to specific ideologies and not bounded territorially and culturally expressed geographical entities.

postulate the ambiguities between Hellene/Romios. In other words, since its inception, the modern Greek state and society have had to indoctrinate western hierarchies regarding the Self/Other. As a result, emphasis on the proximity to Europe produced feelings of pride, whereas, at the same time, there was an innate and perpetual guilt about the Ottoman past, which was often portrayed as a source for present evils in Greece. The Asia Minor refugees provoked a new crisis of identity. Pejorative terms like "*Tourkosporoi*" (sperm of Turks) expressed latent fears regarding the encounter with the East, which was, though, very similar to the Self. Putting these other expressions of Greek-ness (linguistic and cultural varieties) under the umbrella of a formal or high Greek culture became a long-standing project, which culminated during World War II. The war period acted as a unifying glue for the nation.

The Cold War further fed on cultural stereotypes about the eastern borderlands of Europe with political ideology. The countries of the Iron Curtain converted to the 'significant others' of the imagined Free World. Although modernity and nation-states were vital for the formation of societies in both parts of the split post-war Europe, the socialist East was considered as something completely different, which affected the way post-socialist societies were treated since the 1990s. In the Greek context, Cold War ideologies created categories of "dangerous citizens" (Panourgia, 2009), who were stigmatized in order not to contaminate the authentic (white Christian, conservative and capitalist) Greeks. In the 1990s, the post-socialist space emerged as a distinctive social, economic and cultural category. As De Soto and Dudwick (2000) argued in one of the ethnographies published to discuss the specific issues of doing fieldwork in the post-socialist states, there was an a priori feeling of difference among the scholars who did fieldwork in the former socialist societies, which stemmed out of their Cold War prejudices. Their work "emerged out of a feeling, shared by all the authors, that there was something peculiarly post-socialist about the inevitable complexity of fieldwork relationships we were experiencing" (De Soto & Dudwick, 2000, pp. 6–7).

The migration from Eastern Europe and the former Soviet Union caused reactions all over Europe. The fear of an influx of emigrants from the former socialist countries put pressure on the definition of the European identity and borders. Various policies and support mechanisms were invented in that period (1990s) (Europe of Regions, European Neighbourhood Policies, European Policy in West Balkans, Strategic Partnership with Russia), which were made with the goal of shaping the former socialist societies into the image of (western) Europe. As Leontidou (2004) stressed, "[t]he Balkan people are one boundary shift away from European citizenship (…)" (p. 608). The emigration from the former socialist countries in Greece was coincided with the rediscovery of the former Soviet Greeks. Earlier work (Sideri, 2006) among Pontic-Greeks from Georgia showed that brotherly solidarity in Greece emerged as an outcome of the so-called "return" of the Greek population, living in the former Soviet territory, to the "homeland". However, as in the case of Asia Minor Greeks, the initial feelings of support were substituted by rumours of mistrust and xenophobia reinforced by the media, which called those immigrants "*Rossopontioi*" (Russian–Pontics), and thus challenged their bonds to Greece (Sideri, 2006).

Since the 1990s, globalization and neo-liberalism have increased economic inequalities and mobilities, especially towards the urban centres. Environmental changes provoked the uprooting of millions of people. Furthermore, new technologies disseminated images and lifestyles that generated the imagination of a better life out there. Similarly, the improvement of life in various parts of the world motivated people to dream of a better future (Salazar & Glick-Schiller, 2014). However, the mobility turn in the late twentieth century might have increased the circulation of economic capital and ideas. Nevertheless, the corresponding mobility of humans became more and more scrutinized with various biotechnologies and regimes of mobility. These regimes did not stop mobility, but rather they deepened the hierarchal perceptions of Otherness. As Shamir stated (Shamir, 2005),

> [T]he mobility regime is constructed to maintain high levels of inequality in a relatively normatively homogenized world. In practice, this means that local, national, and regional boundaries are now being rebuilt and consolidated under the increased normative pressure of, and as a counterbalance to, the universal human rights regime. (p. 199)

In this context, although immigrant and refugee flows were motivated by the global economic and political shifts, they were also regimented and regulated in a framework that privileged certain types of mobilities and criminalized others.

In the last decade, Europe (and especially Greece) had to face a double crisis, an economic and a humanitarian one. The first crisis deregulated the market. The latter deregulated the society. Because of this double crisis, the increasing refugee and migrant flows in the last years postulated even further the significance of stereotypes.

Mental maps produced categories of Otherness trying to understand the complex social conditions produced by the formation of the diverse European societies. The above brief historical examination of diachronic conditions, in Greece and in Europe as a whole, produced generalized conditions of Otherness that stressed that stereotypes were not only psychological categories but generative categories of meaning shaped by economic and political conditions of power.

Stereotypes as Signifying Practices

> *Look a Negro ... Mama, see the Negro! I'm frightened ...*
> (Fanon, 1952, 2000, p. 257)

> Give me the soap, daddy, I want the other kids to play with me
>
> 10 year-old school child from Nigeria. (Robert C., personal communication, 13 July, 2013)

In his study of representation as the production of meaning through language, discourse and image, Stuart Hall (1997, pp. 257–259) argued that stereotypes played a significant role in the production of this meaning by constructing and organizing reality into specific types that were used to help us understand, remember and recall knowledge about reality at fast speed and in diverse contexts. For example, an old lady with a child on the street will be considered to be his/her grandmother because of the age difference, the white hair, maybe the more conservative dress code, the protective and caring relation with the child, and all these attributes that are often linked to the role of a grandmother in Greece. How do these stereotypes function?

First, there is over-simplification and reductionism. In the example with the white-haired woman, one physical characteristic, her white hair, became her identity. In the quotes from Fanon and the author's fieldwork, Blackness had an all-encompassing role for the French doctor and the Black child. They were Black as opposed to the white French colonial society and the white society in Greece. There is an internal, instant comparison stemming from an exterior characteristic, colour, which became a dominant feature for the man and the child. There was no discussion about any other information regarding the profile of these two people, their education, nationality, where they were born etc. A physical trait was turned into the dominant trait of the Self. This trait became who they were as opposed to the rest of the society. This practice of "*I am the opposite of the Other*" generates dominant inclusions and exclusions in social contexts.

Secondly, in the above case, there was no consideration of how Fanon or the child identified themselves. What were their names? How would they describe themselves? What would be the most important information through which they would like to become known? They both became recognized through the attributes we used to describe them. At the moment of the encounter, they were recognized through their Blackness, which became their identity. In that moment, the inequality in the power geometry of that encounter fixed the boundary and produced a bounded identity.

Thirdly, as Hall (1997, p. 263) pointed out, stereotypes have their own "poetics" and "politics". The history of French colonialism—centuries of domination and economic exploitation, slavery and imperialism—was projected in an essentialist way on the body and skin of that Black man. The child was scared. Blackness as a sign of evil, primitivity and savagery was constructed through the encounters of missionaries, mercenaries, bureaucrats and artists. The fear of revolt, resistance and fighting became a constitutive part of violence used to keep the colonies in order. "*The Black will come and eat you*" (*o mavros tha erthei na se faei*) is a primal story in Greek tradition, which substituted in many cases of the bad wolf. Did the Black substitute the animal or did the Black figure simply become the animal? The use of the general term "black" in Greek comprised different categories, for example, the Roma people or the Black people. However, as stated above, the boundaries move not in order to become obliterated but in order to become fixed again. The Black is not only connected to the primal fear but also to filth. The Black child should be washed with soap in order to become clean and play with the white Greek kids at school. Mary Douglas, in her seminal work of Purity and Danger (1966), proved that categories of filth and cleanness in food, drink or social behaviour were used to shape and popularize categories of inclusion and exclusion. Imagining the Black kid or the Black man as filthy or terrifying is a way to distinguish them from Us, to exclude them as different, and this is the work of power and fantasy.

Finally, there is a process of substitution and fetishism in stereotyping and representation. In the above example, one physical trait substituted all other characteristics. It became dominant. This trait also was connected to histories of colonial power, not only literally but symbolically, at the level of imagination of the Other. However, in both encounters, the gaze was fixed. The woman and the child did not run to hide when they saw the Black man. The children in the Greek school did not leave him alone. The child fixed his gaze and asked his mother to look at this man as well. The children in school asked the child to clean himself. Embodied difference was marked through a gaze, and a thing (a body part, a colour) substituted the entity in its totality. This characteristic often embeds insinuations not only of fear but also of sexual desire. This was succeeded through fetishism, according to Hall (1997, p. 266).

The above brief examination of the stereotypes as signifying practices postulates how these categories of meaning are part of everyday communication and understanding of the world. They are flexible and become contextualized in specific histories and traditions. They are there, almost unmarked and thus powerful. They fixed the boundaries and provoked dominant perceptions about the Self and the Other. They are also produced by hegemonic ideas and images that circulate all around, especially in the last decade of the global media domination. They circulate but they end up in closure and fixity. They reduce diversity, they oversimplify social and historical complexity and they naturalize the boundary until it becomes invisible. In this way, they can become persistent to time and changes. Nevertheless, why do stereotypes persist, being such precious currency in everyday communication and exchanges? What is the cultural value of stereotypes? How can they be used in order to make us understand the current refugee crisis?

The Everyday Value of Stereotypes

> *We are hospitable people but they [the refugees] should not take advantage of our good faith"* the taxi driver said. *"You see what happened with Makedoniko [the question of name of North Macedonia].* (Dimitris K., personal communication 17 September, 2019)

Until this point, the examination of stereotypes had to do with their structure and function. But what is their use? Stereotypes are used as cultural currency in our everyday communication. Studying this use could help us understand how the other is usually perceived, categorized, imagined and objectified and why these processes are valid in daily contexts. But why do stereotypes become so popular? What is their power of circulation and persistence? Are they only used to stigmatize and set the boundary with Otherness or do they provide significant self-perceptions? And of what kind?

Dimitris Theodossopoulos (2003), in a collected volume, provided a study of how neighbors of different ethnicities from Southeast Europe demoted each other, although they all belonged to the same periphery and were in weak economic and political positions. Theodossopoulos and his co-writers argued that stereotypes in the region often drew from the feeling of injustice, weakness and disempowerment due to power imbalances, vulnerability and discrimination. Degrading neighbors often provided explanations and justification of their own social and political conduct and their failures. This indoctrinated fear and discrimination due to the unpredictability of their life was often considered the result of great powers or of the privileged ones. Stereotyping is fixing, and fixing can provide safety and give back a sense of control regarding the unknown.

The abovementioned taxi driver made a direct connection between the current refugee crisis as it is known in Greece (the increase of the flow of refugees from the Middle East and North Africa since 2015) and the question of the name of North Macedonia/FYROM; in other words, the problem of recognition of North Macedonia by Greece. In the context of the question of recognition, the general impression of the Greek public was that political allies of Greece within the EU and NATO did not help the country. They betrayed the confidence of Greece despite their belonging to the same alliance of nations. The political and economic interests of other European countries and the USA predominated and impeded justice to be served and the name of Macedonia to be attributed only to Greece. The taxi driver also felt that, in the context of the refugee crisis, what is expected from Greece, in terms of accommodating increasing numbers of refugees, is overwhelming. At the same time, the denial of many EU member states to receive and host refugees worsens the plight of Greece and, especially, of the Greek Aegean islands. In this respect, there is an analogy. Western powers are not willing to support Greece; thus, another tragedy is unavoidable.

However, there is an ambiguity in his remarks. In the first half of his statement, the taxi driver stresses the hospitality of the Greek people. Hospitality is opposed to what is implied, the trickiness of the Others, the refugees or even of the Northern neighbors and allies. Hospitality is a cultural idiom that exists in the tradition of the Eastern Mediterranean and negotiates categories of inclusion and exclusion beyond the strict kinship relations. Hospitality tests the boundaries and transforms the stranger into a familiar category but in an intimate context, that of the host's house, and for a specific period within which the guest should respect the rules. Hospitality is not about equal recognition. It is about the promise of reciprocity. In the meantime, the guest should only adapt to his host's expectations (see Papataxiarchis, 2006, pp. 1–85). Yet, the belief of being cheated puts Greeks in an inferior position, portraying them as powerless, gullible and naive.

These exact characteristics of inferiority, shame and negativity can play a significant role in the community. The traditional communities whose coherence, according to Durkheim (2010), was rooted in kinship during the last decades seem to become transformed into communities of blurred boundaries (sometimes immaterialized on the web). These new types of communities seem to be a working project produced by different forms of practices and agents in late capitalism (see Zaimakis, 2011). Thus, as the concept of community becomes harder to define and delineate, these kinds of hidden emotions, expressed by the taxi driver's statement, contribute to the sense of belonging. Michael Herzfeld (1997) stressed that the expression of these feelings of vulnerability to outsiders can often become the glue for the production of membership. This "cultural intimacy" consists of characteristics, beliefs which are "considered a source of external embarrassment but that nevertheless provide insiders with their assurance of common sociality (…)" (Herzfeld, p. 3). As Herzfeld argued (2014), this intimacy developed creatively in relation to state ideologies and nationalism and is expressed in a variety of ways, often contradictory ones.

The taxi driver's statement reiterated a contradiction: the sense of pride for the hospitality of the Greeks and the sense of shame for their gullibility which makes them easy victims. Still, this contradiction was also postulated in the way he connected two different histories of national crises, as he interpreted them, where the intervention (or the lack there of) of exterior factors was decisive. If we look closer at this statement, this feeling of inferiority and mistrust implies, at the same time, pride for the Greek trustworthiness, good faith and sincerity which separates them from the behaviour of the Others. Thus, as Theodossopoulos argued (2003, p. 11), (ethnic) stereotypes "ha[ve] as much to say about categorizing difference as about explaining it; it is as much about 'structure' (…) as about 'agency'". This double use of stereotypes as categories of meaning and practice is their value in everyday life. They do not simply produce or reiterate knowledge and belief of oneself and its Others; they can also negotiate ways to challenge it.

Challenging Stereotypes

If stereotypes have this all-encompassing power, is there a way to overcome them? Or if we cannot overcome them, are there any ways to work through or with them in order to challenge them? Firstly, I strongly believe that stereotypes should not be dismissed as by-products of ignorance or symptoms of limited education. Stereotypes produce meaning and therefore, they should be studied in order to become understood, to explore the conditions of their production, the depth of their content and the strength of their persistence. Furthermore, we should also study their communicative use, where and who uses them, what kind of stereotypes we use and how this use can change. This is important.

Stereotypes are not static. They become contextualized in a protean way. Their ultimate goal is to create closure, not to be faithful to their content or to have a constant and permanent target. This fluidity is an opportunity. Contradictions in the use of stereotypes produce doubts and challenge their innate role to produce unifying meaning. Putting forward these contradictions is a way to challenge stereotypes, to underline their constructed nature, and to make them visible and explicit. Moreover, working through these contradictions can give off their fragile nature and give us a glimpse into our own prejudices, increasing the opportunity for intercultural dialogue.

The Twist

I started my paper with a story. The story of a young girl who arrived in Greece with her family. Without any further contextualization, we can easily believe that the story belongs to a recent refugee. However, the story of the young girl does not belong to a refugee from Syria, Iraq, Somalia etc. The story belongs to a refugee from Aival (Asia Minor). She belongs to a "tourkosporo". She arrived in Lesvos with her family. She lived there in a tent with many other people. Then, the family moved to another camp in the biggest port of Greece, in Piraeus. There, she had to take care of her little brothers and sisters, although she had just reached puberty, as her mother looked for a job in the industrial zone of the port. There, she was raped by a member of her extended family. Later on, she moved to in Thessaloniki where she learnt on her own to read and write. She worked in a tobacco factory, and she got married and gave birth to three children and many grandchildren. Her name was Sophia and she was my grandmother.

References

De Soto, H. G., & Dudwick, N. (Eds.). (2000). *Anthropologists in postsocialist states*. University of Wisconsin Press.

Douglas, M. (1966). *Purity and danger. An analysis of pollution and taboo*. Routledge & Kegan Paul.

Durkheim, E. (2010). From mechanical to organic solidarity. In A. Giddens & P. W. Sutton (Eds.), *Sociology: Introductory readings* (Vol. 2, pp. 25–29). Polity Press.

Dyer, R. (Ed.). (1977). *Gays and film*. British Film Institute.

Galeano, E. (2009). *Mirrors: Stories of almost everyone*. Nation Books.

Gazi, E. (1999, January 1).«Οριενταλισμός». Το κείμενο ως γεγονός. ["Orientalism". The "text" as "event"]. *Mnemon*, 21, 237–246. (in Greek). https://doi.org/10.12681/mnimon.795

Gilman, S. (1991). *Inscribing the other (1)*. University of Nebraska Press.

Hall, S. (1997). The work of representation. In *Representation: Cultural representations and signifying practices* (Vol. 2, pp. 13–74). Sage Publications, Inc; Open University Press.

Herzfeld, M. (2014). *Cultural intimacy: Social poetics in the nation-state*. Routledge.

Herzfeld, M. (1987). *Anthropology through the looking-glass: Critical ethnography in the margins of Europe*. Cambridge University Press.

Herzfeld, M. (1997). Anthropology: a practice of theory, *International Social Science Journal*. https://doi.org/10.1111/j.1468-2451.1997.tb00025.x

Katz, D., & Kenneth, B. (1933). Racial stereotypes of one hundred college students. *The Journal of Abnormal and Social Psychology, 28*(3), 280.

Kohut, H. (1971). *The analysis of the self: A systematic approach to the psychoanalytic treatment of narcissistic personality disorders*. International Universities Press.

Leontidou, L. (2004). The boundaries of Europe: Deconstructing three regional narratives. *Identities: Global Studies in Culture and Power, 11*(4), 593–617.

Papataxiarchis, E. (2006). The burdens of alterity: Dimensions of cultural differentiation in early 21st century Greece. In E. Papataxiarchis (Ed.), *The burdens of alterity: Dimensions of cultural differentiation in early 21st century Greece* (pp. 1–85). Alexandria. (in Greek).

Panourgia, N. (2009). *Dangerous citizens: The Greek left and the terror of the state*. Fordham Univ Press.

Said, E. (1994). *Orientalism*. 1978. Vintage 25.

Salazar, N. B., & Glick-Schiller, N. (2014). Introduction. Regimes of Mobility Across the Globe. In *Regimes of Mobility. Imaginaries and Relationalities of Power* (pp.1–19). Routledge.

Shamir, R. (2005). Without borders? Notes on globalization as a mobility regime. *Sociological Theory, 23*(2), 197–217. https://doi.org/10.1111/j.0735-2751.2005.00250.x

Sideri, E. (2006). In quest of Eastern Europe: Troubling encounters in the post-cold war field. *Anthropology Matter, 8*(1). https://doi.org/10.22582/am.v8i1.77

Theodossopoulos, D. (2003). Degrading others and honouring ourselves: Ethnic stereotypes as categories and as explanations. *Journal of Mediterranean Studies, 13*(2), 177–188.

Zaimakis, Y. (2011). *Koinotiki Ergasia ke topikes koinonies. Anaptyksi, syllogiki drasi, polypolitismikotita [Community work and local societies. Development, collection action and multiculturalism].* Plethron.

European Media Discourses of the Refugee "Crisis" and Human Rights

Christos A. Frangonikolopoulos

Abstract

The refugee is trapped between these two positions: moral responsibility/solidarity versus threat/exclusion. How can we, therefore, transcend the resistances (often emotional) and heated tones vis-à-vis the phenomenon of migration? How can we overcome the stereotypes and prejudices faced by migrants and refugees? How can we promote a representation of the other and of alterity? There is a need for a communication strategy in which it is no longer ministries, associations or international organisations speaking to us about "migration and migrants", but the migrant who speaks to us, who requests our attention and our gaze. What is lacking in most public communication is precisely *their own self-representation*: their voice, their story, their gaze on us and on the hosting society.

The refugee is trapped between these two positions: moral responsibility/solidarity versus threat/exclusion. How can we, therefore, transcend the resistances (often emotional) and heated tones vis-à-vis the phenomenon of migration? How can we overcome the stereotypes and prejudices faced by migrants and refugees? How can we promote a representation of the other and of alterity? There is a need for a communication strategy in which it is no longer ministries, associations or international organisations speaking to us about "migration and migrants", but the migrant who speaks to us, who requests our attention and our gaze. What is lacking in most public communication is precisely *their own self-representation*: their voice, their story, their gaze on us and on the hosting society.

C. A. Frangonikolopoulos (✉)
School of Journalism and Mass Communications, Jean Monnet Chair on European Union Public Diplomacy, Aristotle University of Thessaloniki, Thessaloniki, Greece
e-mail: chfragk@gapps.auth.gr

D. Anagnostopoulou (ed.), *European Identities, Inclusion and Equality*, Diversity and Inclusion Research, https://doi.org/10.1007/978-3-031-90602-2_3

The "European refugee crisis", referring to the influx of migrants into Europe since 2015 (Krzyżanowski et al., 2018), not only introduced *practical challenges* to the political and civil sphere but also introduced equally *challenged* common human rights narratives. Unfolding in close range of and within European territory, one could rarely speak of a distant crisis any longer, even if the initial circumstances (the war in Syria) still feel distant to many Europeans. As such, at least a part of civil society has either witnessed the situation directly (inhabitants of Greek islands, for instance) or has been involved in active responses (volunteer organizations, refugee camp staff, donors of material supplies etc.).

Research suggests the view that there are two dominating frames in European media coverage (Nerghes & Lee, 2019; Eberl et al., 2018; Triandafyllidou, 2018; Gevisa La Rocca, 2017). On the one hand, the refugee is portrayed as a "threat" (to national security or cultural identity) and is, hence, to be excluded from "our" community. On the other hand, the refugee appears as a "victim" figure. In that way, the refugee is trapped between these two positions: moral responsibility/solidarity versus threat/exclusion (Musarò & Parmiggiani, 2017).

The depiction of refugees as a threat has contributed to an increasingly anxious and hostile climate, because it has led to very tangible changes within the political landscape of Europe, most notably to the sharp rise of right-wing/nationalist movements and parties. In that context, the non-hostile "victim" frame seems to do less harm, because it might originate in the well-intended aim to trigger empathy, instead of rejection, among the audience. However, the "victim" frame is equally potent to produce problematic, if not damaging, perceptions in the long run: linked to visualities of collective misfortune—most prominently, images of refugees squeezed on unstable rubber boats or overcrowded camps with only a minimum of material supply—the refugees are situated within "a field of representation that reduces their human life to corporeal existence … fully reliant on Western emergency aid or rescue operations to survive and so inevitably dispossessed of will and voice" (Chouliaraki & Stolic, 2017).

In fact, the UN-EU-NGO-centred Humanitarian Club has cultivated a Savage-Victim-Savior metaphor, according to which vulnerable and defenceless individuals and communities are framed as figures of victimhood who fall prey to a perpetrator, usually a particularly repressive, autocratic or criminal "savage" state apparatus (Mutua, 2001). In this context, the human rights corpus/humanitarianism itself emerges as the authorized source of relief and hence the sole "savior" figure. By casting actors into "superior and subordinate positions", the basic claim of "universality" (as enshrined in the title of the UN Declaration) is undermined. Instead, the narrative contributes to a process of "othering". Reduced to a life context of naked survival, the refugees/migrants as "visualities of misfortune" suggest a "lack of civic status" and, in the broader sense, nullify not only the migrant's dignity but essentially his entitlement to human rights as a whole (Herrero-Jiménez et al., 2018; Meyer et al., 2018).

This is important when considering how the complexity of migration and asylum is reduced to an abstract technical and emotional issue that *prioritises security over concerns of human rights*. This depoliticised politics, based on compassionate care and technocratic control, contributes to the construction of the image of the Mediterranean as a "migration crisis space", in which *culpability* is totally misperceived. The policy to keep refugees out by making it clear that they are unwanted and unworthy allows for the deaths of certain populations to take place without sanctions or repercussions. Toleration of border deaths involves not only a denial of culpability through the identification of deaths as a product of "natural" forces, but also the shifting or displacement of responsibility onto the person at risk of death. In a context of increased border deaths, this occurs through a process of victimisation embedded in humanitarian operations, such as search and rescue, which has become integral to governing migration in the Mediterranean context. Here, culpability is not simply denied; rather, the rescuer enacts responsibility while passing irresponsibility onto the victim. Instead, it implies an endless present: they are migrants; they move; it's what they do (Musarò & Parmiggiani, 2017).

Framing migrants in terms of victimisation, sensationalism and stereotypes in a narrow humanitarian context takes no account of the bigger picture, neither does highlighting the benefits of migration flows nor does addressing the challenges that they raise in our societies. With debate raging over whether people crossing the Mediterranean via unofficial routes should be regarded as deserving candidates for European sympathy and protection, many questions go unanswered and myths circulate:

- who are these people and what do they want from us?
- why don't they stop in the first safe country they reach?
- why don't the men stay behind and fight?
- how can we make room for everyone?
- are they bringing their problems to our shores?
- do they threaten our culture and values?

All this creates the false impression that the crisis was a problem from elsewhere that landed unexpectedly on European shores. Wrong:

1. Europe has played a key role, historically, in the shaping of a world where power and wealth are unequally distributed, and European powers continue to pursue military and arms trading policies that have caused or contributed to the conflicts and instability from which many people flee.
2. The crisis of 2015 was a direct effect of the complex system of policing immigration from outside the EU that has been constructed in the last few decades. In short, this has involved the EU and its member states signing treaties with countries outside its borders to control immigration on its behalf, and also by introducing an internal system for regulating the movements of asylum seekers that aims to force them to stay in the first EU country they enter (Dublin Regulation (EU) 604/2013, 2013). This, cumulatively, had the effect of forcing desperate people to take narrower and more dangerous routes by land and sea, while the prioritising of border control over safe and dignified reception conditions compounded the disaster.

Europe's refugee crisis, or more properly, a disaster partly caused by European border policies, rather than simply the movement of refugees towards Europe, not only is one of the most heavily mediated world events, but also unfolds around the edges of a wealthy and technologically developed region, home to several major centres of the global media industry. Scenes of desperation, suffering and rescue that might normally be gathered by foreign correspondents in harder-to-access parts of the world are now readily available to reporters, news crews, filmmakers and artists at relatively low cost (Thrilling, 2019).

How can we, therefore, transcend the resistances (often emotional) and heated tones vis-à-vis the phenomenon of migration? How can we overcome the stereotypes and prejudices faced by migrants and refugees? How can we promote a representation of the other and of alterity? There is a need for a communication strategy in which it is no longer ministries, associations or international organisations speaking to us about "migration and migrants", but it should be the migrant who speaks to us, who requests our attention and our gaze. What is lacking in most public communication is precisely *their own self-representation*: their voice, their story, their gaze on us and on the hosting society.

Therefore, a strategy is required, which involves the following:

- *establishing a relationship with someone*, giving him or her the *opportunity to be heard, together negotiating potential solutions* to address their problems,
- opening *the circle of "us"* by accepting the stories of lives that are different from one's own and therefore placing oneself in the condition of being welcoming, respecting, desiring, and curious to know the "other" and share his or her world,
- giving voice to the protagonists of migration, giving space to their gaze, their narrations, their stories, being open to dialogue by listening to what they have to say and striving to understand what they are telling us,
- allowing for a shift from a communication "on" the theme of migration to a communication "with" the people directly involved, through a search for languages, techniques, and processes able to create dialogue,
- developing new discourses favouring the development of an image of immigrants and refugees as people with their own story and identity, active subjects who have a voice and an idea concerning their own lives, who make choices and fight to carry them out, determined to reach, despite the difficulties, important objectives, and therefore, as people deserving of our respect, attention, and empathy.

Through the transformation of the migrant from *object*—of our compassion, our collective fear, our discrimination, tolerance and integration—to an *active subject*, public communication will be able to produce alternative discourses to the pathos-securitarian emergency frame, to the culture of aid (fed by the bleeding-heart-liberal spirit of the philanthropic gesture) and to the culture of legality (fed by the suspicion, fear, control and negation of the other). Good examples in this direction are:

- BBC's 25-episode podcast series, which followed a middleclass Syrian family along its precarious journey from Turkey to Germany.
- Time Magazine's yearlong coverage of three refugee families and their new-born babies in a special series entitled "Finding Home".
- Guardian's "The Long Read". As part of the "slow news movement," the Guardian devotes a section of its coverage to long-form pieces that teach readers more about a topic rather than just giving them the headlines.
- The specialized news site, Refugees Deeply, allotted sections of its coverage to refugee journalists, as well as to the conflicts from which individuals have fled, in order to help its readers better understand why someone would feel compelled to risk their life attempting to cross the Aegean.
- The Refugee Journalism Project, which supports refugees and exiled journalists to re-start their careers in the UK. It was founded in 2016 and since 2018, the project has been based exclusively at London College of Communication, part of the University of the Arts London. The project's core aims are to help prepare refugee journalists to work in the UK media industry, create opportunities for refugee journalists to publish their work and build a wider network, engage with new audiences, key policy and opinion-makers in order to debunk negative, institutional and public perceptions of refugees.

In conclusion, human rights narratives are rightfully an integral component of the "refugee crisis". However, they often appear disconnected from their legal basis and that makes them vulnerable to political manipulations. In addition, their dual existence as both a legal code and a loose moralistic language allows human rights to be deployed as a potent narrative with little or no attempt to provide clarity and context. Thus, as an essential transmitter of these discourses, the media and journalists have the potential to neutralise inflammatory rhetoric and vague appeals to moral standards by providing the audience with sufficient context. In this direction, as Ibrahim Seaga Shaw (2012) has argued, it is important to begin by comparing and contrasting the terms "human wrongs journalism" and "human rights journalism". That will identify and critique the often-subtle ways in which journalism is implicated in the structural imperatives of politics and economics, which more often than not, underpin human rights abuses. That is to say, to find new ways to disrupt the ideological purchase of official truth claims, not least where the waging of war by "us" against "them" is effectively normalised to the point that peace-centred alternatives are trivialised, marginalised or excluded altogether as being less than newsworthy.

This begins by educating the public about their own rights, the rights of others and to what extent a state is capable of or responsible to safeguard them. Tracing back notions of human rights to their historical, political or legal origins and documents can not only demystify perceptions of human rights as moral truths, but also it would contribute to a more rational, productive approach, in which the audience better understands its own duty of respecting rights. Only in this way, can we overcome the role of a passive spectator and, at the same time, engage with the human rights debate in a more grounded way. In covering conflict and crisis, Galtung

(2006a, 2006b) explains that media focuses mainly on direct and visible violence (the dead and the injured), on dichotomies (us and them) and on the elites. As an alternative to this kind of reporting, he proposes a framework for what he calls "peace journalism". Peace journalism, conversely, seeks to offer counter-narratives and to frame stories in a way that fosters a more constructive societal debate (Youngblood, 2017). It enriches the news agenda beyond current events and the guise of "reporting the facts" and broadens the range of sources and voices used in the news beyond officials and technocratic experts. It provides comprehensive reporting on the roots of a conflict while it simultaneously reveals its long-term consequences and possible solutions. This is because analyzing a conflict through a peace journalism lens involves the definition of a problem, a diagnosis of causes, a moral judgement and the suggestion for its resolution (Nicolás-Gavilan, 2011; Kalfeli & Frangonikolopoulos, 2019).

There is a need to stop framing these newly arrived people as *others*; people from "over there", who have little to do with Europe itself, are antagonistic to its traditions and culture. As confirmed by demographic and economic reports, migration to Europe will continue over the next few years, both due to the factors pushing migrants and the fact that European economies and societies need migration. Therefore, it is fundamental to consider that stopping migration is not only an unrealistic prospect that would produce concrete effects on the everyday lives of millions of vulnerable people on the move, but also would contribute to worsening the conditions under which migration will take place in the near future as well as of the lives of migrants already established in Europe.

References

Chouliaraki, L., & Stolic, T. (2017). Rethinking media responsibility in the refugee "crisis": Visual typology of European news. *Media, Culture & Society, 39*(8), 1162–1177. https://doi.org/10.1177/016344371772616

Dublin Regulation (EU) 604/2013. (2013). *Regulation (EU) No 604/2013 of the European Parliament and of the Council of 26 June 2013 establishing the criteria and mechanisms for determining the Member State responsible for examining an application for international protection lodged in one of the Member States by a third-country national or a stateless person (recast)*, OJ L 180, 29.6.2013, pp. 31–59, https://eur-lex.europa.eu/eli/reg/2013/604/oj/eng

Eberl, J. M., Meltze, E. E., Herrero, B., Theorin, N., Lind, F., Berganza, R., Boomgaarden, H. G., Schemer, C., & Strömbäck, J. (2018). The European media discourse on immigration and its effects: A literature review. *Annals of the International Communication Association, 42*(3), 207–223. https://doi.org/10.1080/23808985.2018.1497452

Galtung, J. (2006a). Journalism as an ethical challenge. *GMJ [Mediterranean Edition], 1*(2).

Galtung, J. (2006b). Peace journalism as an ethical challenge, *GMJ* [Mediterranean edition].

Herrero-Jiménez, B., Calderón, A. C., Carratalá, A., & Berganza, R. (2018). The impact of media and NGOs on four European Parliament discourses about conflicts in the Middle East. *Media, War and Conflict, 11*(1), 65–84. https://doi.org/10.1177/1750635217727310

Kalfeli, N., & Frangonikolopoulos, C. (2019, April 29). Peace Journalism. In *The International Encyclopedia of Journalism Studies. Advance Online Publication*. https://doi.org/10.1002/9781118841570.iejs0139.

Krzyżanowski, M., Triandafyllidou, A., & Wodak, R. (2018). The Mediatization and the politicization of the "refugee crisis" in Europe. *Journal of Immigrant & Refugee Studies, 16*(1–2), 1–14.

La Rocca, L. (2017). Media, migrants and human rights. *International Review of Sociology, 27*(2), 225–229.

Meyer, C. O., Sangar, E., & Michaels, E. (2018). How do non-governmental organizations influence media coverage of conflict? The case of the Syrian conflict, 2011-2014. *Media, War and Conflict, 11*(1), 149–171. https://doi.org/10.1177/1750635217727309

Musarò, P., & Parmiggiani, P. (2017). Beyond black and white: The role of media in portraying and policing migration and asylum in Italy. *International Review of Sociology, 27*(2), 241–260.

Mutua, M. (2001). Savages, victims, and saviors: The metaphor of human rights. *Harvard International Law Journal, 42*(1), 201–209.

Nerghes, A., & Lee, J. S. (2019). Narratives of the refugee crisis: A comparative study of mainstream-media and twitter. *Media and Communication, 7*(2). https://doi.org/10.17645/mac.v7i2.1983

Nicolás-Gavilan, M. T. (2011). Framing the news: Form political conflict to peace. How the "framing theory" and the "political context model" can enhance the peace journalism model. *Journal of Latin American Communication Research, 1*(2).

Shaw, S. I. (2012). *Human rights journalism*. Palgrave.

Thrilling, D. (2019). How the media contributed to the "refugee crisis". *The Guardian Long Read*. Retrieved from https://www.theguardian.com/news/2019/aug/01/media-framed-migrant-crisis-disaster-reporting

Triandafyllidou, A. (2018). A "refugee crisis" unfolding: "Real" events and their interpretation in media and political debates. *Journal of Immigrant & Refugee Studies, 16*(1–2), 198–216.

Youngblood, S. (2017). *Peace journalism principles and practices: Responsibly reporting conflicts, reconciliation, and solutions*. Routledge.

Instrumentalizing Refugees: Turkey, Greece and the European Union

Sophia Kaitatzi-Whitlock

Abstract

By its very nature migration constitutes a transnational phenomenon, affecting various geographies, transit or end-destination countries, occasionally gravely. This study focuses on *refugees' flows*. Namely, refugee flows from the Middle Eastern and Eastern Mediterranean regions towards European countries, which however, originate from externally caused and indeed imposed "endless wars". External state-destruction practices by NATO members, inter alia, have been going on in the region at least since 2003, with the invasion of Iraq, and are currently accentuated acutely.

To grapple with the syndrome of such incited, complicated international and transnational problems, I retrace the sequence of war events that triggered mass eradication and the original fleeing of main refugees' hordes and subsequently follow their changing fates and life trajectories. Then, I highlight relevant national border conflicts through *the lens of refugees'* management and instrumentalizing and their dire "utility adventures". In this respect, I assess the key international humanitarian part, which was formally assigned to Turkey by the EU, following which Turkey holds centre stage in this frame. Ever since, it has acquired crucial *power* via refugee hosting, handling or even blackmailing with. Through this process Turkey became the de facto host of circa four million of dislocated individuals, mostly refugees from Syria, Iraq and Libya, who are unwelcome elsewhere. I observe that by dealing with such hugely burdensome "collateral damage", indeed, the humanitarian disaster of "other countries' wars", gave Turkey a unique opportunity to acquire a powerful role in negotiat-

S. Kaitatzi-Whitlock (✉)
School of Journalism and Mass Communication, Aristotle University of Thessaloniki, Thessaloniki, Greece
e-mail: sophiakw@otenet.gr

D. Anagnostopoulou (ed.), *European Identities, Inclusion and Equality*, Diversity and Inclusion Research, https://doi.org/10.1007/978-3-031-90602-2_4

ing with important international actors through instrumentalization of refugees systematically.

The study documents modes employed in performing such tasks, including investigation of manipulative stances and instances of instrumentalizing refugees. In this respect, analysis suggests a *transformation* in Turkey's standing, in its relationship with involved counterparts, but also with refugees themselves. Turkey's tactics in handling refugees as a means of negotiation leverage not only explain but also prove that country's strategic advances to elicit power and prevail as a major regional power. Conversely, passive, absentee or belated reactive moves were observed on the part of key actors such as NATO and the EU. What prevails, then, on this side is a policy aversion or paralysis, especially on the part of the Union, resulting effectively in an inability to defend EU interests, its border-countries and hence its territorial integrity. Hence, the study infers that incapacity to pre-empt deterioration of refugee humanitarian disasters, at the stage of inception, is crucial both for state self-defence and also for international law principles. Overall, the combination of EU policy and non-policy outcomes has resulted in debilitating international law and in intensifying lawless recklessness.

Introduction

In October 2019, a new invasion took place in Syria. Turkish military forces occupied the Northern Syrian border zone, thereby exacerbating matters in an already extremely complex situation. Rather than peace, stability or modestly improved conditions in the internationally multi-conflict-stricken area of the Eastern Mediterranean region, more subversive changes ensued. The crisis escalated into a broader and more complex vicious circle ever since Turkey revamped its role and status altogether, thereby assuming commanding strategies and launching expansive projects with new claims that endanger the security in the Eastern Mediterranean.

This study focuses on *refugees and their flows* as an acutely accentuated transnational social phenomenon, deriving from such "endless wars" in the Middle East and surrounding areas. Firstly, I retraced the sequence of war events that triggered mass fleeing. Secondly, I followed up on the trajectories and the attendant changing fate of refugees by highlighting conflicts through *the lens of refugees* transformative adventures. The role of implicated key actors is examined, especially of Turkey, which holds centre stage in this frame, as it obtained a key *role* in refugee trajectories as the de facto host of millions of elsewhere unwelcome individuals. Given the international legal framework concerning *refugees*, the 'Geneva Convention', (UN General Assembly, 1951), the "enterprise" of hosting refugees granted a *sui generis* power to it. By dealing with such burdensome "collateral damage"—the humanitarian disaster of "others' wars"—Turkey acquired a key role in negotiating with powerful third actors. Following such a massive exodus, the country has been hosting over three million refugees from Iraq, Syria and Libya, among other countries. The aim of this study is to document the modes employed in performing this task, including investigation of manipulative stances or instances of instrumentalizing refugees. Analysis suggests a *metamorphosis* in Turkey's role in its relationship with involved counterparts but also with refugees. **By studying the tactics used in handling refugees as a means of negotiation leverage by Turkey, that country's strategic advances to elicit power and prevail as a regional superpower can be scrutinized and explained.**

Respectively, I monitored the reactive moves triggered by key involved actors, notably NATO, the USA and the European Union (EU) member states. Indeed, some international actors have emerged as "complicit" in Turkey's invasion of Syria. This outcome encouraged the country to defy international law and intensify its recklessness. Given such encouraging nods, Turkey upgraded its instrumentalization of refugees. Such practices and strategies elucidate Turkey's goal to promote its geopolitical position. Lastly, I concluded by discussing the impact on international law and on undermining and weakening legitimate stakeholders' interests in the Eastern Mediterranean.

The Syrian Crisis in the Background of the Middle Eastern Crises

Several actors have gotten involved in the unfolding of the successive and intersecting war conflicts. Broadly, they belong in two separate categories: the Intra-Syrian or intra-territorial forces (e.g., civil war insurgents) and the alien external forces.

Identifying and Categorizing Diverse Types of Implicated Actors and Relations

The embattled home actors and forces are comprised of two main sub-groups. The first group would be the anti-Assad "Free Syrian Army", which launched the civil war in 2011. Various liberal sections joined forces to fight against the autocratic Assad regime, aiming to democratize the political system (Augier, 1917/2020). This was a branch of the *Arab Spring* movements sponsored mainly by the USA.[1] The second group is the ethnically distinct Kurds: the Syrian Democratic Forces (SDF/YPG), who fought to gain state autonomy from central Syria and to eliminate the Islamic State (ISIS). To this effect, they fought in a strategic alliance with US forces successfully.[2] ISIS, a jihadist group that sprang off from al-Qaeda, originally under the name "Islamic State in Iraq and the Levant", was first established in Iraq in

[1] "Since at least 2006, the US has been funding political opposition groups in Syria, including a satellite television channel that beams anti-government programming into the country" (Blum, 2013, p. 145).

[2] See Conflict Monitor by HIS Markit, BBC.

2013. There they established their "Islamic Caliphate"[3] and subsequently expanded into Syria and fought to solidify it.

Among the external powers participating permanently or meddling in phases in the entangled Syrian wars, we have observed that the USA transferred military forces from its Iraq base to Syria to combat ISIS branches there. Ever since its invasion of Iraq in 2003, the USA has maintained military troops and personnel in the region and operated against Islamists in Syria in alliance with local forces, notably Syrian Kurds. Following the defeat of ISIS in March 2019 (Islamic State group defeated as final territory lost, US-backed forces say, 2019),[4] the USA announced the withdrawal of military forces from the Syrian ground. This act worked as a nod for Turkey to move in. During the various conflicts and wars in Syria, Turkey emerged with manifold roles. Turkey maintained close relations with ISIS and supported ISIS (Sassounian, 2014) militarily by providing them with weaponry and materials for combatants (The European Parliament, 2015)[5] against its NATO allies. Meanwhile, Turkey has also evolved into a quasi-"institutional" host of refugees. Moreover, they have closely checked Kurdish-Syrian developments, aiming to deter the independence of Syrian Kurds, thereby securing its national interests, by opposing any encouragement of irredentism among Kurds in Turkey. The country concluded the cycle of its roles by invading Syria and occupying Syrian territory illicitly. In this way, Turkey gradually prevailed as a momentous protagonist, achieving indeed to check and shape outcomes in the Syrian wars. Next, in the opposite camp, the Russian Federation (RF), a long-established ally of the Hafez Al Assad regime, got to enjoy a partner position. The RF supported the ruling Assad regime in many ways: through military operations in the civil war fights, by provision of weaponry and diplomatically.[6] Furthermore, Iran and religious Iranian forces sided up with the Shiite sections of Muslim populations in the country, opposing both the USA and Israel. Another factor is that Israel, a strategic US ally that keeps many of its Islamic neighbours in check, also fought against ISIS and contributed operationally in support of the USA. They have been positioned against most Islamic states, notably, those supporting the Palestinian state and people. Lastly, although not involved in any in situ territorial conflicts, the EU featured evidently in these wars, as they became the destination for millions of refugees but also a policymaker regarding this major humanitarian crisis.

[3] It was supported by Turkey and Arabic states, such as Qatar.

[4] On 23 March 2019, Mustafa Basli, of the SDF, announced proudly on Twitter, "the total elimination of the so-called Caliphate and the 100% territorial defeat of ISIS". Likewise, SDF General Mazloun Kobani confirmed this victory and added that fighting would continue against any remaining "pockets" held by ISIS forces.

[5] According to evidence by Cumhuriyet journalist Can Dündar, in Turkey, this was not denied, also inducing a question in the European Parliament. According to further concurring evidence, Turkey supported ISIS systematically and intensely.

[6] The Hafez al Assad regime is based on family autocracy, like in many other Arab countries. It has been reigning in Syria for decades. The Arab Spring Movement of the country pursued democratization, a change of the regime towards transparency and accountability.

The Apples of Discord

The formerly semi-autonomous Kurdish province, under the Syrian Democratic Forces (SDF) in northeastern Syria, joined the alliance in the concerted anti-ISIS offensives. All along, the SDF pursued their independence from Syria. Thus, Kurds fought a dual war: a liberation war and an anti-ISIS war, conditioning the former on the success of the latter. They admittedly proved to be the most crucial, valiant fighters among the allied anti-ISIS forces. The USA had promised to reward them with the establishment of their independent state and raised their hopes. An SDF independence would open the road to resolution of the longstanding Kurdish national problem. Inevitably, this entailed secession from Syria, which in its turn, entailed intricate geopolitical reshufflings and broader challenges, also involving Turkey. Yet, as soon as the SDF delivered their victory to the anti-ISIS camp, the Trump administration reneged on previous promises and betrayed them ungratefully. With hindsight, one may speculate whether, and to what extent, SDF/YPG goals were realistic.

The crucial apple of discord in Syria consists in the wealth of natural resources of the country, notably oil fields in the Northern Syrian provinces. Similarly, its strategic position, at the heart of the Eastern Mediterranean coast, enticed external international forces with interests, aspiring stakes and claims. Yet another conflict source stems from ethnic differences and divisions, notably concerning the irredentism of the Kurds. The making or the curbing of Kurdish state independence was crucial. By deterring it, Turkey avoided, at least provisionally, a catalytic internal change or an ethnological meltdown. So, it is elucidated why such quite heterogeneous international actors fought to impose their antagonistic agendas and to influence developments. Combined, these factors form an entangled vicious circle, fraught with tensions, divisions and claims on diverging but also crossing axes of interests: national, religious, political and economic.

Trends and Forms of Instrumentalizing Refugees

Over the last ten to fifteen years, Syria emerged as the epicentre of a multi-axial conflict zone, including a civil war, involving also external attacks on several fronts and provinces, plus religious and ethnic conflicts. Political, geopolitical and geoeconomic claims and controversies lay at the bottom of such turmoil. The embattled situation can, perhaps, be likened to a "war of all against all"—indeed, a humanitarian and geopolitical quagmire from where diverse kinds of fleeing individuals originate. Due to such complex wars, millions of inhabitants were forced to flee for their lives; hordes of persecuted individuals and families left their homes in Syria.

The International Legal Framework Concerning Refugees and Humanitarian Crisis

Given the international legal protection afforded to refugees by the UN Geneva Convention of 1951 (Weis, 1951), the *refugee entity* became a crucial international "unit" but also an agency per se. Indeed, it was destined to become pivotal in current international affairs. Populations fleeing from these regions can escape inevitably towards Turkey, which receives hosts and manages their insecure existence as a "captive entity". Ever since the eruption of the fleeing phenomenon, the trafficking industry has soared. Similarly, tens of NGOs emerged to assume diverse care roles around such crisis situations (Frangonikolopoulos, 2007), variously facilitating fleeing refugees. They organized their travelling movements step by step, often illegally. By the same token, they mediated in "exporting" these groups to their next transit venue, in this case, some Greek islands or the mainland. After a transit stay in Greece, most refugees continued towards northern European destinations (Barlai et al., 2018). Fleeing influxes soared, but there came a point of saturation, culminating in the "EU refugee crisis" in 2016, when refugee trajectory flows were interrupted abruptly (Barlai, ibid.; Kaitatzi-Whitlock & Kenterelidou, 2018).

Heterogeneity of Refugees: A Crucial Aspect

Refugees are the direct victims and "damage-products" of dictatorships and wars but, recently, also of natural disasters.[7] Their lives are either ruined or totally subverted. The Syrian "multi-war" churned out several kinds of refugees, such as civil war refugees, ISIS terror-victim-refugees and those escaping from bombardments and operations of anti-ISIS allied forces, both local and foreign. The latest batch of refugees stemmed from the Turkish invasion of Syria. Paradoxically, people escaped from Turkish military shelling to end up in Turkey. All of them escaped from Syrian territories, yet from diverse campaigns and battles. Many met in Turkish or Greek refugee camps, crossed roads and familiarized themselves as camp inmates. Yet, their cultural identities, political affiliations or orientations may differ considerably. Many share the Islamic religion by origin, or Islam, as their culture. Others are secularized or agnostic, while some are politically, rather than religiously, minded. Hence, Islam cannot be thrown on all as a blanket attribution. Nevertheless, generic outlooks prevail on victim populations. They tend to be treated "uniformly", even by NGO officials. For individuals in such exposed conditions, notions like individuality, privacy and intimacy lose their meaning. This is implicit in their condition. Crucially, it is mostly North European countries that are the preferred destinations of most *refugees*.

[7] The official legal definition of "refugee" in the rather old Geneva Convention does not include those forced to flee because of natural disasters. Evidently, though, "climate refugees" or "disaster displacement" peoples have been growing enormously since global warming and climate collapse.

Refugees' Passage Through Turkey

To escape wounds, unbearable suffering or death, refugees will try anything. Given the complex geopolitical situation they are entangled in, these individuals, families or groups must, often inevitably, pass through Turkey. This "Passage through Turkey" becomes significant, perhaps determinant for their future. The Turkish state is the *commanding subject* of their life story. Apart from everything else, until they reach their desired destination safely, refugees risk death from famine, drowning or trafficking. Moreover, exposed foreign individuals face several other forms of subjugation. Implicit in their condition is that they become *victim objects* in refugee handling processes. Although the United Nations Human Rights Council (UNHRC) plays an important watchdog role, their lives remain still quite at risk. Either they are in the hands of the Turkish or the Greek state, among NGO professionals, or in the hands of profiteering traffickers; they face risks. Put differently, during the fleeing process, human beings are not *in control* of their lives, especially those most vulnerable. Hence, escaping and fleeing are synonymous with dependency and risk. Freedom, balanced power relations and redemption may be obtained on arrival at a safe haven. Yet, they are elusive.

In 2015, Turkey struck an accord with the EU to receive funds in exchange for hosting and caring for refugees. So, Europeans paid many billions of euros to rid themselves of this refugee burden, which was caused by USA-led invasions, anti-terrorist campaigns or democracy-planting civil wars, ever since invading Iraq in 2003. Evaluating these processes, on the backdrop of corresponding international legal provisions, reveals how Turkey advanced from *instrumentalizing* refugees partially to gradually, manipulating them massively. In this way, Turkey fortified its strategic position and role, to the detriment of its adversaries. Such *role transformation* has caused problems, yet it was facilitated by the EU through its unwillingness or incapacity to adopt a coherent, timely, lasting, common immigration policy. The EU trickled to appeasing policies towards Turkey, which held the refugee-host key and kept twisting it opportunely. In this regard, there is uncertainty concerning how far Turkey will go, since it started disturbing the legitimate stakeholders' rights through various provocations. The crucial question is whether the now debilitated counterparts can determine the terms in the Eastern Mediterranean region from the perspective of their own interests.

Producing, Using and Abusing Refugees

In the past, refugees leaving Turkey got transported secretly to the shores of Greek islands, like Lesvos or Samos. According to the terms of the 2015 agreement with the EU, Turkish authorities are expected to police illicit trafficking and curb it. This was hardly the case. Illegal moves by traffickers, usually under extremely insecure and precarious conditions, often led to refugees drowning. Nevertheless, refugees will continue paying exorbitant sums of money and undertaking many risks in exchange for their perceived safety and freedom and so to keep moving to survive.

At the end of February 2020, TV news viewers witnessed an impressive but odd happening. Transporting of refugees to the Greek frontier of Evros—Alexandroupolis was executed by official Turkish services. Likewise, after the deterrence and failure of that ambushing project, official forces drove them back again to Constantinople (IN, 2020; Greece/Turkey: Asylum-seekers and migrants killed and abused at borders, 2020).[8] As evidenced in relevant news reports (BBC, The Guardian, NYT), refugee families and groups were shoved and utilized as pawns in an international border conflict between Greece and Turkey. Importantly, this signalled the adoption of quite new practices and alarming tactics by Turkey, namely, in treating refugees as pawns, playing with their pain.

Initially, refugees were a tool for negotiations. Later, they were converted into tools to threaten the terrified Europeans. More recently, they got shepherded as "forced trespassers" of locked borders. However, when President Recep Tayyip Erdoğan stated, "I opened the gates" (Stevis-Gridneff & Gall, 2020) (Western borders) inviting them to rush massively to Evros, he cruelly deceived refugees patently, because those borders are closed with erected walls on the Greek-European side. Presumably, without themselves realizing the deception and the exploitation of their refugee identity, they got embroiled in an international conflict. This was due to a seemingly common interest between Turkey and the refugees, so they trustingly followed them. The Geneva Convention (1951) addresses individual refugee rights. Here, though, observers witnessed masses of refugees being herded around, by a state leader, on false allegations. An unprecedented, extraordinary strategy was deployed, setting in motion new phenomena. But do such practices comply with legality? Are they compatible with Geneva Convention provisions? By shoving large groups around, boarding them on buses and driving them to closed border sites and back, one utterly exploits helpless and dependent refugees for the ulterior motives of the manipulator. Scruton's definition of exploitation suggests that it is undertaken precisely for the benefit of manipulators (1982, p. 162):

> In common parlance, John exploits Alfred when John uses Alfred to John's advantage, and to Alfred's detriment, without making just recompense […] Exploitation may involve deception (as in fraud), or force (as in slavery), or "undue influence" […] but its essence does not consist in any of these, which are invoked only to explain the position of the victim. Some find its essence in the idea of "just recompence".

In this case, instrumentalization of the entity of refugees was organized by a host state, aiming to expose the "heartlessness" and inhumanity or, plainly, policy weakness on the part of the Europeans. Indeed, President Erdoğan went public instantly to accuse Greece and the EU for not hosting refugees, while Turkey hosts millions

[8] The Evros-Alexandroupolis border incident erupted on 28 February and lasted till Monday, second of March 2020. The images of such organized massive population mobilizations were disturbing. Even more so, since this country has a history of forced and goaded mass mobilizations of refugees in its past; during WW I and up until 1922 Armenian and Greek refugees were pushed out and around till their extermination, in the Ottoman Empire, a century ago. See Bryce et al. (2000) and Milton (2008). See also: https://www.aljazeera.com/news/2020/03/turkish-police-bolster-greek-border-stop-migrants-return-200305114014230.html

of them. Thus, soon after invading and occupying Syria in 2019, Turkey "advanced" qualitatively in exploiting refugees in novel ways, including the refugees that Turkey created themselves by their invasion. In this way, any trusting partner relations between the EU and Turkey are totally undermined. Apart from anything else, such events both generated and manifested hostility between NATO partners, or ostensibly "friendly neighbors". Yet, this transpired as the objective of President Erdoğan.

Refugees are thus not just war victims but also pawns and ploys of Turkey, their institutional protector and host. Hence, the masses of shoved refugees were handled as an asset. Compared to slaves, they too confer use-value while in captivity to their host-dealer. It may also be correlated with "trafficking", currently a thriving global industry. Refugees may become "trafficked", bought and sold, blatantly used, individually or *en group*. They are unfree, manipulated, sent back and forth in the interest—monetary or otherwise—of the intermediary controlling party, for their own gain. This highlights, then, a manifest *transmutation*, documented in the spectacular Evros "adventure". In disagreeable, coercive, yet "official ways", refugees got converted into the "wedge" or leverage pawns through which President Erdoğan aimed to fulfil his ulterior motives. Refugees have been caught in an unprecedented trap. Undoubtedly, this is a reckless (or at the very least undiplomatic) misuse of playing with the "humanitarian card", and it should be unacceptable by all human rights standards accepted today. This novel consequence was generated following Turkey's invasion of Syria.

Greece: The Next Refugee Passage and Consequences for the Country

Apart from dire consequences incurred on persecuted refugees themselves, several more actors have suffered from Turkey's tactics and unusual strategic challenges. These include adjacent countries such as Cyprus, Greece and other neighbouring Middle Eastern nations. Thus, Greece also forms an often inevitable, key passageway for fleeing people. Consequently, it is de facto vulnerable to pressures. Indeed, Greece belongs to the worst-hit countries both by the sheer volumes of refugees transiting it and by the attendant humanitarian crisis, but also due to combined aggressive Turkish acts.

The Impact on Greece of Refugees' Arrivals and Inevitable Passing Through

In what follows, I shall therefore present the impact of Turkey's moves, particularly concerning Greece. A new set of provocative, if not plainly aggressive, Turkish moves threatened Greece on several fronts. Primarily through the management of refugee movements, but not exclusively, and by shepherding and directing them to illegal incursions into Greece while operating from Turkish territory. As documented in several reports, the mobilization of refugees by Turkish authorities involved regularly deceiving them[9] and blackmailing Europeans. Through such moves, Turkey has aimed at "expelling" refugees to European countries so as to alleviate its own unbearable burden, as is understandable. Nevertheless, the method of blackmail and of extorting changes remains an act of aggression towards a partner: the EU since Turkey had already agreed with the EU (2015), on hosting refugees. Thus, the true and deeper aims of Turkey remain unclear or enigmatic.

Because the potential of new refugee influxes petrifies several EU countries (Barlai et al., 2018; Kaitatzi-Whitlock & Kenterelidou, 2018), the entrapping of refugees in distant countries became the next, least bad option for them. Short-sightedly, this has satisfied all those intransigent EU member states that have refused to host refugees. Given such an EU-fixed absurd situation, Greece ends up trapped by both sides. It has become the main or sole European member state forced to be an intermediary host of refugees, without a corresponding EU programme nor equivalent funding, at that (To Pontiki, 2023). Despite all efforts by the former SYRIZA-led government, the country has proven quite incapable of coping with such disproportionately large numbers of refugees (ca 90.000). While most member states have refused to accept their proportionate quota of refugees, Greece has gotten inundated and trapped. The country sought EU assistance that did not materialize in due time. Thus, in direct contravention to the "Solidarity Principle," partners have denied alleviating Greece from its excessive burden of refugees.

Moreover, in the face of such an insensitive stance, central EU authorities have failed to either discipline or accommodate such member states duly. Thus, union fairness remains non-existent. Time and again, the EU has appeared to not command authority. Such inability reflects on the EU's lack of a coherent and sustainable immigration policy. In this light, the threats of perpetually growing influxes, due also to the new arrivals from the recent invasion, have been experienced as suffocating local citizens. Turkey was seemingly banking exactly on this. Worse, its strenuous pressurizing strategy against Greece has been comprised of a broad spectrum of actions to exhaust it. In short, "Turkey the bully" awoke, pursuing territorial and other assets under its new guise.

Attacking Greece on Several Fronts

Militarily, Turkey has been sustaining incessant daily aviation violations involving dangerous provocations against Greece. Tensions of illegal overflights over the FIR of Athens or coastal violations have been going on for decades but intensified further recently. From a Greek perspective, this has been a specimen of properly gratuitous violence, but from the opposite side, Turkey has been advancing by marking its territorial claims. From a legal standpoint, Turkey has ignored certain international law provisions, opting for its own, *sui generis* "reading" of them. Notably, the

[9] Even if we presume that refugees agreed willingly, could this occur *en masse*? Even if they offered their consent to be travelled to the border of Greece, this remained still an elicited outcome based on deceptive promises.

country is not a signatory to the International Maritime Law (UNCLOS)[10] and has unilaterally refused to recognize its indisputable global validity. Hence, it has been violating it, notably, in the Aegean Sea, indicatively, by declaring an illegal "*Casus Belli* on Greece". Economically, Greece has been badly affected in multiple ways since Turkey has laid claims to Greece's exclusive economic zones, extending as far south as the Libyan Sea and affecting the island of Crete. There have also been geopolitical threats. Thus, following the invasion of Syria, Turkey's appetite has grown so much that it has launched aggressive rhetoric daily while deploying hostile moves, targeting even mainland territories, like Evros. Such acts have confirmed a revamped, "new Turkey", which aims at the abolishing of international treaties on maritime territorial delimitations. Inter alia, such claims and sustained pressures have counteracted economic development, notably, in the Greek archipelago. Combined, these moves have composed a new *subversive* strategic approach and an aggressive "program". To even dare these acts has signalled Turkey's insatiable power thirst. Unless contained urgently, drastic changes are imminent. Such outcomes have perplexed and upset Greeks, causing tension and disarray. Statements by the Foreign Affairs and Defence ministers, N. Dendias and N. Panagiotopoulos, respectively, are indicative of this. To come to grips with Turkey's polemical shifts, they have introduced new terminology. Greeks now learn about "quasi wars" or that "Turkey is launching hybrid threats" (To Pontiki, 2023, pp. 6–7; Kossioni, 2020; Gialouridis, 2020). Through such notions, the Greek ministers have been attempting to reflect threatening developments and come to grips with a war-mongering neighbour.

Turkey: A New Actor—A New Factor

Turkish forces occupied Syrian territory on the pretext that they must protect their southeastern borders (Bellut & Levent, 2019; Euronews & Reuters, 2019). Thus, a sovereign state was invaded at a scale of 8/835 square kms. What were the causes of this particular offensive action by Turkey?

Eliminating the Goal of a Free, Independent Kurdistan

This prompt and large-scale military action by Turkey effectively entailed curbing the Kurds from achieving their long-standing goal for an independent Syrian Kurdistan. The implicit logic was that if SDF/YPG Kurds gained independence, then Kurdish populations in Turkey would be encouraged to pursue independence as well. Kurdish independence has been a veritable international problem, while it

[10] The United Nations Convention on the Law of the Sea (UNCLOS) provides for 12 nautical miles of national territorial prerogative and control. Nonetheless, this is denied to Greece with a "Casus Belli' declaration from Turkey. The effect of this intimidation is that Greece's territorial sovereignty officially extends only to 6 nautical miles, unlike everywhere else in the world.

poses an existential threat to Turkey as Turkish borders would be cut back considerably. So, Turkey intervened to deter this danger. Remarkably, while it intervened *illegally* to "secure" its southeastern border, it concurrently has been pursuing the breakup and change of its European borders with Greece at Evros. Hence, the expansionist strategy of Turkey is indisputably manifest.

Hence, President Erdoğan's Turkey has acted inimically across the entire Eastern Mediterranean, concurrently, on many fronts. Firstly, Turkey has been drilling and exploring for gas within the exclusive seawater zones of Cyprus. Secondly, they have launched the refugee-led attacks to break through the Greek border at Evros (February 2020). Thirdly, the Turkish military has intervened operationally in the Libyan Civil War. This extraordinarily expansive chain of operations has subverted several actors: Syria and the Syrian refugees, Kurs, Greece, Cyprus, the EU and Egypt. Thus, Turkey has been acting offensively on southern, western and northern bordering nations. So far, it has successfully forged its own *status* transformation by: [a] officially intervening in the Syrian Crisis and by curbing options for a future Kurdish state, [b] initiating a new type of refugee weaponizing-exploitation, thereby accentuating and exacerbating the refugee crisis, and [c] destabilizing and threatening Greece, Cyprus and the EU. Through such multi-faceted and escalating provocations, Turkey has wielded substantial power and has been pursuing its strategic goals to control the entire Eastern Mediterranean region and to check "all game" there. By contrast, neighbouring countries and the EU, as such, have been weakened.

Turkish Goals Fulfilled

Through astute brinkmanship and strategic, bold and reckless moves, Turkey has undergone a drastic shift, bordering though on illegality: [a] They militarily invaded North Syria, presumably, after the tacit nod of the Trump administration. In doing so, [b] Turkey started causing new refugees of its own making. [c] They introduced a hybrid, *quasi-official* sort of manoeuvring of refugees, when shoving them to break into Greece, across Evros-Alexandroupolis (Stevis-Gridneff & Gall, 2020). President Erdoğan argued that Turkey cannot bear the mounting weight of refugees. Proportionately, though, the same applies for Greece too. Notwithstanding this, [d] Turkey also orchestrated a media blame-game against both Greece and the EU. President Erdoğan has personally blamed them as in-humanitarian, due to their anti-refugee stance (Turkey rejected 1 billion euro in migrant aid from EU: Erdogan, n.d.). Through such organized media blame-games, Turkey has additionally passed moral judgements. In all, Turkey has come out as "producer" of refugees but concurrently also as host and *utilizer* of them. Put in economic terms, this amounts to vertical integration of monopoly power control.

What do such unorthodox events signal to the world, to Greece and to the EU? Media presumptions suggest ordinary "exerting pressure", in the "Turkish bazar style" to achieve more profitable refugee "deals" from the EU. This time, however, the game has turned. Turkey has not only been blackmailing both Greece and the EU, but has also been claiming actual Aegean, Eastern Mediterranean and European asset-rich territories. Given such bold moves, Turkey seems to have succeeded in destabilizing, or even in "neutralizing", the EU. Thus, we can remark that by invoking its "right to border protection" after having secured the NATO approval, in view of worries about Kurdish insurgency, Turkey has subsequently been pursuing the dismantling of the borders with the rest of its neighbours. Turkey's movements have entailed, or at least they forebode, expansive border changes to their exclusive benefits. The most unusual aspect of this is that it has advanced, so far, without any opposition. Thus, in a Middle East situation that was already "out of control", Turkey's invasive inroads exacerbated matters while patently violating international law. All along, the ongoing violence in Syria, Iraq and Libya has continued provoking fresh hordes of *refugees*, thereby deteriorating the humanitarian disaster gravely. Such conditions have perpetuated unresolved conflicts, multiplying the suffering of refugees who wish to knock on European doors. Certainly, refugee challenges will not evaporate. They will persist, contributing to home social crises and problems. The refugees have been, and continue to be, the primary link in the vicious circle in which the EU is entrapped.

Humanitarian Crisis and the Consequences for the EU

Contrary to Stoltenberg, some EU leaders denounced the invasion in Syria and called for sanctions against Turkey, albeit not that vocally. Chancellor A. Merkel publicly denounced the invasion, demanding that President Erdoğan pull back his forces. However, in spite of leading EU member states, including Germany and France, threatening Turkey with sanctions (i.e. imposing an arms embargo), such threats had no effect whatsoever on Turkey. To the contrary, despite the EU-Turkey agreement (2015) on refugee care, the country has unilaterally initiated subversive challenges in this respect too. On the EU's offer of 1 billion euros of extra funds for refugee care during the Evros border crisis, President Erdoğan mockingly retorted that he does not want the money at all. Hence, not only is Turkey undeterred but also, on the contrary, they have persisted in pursuing their illegal goals in Syria. Ignoring European leaders is not simply humiliating. It is, rather, the proof of the EU's reticence, if not weakness in this tug-of-war. Regional leaders may, thus, view the EU as irrelevant in their international handlings, incapable of protecting peace and stability in their own and adjacent territories.

Was the "battle" between these two camps won by the aggressor, or not? Surely, Turkey's corrosive impact is identified primarily on the drastically transformed mode of conducting international relations and politics, which appear as neither legal nor tolerable. Furthermore, illegalities are manifest concerning the respect and protection of refugees in Turkey. At the very least, the impact has been severe on the geopolitical positions of Cyprus and of Greece, a NATO ally, and by extension on the EU itself and the Eastern Mediterranean. They also put pressure on the operational principles of NATO, which are gravely cast into question. Violations of international law cannot be ignored or go unpunished. Undoubtedly, the effects of the

Turkish invasion have been disastrous for local peoples and refugees alike, but also for "International Law" and the "Rule of Law" per se.

NATO's General Secretary Jens Stoltenberg declared that it is Turkey's "right' to invade Syria (Reuters Staff, 2019).[11] Notwithstanding other concerns, such express approval of the invasion, rather than the opposite, is flabbergasting. Interestingly, other international powers, too, held back from criticizing international law violations by Turkey. Overall, third-party aggressive military actions in combination with EU policy inertia foster a perpetual *humanitarian crisis and a security challenge, burdening particularly in Mediterranean, Middle Eastern and European regions*. In short, while offenders succeed in reaping advantages and in safeguarding positions of power in European regions, the EU ends up receiving collateral damages and problems.[12] Nonetheless, to the extent that a measured, common immigration policy based on sustainable country quotas is absent, haphazard refugee influxes are doomed to induce extremism and social consequences, also in terms of rises in neo-Nazi stances in European societies.

Concluding Remarks

Over the last decades, the EU has appeared reticent, unwilling, stiff, or incapable of tackling its crises and defending its own territories effectively. Threats and risks were not as severe in the past, but conditions have changed. The EU has neglected or alienated itself from its Middle Eastern areas, although two of its member states, Cyprus and Greece, are bordering with these regions. Nowadays, speedy invasive reactions by aggressive forces have exposed such incapability of the EU to secure its interests. The Mediterranean, alias *Mare Nostrum*, is thus open to ambitious invasive powers. Policy inertia and lack of unitary governance do cost. If such vital European areas and their surroundings are abandoned, this stands for the EU's existential peril. Conversely, however, separate national moves by European member states are observable, contradicting or even antagonizing one another. Scattered national initiatives cannot offer substitutes to grant security. The opposite holds. They damage the EU. Hence, the issues of governance and of unity of the EU persist, and these are existential. Unless European member states pull their act together fast, this region is endangered. The EU has legitimate rights to self-protection, peace and stability. Through proactive stances, it could act catalytically on protecting its maritime zones, for instance, by due delimitations in the Eastern

[11] NATO's S. G. J. Stoltenberg Defends Stance on Turkey's Offensive in Syria (14-10-2020). As comparisons are elucidating, a relevant and pertinent question is addressed to Jens Stoltenberg: "Should Russian Federation military forces be allowed to invade bordering Norwegian territory on similar pretexts? Namely, concerning the national ambitions of the Sami peoples?" (Reuters Staff, 2019).

[12] The EU could benefit from the refugee crisis if it stopped its phobic, inert approaches. Indeed, the EU needs population rejuvenation urgently. However, problems could be turned into prospects only by committed decision makers. The EU cannot avoid security and migration policies concerning its own Mediterranean Responsibility to Protect (R2P), without getting involved.

Mediterranean. Moreover, it could secure the EU member states' Mediterranean Energy pipelines.

Many scholarly analysts have highlighted the importance for the EU to adopt a common, principled migrant and refugee policy: a realistic policy within its capacities and compatible with its plans and interests. Yet, the vital necessity of such a policy has been misrecognized and misconstrued. Centrifugal forces prevail, thereby endangering the very project of the Union. As things turned out, the EU failed in the test of *intergovernmental governance* and leadership. Enrico Letta, a leading Italian politician, put it succinctly. "Truly, euro-skepticism exists, especially so, in my country. It is mainly due to the way the EU handled the previous two crises: the economic crisis of 2008-2012 and the refugee crisis of 2015. Part of this EU-crisis is due to lack of solidarity, in both cases" (Matsi & Fabien, 2020, pp. 26–27).

The EU's "hesitancy" to intervene proactively as a commanding stakeholder, especially when facing vital challenges, does not only paralyze the Union. It proves its inability to defend EU interests, causes, borders and territories. Incapacity to resolve or pre-empt deterioration of the humanitarian disaster, apart from tyrannizing refugees themselves, foments ultra-right extremism in European societies. Policy inertia is lethal on such internal and external security issues and on stability challenges in foreign affairs. Denial of reality recognition inevitably leads to policy impasses. Even if explicable by the EU's intergovernmental decision-making paralysis and deadlocks, it remains disturbing and, crucially, destructive. Especially when heedless antagonistic powers exploit such gaps and expand and fortify their presence, such weaknesses touch on the very existence of the EU.

References

Augier, J. (1917/2020). *De L'ardeur, histoire de Razan Zaitouneh, Avocate Syrienne* (A. Moshona Trans, 2nd Ed.). Polis. (Original work published in 1917).

Barlai, M., Fähnrich, B., Rhomberg, M., & Griessler, C. (2018). *The migrant crisis: European perspectives and National Discourses*. LIT Verlag.

Bellut, D., & Levent, H. (2019, August 13). Turkey, US work to create buffer zone in Syria. In *Conflicts*. Deutsche Welle. https://www.dw.com/en/turkey-us-work-to-create-buffer-zone-in-northern-syria/a-50013705

Blum, W. (2013). *America's deadliest export–democracy: The truth about US foreign policy and everything else*. Zed Books.

Bryce J., Toynbee, A. J. & Toynbee, A., (2000). *The Treatment of Armenians in the Ottoman Empire, 1915–1916: Documents Presented to Viscount Grey of Falloden by Viscount Bryce* (Uncensored Edition) aka "The Blue Book" Paperback–December 11, 2000.

Euronews, & Reuters. (2019, October 10). Turkey threatens EU critics with open border as Syria conflict intensifies. *Euronews*. https://www.euronews.com/2019/10/09/turkey-begins-military-offensive-in-northern-syria-after-us-pulls-out-troops

Frangonikolopoulos, C. (2007). *ΟΠαγκόσμιοςΡόλοςτωνΜη-ΚυβερνητικώνΟργανώσεων: ΔυναμικήκαιΑδυναμίεςστηνΠαγκόσμιαΔιακυβέρνηση [The global role of NGOs: Dynamics and weaknesses in global governance]*. Sideris. (in Greek).

Gialouridis, C. (2020). Απουσίαπολέμουωςψευδαίσθησηειρήνης [the absence of war, as an illusion of peace]. *Boulvard, 48*, 12–44. http://www.eboulevard.gr/np/newspaper.php?issue=58#page/13

"Greece/Turkey: Asylum-seekers and migrants killed and abused at borders". (2020, April 3). *Amnesty International*. https://www.amnesty.org/en/latest/news/2020/04/greece-turkey-asylum-seekers-and-migrants-killed-and-abused-at-borders/

INnewspaper. (2020). Έβρος: Νέα ένταση στα σύνορα μεταξύ προσφύγων—αστυνομίας. https://www.in.gr/2020/02/28/greece/evros-nea-entasi-sta-synora-metaksy-prosfygon-astynomias

"Islamic State group defeated as final territory lost, US-backed forces say" (2019, March 23). *BBC*. https://www.bbc.com/news/world-middle-east-47678157

Kaitatzi-Whitlock, S., & Kenterelidou, C. (2018). The Greek paradigm. In M. Barlai, B. Fähnrich, C. Griessler, & M. Rhomberg (Eds.), *The migrant crisis: European perspectives and national discourses*. LIT Verlag.

Kossioni, S. (2020, May 26). *Panagiotopoulos Nikos [interview]*. Skai News.

Matsi, A., & Fabien, P. (2020, May 2-3). Enrico Leta: *ΟΚορονοϊόςθέτεισεαμφισβήτησητομέλ λοντηςΕνωμένηςΕυρώπης* [coronavirus puts the future of Europe in question], [interview]. Efimerida ton Syntakton, 26-27.

Milton, G. (2008). *Paradise lost: Smyrna 1922: The destruction of Islam's City of tolerance*. Sceptre Books.

Reuters Staff. (2019, October 14). NATO's Stoltenberg defends stance on Turkey's offensive in Syria. *Reuters*. https://www.reuters.com/article/us-syria-security-turkey-nato-idUSKBN1WT1C8.

Sassounian, H. (2014). Columbia University researchers confirm Turkey's links to ISIS. *Armenian National Committee of America*. https://anca.org/columbia-university-researchers-confirm-turkeys-links-to-isis/

Scruton, R. (1982). *Dictionary of political thought*. Palgrave Macmillan.

Stevis-Gridneff, M. & Gall, C. (2020, March 1). Erdogan Says, "We Opened the Doors," and Clashes Erupt as Migrants Head for Europe. *The New York Times*. https://www.nytimes.com/2020/02/29/world/europe/turkey-migrants-eu.html

The European Parliament. (2015). *The journalist Can Dündar and Turkish support for ISIS*. E-009186/2015. https://www.europarl.europa.eu/doceo/document/E-8-2015-009186_EN.html

To Pontiki. (2023). "Εκείπουμαςχρωστούσανε, μαςπήρανκαιτοβόδι" [Although they owed us, they made us pay]. (2020, April 30). To Pontiki, 2023, 11.

"Turkey rejected 1 bln euro migrant aid from EU: Erdogan". (n.d.). *Arabiya News*. https://english.alarabiya.net/en/News/world/2020/03/03/Turkey-rejected-1-bln-euro-migrant-aid-from-EU-Erdogan-.html

UN General Assembly. (1951, July 28). Convention Relating to the Status of Refugees, United Nations, Treaty Series, Vol. 189, p. 137. https://www.refworld.org/legal/agreements/unga/1951/en/39821 [accessed 16 April 2025]

Weis, P. (1951). *The refugee convention*. UNHCR. https://www.unhcr.org/media/refugee-convention-1951-travaux-preparatoires-analysed-commentary-dr-paul-weis

Zillennials Versus Millennials: Attitudes Toward Gender, Culture, and Migration

Marianthi Karatsiori

Abstract

This study explores the interrelation between attitudes on gender, culture, and migration among Millennial and Zillennial students at a Greek university. These attitudes, often framed dichotomously, are frequent sources of discrimination in contemporary societies. The interplay between culture and migration is evident, focusing strongly on the dynamics developed at a destination through peoples' interaction, coexistence, and the dilution of different values from one culture to another. The gender dimension may be distinct from the concepts of culture and migration, but still, there is this suspicion that even within the most developed western societies, women are less favored than men. The research aims to uncover underlying assumptions about these topics among the youngest two generations of university students in Greece. Using a survey questionnaire, this case study analyzes students' perceptions through descriptive analysis. Results indicate that participants demonstrate open-mindedness toward gender equality, value intercultural competencies, employ appropriate linguistic strategies in cross-cultural communication, and hold positive attitudes toward migration. Notably, no significant differences were observed between millennial and zillennial cohorts. Participants did not validate social stereotypes and emphasized the importance of openness, flexibility, and empathy in intercultural interactions. The majority of respondents employed appropriate linguistic strategies when communicating with people who do not speak their mother tongue. This study, the first of its kind conducted in a Greek university context, contributes valuable insights into evolving attitudes on critical social issues among emerging generations, providing a foundation for further research and potential policy implications in higher education and beyond.

M. Karatsiori (✉)
Department of Educational and Social Policy, University of Macedonia, Thessaloniki, Greece
e-mail: mkaratsiori@uom.edu.gr

D. Anagnostopoulou (ed.), *European Identities, Inclusion and Equality*, Diversity and Inclusion Research, https://doi.org/10.1007/978-3-031-90602-2_5

Introduction

Deconstructing stereotypes by critically analyzing their perceived "naturalness" is a daunting task. This is because beliefs, models, principles, ethics, and practices are deeply embedded in our culture, our language, and in the way social norms and family ties intervene in forming our identity. This study aims to capture the outlook on genders, culture, and migration of "millennial and zillennial" students in a Greek university. Zillennials (or Generation Z) were born between 1994 and 2012/15. Millennials (or Generation Y) were born between 1981 and 1994/6. The Gen Z generation is the first generation to be "digital natives" as opposed to all previous "digital immigrant" generations. Research suggests that trying to understand people's beliefs based on their generation is both complicated and contradictory, as it may involve inferences that are generalizations. Conversely, it is acknowledged that people "do have generational identities" (Purhonen, 2016, p. 176) and, in this sense, a generational interpretation could shed light on the ways social stereotypes on gender, culture, and migration are formed and how they differ from one generation to another.

As populations across the world become more diverse, it is critical to understand how the younger generations, Millennials and Zillennials, construct their beliefs and values toward otherness. The theory of the sociological generation advocates that experiencing childhood, adolescence, and adulthood at about the same period instigates similar beliefs, principles, and attitudes toward life for the people belonging to the same generation (Edmunds & Turner, 2005; Kupperschmidt, 2000). The dissimilarities between generations are mainly associated with the strong societal and environmental impact during the years of socialization, which influence the development of one's character, the formation of principles, and life purposes (Macky et al., 2008). Lifestyle, traumatic events, socioeconomic and cultural events, along with important advances in technology, play a significant role in deciding one's life expectations (Cennamo & Gardner, 2008). The discourse around attitudes on gender, culture, and migration suggests that there might be an interrelation between these three factors and generational cohorts. These attitudes are often captured by dichotomous categories: gender biased or not, intercultural awareness or intercultural insensitivity, anti-migrant attitudes or pro-migrant attitudes. This dichotomous categorization implies that all three (gender, culture, and migration) are frequent discriminatory issues that are common in current societies. The interplay between culture and migration is evident, since it focuses strongly on the dynamics developed at a destination through peoples' interaction, coexistence, and the dilution of different values from one culture to another. The gender dimension may be distinct from the concepts of culture and migration, yet there is this suspicion that, even within the most developed western societies, women are less favored than men. This study attempts to uncover the underlying assumptions the youngest two generations of students in a Greek university have on gender, culture, and migration bias. Sparse investigation of students' attitudes and beliefs on gender, culture, and migration has been done so far.

The following research questions guide the current study:

Research Question 1: Are there any factors that influence students' beliefs about gender, culture, and migration? If yes, which are they?

Research Question 2: What are students' attitudes toward diversity? Do they construct an ethic of social justice, or do they settle for social stereotypes? Do the views of Millennials differ from the views of Zillennials?

This study, guided by a social constructivist perspective, constructed an instrument-questionnaire to capture the diversity and nuances in students' thinking about gender, culture, and migration. First, factors that could influence students' attitudes toward diversity, such as languages spoken, travelling abroad, friends or family members from other countries, cognitive strategies that facilitate communication, and language acquisition, were examined. Next, a separate set of questions for gender, culture, and migration was constructed. Questions and sub-categories from previously tested instruments were used, such as *the Developmental Model of Intercultural Sensitivity* (DMIS) by Bennett (2013), *the Model of Intercultural Communicative Competence of Byram* (1997), *the PISA 2018 Global Competence Questionnaire*, and *The Social Roles Questionnaire: A New Approach to Measuring Attitudes Toward Gender* (Baber & Tucker, 2006). In the end, the recommendations of students for enhancing the intercultural competence and respect toward otherness were also presented.

Theoretical Considerations on Gender, Culture, and Migration

Interest in gender, culture, migration, and the conceptualization of ways beliefs form our identity provide a strong impetus for research. Individuals' beliefs about attitudes toward gender, culture, and migration in society can be useful to researchers who are interested in understanding people's thinking about equity and social justice. People's attitudes toward these three variables—gender, culture, and migration—can produce inequalities that intersect with other social and economic inequalities. It is difficult to capture the complexity of the way people form their beliefs and attitudes, but it could be said that these three variables are dichotomous—in the sense that a person can be gender biased, culture biased, and biased toward migrants. One theory is that if a person is biased in one of these three variables, they will also be biased in the other two variables. There are many forms of discrimination in today's societies, but gender, culture, and migration are the most common and traceable in almost all societies, from the most traditional to the most progressive and unconventional.

Presumably, gender equality should be an outdated issue to research, especially in the western world, where gender issues should have been resolved many years ago. Conversely, the Gender Equality Index 2024 indicates that the EU still has significant progress to make, with an average score of 71 out of 100 (European Institute for Gender Equality, 2024). This score reflects persistent challenges, including gender gaps in the labor market and underrepresentation in decision-making positions (European Commission, 2024). Notably, Greece ranks low among EU countries, highlighting substantial disparities (European Institute for Gender

Equality, 2024). Although there are diverse convictions on the ontogeny and evolvement of gender, several thinkers (Bockting, 1999; Bohan, 2002; Butler, 1986 and 1990; Kimmel, 2000; Maurer, 1999) have advocated that gender is socially constructed and stressed the intricacy of the concept. The World Health Organization on its webpage on gender and health states that "*Gender refers to the characteristics of women, men, girls and boys that are socially constructed. This includes norms, behaviours and roles associated with being a woman, man, girl or boy, as well as relationships with each other. As a social construct, gender varies from society to society and can change over time*." The conviction that men and women differ biologically usually liaises with pre-established conceptions that, for specific social roles, one gender is more suited than the other (Martin & Ruble, 2004). Recent research in Greece highlights the continued relevance of gender equality in education, with teachers expressing a growing interest in addressing these issues in schools (Peleki & Nikolaou, 2024). Studies continue to explore how societal expectations and power dynamics contribute to observed gender disparities in various aspects of life (Galinsky et al, 2024). Therefore, the pursuit of gender equality remains a critical and contemporary concern in Europe and beyond (Bajraktari et al., 2024).

Understanding attitudes toward cultures is a complicated task. The complexity of understanding culture is reflected in the difficulty of defining what culture is. In 1952, Kroeber and Kluckhohn critically appraised 164 different definitions of culture, and today there is an even greater abundance of culture definitions. Hall (1976, pp. 16) argues that culture "*is not innate, but learned; the various facets of culture are interrelated – you touch a culture in one place and everything else is affected; it is shared and in effect defines the boundaries of different groups.*" Similarly, Hofstede (1991, p. 180) defines culture as "*the collective programming of the mind which distinguishes the members of one group or category of people from another.*" Both these definitions view culture as a social construct that influences group dynamics. The concept of intercultural awareness is linked to linguistic competence, since language is the means to communicate and understand the others. To Kramsch (1993) and Byram (1997) the optimal is not a native speaker but an "*intercultural speaker.*" Kramsch (1998, p. 27) defines this intercultural speaker as not someone able to implement the grammatical and syntactical norms but as someone who has the competence to use the linguistic elements they know in different contexts of interaction to facilitate communication. The Council of Europe advocates that "*People's cultural affiliations are dynamic and fluid; what they think defines them culturally fluctuates as an individual move from one situation to another. These fluctuations depend on the extent to which a social context focuses on a particular identity, and on the individual's needs, motivations, interests and expectations within that situation*" (Council of Europe, 2016). An open-minded approach to cultural diversity forms the foundation for respecting human rights. This openness helps us appreciate differences, which is essential for learning to live together in participatory democratic societies.

Our conception of culture directly affects our approach to migration issues. Many studies have investigated the attitudes toward migration from different views, such as analyzing general migration attitudes (Masso, 2009), emphasizing ethnic bias (Onraet & Van Hiel, 2013), focusing on possible advantages of migration (Esses et al., 2012), on diversity of exclusion criteria (Alexseev, 2015), on tensions between locals and migrants (Dustmann & Preston, 2007; Hainmueller & Hiscox, 2010; Malchow-Møller et al., 2008; O'Rourke & Sinnott, 2006), and on ethno-racial antipathy and the belief that migrants damage the welfare state (Ceobanu & Koropeckyj-Cox, 2013). The idea that a strong connection to one's national identity fosters anti-immigration attitudes (Mayda, 2006) continues to find support in more recent research. For instance, Lee's (2023) study in Taiwan revealed that educational content emphasizing an exclusive national identity based on shared ancestry and birthplace actually increased anti-immigrant sentiments among students. Similarly, another experimental work in Mexico demonstrated that priming individuals with an ethnic conception of Mexican national identity led to more negative attitudes specifically towards Chinese immigrants (Acevedo & Meseguer, 2022; Rossi, 2022). Furthermore, research in Germany during the 2015/2016 refugee crisis (Lindstam et. al., 2021) highlighted that a stronger adherence to an ethno-cultural understanding of German national identity was associated with greater opposition to immigration. These findings underscore how the introduction of new traditions and beliefs by migrants can be perceived by locals with a strong national identity as undermining their country's identity and social norms, consequently fueling opposition towards migrants.

Methodology

This survey was conducted at the University of Macedonia in Thessaloniki, Greece. The survey of attitudes toward gender, culture, and migration was conducted using an online questionnaire developed using Google Forms. For this case study, the questionnaire was addressed to undergraduate students of all departments. The significance of this study is that it is the first study conducted in a Greek university that attempts to gauge students' attitudes on gender, culture, and migration themes.

Participants

The University of Macedonia is a small public university in Greece that has eight academic departments comprised of two main scientific fields: (a) Social sciences, humanities and arts (department of European and international studies, department of educational and social policy, department of music science and art) (b) Economic studies and information sciences (department of economics, department of Balkan, Slavic and Oriental studies, department of business administration, department of accounting and finance, department of applied informatics). The questionnaire was posted to Facebook groups created by students and was also forwarded to students mails by three tutors teaching at the university. A total of 126 students participated in the survey, from all departments of the university. There were 107 who identified

Table 1 Categorization of participants by academic field and age group

	Age			
	18–23		>24	
University department	N	%	N	%
Educational and social policy	55	61.8	19	51.4
Management	7	7.9	1	2.7
Informatics	9	10.1	5	13.5
Logistics	1	1.1	0	0.0
International and European studies	17	19.1	5	13.5
Music studies	0	0.0	2	5.4
Balkan and slavic studies	0	0.0	2	5.4

themselves as female, and 19 as male: 89 students (71.7% of the participants) were 18–23 years old (the Zillennial generation), and 37 students (28.3%) were from 24 to 45+ years old (the Millennial generation). The majority of the students were Greek (98%) with Greek as their mother tongue, which reflects the demographic features of the region. One student was Bulgarian and one was Romanian, their mother tongues being Bulgarian and Romanian, respectively. Students represented a variety of scientific fields, and they were primarily from working-class and middle-class families. Table 1 below depicts the number of students per department.

Participants were asked about the languages they speak, as well as the languages of their mother and father. Five participants stated that they speak only their mother tongue, 98 participants stated that they speak 2 languages, 7 that they speak 3 languages, 14 participants speak 4 languages, and 2 participants speak 5 foreign languages. Compared to the language competence of their parents, participants speak more languages than their parents; 53 mothers and 66 fathers of the participants speak only their mother tongue. Concerning the languages that they speak and the level of proficiency in each language, 38 participants state that they speak English fluently. English is the only language to be acquired by the participants at an excellent level. Fifty-nine participants speak English at an advanced level and 17 at an intermediate level. Eleven participants speak French and six participants speak German at an advanced level. Sixteen participants speak German and 14 speak French at an intermediate level. Eighty-eight participants (69.8%) communicate regularly in a foreign language with a friend, colleague, or family member and 87 participants (69%) have friends from other countries.

Participants were also asked whether they had travelled abroad. 103 participants (81.7%) have travelled abroad, while 23 participants (18.3%) have not. Of those that have travelled abroad, 45 participants (43.7%) have travelled 1–3 times, 36 participants (35%) have travelled abroad 4–10 times, and 22 participants (21.3%) have travelled abroad more than 10 times. Twenty-five participants (65.8%) have lived abroad for a month, while 7 participants (18.4%) have lived abroad for 3–6 months, and 6 participants (15.8%) have stayed abroad for more than a year. The majority of respondents had travelled abroad multiple times, and most of them had extramural communication with someone from another country in a foreign language.

Results

The results will be presented in two sections. In the first section, the more general findings will be presented that are related to the intercultural awareness of the participants, the intercultural ommunicative competence, and the linguistic strategies they use to facilitate interaction. In the second part, the attitudes toward gender, culture and migration will be analyzed, along with an open-ended question where students recommend ways the university could offer a more intercultural experience to the students.

Within the research, a key element was the classification of students into two categories based on their age: the Millennial (37 students) and the Gen Z (89 students) generation. This classification assisted in understanding whether there is a difference in attitudes on gender, culture, and migration themes that could be explained by the different influences and set of values and beliefs each generation may embrace.

Bennett's Developmental Model of Intercultural Sensitivity and Byram's Model of Intercultural Communicative Competences

The first set of questions was based on the Developmental Model of Intercultural Sensitivity (DMIS) by Bennett (1986, 1993, 2004, 2013). The DMIS continuum extends from *ethnocentrism to ethnorelativism*. Ethnocentrism includes the first three stages, "denial-defense-minimization," that are conceptualized as more ethnocentric and focus on the experience of one's own culture as "central to reality," whereas *ethnorelativism* includes the last three stages, "acceptance-adaptation-integration," that focus on the experience of one's own and other cultures as "relative to context." The "denial" stage is based on the conviction that a person's culture is the only real culture. People in the denial stage are not able to perceive cultural differences and tend to isolate themselves from other groups (Cushner et al., 2012, p. 155). Through the "defense" stage, people are usually judgmental of other cultures and use negative stereotypes (ibid. p. 157). Through the "minimization" stage, people find common ground between themselves and people of other cultures; acknowledging that all people are people (ibid., p. 158). During the "Acceptance" stage, people recognize that there are many different ways of going about certain situations (ibid., p. 160); they appreciate the plethora of cultural differences, attitudes, and beliefs. "Adaptation" is the fifth stage where one can understand the world through another's "eyes." It could be alleged that it is characterized by empathy and the willingness to understand the other. People that attain the final stage of "integration" could be regarded as culture mediators, since they can understand different cultures and promote unity between different cultures (ibid., p. 165) (Fig. 1).

Six statements, one for each stage, were given to the participants. The seventh statement was added later to make the stage of integration, the openness toward

Fig. 1 The Stages of Development by Bennett: From Ethnocentrism to Ethnorelativism

Table 2 Responses of Zillennials vs. Millennials based on the DMIS by Bennett

		Age		
		18–23 (N = 89)	>24 (N = 37)	*p*-value
1. I believe that my cultural experience derived from the culture and society I live is the only real and valid cultural experience.	**Yes**	**5(5.6%)**	**6(16.2%)**	**0.055[a]***
	No	**84(94.4%)**	**31(83.8%)**	
2. There are inferior and superior civilizations	Yes	20(22.5%)	13(35.1%)	0.141[a]
	No	69(77.5%)	24(64.9%)	
3. I am not objective with cultures I do not know about. They can take a more romantic or less important dimension in my mind. I try to disregard the differences and to focus on similarities between cultures.	**Yes**	**38(42.7%)**	**22(59.5%)**	**0.086[a]**
	No	**51(57.3%)**	**15(40.5%)**	
4. I accept other civilizations though I may not agree with them	Yes	86(96.6%)	35(94.6%)	0.630[b]
	No	3(3.4%)	2(5.4%)	
5. I want to learn for other cultures and I respect them all	Yes	88(98.9%)	37(100%)	1.000[b]
	No	1(1.1%)	0(0%)	
6. I see the world from different cultural perspectives and I adapt accordingly my attitude and way of thinking.	Yes	77(86.5%)	33(89.2%)	0.682[a]
	No	12(13.5%)	4(10.8%)	
7. All human beings must have equal rights	Yes	88(98.9%)	35(94.6%)	0.206[a]
	No	1(1.1%)	2(5.4%)	

[a]Chi-square test, [b]Fischer's exact test, *$p < 0.1$

otherness, and the human rights dimension straightforward and explicit. Table 2 depicts the results per statement and per generation.

As it is evidenced from the analysis of Table 2 Gen Z and Millennials responded in a similar way to all statements with the exception of the first and third statement. It could be derived that the Millennials exposed a more ethnocentric attitude, as 16.2% of them, compared to 5.6% of Zillennials, consider the culture and society they live in as the only real and valid cultural experience, a statement that could denote the "denial" stage. A higher percentage of Millennials, 59.5%, compared to 42.7% of Gen Z, try to disregard the differences and focus on similarities between cultures, a statement that could prescribe the "minimization stage" of DMIS.

The second set of questions is based on Byram's model of intercultural communicative competence (ICC) (1997). Byram embraces a critical culture awareness standpoint and refers to the speaker's competence to evaluate practices and perspectives in their own or other cultures. For developing this intercultural communicative competence, the individual must be able to recognize and interpret implicit or explicit values expressed in all types of interactions. Byram focuses on the ability to

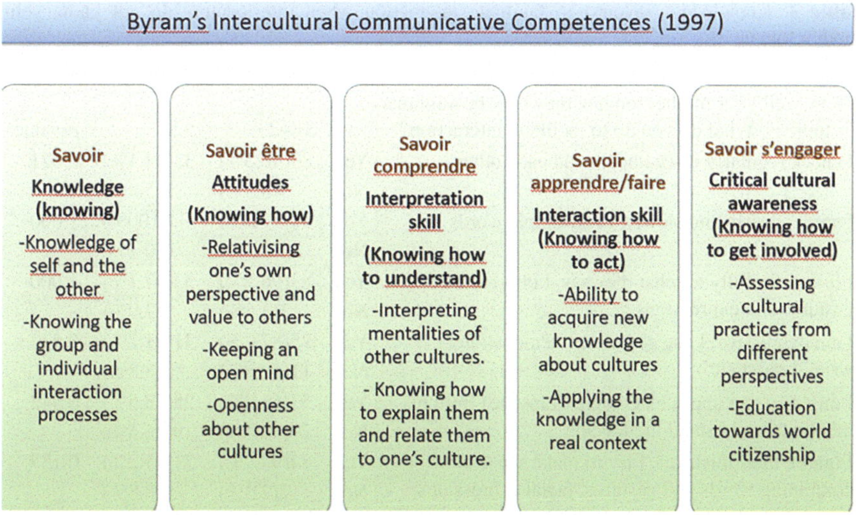

Fig. 2 Byram's Model of Intercultural Communicative Competences

mediate in interactions using knowledge with a degree of necessary acceptance and understanding of the other (1997, p. 53). For attaining intercultural communicative competences, Byram acknowledges 5 "savoirs." Figure 2 depicts the 5 savoirs of Byram's model of intercultural communicative competence.

Two different sets of questions were inspired by Byram's ICC model. The first set (Table 3) addresses mediation skills and examines all savoirs proposed by Byram to some extent. Ideally, an interlocutor who embraces interculturalism and is culturally aware of the challenges non-native speakers face in a foreign country should implement strategies to facilitate communication when interacting with people who may be tourists or migrants and do not speak the interlocutor's native language (which is also the official language of the country) fluently.

The second set (Table 4) focuses on the cognitive strategies an interlocutor employs when learning a second or foreign language. This set of questions emphasizes knowing how to understand (savoir comprendre), knowing how to act (savoir apprendre/faire), and knowing how to engage (savoir s'engager). The questions were adapted to the current context, where interaction can also be facilitated by technology. These sets of statements/questions assess the extent to which Zillennials and Millennials are willing and able to facilitate interaction and overall communication with people from diverse linguistic and cultural backgrounds.

Table 3 depicts a set of savoirs that facilitate interaction when speaking with people from different linguistic and cultural backgrounds. The majority of students employ these techniques, and there are no differences between the two generations, Zillennials and Millennials. The only technique/savoir that is less employed by both generations (Zillennials: 66.3% and Millennials: 73.5%) is the use of an application

Table 3 Knowledge (savoirs) to facilitate interaction when interlocutors do not know your mother tongue

Imagine that you are speaking with people that do not know well your mother tongue, they may be migrants or tourists. What do you do to facilitate interaction?		Age		
		18–23	>24	p-value[a]
I check regularly if we understand each other	Yes	83(96.5%)	32(94.1%)	0.621
	No	3(3.5%)	2(5.9%)	
I speak clearly and slowly, I use simple words	Yes	84(97.7%)	34(100%)	1.000
	No	2(2.3%)	0(0%)	
I listen carefully to what they say, I observe their gestures and expressions	Yes	83(96.5%)	33(97.1%)	1.000
	No	3(3.5%)	1(2.9%)	
I am expressive, I use gestures, I demonstrate, I write, I paint etc	Yes	75(87.2%)	31(91.2%)	0.542
	No	11(12.8%)	3(8.8%)	
I might use an app (i.e., Google Translate) from my mobile to understand them better	Yes	57(66.3%)	25(73.5%)	0.442
	No	29(33.7%)	9(26.5%)	
I ignore their mistakes, I try to make sense by combining words and gestures, facial expressions.	Yes	84(97.7%)	31(91.2%)	0.137
	No	2(2.3%)	3(8.8%)	
I use words from other languages that may be more familiar to them	Yes	74(86%)	29(85.3%)	0.915
	No	12(14%)	5(14.7%)	
I try to make sense by the context and by the knowledge I have for their civilization	Yes	72(83.7%)	30(88.2%)	0.533
	No	14(16.3%)	4(11.8%)	

[a]Pearson chi-square test

Table 4 Knowledge (savoirs) to facilitate language learning

Which are the cognitive strategies you employ when you learn a foreign language?		Age		
		18–23	>24	p-value[a]
I try to understand the way the language functions	Yes	68(79.1%)	26(76.5%)	0.755
	No	18(20.9%)	8(23.5%)	
I observe the way the words are formed	Yes	60(69.8%)	25(73.5%)	0.683
	No	26(30.2%)	9(26.5%)	
I watch movies in the language I learn	Yes	56(65.1%)	17(50%)	0.126
	No	30(34.9%)	17(50%)	
I listen to songs in the foreign language	Yes	58(67.4%)	18(52.9%)	0.137
	No	28(32.6%)	16(47.1%)	
I observe the pronunciation of native speakers	Yes	53(61.6%)	20(58.8%)	0.777
	No	33(38.4%)	14(41.2%)	
I read blogs in the language I learn	Yes	18(20.9%)	6(17.6%)	0.685
	No	68(79.1%)	28(82.4%)	
I try to make friends whose mother tongue is the language I learn	Yes	15(17.4%)	7(20.6%)	0.688
	No	71(82.6%)	27(79.4%)	
I try to find videos that explain a grammatical phenomenon I wish to understand better	Yes	44(51.2%)	18(52.9%)	0.861
	No	42(48.8%)	16(47.1%)	

[a]Mann Whitney test

(i.e., Google Translate) that could facilitate communication between interlocutors of different languages.

Table 4 presents a set of savoirs that facilitate language learning. The majority of students employ these cognitive strategies, with the exception of "reading blogs" in the language they learn and trying to make friends whose mother tongue is the language they learn. There are no differences between the two generations.

Attitudes Toward Gender, Culture, and Migration

In this section, students indicate their agreement with each item on a 4-point scale from *Agree Strongly (4)* to *Disagree Strongly (1)*. The first set of questions aimed at detecting Millennials and Zillennials attitudes toward gender. The first seven questions were based on *The Social Roles Questionnaire: A New Approach to Measuring Attitudes Toward Gender* (Baber & Tucker, 2006). The rest were added. Table 5 presents the responses of the participants. Students' attitudes toward gender are open-minded and non-biased; no differences between the two generations are noted.

Table 5 Attitudes toward gender

	Age		
Attitudes toward gender	18–23	>24	*p*-value[a]
Tasks around the house should not be assigned by sex	4.00	4.00	0.875
Some professions (i.e., pilots, truck drivers) are not appropriate for women	1.00	1.00	0.469
Mothers should be more involved to the upbringing of children	2.00	2.00	0.261
Mothers should work only if it is necessary	1.00	1.00	0.146
Men are more fit for professional positions that have great responsibility	1.00	1.00	0.909
A father's main responsibility is to provide financially for his children	1.00	1.00	0.386
Men are more aggressive than women	2.00	2.00	0.853
In Greece, there are not inequalities between men and women in the professional positions in the private domain	1.00	1.00	0.913
The mother of a family must have the main responsibility for household chores	1.00	1.00	0.932
It is reasonable and justified that men are preferred for some professional positions (i.e., bus drivers, engineers etc.)	1.00	1.00	0.561
It is preferable for a father to have a better job than the mother	1.00	1.00	0.092
Girls are by nature more adept than boys at household chores	1.00	1.00	0.856
I am informed about inequalities between men and women in different parts of the world	4.00	4.00	0.970
In Greece, there are not inequalities between men and women in the professional positions in the public domain	1.00	1.00	0.931
Boys have an inclination to science	2.00	2.00	0.340
Girls have an inclination to theoretical studies	2.00	1.50	0.345
The sex of a child must not guide its upbringing	4.00	4.00	0.610

[a]Mann Whitney test

Table 6 Attitudes toward culture

Attitudes toward culture	Age		p-value[a]
	18–23	>24	
I learn about the history and culture of other countries	2.00	3.00	**0.005**
I keep an open mind on cultures and ideas	4.00	4.00	0.827
I can understand a different viewpoint from my own and I can change my opinion	3.00	3.00	0.707
I learn about different civilizations and traditions	3.00	3.00	0.122
I am informed about the political situation in other countries	3.00	3.00	0.100
My interpersonal skills are improved when I speak with people from other countries	3.00	4.00	**0.040**
I can recognize and I refrain from using words that reinforce stereotypes	4.00	4.00	0.277
I try to have friends from different countries	3.00	2.00	0.150
I respect beliefs and traditions from other countries	4.00	4.00	0.543
I respect different values of my own	4.00	4.00	0.643
I respect the religion of other countries	4.00	4.00	0.858
It is important for children to learn from a young age to respect other cultures	4.00	4.00	0.744
I understand that my viewpoints are the result of my experiences; I acknowledge that different opinions may also be valid	4.00	4.00	0.406
When I speak with other people their appearance does not influence me in the opinion I form about them	4.00	4.00	0.794
I have a sense of belonging in a global humanity	3.00	3.00	0.522
I respect diversity	4.00	4.00	0.194

[a]Mann Whitney test

The second set of statements/questions explores attitudes toward culture, as presented in Table 6. Students' responses indicated openness to people from different cultural backgrounds and respect for others. While no significant differences emerged between the two age groups, the Millennial generation responded more positively regarding learning about other countries' history and culture and improving their interpersonal skills when interacting with people from other countries. However, these subtle differences might be attributed to the age gap between the groups rather than a conscious attitude toward culture. As we age, we tend to learn more about other cultures and their history, recognizing that our interpersonal skills are enhanced through interaction.

The final set of statements/questions targeted the revealing attitudes toward migration and migrants. The first four questions were translated from the PISA Global Competence Framework (OECD, 2018) and, in particular, from the PISA 2018 Global Competence Questionnaire and the construct *Attitudes towards immigrants*. The PISA Global Competence Framework (OECD, 2018) aims at preparing youth for an inclusive world, and it is addressed to adolescents, to 15-year-old students.

Table 7 displays students' responses. The responses displayed a positive attitude toward migrants. It could be noted, though, that although the vast majority of

Table 7 Attitudes toward migrants

Attitudes toward migrants	Age		
	18–23	>24	*p*-value[a]
The minor migrants should have access to the education system, even if they do not know the language of the country	4.00	4.00	0.130
The migrants should have the right to vote after living for some years in the host country	3.00	3.00	0.764
Migrants should be able to practice their traditions	3.00	3.00	0.383
Migrants should have the same rights with everybody else	4.00	4.00	0.908
The minor migrants should use their mother tongue in the school	3.00	3.00	0.843
The minor migrants do not deteriorate the level of students within a classroom	4.00	3.00	**0.031**
The state should support more the smooth integration of migrant students in the education system	4.00	3.50	0.288
I feel empathy for migrants	3.00	3.00	0.325
I am not afraid of migrants	3.00	4.00	**0.004**
Minor migrants do not cause problems in the classroom	3.00	4.00	0.344
It would not be better neither for the migrants nor the host country for migrants to return to their country of origin	4.00	4.00	0.911
I am informed about migration issues	2.00	2.00	0.379
Migrants that come to live in Greece do not worsen the situation of poor citizens	4.00	4.00	0.984
Migrants do not harm the economy of Greece	3.00	4.00	0.118
It's right and humane for a country to host migrants	4.00	4.00	0.574
The optimal is for a country to have one religion	1.00	1.00	0.572

[a]Mann Whitney test

respondents strongly agreed that migrants should have the same rights as everybody else, they did not respond so positively (the mean score is 3, "agree" and not 4, "strongly agree") in related questions such as "Migrants should be able to vote, … practice their traditions, … use their mother tongue in the school," and to the question "I feel empathy for migrants." The only differences between the responses of Millennials and Zillennials are spotted in the questions "The minor migrants do not deteriorate the level of students within a classroom" and "I am not afraid of migrants." To this question, a further analysis was effectuated based on sex, and it was evidenced that Zillennial women were those that responded less favorably, making it possible to assume that women of a young age might feel less secure when in public alone, a feeling that might not correspond to their overall attitude toward migrants but to more general insecurity of being young and alone outdoors.

An open question was inserted at the end of the questionnaire asking students to propose ways that the university could help them develop their intercultural communication skills. Sixty respondents answered that question, 21 of them asking for more mobility schemes in other countries via the Erasmus+ and other similar initiatives. Twelve students suggest that the university should encourage the admission and attendance of students from other countries for the university to have a multicultural and multilingual audience. Nine students propose that the academic programs should be offered in English and other languages and not merely in Greek. Eight students suggest more synergies with universities from other countries where they could attend online courses in other parts of the world by the use of contemporary technological means (teleconference platforms). Four students suggest the introduction of more courses related to intercultural communication. Two students suggest the creation of a unit within the university that will encourage volunteer participation of students in refugee shelters and will also inform students about current global social emergencies around the world. All these suggestions are constructive and presuppose a transformative engagement from all stakeholders (ministry of education, university rectors and managerial services, academic staff, and students). The proposal to admit students from other countries raises significant educational policy considerations, as it necessitates a shift in how publicly funded universities in Greece evaluate and admit students to undergraduate programs, which currently relies on a nationwide examination system ("panellinies exams"). At present, the majority of international students in Greek universities in undergraduate programs (Bachelor Degrees) are those participating in mobility programs such as Erasmus+ or similar initiatives. Other proposed measures could be more readily implemented, enhancing intercultural awareness in non-academic settings on campus, as much of the learning takes place outside the classroom environment. Currently, publicly funded Greek universities foster intercultural awareness within academic curricula through mandatory language courses offered by nearly all academic departments, opportunities for overseas experiences, and graduate programs (Master's Degrees, PhD programs). Additionally, universities regularly organize and collaborate with other institutions to host international and European conferences, workshops, seminars, webinars, hybrid courses, and professional development activities focusing on international and intercultural themes.

Limitations

This study, while providing valuable insights into generational attitudes toward gender, culture, and migration in a Greek university context, has several limitations that should be considered. First, the sample size (N=126) was relatively small and geographically limited to a single institution, the University of Macedonia in Thessaloniki. This restricts the generalizability of findings to the broader Greek student population or to other educational contexts. Second, the demographic composition of participants was notably skewed, with 85% identifying as female, which may have influenced the results, particularly regarding gender-related attitudes. Third, the participants were predominantly Greek (98%), limiting the study's ability to capture diverse cultural perspectives within the university setting. Fourth, as a cross-sectional study, it provides only a snapshot of attitudes at a single point in time rather than tracking how these attitudes might evolve. Fifth, the self-reported nature of the data collection method may introduce social desirability bias, particularly on sensitive topics like migration and gender equality where participants might respond according to perceived socially acceptable views rather than their authentic beliefs. Future research would benefit from a larger, more diverse sample across multiple Greek universities, longitudinal design to track attitudinal changes over time, and mixed-methods approaches incorporating qualitative elements to explore the nuances behind the quantitative findings presented here.

Discussion

Attitudes toward gender, culture, and migration are evidenced to be positive. As a response to the first research question, neither the number of foreign languages spoken by the participants or their parents, nor travelling and staying abroad and having friends from other countries, evidenced that influence students' attitudes toward gender, culture, and migration. Consequently, no external factors were identified to undermine or reinforce attitudes toward gender, culture, and migration. In regards to the second research question, students' attitudes toward diversity were positive. Students did not settle for gender social stereotypes; they also demonstrated respect for cultural otherness and understood the difficulties faced by migrants. They adopted a positive attitude toward migration, and the attitudes of the two generations, Millennials and Gen Z, do not differ.

Participants in the study demonstrated an open mind toward gender inequalities. They did not validate social stereotypes, they valued attitudes of openness, flexibility, and empathy as being the most important when communicating with someone from another culture. In addition, the majority of respondents employed appropriate linguistic strategies when communicating with people who do not speak their mother tongue, which is, according to Byram (1997), a significant step of being an intercultural speaker, a person who uses language to enable communication between different cultures. The majority of respondents have a positive attitude toward migration. The suggestions made by students for the University to support them in enhancing their intercultural competences were valid and, if implemented, the Greek universities could have a more dynamic international presence; the survey conducted was limited in its sample size and geographical scope.

The findings of this study align strongly with the ethnorelativism stages of Bennett's Developmental Model of Intercultural Sensitivity (DMIS), with participants overwhelmingly rejecting ethnocentric perspectives in favor of more culturally relative positions. This positioning within the ethnorelativism end of Bennett's continuum suggests that Greek university students have developed a nuanced understanding of cultural diversity despite Greece's relatively homogeneous demographic composition. This apparent contradiction raises important questions about how students develop ethnorelative perspectives with limited exposure to cultural diversity in their immediate environment. For Greek higher education institutions, these findings suggest students may be intellectually prepared for more advanced intercultural learning experiences than currently offered. Participants demonstrated uneven development across Byram's five savoirs. Their savoir être (attitudes) and savoir comprendre (skills of interpreting) appear well-developed, as evidenced by their openness toward different cultures and ability to facilitate cross-cultural communication. However, gaps emerge in savoir apprendre/faire (skills of discovery and interaction), with fewer students engaging in interactive approaches to language learning. Similarly, while savoir s'engager (critical cultural awareness) appears strong in theoretical terms, the study doesn't fully explore how students might critically evaluate cultural practices beyond abstract positions. This imbalance suggests stronger theoretical foundations than practical skills of interaction, consistent with limited opportunities for authentic intercultural exchange within a predominantly homogeneous university context. The minimal differences observed between Millennial and Gen Z cohorts challenge aspects of sociological generation theory. While this theory suggests distinct generations should show meaningful differences due to unique formative experiences, our findings suggest otherwise in the Greek context. This may indicate that the formative experiences of these two generations in Greece have been more similar than different, despite technological distinctions. The economic crisis that began in Greece in 2009 affected both generations during formative periods, potentially creating shared perspectives that transcend typical generational boundaries. This suggests that national socioeconomic conditions may sometimes override global generational patterns in shaping attitudes toward critical social issues.

References

Acevedo, J., & Meseguer, C. (2022). National identity and anti-immigrant sentiment: Experimental evidence from Mexico. *Migration Studies, 10*(4), 608–630. https://doi.org/10.1093/migration/mnac024

Alexseev, M. (2015). The asymmetry of nationalist exclusion and inclusion: Migration policy preferences in Russia, 2005–2013. *Social Science Quarterly, 96*(3), 759–777.

Baber, K. M., & Tucker, C. J. (2006). The social roles questionnaire: A new approach to measuring attitudes toward gender. *Sex Roles, 54*, 459–467.

Bajraktari, H., Faiku, M., & Qatani, V. (2024). Gender equality: Progress, and challenges in european society. *Humanities Journal, 1*(1), 2024005-2024005. https://doi.org/10.31893/humanitj.202400

Bennett, M. (1986). A developmental approach to training for intercultural sensitivity. *International Journal of Intercultural Relations, 10*(2), 179–195.

Bennett, M. (1993). Towards ethnorelativism: A developmental model of intercultural sensitivity. In M. Paige (Ed.), *Education for the intercultural experience*. Intercultural Press.

Bennett, M. (2004). Becoming interculturally competent. In J. Wurzel (Ed.), *Toward multiculturalism: A reader in multicultural education* (2nd ed., pp. 62–77). Intercultural Resource.

Bennett, M. (2013). *Basic concepts of intercultural communication: Paradigms, principles, & practices*. Intercultural Press.

Bockting, W. O. (1999). From construction to context: Gender through the eyes of the transgendered. *SIECUS Report, 28*, 3–7.

Bohan, J. S. (2002). Sex differences and/in the self: Classic themes, feminist variations, postmodern challenges. *Psychology of Women Quarterly, 26*, 74–88

Butler, J. (1986). Sex and gender in Simone de Beauvoir's Second Sex. *Yale French Studies, 72*, 35–49.

Butler, J. (1990). *Gender trouble: Feminism and the subversion of identity*. Routledge.

Byram, M. (1997). *Teaching and assessing intercultural communicative competence*. Multilingual Matters.

Cennamo, L., & Gardner, D. (2008). Generational differences in work values, outcomes and person-organisation values fit. *Journal of Managerial Psychology, 23*(8), 891–906.
Ceobanu, A., & Koropeckyj-Cox, T. (2013). Should international migration be encouraged to offset population ageing? A cross-country analysis of public attitudes in Europe. *Population Research and Policy Review, 32*, 261–284.
Council of Europe. (2016). *Competences for democratic culture: Living together as equals in culturally diverse democratic societies*. Council of Europe.
Cushner, K., McClelland, A., & Safford, P. (2012). *Human diversity in education*. McGraw Hill.
Dustmann, C., & Preston, I. P. (2007). Racial and economic factors in attitudes to immigration. *The BE Journal of Economic Analysis and Policy, 7*(1), 62.
Edmunds, J., & Turner, B. (2005). Global generations: Social change in the twentieth century. *British Journal of Sociology, 56*(4), 559–578.
Esses, V. M., Brochu, P. M., & Dickson, K. R. (2012). Economic costs, economic benefits, and attitudes toward immigrants and immigration. *Analyses of Social Issues and Public Policy, 12*(1), 133–137.
European Commission: Directorate-General for Justice and Consumers. (2024). 2024 report on gender equality in the EU. Publications Office of the European Union. https://data.europa.eu/doi/10.2838/401813
European Institute for Gender Equality. (2024). Gender Equality Index 2024: Greece. https://eige.europa.eu/gender-equality-index/2024
Galinsky, A. D., Turek, A., Agarwal, G., Anicich, E. M., Rucker, D. D., Bowles, H. R., Liberman, N., Levin, C., & Magee, J. C. (2024). Are many sex/gender differences really power differences? *PNAS Nexus, 3*(2). https://doi.org/10.1093/pnasnexus/pgae025
Hainmueller, J., & Hiscox, M. J. (2010). Attitudes toward highly skilled and low-skilled immigration: Evidence from a survey experiment. *American Political Science Review, 104*(01), 61–84.
Hall, E. T. (1976). *Beyond culture*. Anchor Books/Doubleday.
Hofstede, G. (1991). *Cultures and organisations: Software of the mind*. McGraw-Hill.
Kimmel, M. S. (2000). *The gendered society*. Oxford University Press.
Kramsch, C. (1993). *Context and culture in language teaching*. Oxford University Press.
Kramsch, C. (1998). *Language and culture*. Oxford University Press.
Kupperschmidt, B. (2000). Multigenerational employees: Strategies for effective management. *The Health Care Manager, 19*(1), 65–76.
Lee, B. (2023). Educational content, exclusive national identity, and anti-immigrant attitudes. *The Journal of Politics, 85*(4), 1182–1197.
Lindstam, E., Mader, M., & Schoen, H. (2021). Conceptions of national identity and ambivalence towards immigration. *British Journal of Political Science, 51*(1):93–114. https://doi.org/10.1017/S0007123418000522
Macky, K., Gardner, D., & Forsyth, S. (2008). Generational differences at work: Introduction and overview. *Journal of Managerial Psychology, 23*(8), 857–861.
Malchow-Møller, N., Munch, J. R., Schroll, S., & Skaksen, J. R. (2008). Attitudes towards immigration-perceived consequences and economic self-interest. *Economics Letters, 100*(2), 254–257.
Martin, C. L., & Ruble, D. (2004). Children's search for gender cues: Cognitive perspectives on gender development. *Current Directions in Psychological Science, 13*(2), 67–70.
Masso, A. (2009). A readiness to accept immigrants in Europe? Individual and country-level characteristics. *Journal of Ethnic and Migration Studies, 35*(2), 251–270.
Maurer, L. (1999). Transgressing sex and gender: Deconstruction zone ahead? *SIECUS Report, 28*, 14–21.
Mayda, A. M. (2006). Who is against immigration? A cross-country investigation of individual attitudes toward immigrants. *Review of Economics and Statistics, 88*(3), 510–530.
OECD. (2018). PISA 2018 Global Competence Questionnaire. https://www.oecd.org/content/dam/oecd/en/topics/policy-sub-issues/global-competence/PISA-2018-Global-Competence-Questionnaire.pdf

O'Rourke, K. H., & Sinnott, R. (2006). The determinants of individual attitudes towards immigration. *European Journal of Political Economy, 22*, 838–861.

Onraet, E., & Van Hiel, A. (2013). When threat to society becomes a threat to oneself: Implications for right-wing attitudes and ethnic prejudice. *International Journal of Psychology, 48*(1), 25–34.

Peleki, A., & Nikolaou, S. (2024). Teacher education and gender equality in Greece: A case study. *International Journal of Social Science and Economic Research, 9*(9), 3487–3514. https://doi.org/10.46609/IJSSER.2024.v09i09.020

Purhonen, S. (2016). Zeitgeist, identity and politics: The modern meaning of the concept of generation. In I. Goodson, A. Antikainen, P. Sikes, & M. Andrews (Eds.), *The Routledge international handbook on narrative and life history* (pp. 167–178). Routledge.

Rossi, F. (2022). National identity and anti-immigrant sentiment: Experimental evidence from Mexico. *Political Science Research and Methods, 10*(4), 775–791.

World Health Organization. (n.d.). *Gender and health*. https://www.who.int/health-topics/gender#tab=tab_1

Politics and Identity Issues: The Case of North Macedonia After the Prespa Agreement

Vlasis Vlasidis, Athanasios Grammenos, Eleni Siapikoudi, and Anna Korneeva

Abstract

The Balkan region after the collapse of the big empires and the formation of nation-states had to deal with many bilateral disputes. These disagreements focus on territorial integrity, sovereignty and borders and identity issues. One of these cases is North Macedonia. After the dissolution of the former Yugoslavia, the creation of a new state in the region has created many controversies with the neighboring states, questioning the whole existence of the state. As we are going to analyze, there are two ways: either the state creates the nation or the nation creates the state. In our case study, the newly established state tried over the years to shape and popularize the national identity of the population. For that reason, contradictory elements have been used to support these arguments and caused bilateral disputes with Greece, Serbia, Bulgaria and others. The purpose of this chapter is to analyze the creation of the national identity in North Macedonia, to describe the socio-political developments that led us to the Prespa Agreement, and to examine how the Agreement has been implemented.

V. Vlasidis (✉)
University of Macedonia, Thessaloniki, Greece
e-mail: vvlasidis@uom.gr

A. Grammenos
Council for International Relations, Athens, Greece

E. Siapikoudi
Department for Balkan, Slavic and Oriental Studies, University of Macedonia, Thessaloniki, Greece

A. Korneeva
Department of History and Ethnology, Democritus University of Thrace, Komotini, Greece

D. Anagnostopoulou (ed.), *European Identities, Inclusion and Equality*, Diversity and Inclusion Research, https://doi.org/10.1007/978-3-031-90602-2_6

Introduction

The identity of the people of North Macedonia and its recognition by the neighboring states (Greece, Bulgaria, Serbia, and Albania) has been at the epicenter of a long dispute in the Balkans and part of the "Macedonian Issue." Historically, the Macedonian issue begins with the gradual retreat of the Ottoman Empire from Europe and the loss of power after the defeat it suffered in the Ottoman-Russian War of 1877–1878 and the following treaties of San Stefano (1877) (Holland, 1885, pp. 335–348) and London (1878) (Hertslet, 1891, pp. 2759–2798). The declining Empire fed the aspirations of the Greeks, Bulgarians, and Serbs, who had their own minorities living in the wider region referred to as Macedonian lands as well as vested interests pressing for territorial expansion.

These minorities started their territorial expansion war that had two phases. At first, they made use of propaganda, utilizing priests and teachers in the last decades of the nineteenth century, but, in the first decade of the twentieth century, it escalated and went wild with armed bands (andartes, komitadjis, and chetniks) fighting for the actual control of the Macedonian cities and peoples. Finally, the withdrawal of the Ottoman Empire from Europe became a reality with the Treaty of Bucharest (1913) (Anderson & Hershey, 1918, pp. 1870–1914) bringing to an end to the Balkan Wars; Greece incorporated the entire South Macedonia, Serbia the Northwest, and Bulgaria a small part of the East. A few years later, the Treaty of Neuilly-sur-Seine (1919) (Nestor, 1962) closed some pending issues with the Bulgarian borders, settling many side issues, too (Barker, 1950; Kofos, 1964; Petiffer, 1999).

Despite that settlement, a significant minority of the people living in the Serbian part of Macedonia declared openly their ethnic affiliation with Bulgaria, something that could be substantiated by the way they chose sides in the First and Second World Wars. However, Bulgaria's failure to win either war disappointed the aforementioned minority. In this vein, they accepted to participate in the creation of the socialist federation of Yugoslavia, with Tito to be as their leader. With Tito, the local communists declared the Anti-Fascist Assembly for the People's Liberation Front of Macedonia (ASNOM) on 2 August 1944, which provided the base on which the People's Republic of Macedonia as a federal state of Yugoslavia was built in late 1945.

The Making of the Republic of Macedonia: Identity Building

During the Cold War, the "Macedonian" issue was a useful political tool to exert some influence on the geopolitical sub-system of the southern Balkans by communist Yugoslavia. In particular, Tito believed that Greece, a NATO member, could potentially provide the desired access to the Aegean. To achieve this goal, he promoted the idea of a different "Macedonian" ethnic identity for the inhabitants of the southern part of his country in order to put pressure mostly on Bulgaria and, secondly, hoping for Greece's concessions. His full support for the new Yugoslavian federate state aimed at enabling the creation and anticipated prosperity of a nation that, after the breakup of Yugoslavia, would play a leading role in Macedonia's wider region, claiming the entire Macedonian history and cultural heritage (Palmer et al., 1971).

Within Yugoslavia, the country acquired its constitution, a government, a local parliament, an official language, and state symbols, and in brief, every structure that is needed for a state to have sovereignty and autonomy, absolute or limited, as part of a federation. Social and political scientists always pose the question of whether a nation creates the state or the other way around; in this case, the authors argue that the latter has occurred. In the period between 1945 and 1990, designated policies in Belgrade boosted the creation of a distinct "Macedonian" language, the foundation of a national "Macedonian" Orthodox Church (which was uncanonical and remains unrecognized by other churches to date), and more importantly, the invention of a direct line for the "Macedonian" nation from antiquity to the present day, which would feed the sense of belonging and national pride of the "Macedonian" people, preventing them from dissolution. The Yugoslav efforts were facilitated by the Greek Civil War (1946–1949). The total destruction of the communist army (DSE) made thousands of Greek or Slavic-speaking fighters into refugees who fled the country and moved to Yugoslavia, especially in the Skopje and Bitola regions. Their anti-Greek sentiments for their defeat made them vulnerable to the Yugoslav propaganda, with the hope that 1 day they could revenge their opponents (Vlasidis, 2017, p. 23).

Regarding the language, the regime chose the dialect of Prilep (Koneski, 1945, 1949) and the scholar Blaze Koneski developed it into a diverse language, changing elements of the alphabet, grammar, and vocabulary (Koneski, 1950, 1952). Concurrently, the (Yugoslavian) federal state created an educational system and promoted a certain political ideology, ranging from "Macedonian consciousness" to "Yugoslav patriotism." Eventually, it can be argued that the role of the educational system was not to prepare students for professional and scientific careers; it rather served the cohesiveness of a nation-in-process, advocating that history is not fair with "Macedonia" as long as there are still "Macedonians" under foreign rule (Mavrogeni, 2010, p. 273; Vlasidis, 2017, pp. 19–20).

In order to facilitate these efforts and assist similar efforts in Bosnia-Herzegovina and Montenegro, Yugoslavia founded the Institute of National History as part of the Macedonian Academy of Sciences and Arts (MANU). This institute was solely responsible for the creation of the national history of the Macedonians (Ivanovski, 1978).

In the beginning, the prevailing opinion was to present the "Macedonians" as descendants of the Medieval Bulgarian King Samuel (Kofos, 1962, pp. 375–396). This doctrine was followed during the time that the Socialist Republic of Macedonia was part of Yugoslavia. This way, a feeling of solidarity was cultivated among all Yugoslav nations. But when Yugoslavia collapsed and a new independent state was formed (1991), adherence to Slavic origin and identity was no longer necessary. In desperate need of a strong national identity, the independent newly founded "Republic of Macedonia" adopted the narrative they were told about their alleged ancient origins, and the beginnings of the nation's history were placed in the dynasty of Philip and Alexander, claiming all Greek and Bulgarian history and heritage of the region as "Macedonian" (Michailidis, 2010, pp. 222–226).

A very interesting case study for the "Macedonian" nation-building is the Church. The dominant churches in the region are the Serbian Orthodox Patriarchate and the Orthodox Church of Greece, which is spiritually connected to the Ecumenical Patriarchate. The people of the "Macedonian" state are also Orthodox and any influence upon them, from either Belgrade or Athens, could be catastrophic for the Yugoslav plans. To avoid any complications, already from 1945, the communists in Skopje declared unilaterally the restoration of the Ohrid Archbishopric, which was abolished in 1776. It is noted that only the Ecumenical Patriarch has the authority to establish, restore, or annul a Christian Orthodox Metropolis or a bishopric. Thus, the foundation of the autonomous "Macedonian Orthodox Church" (MOC) was uncanonical. The Serbian Patriarchate reluctantly accepted communion under the pressure of Tito; however, when in 1967 MOC declared autocephaly, the crisis ended up in a schism, and the MOC was declared as schismatic. The Serbian Church officially announced that the decision was taken considering only the Holy Canons despite the political pressure from the communist regime (Marusic & Cheresheva, 2017; Papastathis, 1967, pp. 151–154).

An Independent "Macedonian" State and a New Nation

Since 1991, all scholars from North Macedonia promoted the idea of the Macedonian identity and claimed from the neighboring states what they believed to be their heritage. In addition, they received unexpected publicity due to Greek concerns. The international community was interested in the small, newly formed state and was informed of its identity from scholars such as Hugh Poulton (1995) and Loring Danforth (1995). In addition, immigrants from FYROM to the USA, Canada, and Australia used the Internet to promote their narrative about their Macedonian identity and their views on the Macedonian Issue (Vlasidis, 2010, pp. 301–315). In addition, they raised the claim that a large "Macedonian" minority resided in Greece and Bulgaria, with the two countries refusing to recognize it and its rights, proposing irredentist scenarios for establishing alleged justice (Aarbakke, 2010, pp. 204–208; Macedonian Academy, 1993; Whitman, 1994).

Greece and Bulgaria have not accepted the claims by scholars and institutions from the Former Yugoslav Republic of Macedonia. More precisely, Bulgaria considers that the creation of the modern Macedonian nation was an unfortunate development for the Bulgarian nation, and it is a "trauma" for the Bulgarian people (Sfetas, 2012, pp. 243–245). Nevertheless, despite efforts to converge, Bulgarians highly disagreed about the historical creation of the Macedonian nation (Aarbakke, 2010, pp. 196–212). The disagreements are even more intense from the Greek side (Sfetas & Kentrotis, 1994, pp. 337–377; Roudometov, 2002; Vlasidis, 2005, pp. 288–316).

Many scholars from North Macedonia argue that the Bulgarian and Greek perspectives and grievances about the Macedonian identity, as structured and promoted in the years of independence, are unfounded and characterized as nationalistic (Al-Bander, 2017, p. 37; Vankovska, 2010, p. 453), and they have a different view about the modern history. Other journalists and scholars simply note that mainly Greece's objections have left North Macedonia out of the European Union, with no invitation to be a candidate member. (Kafedjiska, 2018, pp. 1839–1840).

In order to protect the sovereignty of the state and the cohesion among the people, current North Macedonia invested again in heritage, claiming they are direct descendants of the ancient Macedonians. Simultaneously, they portrayed themselves as victims of the Greek—among others—expansionism which oppressed their people and occupied "Macedonian" territories (Pod robstvo), namely the part of Macedonia that belongs to Greece since 1913 (Vlasidis, 2005, p. 293).

From the political perspective, Bulgaria was the first country to recognize the independence of the new state as "Republic of Macedonia", on 15 January 1992; nonetheless, the Bulgarians emphasized that the ethnic roots of the "Macedonians" are Bulgarian, and the "Macedonian" language is nothing more than a Bulgarian dialect (Mus, 2016). Greece refused to recognize the "Republic of Macedonia" under that name, arguing that it imposed de facto territorial aspirations and historical falsification that would not be tolerated.

To break the deadlock, after long negotiations under the UN mediation, Athens and Skopje signed an Interim Accord in 1995 (Interim Accord, 1995), according to which Greece recognized its neighbor with the provisional name "Former Yugoslav Republic of Macedonia" (FYROM), setting the temporary conditions for the bilateral relations. The same document mandated that negotiations for a permanent solution should start immediately, and a special UN envoy was employed. Cyrus Vance, an experienced diplomat, was the first UN representative, who was succeeded later by Matthew Nimetz. The situation was not easy either for Athens (Kofos, 2005, pp. 125–224) or for Skopje (Tziampiris, 2005, pp. 225–252).

Politicians, journalists, and political scientists in Skopje argued that the Greek foreign policy was stiff due to domestic political disagreements and thus pressure was exerted upon their side to proceed to concessions (Vankovska, 2010, pp. 437–438, 449–458). Moreover, they claimed that it is only their country that is forced to make concessions on the issue of their name (Vankovska, 2010, pp. 442–443) and that all the other countries worldwide are allowed to become members of international organizations by their constitutional name. However, the latter claim is not really the case (Zaikos, 2010, pp. 338–344).

Taking into account the stance of each side, this chapter argues that the name is not the first or the most difficult issue; the actual conflict relates to the content of the "Macedonian" identity and the determinants for the national narrative of the people living in current North Macedonia. History, culture, tradition, heritage, and language were connected in a way that disputed the Greek and Bulgarian self-determination, notwithstanding the established arguments from the scientific community. It seems that for them, when history is not convenient, individual and collective memories are employed (Vankovska, 2015, pp. 9–12).

Macedonian Identity in the New Century

The ambitions of FYROM to become a member of NATO collapsed in 2008 at the Bucharest Summit. Although the US administration was very supportive of that prospect and no technical objections existed, the invitation was blocked by second thoughts from France and Greece. The reason was France's denial to vote for a "package invitation" to both FYROM and Ukraine as planned by the USA, but eventually, the incident was understood in the public opinion as a "Greek veto." In any case, the result was the same for FYROM, leaving politicians and the population of the country devastated.

In this vein, the government decided to enforce people's psychology, after the veto, with a new program that would tone up national pride. Several changes were planned, with the aim to celebrate the local version of history and identity. A prominent activity was the "Skopje 2014" program, which was launched in 2010. That program aimed at restoring buildings of the 1920s–1930s that were destroyed after an earthquake in 1963. It also aimed to build the national opera house, public offices, and bridges across the Vardar River and install a large number of statues depicting the country's view of cultural heritage. The new style incorporated baroque and neoclassical elements, hiding the socialist style of the city (Harwell, 2011; Ilieski, 2017). This project was spread all over the city of Skopje, and it was fully supported by the conservative ruling party of VMRO-DPMNE (Janev, 2011, pp. 34–38).

The architectural style of the city's renovation was planned in order to highlight the links with ancient times and, more precisely, the Kingdom of Macedonia. Several monuments started to emerge all over the country. The most famous statue is 22 m high and illustrates Alexander the Great surrounded by eight lions. Other statues of Alexander the Great and Phillip II were built in Prilep and Bitola. In Skopje, several buildings were put up with a neoclassical style in order to resemble an ancient Greek agora. Serbian architect Srdan Jovanovic has called it "Turbo Architecture", meaning that it was "a post-socialist mainstream in nationalizing collective identity through architecture" (Cvoro, 2018, p. 103). Public art was used as a political tool in mapping areas to promote a new national identity (Mavrogeni, 2015, p. 71). These attempts promoted a direct connection with ancient Macedonians, claiming the whole of ancient Macedonian heritage to make up for the failures of the state's foreign policy.

Thus, in the spring of 2017, a new multi-party government was formed under the premiership of Social Democrat Zoran Zaev, leader of SDSM. Zaev prioritized the European and Atlantic membership of FYROM. He understood at that time the critical role that both Greece and Bulgaria had in order to achieve the European perspective of the country. That being said, the government realized for the first time that a compromise with its southern neighbor was necessary, in order to solve the longstanding dispute. In this connotation, a change to the maximalist claims of identity and a restart to the national narrative were needed. To achieve that, Zaev started the negotiations firstly with Bulgaria. After 18 years of bilateral negotiations, on 1 August 2017, the two governments signed a Friendship Agreement to enhance the relations between the two Balkan states and facilitate further cooperation (Testorides, 2017).

At the same time, Zaev initiated negotiations with Athens in order to resolve the name dispute and a series of other issues. On 12 June 2018, Zaev and the Greek Prime Minister Alexis Tsipras, accompanied by their Foreign Ministers Dimitrov and Kotzias, signed the Prespa Agreement, with the aim to put an end to the long-lasting issues between the two countries. FYROM agreed on the challenging decision to change the official name of the country to "North Macedonia." This Agreement was ratified by the parliaments of both countries and it went into force on 12 February 2019 (UN Statement, Feb. 13th, 2019). Until today, the two sides face difficulties implementing this Agreement, but the main problem burdens the shoulders of North Macedonia because they need to rationalize much of its recent political tradition and historical claims.

Identities After the Prespa Agreement-Hard Decisions

National identity is an essential relay of a society's cohesion and is defined by specific characteristics, such as origins, territory, occupation, language, culture, state, and religion. The sense of common ancestry provides the feeling of continuity, giving a sense of heritage within a defined geographical area, and is the core of national identity, because it is from this standpoint that the national identity's evolution is unavoidable can evolve. Moreover, the native language and the culture contribute to the cohesion among the members of the society, while they create a national and collective heritage and a sense of belonging. Therefore, the state penetrates actively into the configuration of national identity by using the educational system or the army (Veikos, 1999, pp. 28–43).

National identities are not static; they develop and change their characteristics. Cultural memory creates heritage and vice versa and is also expressed through public monuments and statues. Great importance is attributed to nationalism as it provides a new essence to existing identities and, therefore, to the ability to survive. According to Marcel Mauss, "Heritage is from us to us" (Mauss, 1985, p. 22) because national identity is an inextricable element of heritage, hence it must be seen as "between us and the others" (Koppa, 2013, p. 123).

The daily recollections and narrations of these memories serve to construct the collective memory. Due to the connection between the memory of events and representations that social groups create and replicate, sociologists and anthropologists believe that collective memory can endure under certain, predetermined social conditions (Roudometov, 2002, p. 6).

Some basic elements of the Prespa Agreement shape the way in which the terms "Macedonia" and "Macedonian" have to be used after the ratification of the Agreement. First of all, the Agreement clarified the cultural and historical differentiation of the terms "Macedonia" and "Macedonian" in the understanding of the two parties (Greece–North Macedonia). The importance of this element can be understood in the context of the clarification that when Greece refers to the geographical term of Macedonia; it denotes not only the area and the people of the northern region of Greece but also attributes to it the Hellenic civilization, culture, and history that is distinct from that of North Macedonia's civilization. In this vein, it is recognized that the historical context and the cultural heritage of North Macedonia are not identified in the same context (Prespa Agreement, 2018, Art 7, Para. 1: 9).

Identities can also be acknowledged in different ways. Language, history, religion, and cultural heritage are some of the ways used throughout the years by many states in order to shape a specific collective identity that could be understood and identified not only by the members of the state but also by other states. Moreover, in order for a state to identify itself, it seeks or even creates discerning aspects from its neighbors in order to differentiate itself from the "others." In this context, the "Republic of Macedonia" tried to establish a collective identity through the years. The Prespa Agreement challenges that identity and prepares the people for a smooth transition. Firstly, the language is identified as a "Macedonian language" in the group of South Slav languages. It is clarified at this point that the identification of the language has nothing to do with the Macedonian cultural heritage of Greece (Prespa Agreement, 2018, Art. 7: 9).

Another important element of the Agreement is the identification of the nationality of the people of North Macedonia. More precisely, the nationality is referred to as Macedonian/citizens of the Republic of North Macedonia. It is clear that nationality is given to the citizen because of their staying in this specific country, and it is irrelevant to their ethnicity. Briefly, nationality is commonly understood as a person's relationship with the political state to which he/ she belongs or is affiliated. Ethnicity is the identification of a person with a particular racial, cultural, or religious group. In North Macedonia among the Slavs, Albanians comprise almost 30% of the country's total population. In this respect, an international agreement could not identify the ethnicity of the population, let alone in the case of North Macedonia, that is not contained with one dominant ethnic identity, but is also shared with the numerous Albanian people (Prespa Agreement, 2018, 2 Art. 7, Para. 2–3:9).

Monitoring the Changes of the Prespa Agreement

The rapprochement of the two states is based on two interconnected conditions. Firstly, the EU accession of North Macedonia was discussed again in 2019, but this time it was obscured by the French, Dutch, and Austrian vetoes and, secondly, the implementation of the Agreement in its entirety. The above veto discourages North Macedonia from continuing with the previous enthusiasm for the reforms if it does not see the "rewards" from the European Union.

At this moment the present research finds that:

Governmental web pages have changed their names; however, they tend to use the adjective "Macedonian" frequently. All ministries, all governmental institutions, and all services have changed their official names from Republika Makedonija to Republika Severna Makedonija and from the Republic of Macedonia to the Republic of North Macedonia. Nonetheless, apart from this alteration, they prefer to use the adjective Macedonian and not the name North Macedonia.

A second element that remains unchanged is the name of political parties. The weak point is that the Agreement did not obligate North Macedonia to do the same with private entities, and it is not guaranteed by the law. Although, in practice, it is obvious that even the change in public entities has not been finalized one and a half years after the signing of the agreement. One good example of this situation is that even the name of Zaev's party is still entitled as "Social Democratic Union of Macedonia." Below are the current official names of the parties as they are both mentioned in public and also on their official websites.

- Socialist Party of Macedonia (n.d.) (Socijalisticka Partija na Makedonija/Социјалистичка Партија на Македонија) (n.d.)
- Liberal Democratic Party (n.d.) (Liberalno-Demokratska Partija/Либерално-Демократска Партија)
- New Social Democratic Party (n.d.) (Nova socijaldemokratska partija/Нова Социјалдемократска Партија) (n.d.)
- Citizen Option for Macedonia (n.d.) (Građanska opcija za Makedonija/Граѓанска опција за Македонија)
- Internal Macedonian Revolutionary Organization–People's Party (n.d.) (Vnatrešna Makedonska Revolucionerna Organizacija-Narodna Partija/Внатрешна Македонска Револуционерна Организација-Народна Партија)
- Democratic Renewal of Macedonia (n.d.) (Demokratska obnova na Makedonija/Демократска обнова на Македонија)
- Democratic Union for Integration (n.d.) (Demokratski unija za integracija/Демократска унија за интеграција)
- Party of United Democrats of Macedonia (n.d.) (Partija na obedineti demokrati na Makedonija/Партија на обединети демократи на Македонија)
- United Macedonia (n.d.) (Единствена Македонија)
- The Left (n.d.) (Levica/Левица)

We can observe that not even one party uses the official name of the state.

The third point is the passports. More precisely, passports sealed since February 2019 mention the new name as an intermediate measure until their substitution. The new biometric passports have the new name printed on them in 3 languages: Macedonian, English, and French.

The car plates have changed as well. All new cars have plates with NMK on them, but it is not an obligation for all other vehicles (cars, trucks, coaches) to change their plates with the new one. The road signs have changed as well. All signs at the borders now mention North Macedonia: "Welcome to North Macedonia." Toll booths give receipts mentioning Severna Makedonija, and T-Mobile welcomes us to North Macedonia.

The situation is not the same when we are dealing with authorities not providing services to foreigners. Public buildings and services have not adapted to either the spirit or the letter of the Agreement. All museums in Skopje and other cities (Bitola,

Prilep, Doiran, Gevgelja, Struma, and Ohrid) public or private (these are limited), have on them a small metallic plate in which the new name, Republika Makedonija, is usually mentioned, but all other plates, titles, and, information remain unchanged. Instead, the narrative of "Macedonian continuity" is preserved in the public discourse in violation of Article 7, paragraphs 3 and 4. The same holds for the websites. Even the country's website of the National Tourism Organization of the country (Macedonia Timeless, n.d.) refers to Macedonia, stating on the main page "Macedonia's official tourism site", although the menu mentions "Basic information about North Macedonia", and all information is copyrighted by @ NorthMacedoniaTimeless.

The same can be said for statues all over the country. Starting from the center of Skopje, statues of Alexander and Philip remain where they stand, but the signs at their base were violently detached, probably because in the signs there was mention of the Hellenistic heritage of Macedonia (Prespes Agreement, 2018, Art. 8, par. 2: 10). The same can be observed for the statues of Olympias, mother of Alexander the Great, Macedonian Warrior, Porta Macedonia, in the city center of Skopje, or the statue of Phillip the Second at Bitola and other cities.

Another crucial factor is the school books that remain unchangeable. The Agreement formed a joint interdisciplinary committee of experts that will revise the school textbooks (Prespa Agreement, 2018, Art. 8, Par. 5:11), but this process was postponed for the future. It can be argued that recent political developments in Europe and the election of a new government in Greece and North Macedonia have affected this process.

Another problem is the status and the name of the local church. The Prespa Agreement does not make any provisions for the MOC, but this is another exceptional case with many aspects that require a political solution. For over 35 years, the MOC lived isolated and unrecognized, refusing to compromise with Belgrade. In 2017, Archbishop Stephan asked the Bulgarian Patriarchate in Sofia to assume the parental authority of the MOC (Marusic & Cheresheva, 2017). However, this move would imply a new conflict with Belgrade and possibly with the Ecumenical Patriarchate in Constantinople, thus, so far Sofia has been reserved in replying to the invitation yet. Other sources say that a solution with political encouragement would be for the Ecumenical Patriarchate to take back the jurisdiction of North Macedonia, restore the Archbishopric of Ohrid canonically, and establish a Church deleting the "Macedonian" compound from its name (Marusic, 2018). In his interview, Archbishop Stephan said that the MOC has no nationalist claims or objectives, but it wants to be free to execute its spiritual work. He stated: "Macedonians are not enemies of the Greeks. The Greeks are the closest people to the Macedonians." (Grammenos, *Interview with Archbishop*, 2019).

Our research in Skopje (August 2019) brought us in contact with the youth of the liberal party (LDP) which was in government in coalition with the Social Democratic Union. A ten-member delegation from Greece met with a ten -member delegation from North Macedonia in a 3-day workshop. We noticed that the local team had no Albanian member or member of Albanian origin and, in general, they were cautious about mentioning the Albanian minority.

Also, they avoided raising any historical issues or commenting on the statues of Alexander and Philip, even after the desire for the Greek team to visit them and take photos. In actual fact, their main concerns were about the future of North Macedonia and, more precisely, the EU accession, the liberalization on social issues, and the economic reforms.

Another mission of 40 students from the Université Libre de Bruxelles, the Aristotle University of Thessaloniki, and the University of Macedonia, both of the latter being at Thessaloniki, visited Skopje from 26 September to 6 October 2019. A survey from Belgian and Greek students with their Macedonian partners took place in the capital of North Macedonia and made clear that opinions and feelings differ. Especially, a big percentage of the North Macedonian students advocated that everyone has the liberty to present or consider themselves in a specific manner that they wish or deem true, and, in that way, anyone who lives in the geographical area can be self-determined as Macedonian. However, they corroborate that they are descendants of Alexander the Great and his empire, but also, they admit the political use of this identity by the Gruevski's government after the failed experiment of Yugoslavia. Furthermore, this part of society does not accept or agree with the terms of the Prespa Agreement as, because they strongly believe that, the agreement is an offense to their "Macedonian" identity, and, also they openly request to be self-determined as Macedonians. On the other hand, the supporters of the new circumstances advocate that the Prespa's Agreement is a great opportunity to throw off the yoke of a counterfeit national identity and for the country to become a member state of the EU and NATO, which could not happen without the Agreement with Greece (Lagrou, 2019, p.163 et suiv.).

Conclusion

The Prespa Agreement was a step of utmost importance and necessity for the region in defining the identity boundaries of the people of North Macedonia, at least vis-à-vis Greece. Nevertheless, this re-approach and cooperation for the signing of the Agreement will be fruitless if there will be no continuation and real effort from both sides. The Agreement will yield positive results if both countries show sincere interest in working together. Secondly, the long standby for the EU accession talks can discourage decisively North Macedonia, forcing many people to turn to populism and nationalism, or even to Russia, as they need to see tangible changes in their way of living and a reward for their efforts so far.

The evolution of the identity of North Macedonia affects the people's views and perspectives. The generation that was in school back in 2002–2004, and grew up with the revisionist ideas of that period, today are in a very productive age and practically run the country. For that reason, the embedded beliefs and national narrative are part of their thinking and decision-making.

Lastly, we do not expect a political Agreement to change an established mentality in just a few months. The collective understanding of the self, the common historical perceptions, and the cultural recollections are deeply rooted in public thinking and take time to change.

Substantially, just an agreement cannot change the rhetoric of a specific identity that had been used for years. The collective understanding of the community, the cultural and historical representations of the past, and the public discourse are rooted in society and its way of thinking, and people need time as well as to be willing to change if they are to change. A continuing and organized political plan for North Macedonia could make a difference and show to its people a different way forward into the future.

References

Aarbakke, V. (2010). Who can mend a broken heart. Macedonia's place in Modern Bulgarian History. In I. Stefanidis, V. Vlasidis, & E. Kofos (Eds.), *Macedonian identities through time. Interdisciplinary approaches* (pp. 184–212). Epikentro.

Al-Bander, S. (2017). Blind sides of national histories: Reconciliation between Macedonia and Greece. In B. Lambros, I. Dodovska, & D. Jovanovski (Eds.), *Balkan crossroads. Historical dialogue between scholars in Southeastern Europe* (pp. 28–37).

Anderson, F. M., & Hershey, A. S. (1918). The Treaty of Bucharest, August 10, 1913. In *Handbook for the diplomatic history of Europe, Asia, and Africa 1870–1914* (pp. 439–441). National Board for Historical Service, Government Printing Office. Retrieved from https://archive.org/details/handbookfordipl01hersgoog/page/n442/mode/2up?view=theater

Barker, E. (1950). *Macedonia. Its place in Balkan Politics*. Royal Institute of International Affairs.

"Citizen Option for Macedonia (Građanska opcija za Makedonija/Граѓанска опција за Македонија)" (n.d.). https://grom.mk/

Cvoro, U. (2018). *Transitional aesthetics: Contemporary art at the edge of Europe*. Bloomsbury Academic.

Danforth, L. (1995). *The Macedonian conflict: Ethnic nationalism in a transnational world*. Princeton University Press.

"Democratic Renewal of Macedonia (Demokratska obnova na Makedonija/Демократска обнова на Македонија)" (n.d.). https://dom.org.mk/

"Democratic Union for Integration (Demokratski unija za integracija/Демократска унија за интеграција)" (n.d.). http://bdi.mk/

Grammenos, A. (2019, August 31). Archbishop Stephan of the MOC [Interview]. North Macedonia.

Harwell, S. E. (2011). *Building national anxiety: The "Skopje 2014" project in Macedonia's Capital*. University of Washington.

Hertslet, E. (1891). Treaty between Great-Britain, Austria-Hungary, France, Germany, Italy, Russia, and Turkey, for the Settlement of Affairs in the East, Signed at Berlin, 13th July 1878 (Translation). In *The map of Europe by Treaty; which have taken place since the general peace of 1814. With numerous maps and notes* (Vol. IV (1), pp. 1875–1891). Her Majesty's Stationery Office. https://archive.org/details/mapofeuropebytre04hert/page/2864/mode/2up?view=theater

Holland, T. E. (1885). The Preliminary Treaty of Peace, signed at San Stefano, 17 March 1878. In *The European concert in the eastern question and other public acts*. Clarendon Press.

Ilieski, Z. (2017). *"Skopje 2014"—Between belated nation-building and the challenges of globalisation*. Freie Universität Berlin.

Interim Accord. (1995, September 13). https://peacemaker.un.org/sites/peacemaker.un.org/files/MK_950913_Interim%20Accord%20between%20the%20Hellenic%20Republic%20and%20the%20FYROM.pdf

"Internal Macedonian Revolutionary Organization–People's Party (Vnatrešna Makedonska Revolucionerna Organizacija-Narodna Partija/Внатрешна Македонска Револуционерна Организација-Народна Партија)" (n.d.). http://www.vmro-np.org.mk/

Ivanovski, V. (1978). *30 godini Institut za Natsionalnata Istorija*. Institut.

Janev, G. (2011). Ethnocratic remaking of urban space - Skopje 2014. *European Federation of Landscape Architecture Journal, 1*, 34–38.

Kafedjiska, V. (2018). Macedonia in the waiting room of the European Union: Betrayed hopes. *International Journal of Advanced Research, 6*(2), 1835–1841. https://doi.org/10.21474/IJAR01/6625

Kofos, E. (1962). The making of Yugoslavia's People's Republic of Macedonia. *Balkan Studies, 3*, 375–396.

Kofos, E. (1964). *Nationalism and communism in Macedonia*. Institute for Balkan Studies.

Kofos, E. (2005). The unresolved "difference over the name": The Greek perspective. In E. Kofos & V. Vlasidis (Eds.), *Athens-Skopje. An uneasy symbiosis* (pp. 125–224). ELIAMEP.

Koneski, B. (1945). The Macedonian literature and the Macedonian literary language: teaching that took place at the Skopje people's university. Kultura. [Конески, Блаже, Македонската литература и македонскиот литературен јазик: предавање одржано на Скопскиот народен универзитет, Скопје: Култура, 1945].

Koneski, B. (1949). *Prilep speech*. Faculty of Philosophy of the University. [Конески Блаже, Прилепскиот говор, Скопје: Филозофски факултет на Универзитетот, 1949].

Koneski, B. (1950). *Crossing to the Macedonian Alphabet and Spelling*. Blazhe's Letter to the Editor. [Конески Блаже, Преминување на македонската азбука и правопис. Блаже статија - 1950].

Koneski, B. (1952). *Grammar of the Macedonian Literary Language. Part I, Introduction; For the votes; For the accent*. State Book Publishing House of the People's Republic of Macedonia. [Конески Блаже, Граматика на македонскиот литературен јазик. Дел I, Увод; За гласовите; За акцентот, Скопје: Државно книгоиздателство на НР Македонија, 1952].

Koppa, M. (2013). FYROM: The difficulties have not finished yet (In Greek). In T. Dokos & I. Armakolas (Eds.), *Apo ta Valkania sti Notioanatoliki Evropi: Proklisis kai prooptikes*. Sideri.

Lagrou, P. (2019). La Question Macédonienne. Retour d'un voyage. *Mémoires en Jeu 9*, 2019 (été/automne), 161–166.

"Liberal Democratic Party (Liberalno-Demokratska Partija/Либерално-Демократска Партија)" (n.d.). https://ldp.mk/

"Macedonia and its Relations with Greece" (1993). In *Macedonian Academy of Sciences and Arts*.

"Macedonia Timeless" (n.d.). https://www.macedonia-timeless.com/eng

Marusic, S. J. (2018, May 31). *Macedonian Church gets entangled in 'name' dispute*. BIRN.

Marusic, S. J., & Cheresheva, M. (2017, November 20). *Macedonia's lonely church seeks Bulgarian 'parent'*. BIRN.

Mauss, M. (1985). A category of the human mind: The notion of person; the notion of self. In M. Carrithers, S. Collins, & S. Lukes (Eds.), *The category of the person: Anthropology, philosophy, history* (pp. 1–25). Cambridge University Press.

Mavrogeni, S. (2010). Macedonian Sarissa and Albanian Eagle: FYROM's new school textbooks. In I. Stefanidis, V. Vlasidis, & E. Kofos (Eds.), *Macedonian identities through time. Interdisciplinary approaches* (pp. 273–293). Epikentro.

Mavrogeni, S. (2015). Public art in FYROM. *Macedonian Studies Journal, 2*(1), 63–74. https://www.academia.edu/41422971/PUBLIC_ART_IN_FYROM

Michailidis, I. (2010). What Macedonia for the Macedonians: Politics and history in Yugoslav Macedonia. In I. Stefanidis, V. Vlasidis, & E. Kofos (Eds.), *Macedonian identities through time. Interdisciplinary approaches* (pp. 213–226). Epikentro.

Mus, J. (2016). Between Skopje and Sofia. *Aspen Review Central Europe, 1*.

Nestor, S. (1962). Greek Macedonia and the Convention of Neuilly (1919). *Balkan Studies, 3*(1), 169–184.

"New Social Democratic Party (Nova socijaldemokratska partija/Нова Социјалдемократска Партија)" (n.d.). https://nsdp.org.mk/

Palmer, S. E., Jr., Stephen, E., & King, R. (1971). *Yugoslav communism and the Macedonian question*. The Shoe String Press, Inc. Archon Books.

Papastathis, C. K. (1967). L'autocéphalie de l'église de la Macédoine yougoslave. *Balkan Studies, 8*, 151–154.

"Party of United Democrats of Macedonia (Partija na obedineti demokrati na Makedonija/Партија на обединети демократина Македонија)" (n.d.). https://podem.org.mk/

Petiffer, J. (Ed.). (1999). *The New Macedonian question*. Palgrave.

Poulton, H. (1995). *Who are the Macedonians*. Indiana University Press.

Prespa Agreement. (June 17, 2018). https://www.mfa.gr/images/docs/eidikathemata/agreement.pdf

Roudometov, V. (2002). *Collective memory, national identity & ethnic conflict*. Praeger.

Sfetas, S. (2012). The Bulgarian-Yugoslav Dispute over the Macedonian Question as a reflection of the Soviet-Yugoslav Controversy (1968-1980). *Balcanica, XLIII*, 241–272.

Sfetas, S. P., & Kentrotis, K. (1994). Skopje in search of an identity and international recognition. *Balkan Studies, 35*, 337–377.

"Socialist Party of Macedonia (Socijalisticka Partija na Makedonija/Социјалистичка Партија на Македонија)" (n.d.). http://spm.org.mk/

Testorides, K. (2017, August 1). Macedonia, Bulgaria Sign Historic Treaty, Renounce Rivalry. In *AP NEWS*. https://apnews.com/article/a3bb01ba483e44ad8a49aebe63f4f6fa

"The Left (Levica/Левица)" (n.d.). https://levica.mk/

Tziampiris, A. (2005). The name dispute in The Former Yugoslav Republic of Macedonia after the signing of the interim accord. In E. Kofos & V. Vlasidis (Eds.), *Athens-Skopje. An uneasy symbiosis* (pp. 225–252). ELIAMEP.

"United Macedonia (Единствена Македонија)" (n.d.). https://en.wikipedia.org/wiki/United_for_Macedonia

UN Statement (2019). Secretary-General of the United Nations. (2019, February 13). *Statement attributable to the Spokesman for the Secretary-General on Prespa Agreement*. https://www.un.org/sg/en/content/sg/statement/2019-02-13/statement-attributable-the-spokesman-for-the-secretary-general-prespa-agreement

Vankovska, B. (2010). David vs Goliath: The Macedonian position(s) in the so-called 'Name Dispute' with Greece. *Sudosteuropa, 58*(3), 436–467.

Vankovska, B. (2015). History and memories of the Balkan Wars in the Republic of Macedonia: Debates over the past. In J. Pettifer & T. Buchanan (Eds.), *War in the Balkans: Conflict and diplomacy before World War I* (pp. 1–16). I.B. Tauris.

Veikos, T. (1999). *Ethnicity and ethnic identity (In Greek)*. Ellinika Grammata.

Vlasidis, V. (2005). We and the others: Greece's image in FYROM's press and education system (1995-2002). In E. Kofos & V. Vlasidis (Eds.), *An uneasy symbiosis* (pp. 253–316). ELIAMEP.

Vlasidis, V. (2010). History in mission command: The Macedonian question and the Internet 1990-2007. In I. Stefanidis, V. Vlasidis, & E. Kofos (Eds.), *Macedonian identities through time. Interdisciplinary approaches* (pp. 294–320). Epikentro.

Vlasidis, V. (2017, January). The Macedonian issue in postwar era and the creation of a Slavomacedonian identity. *Notebooks of Macedonian History and Civilisation, 3*, 12–30 [Το Μακεδονικό Ζήτημα στα μεταπολεμικά χρόνια και η δημιουργία της σλαβομακεδονικής ταυτότητας. *Σε Τετράδια Μακεδονικής Ιστορίας και Πολιτισμού*, 3, 12–30].

Whitman, L. (1994). Denying ethnic identity. The Macedonians of Greece. In *Human rights watch*.

Zaikos, N. (2010). The onomastics of States in International Law: The case of The Former Yugoslav Republic of Macedonia. In I. Stefanidis, V. Vlasidis, & E. Kofos (Eds.), *Macedonian identities through time. Interdisciplinary approaches* (pp. 337–361). Epikentro.

Part II

The Role of European Charters and the European Pillar of Social Rights in Fighting Social Exclusion

The European Social Charter and the Charter of Fundamental Rights of the European Union

George N. Theodosis

Abstract

This chapter attempts to explore the interrelations of the European Social Charter (ESC) and the EU Charter of Fundamental Rights (CFREU) in protecting social rights within the difficult relationship of ESC and EU social law, the limitations and the potentials of both instruments regarding the justiciability of their provisions, and the prospects of better inter-institutional cooperation in the field of social rights.

In the first part of this chapter, the main argument is that the ESC and the EU law have a difficult relationship, which from an EU side point of view is mainly due to the *"à la carte"* system of the Charter. These difficulties are shown both in the incorporation into national law of directives deemed by the European Committee of Social Rights (ECSR) not to meet the requirements of the Charter and in the issues related to the implementation of austerity measures in member states like Greece, during the past decade.

These difficulties exist despite the common objectives pursued by the two texts and their clear intertextuality, as analysed in the second part. However, in recent years there seems to be the beginning of a dialogue between the texts in the case law of the EU Court of Justice (CJEU).

Finally, in the third and final part, the author presents the system of monitoring and justiciability of the rights provided for in the two instruments as the effectiveness of protection is inextricably linked to the importance of social

The views expressed in this chapter concern only its author.

G. N. Theodosis (✉)
Department of Law, Democritus University of Thrace, Komotini, Greece

European Committee of Social Rights, Strasbourg Cedex, France
e-mail: gtheodos@law.duth.gr

D. Anagnostopoulou (ed.), *European Identities, Inclusion and Equality*, Diversity and Inclusion Research, https://doi.org/10.1007/978-3-031-90602-2_7

rights. To date the monitoring system of the Charter has been rather imperfect and the justiciability rather limited; however, there are some "cracks" which allow for optimism, particularly concerning the recognition of a horizontal direct effect of certain rights, as regards both the ESC and the CFREU.

The author concludes that the legal constraints presented by the two institutions will be lifted to a certain extent, and the dialogue between the two texts will be intensified as the multicrises call for a review of social policies on the basis of the principle of solidarity.

Introduction

The year 2021 marked the 60th anniversary of the adoption of the European Social Charter in 1961 and the 25th anniversary of the adoption of its revised version in 1996.[1]

The European Social Charter of the Council of Europe (1996), along with the European Convention on Human Rights (1950), which was also adopted within the framework of the Council of Europe in 1950, and the Charter of Fundamental Rights of the EU (2009) collectively form a comprehensive set of legally binding instruments for the protection of human, social, and economic rights on the European continent, despite their varying objectives, scope, and justiciability.

All three of these institutional texts, though not all originating from the Council of Europe, reflect Europe's longstanding tradition and legal culture concerning the protection of fundamental rights, which is as essential today as it was in the period following the two world wars that led to the creation of the Council of Europe in 1949.[2]

Over the past 15 years, the protection of political, social, and economic rights in the European Union has been increasingly challenged due to successive crises. The deep/severe economic crisis, especially in Southern Europe, led to stringent austerity measures that significantly diminished social rights protection, notably in countries such as Greece, Portugal, Ireland, and Italy (Deligianni-Dimitrakou, 2013; Gavalas, 2011; Gavalas, 2012; Nivard, 2012a).

Conversely, European countries face a completely different challenge with the ongoing refugee crisis and the influx of millions of migrants, refugees, and asylum seekers. To date, they have yet to adopt commonly accepted solutions for managing or preventing their entry into European territory and for implementing reception

[1] Henceforth references to both the European Social Charter of 1961 and the Revised European Social Charter of 1996 may be made as ESC or Charter, unless further clarification is required to specifically refer to one or the other text, in which case this will be indicated.

[2] It is reminded that the Council of Europe's fundamental purpose, as stated in Article 1 of its statute, is to promote greater unity among member states, safeguarding their shared ideals and principles. This goal is achieved through discussions on common-interest issues, agreements, and collective actions in various domains, including economics, society, culture, science, law, and administration. Additionally, the Council focuses on preserving and advancing human rights and fundamental freedoms.

policies that ensure decent living conditions. This is critical for the protection of the most vulnerable social groups, such as children and, in particular, unaccompanied minors (European Committee of Social Rights, 2021a).

Thirdly, the crisis of the COVID-19 pandemic, along with the adverse economic consequences associated with it, had significant repercussions, especially on the access of vulnerable social groups to the public good of health (European Committee of Social Rights, 2020), but it also affected other labour and social rights (European Committee of Social Rights, 2021b).

Finally, the ongoing war in Ukraine is having both direct and visible effects on the lives and enjoyment of fundamental human and social rights for Ukrainian citizens, many of whom are forced to flee their homeland (European Committee of Social Rights, 2022). Particularly due to the energy crisis it has triggered, it is also causing largely unforeseen consequences, affecting the social and economic rights and freedoms of European citizens.[3]

Under the above circumstances, if the European Social Charter and the EU Charter of Fundamental Rights did not exist, we would need to both invent them and enhance their institutional significance. They serve as essential safeguards for addressing all the aforementioned "black swans" (as well as potential future ones) that disrupt the normal trajectory of progress.

European Social Charter and EU Charter of Fundamental Rights

Initiated following the establishment of the Council of Europe in 1949, the European Social Charter (ESC) arose from negotiations aiming for a comprehensive pan-European human rights treaty. Although, initially envisioned to mirror the Universal Declaration of Human Rights (1948), member states prioritized the adoption of the European Convention on Human Rights (ECHR) in 1949, emphasizing civil and political rights to reinforce democracy and the rule of law in Europe. This prioritization reflected political compromises in the context of post-war challenges posed by fascist/Nazi regimes and two world wars.

The European Social Charter, adopted in 1961 and revised in 1996, is a comprehensive instrument safeguarding social and economic rights. It complements the European Convention on Human Rights (Brillat, 2017) and has been ratified in one form or another by 42 out of 46 Council of Europe member states, including all European Union states (Council of Europe, 2021). It is monitored by the European Committee of Social Rights (ECSR).

[3] As an example, reference could be made to the risks posed by the war in Ukraine, leading to an increase in energy prices and subsequent inflation, affecting primarily the more vulnerable social groups and their rights derived from Article 30 ESC (revised) regarding protection against poverty and social exclusion, as well as Article 31 ESC (revised) regarding the right to housing (which, of course, includes access to adequate housing, which cannot be ensured without heating during the winter months).

On the other hand, the Charter of Fundamental Rights of the European Union (CFREU or EU Charter) was adopted on December 7, 2000, in Nice. It is monitored by the Fundamental Rights Agency of the European Union (FRA).

Although initially lacking legal effect, the EU Charter of Fundamental Rights acquired legal standing with the entry into force of the Treaty of Lisbon on December 1, 2009 (Treaty of the European Union, 2009), becoming a comprehensive, legally binding document within the EU framework. While facing limitations in judicial enforcement, the Charter has evolved into a crucial text safeguarding civil, political, social, and economic rights of EU citizens. Its integration into the EU Treaty, aligning with the UN Vienna Declaration,[4] has notably strengthened the internal market, reflecting a transformative perspective on universal, indivisible, interdependent, and interrelated human rights (Treaty on European Union, 2009, art. 6, para. 1).

Objectives and Scope of the Two Charters

The ESC (European Social Charter) aims to secure social rights without discrimination based on race, colour, gender, religion, political beliefs, or national origin, as outlined in its preamble, across its member states and contracting parties.

The ESC, in its revised version (1996), with 31 articles, covers a wide scope of social rights, including labor, health, housing, social security, and welfare. It prioritizes protecting vulnerable groups like the elderly, children, individuals with disabilities, and migrants, ensuring their well-being and rights are safeguarded.

In principle, ESC rights typically encompass all workers in States Parties, regardless of sector (public or private) or employment status (employees, home workers, etc.). Exceptions exist, particularly for foreign workers. The ESC's scope, as defined in its Appendix, often extends these rights *"to nationals of other Contracting Parties residing or working regularly in another Contracting Party's territory"*.

On the other hand, the Charter of Fundamental Rights of the European Union (CFREU) has wider-ranging objectives and is founded on the principle that the European Union is built upon the inseparable and universal values of human dignity, freedom, equality, and solidarity (CFREU, 2007, preamble).

The CFREU covers a wide range of civil, political, social, and economic rights across 54 articles grouped into seven chapters. The initial six chapters detail rights related to dignity, freedoms, equality, solidarity, citizens' rights, and justice, while the final chapter contains four horizontal clauses for charter interpretation and application.

[4] The UN Vienna Declaration and Programme of Action was adopted at the World Conference on Human Rights, held in Vienna, Austria, on June 25, 1993, in order to "promote universal respect for, and observance and protection of, all human rights and fundamental freedoms for all" (para. 1), https://www.ohchr.org/en/instruments-mechanisms/instruments/vienna-declaration-and-programme-action

The fundamental rights in the CFREU are primarily "universal rights", meaning they apply to "everyone". Nonetheless, certain provisions aim at protecting specific groups, including "EU citizens" or "third-country nationals".[5]

The Relationship Between the ESC and EU Law

The ESC serves as a comprehensive continental-level framework safeguarding social and economic human rights, complementing the ECHR, which focuses on civil and political rights. However, within EU law, its prominence is comparatively diminished. Although all EU member states are bound by both the ECHR and the ESC,[6] the latter's recognition and impact within EU law fall short of the ECHR's stature, highlighting a disparity in their influence within the Union.

In the Treaty on European Union (TEU) in its current form (Treaty of Lisbon), which has been in force since 2009, there is no mention of the European Social Charter, unlike the significant references made to the ECHR.[7] Additionally, in the CFREU, which, according to Article 6 TEU (paragraph 1), holds "*the same legal value as the Treaties*" of the Union, there is no legally significant mention of the ESC. Notably, Article 52, paragraph 3 of the CFREU stipulates that:

> where this Charter contains rights that correspond to those guaranteed by the European Convention for the Protection of Human Rights and Fundamental Freedoms, the interpretation and scope of those rights shall be the same as those established by that Convention.

To grasp the significance of the ESC in comparison to the ECHR (as well as independently), the CFREU makes only one indirect reference to the ESC, without mentioning it by name. This reference is found in the CFREU's preamble, where it essentially acknowledges the self-evident fact that:

> the rights stem primarily from the shared constitutional traditions of the Member States, the European Convention for the Protection of Human Rights and Fundamental Freedoms, the Social Charters adopted by the Union and the Council of Europe, and the jurisprudence of the Court of Justice of the European Union and the European Court of Human Rights.

---

[5] For example, in Article 15 of the CFREU (Charter of Fundamental Rights of the European Union), in the first paragraph, "*Every person has the right to work and to pursue freely the employment of their choice*" in the second paragraph, "*Every citizen of the Union is free to seek employment, work, reside, or provide services in any Member State*", and in the third paragraph, "*Third-country nationals who are authorized to work in the territory of the Member States are entitled to working conditions equivalent to those enjoyed by Union citizens*". https://fra.europa.eu/el/eu-charter/title/title-ii-freedoms

[6] Council of Europe. (n.d.-a). *Charter Texts*. https://www.coe.int/en/web/european-social-charter/charter-texts

[7] Treaty on European Union (2009), art. 6, paras. 2 and 3. In these paragraphs, it's stated that the Union will join the European Convention for the Protection of Human Rights and Fundamental Freedoms. Fundamental rights (1950), derived from the common constitutional traditions of Member States and the European Convention, will form fundamental principles of Union law.

However, this does not imply that the ESC lacks value and significance in EU law and its institutions. Quite the opposite, the importance and mutual interactions between the Social Charter system and the European Union are evident in numerous points of convergence between these two legal frameworks.

First and foremost, the primary Union law explicitly references the European Social Charter. The Treaty on European Union's preamble underscores member states' *"dedication to fundamental social rights, delineated in the 1961 European Social Charter and the 1989 Community Charter of Fundamental Social Rights of Workers"*, emphasizing their enduring commitment.

Article 151 of the Treaty on the Functioning of the European Union (TFEU) (2009) is significant, directly referencing the European Social Charter (ESC). It outlines shared objectives for the EU and its member states, emphasizing employment promotion, improved living and working conditions, sustained social protection, social dialogue, human resource development, and exclusion combat. This reflects the EU's commitment to fundamental social rights from the ESC, serving as a focal point for social progress. Despite these references, secondary EU legislation seldom incorporates ESC principles, highlighting a gap between member states' intent and the integration of ESC provisions into EU legislation.

In certain instances, such as Decision 50/2002/EC of December 7, 2001 (establishing a program of community action to encourage cooperation between member states to combat social exclusion) (Decision 50/2002/EC, 2001), the European Social Charter (ESC) is referenced in its preamble among legal acts. This decision outlines that both the community and member states must consider:

> fundamental principles, such as those established in the European Social Charter signed in Turin on 18 October 1961, the revised Social Charter of the Council of Europe (1996), notably Article 30, which addresses the right to protection against poverty and social exclusion, and the 1989 Community Charter of the Fundamental Social Rights of Workers. Additionally, we acknowledge the rights and principles recognized in the Charter of Fundamental Rights of the European Union, jointly proclaimed on 7 December 2000 by the European Parliament, the Council, and the Commission, with the objective of combatting exclusion.

In other cases, the ESC is referenced in the regulatory act to clarify that its application should be construed as "'without prejudice" 'to the rights protected by the ESC itself or to any more favorable treatment it may guarantee. For instance, this is evident in Directive 2003/86/EC regarding the right to family reunification (Directive No. 2003/86/EC, 2003), which specifies that:

> it shall apply without prejudice to more favorable provisions: (a) (...) (b) the European Social Charter of 18 October 1961, the revised European Social Charter of 3 May 1987, and the European Convention on the Legal Status of Migrant Workers of 24 November 1977

It is also evident in Directive 2014/36/EU on the conditions of entry and residence of third-country nationals for the purposes of seasonal employment (Directive 2014/36/EU, 2014), which states that:

> (the ESC) should apply without prejudice to the rights and principles contained in the European Social Charter of 18 October 1961 and the European Convention on the legal status of migrant workers of 24 November 1977. (preamble, para. 44)

However, it should also be mentioned that the revised European Social Charter (ESC) draws inspiration from EU Directives, seen in provisions like informing workers about essential aspects of their employment contract or relationship, highlighting a reciprocal influence (Directive No 91/533/EEC, 1991, art. 2 para. 6 of the ESC Statute), setting the minimum age for employment in hazardous or unhealthy occupations (Directive No 94/33/EC, 1994, art. 7 para. 2), implementing measures to enhance the health and safety of pregnant women, recently postpartum workers, or breastfeeding mothers (Directive No 92/85/EC, 1994, art. 8 para. 4), and safeguarding employees in cases of employer insolvency (Directive No 80/987/EEC, 1980, art. 25), among others (Council of Europe, 1996).

Although interaction exists between the Council of Europe's ESC and the EU's social provisions, the closer integration is hindered by the ESC's flexible *à la carte* system,[8] enabling states to selectively adopt provisions as international law obligations. The flexibility inherent in its application creates challenges in maintaining uniformity across member states, complicating their alignment with EU law, primarily structured on the principle of partial harmonization.

Apart from two states, France and Portugal, which have accepted all the articles and paragraphs of the (Revised) ESC, the remaining states have ratified varying numbers of provisions from both versions of the ESC.[9]

This lack of uniformity and inconsistent application across member states of the ESC rules within the member states of the EU explains its limited recognition of EU law. While Article 151 TFEU mentions ESC, it could not be considered as imposing a legal obligation that the ESC is legally binding in the application of EU law; therefore, the ESC can only serve as a source of inspiration for the European legislator and the member states in promoting their objectives in the field of social policy. According to CJEU Advocate General Sir Francis Jacobs, as parties can choose which ESC provisions to be bound by, the rights lack universal recognition, challenging their inclusion in EU law's general principles (De Schutter, 2017).

---

[8] This "à la carte" system has its limitations. As defined in Part III, Article A, paragraph 1 of the revised ESC, the contracting parties undertake the obligation to consider themselves bound by a minimum number of rights. These must include at least six of the nine specified "core" articles of Part II of the Revised ESC, namely, Articles 1, 5, 6, 7, 12, 13, 16, 19, and 20, and an additional number of articles or numbered paragraphs of Part II of the Revised ESC that they may choose, provided that the total number of articles or numbered paragraphs to which they are bound is not less than 16 articles or 63 numbered paragraphs. The original 1961 ESC already provided for such an "à la carte" system. According to Article 20 of the 1961 ESC, states must accept at least five of the seven articles (Articles 1, 5, 6, 12, 13, 16, and 19) and certain articles or numbered paragraphs of Part II of the ESC, according to their preference, provided that the total number is not less than 10 articles or 45 numbered paragraphs.

[9] Council of Europe. (n.d.-c). *Accepted provisions of the European Social Charter.* https://www.coe.int/en/web/european-social-charter/provisions-of-the-charter

The rare and limited reference to the ESC regarding legislative activity and the formulation of EU social policy in the field of social rights can also partly be explained, at least in recent decades, by the fact that the CFREU includes a part—under Title IV—dedicated to solidarity, covering many areas included in the ESC. It is therefore more direct for the Union's institutions to refer to the CFREU rather than the ESC regarding legislative and policy initiatives in the field of social rights.

In Particular, the Influence of the ESC on Shaping the Content of the CFREU

Based on the analysis above, it is evident that the ESC plays a minor role in EU law. However, despite its brief mention in the CFREU preamble, it undeniably inspired numerous rights and principles within the CFREU.

This conclusion can be derived from the explanations concerning the CFREU (Charter of Fundamental Rights of the EU, 2007); even though they do not possess inherent legal authority, they serve as a valuable interpretive tool for elucidating the provisions of the Charter. Based on these explanations, the ESC served as the source of inspiration for the following rights and principles within the CFREU (Stangos, 2013):

- the right to education (Article 14 CFREU), specifically regarding access to vocational and continuing training, drew inspiration, among other sources, from Article 10 ESC;
- the freedom to choose an occupation and the right to engage in work (Article 15), which are generally encompassed by Article 1 paragraph 2 ESC and Article 19 paragraph 4 ESC, find resonance in the CFREU, as they stipulate that third-country nationals authorized to work within member states are entitled to working conditions equivalent to those enjoyed by Union citizens (Article 15 para. 3 CFREU);
- the principle of equality between women and men (Article 23 CFREU) was influenced by Article 20 ESC, as regards equality in employment, occupation, and pay;
- the rights of the elderly (Article 25 CFREU) were inspired by Article 23 of the revised ESC;
- the inclusion of persons with disabilities (Article 26 CFREU) was influenced by the corresponding Article 15 ESC;
- the right of workers to information and consultation within the undertaking (Article 27 CFREU) derives from the provision added to the ESC by the 1988 Protocol (Council of Europe, 1988);
- the right of collective bargaining and action (Article 28 CFREU), corresponds to Article 6 ESC;
- the right of access to employment services (Article 29 CFREU), corresponds to Article 1 para. 3 ESC;

- protection of the worker in the event of unjustified dismissal (Article 30 CFREU), was inspired by Article 24 of the revised ESC;
- fair and just working conditions (Article 31 CFREU), is based on three articles of the ESC: Article 3 ESC as regards the part relating to safety and health at work; Article 2 ESC itself as regards the principle of maximum working hours and the right to daily and weekly rest periods and paid leave; as well as Article 26 of the revised Charter on the right to dignity at work;
- prohibition of child labour and protection of young people in the workplace (Article 32 CFREU), is based on Article 7 ESC;
- balance of family and professional life (Article 33 CFREU), is based on Article 16 ESC, as regards the social, economic, and legal protection of the family, as well as Article 8 ESC and Article 27 of the revised Charter, as regards the right to protection from dismissal on grounds related to maternity and the right to maternity and parental leave;
- insurance and social assistance (Article 34 CFREU), is based on Article 12 ESC as regards social security benefits, Articles 12 and 13(4) ESC as regards the right of persons legally residing or moving within the Union to social security and social benefits; and Article 13 of the ESC as well as Articles 30 and 31 of the revised ESC on the right to social assistance and housing to ensure a decent life for all those who lack sufficient resources and the principle of combating social exclusion and poverty;
- health protection (Article 35 CFREU): its principles are based on Article 11 ESC, as well as Article 13 for the part concerning medical assistance for persons in need.

It is thus evident from this catalog, that the European Social Charter (ESC) significantly influences social and labour rights in the EU. In this context, it would indeed be appropriate for explicit references to the European Social Charter to be made not only in the explanatory notes but also in the text of the CFREU. Such references would offer crucial guidance for interpreting Title IV (Solidarity) and other social provisions of the CFREU in a manner consistent with the content of the rights and principles enshrined in the provisions of the ESC. This would ensure alignment for all EU member states within the framework of the European Social Charter and the interpretation provided by the European Committee of Social Rights (Garben, 2020).[10]

[10] In the past decade, the European Committee of Social Rights (ECSR) has observed disparities in the laws of EU member states concerning rights outlined in the ESC and EU social law. Notable cases include Sweden post-Laval CJEU judgment and France's implementation of the Working Time Directive. Disagreements also arose over economic crisis measures under troika agreements, particularly in Greece. See ECSR, 2010a, Complaint 55/2009, 2010; ECSR 2010b, Complaint 56/2009, 2010; ECSR, 2012b, Complaint 76/2012, 2012; ECSR, 2012c, Complaint 77/2012, 2012; ECSR, 2012d, Complaint 78/2012, 2012; ECSR, 2012e, Complaint 79/2012, 2012; ECSR, 2012f, Complaint 80/2012, 2012; ECSR, 2013, Complaint 85/2012, 2013.

The Shortcomings of the CFREU in Relation to the ESC

While the CFREU draws inspiration from the ESC, it doesn't provide the same comprehensive treatment of outlined rights. The CFREU lacks certain social and economic principles integral to the human condition, a gap unjustifiable in a Charter of *Fundamental* Rights. In terms of comparison, the ESC offers fuller protection of social rights than the CFREU. For example, on the right to work, the CFREU includes the freedom of work but doesn't endorse full employment as the primary goal, deviating from the commitment to maximize job opportunities. This commitment represents, on the contrary, a prioritization of the content of the right to work, as enshrined in the ESC (Art. 1, para. 1).

The CFREU is also silent on another crucial workers' right: the right to fair remuneration, which ensures that workers receive adequate pay to maintain a decent standard of living for themselves and their families. This right is essential to the ESC's framework (ESC, art. 4).

Certain rights, protected in secondary EU law and part of the revised ESC, are absent from the fundamental rights in the CFREU. Notably, rights related to the safety and health of pregnant women and workers' claims protection in cases of employer insolvency are excluded (Article 8 paras. 4 and 5, and Article 25 of the revised ESC, respectively). The omission of the first right, tied to the broader principle of maternity protection, from CFREU principles, despite inclusion in secondary law, is surprising.

The difference between the two Charters and the lack of relevant provisions in the CFREU, in the (highly interconnected) areas of social welfare, the right to housing, and the fight against poverty and social exclusion, is characteristic. The revised ESC explicitly safeguards these rights in Articles 13, 30, and 31. In contrast, the CFREU vaguely acknowledges them in Article 34, paragraph 3, related to security and social protection. This approach lacks substantive content, affirming Union respect for these rights *"in accordance with procedures provided for by community law and national legislation and practices"*.

In summary, it was a positive development that the CFREU included social rights among the fundamental rights, albeit with some ambiguity, alongside the so-called civil and political rights and fundamental freedoms. However, a common critique is that the CFREU has not fully utilized the potential to incorporate the rights outlined in the ESC system, with the result of a lower level of protection for these rights in EU law compared to the protection recognized by the ESC (without disregarding, of course, the imperfections inherent in the 'à la carte' system of ratification of ESC provisions, as it pertains to the uniformity of protection).

Control Mechanisms and Justiciability

Regarding the enforcement and justiciability of the rights established by the European Social Charter (ESC), States Parties are subject to the oversight of the European Committee of Social Rights (ECSR). The Committee comprises 15 independent members, appointed by the Committee of Ministers of the Council of Europe for a 6-year term, which can be renewed once.

The ECSR ensures compliance by States Parties with the provisions of the ESC through two distinct procedures: reporting, in which member states regularly submit national reports,[11] and collective complaints. The collective complaints procedure was adopted in 1995 and came into effect in 1998 through the Additional Protocol to the European Social Charter Providing for a System of Collective Complaints (Council of Europe, 1995a). To date, only 16 states parties (out of a total of 42 states parties to one of the two versions of the ESC) have ratified the collective complaints procedure.[12]

As part of the periodic reporting process, States Parties submit periodic reports on the implementation of the Charter in their national legislation and practice. These reports are reviewed by the European Committee of Social Rights (ECSR), which decides whether the national legislation and practices described in the national reports are compatible with the provisions of the ESC. The "Conclusions" of the ECSR are published annually, and when the ECSR concludes that a situation is not in conformity with the ESC, the Contracting State is required to take all necessary measures to address the situation and ensure compliance. Oversight of this process falls to the Committee of Ministers, intervening in the final stage of the reporting system. The Committee of Ministers of the Council of Europe ensures the monitoring and implementation of the ECSR's conclusions and intervenes in the final stage of the reporting system.

The Committee of Ministers may issue a resolution for the closure of each supervision cycle, which may include proposals to the States Parties found to be in violation of the provisions of the ESC. If a state takes no action, the Committee of Ministers may address a recommendation to that state, requesting it to amend its legislation and/or practices.

The collective complaints procedure complements judicial protection from the European Convention on Human Rights, though it differs in scope. Unlike individual appeals to the European Court of Human Rights, the ECSR cannot consider individual appeals due to the collective nature of social rights. Only employers' and workers' organizations, as well as NGOs, are eligible to initiate a collective complaint. Competent organizations include international social partners, approved international NGOs, and national social partners. Additionally, each state may grant the right to bring collective actions to specific national NGOs with expertise in ESC matters, as outlined in Article 2 of the 1995 Additional Protocol (Council of Europe, 1995a).[13]

In collective complaint procedure, organizations can initiate legal action before the ECSR without the need to exhaust domestic remedies, thereby avoiding potential delays. If the ECSR determines that a State is not fulfilling its obligations under

[11] Council of Europe. (n.d.-b). *Reporting system of the European Social Charter*. https://www.coe.int/en/web/european-social-charter/reporting-system

[12] Belgium, Bulgaria, Croatia, Cyprus, Czech Republic, Finland, France, Greece, Ireland, Italy, Netherlands, Norway, Portugal, Slovenia, Sweden, and Finland (Council of Europe, 1995b).

[13] So far, only Finland has granted this possibility to national NGOs.

the Charter, corrective actions to address the violation are mandated. The State must inform the Committee of Ministers about actions taken to align with the ESC. The Committee of Ministers may issue a resolution that takes into account the intention of the "respondent" state to take appropriate measures to remedy the situation in order to make it compatible with the ESC. If the State doesn't signal intent to remedy the situation, a recommendation may be issued, requiring a two-thirds majority vote.

The ECSR's decisions, stemming from binding provisions, must be respected by states but are not self-executing domestically. Effective ESC rights implementation depends on national courts interpreting legislation in line with ECSR decisions (Papadopoulos, 2019).

Additionally, the effective implementation of the rights under the ECS is closely linked to the legal nature of its provisions, namely whether they are provisions of direct applicability or declarative rights. Only the former can be directly applied within the domestic legal order, as declarative provisions require additional regulatory measures to be adopted by the contracting states. It is challenging to predetermine which right under the ECS has direct applicability and which is declarative, as this issue depends on the constitutional and legal traditions of the contracting states. It is not surprising that, even within the same state, there are conflicting judicial decisions regarding the direct application of the same right!

For instance, the French Court of Cassation has accepted the direct horizontal application (meaning application in disputes solely between individuals) of certain articles of the ESC, such as Article 5 (right to organize) and Article 6 (right to collective bargaining) (Nivard, 2012b).[14] Regarding Article 24 (protection against dismissal), the Court of Cassation has expressed doubts about its direct effect.[15] Similarly, the Greek Supreme Court, the Areios Pagos does not recognize the direct applicability of Article 24 ESC, questioning its direct effect in domestic law (Greek Supreme Court, 2018; Greek Supreme Court, 2020), although some lower courts have acknowledged it.

In Spain, an interesting application of ESC rights involved labor courts annulling legislation permitting employee dismissal without notice or compensation during the probationary period. Spanish courts cited the ECSR decision on Greek

[14] French Court of Cassation, Lab. Div. (2010, April 14; 2010, November 10; 2010, December 1; 2011, February 16; 2011, March 23; 2011, September 28). *Nos. 09-60,426, 09-60,429, 09-72,856, 10-60,117, 10-60,189, 10-60,191, 10-60,185, 10-19,113.*

[15] See French Court of Cassation, plenary for opinion, 17 July 2019, opinion n°15,012 et n°15,013: Article 24 of the revised European Social Charter does not have direct effect in domestic law in a dispute between private individuals. This position was recently confirmed: Cour de cassation, Chambre sociale, arrêt du 11 mai 2022, pourvoi n° 21-15.247. And this, despite the initial recognition of direct effect by the French Council of State in the Fischer case. Conseil d'État, 7ème et 2ème sous-sections réunies, 10/02/2014, 358,992. https://www.legifrance.gouv.fr/ceta/id/CETATEXT000028583868, which held that the provisions of Article 24 do notbexclusively govern relations between States and do not require any additional regulatory intervention to have legal effect among individuals ("*ces stipulations, dont l'objet n'est pas derégir exclusivement lesrelations entre les Etats et qui nerequièrent l'intervention d'aucun acte complémentaire pourproduire deseffets à l'égard des particuliers* …").

complaint no. 65/2011 (European Committee for Social Rights, 2012a), aligning measures imposed on Greece by the Troika with those in Spain.[16] This Spanish case law showcases how ECSR jurisprudence can impact national court decisions. Conversely, in Greece, which was found in violation of the ECSR, there's no compliance with national legislation on the matter, and the courts don't address the issue, highlighting contrasting approaches in enforcing ECHR rights at the national level! (Deligianni-Dimitrakou, 2013).

Finally, the possibility of judicially claiming the social rights of the CFREU included in its chapter on "Solidarity" is limited, on the one hand, by the scope of application of the CFREU and, on the other hand, by the rules of procedure of the CJEU, which does not allow direct recourse by EU citizens to it.[17] On the other hand, according to Article 51 CFREU, its provisions are addressed to the Union's institutions and bodies, respecting the principle of subsidiarity, as well as to member states only when they are implementing EU law.

The CJEU has stressed that the term implementation of Union law "*means that fundamental rights guaranteed in the legal order of the European Union apply to, but not outside all situations governed by EU law*" (CJEU, 2010, *Åklagaren v Hans Åkerberg Fransson*, para. 19; CJEU, 2014, *Pfleger*, para. 33; CJEU, 2015, *Thierry Delvigne v Commune de Lesparre Médoc* and *Préfet de la Gironde*, para. 26). This reasoning was also used when the CJEU was asked to examine the application of the CFREU in cases involving austerity measures against the economic crisis. According to the CJEU, financial assistance programs, agreed between some member states (including Greece) and the Troika, fall outside the scope of EU law (CJEU, 2012, Pringle, paras 178–181). Therefore, due to this approach, CFREU rights cannot be applied.

The CJEU is quite reluctant to give direct effect to social rights under EU law. According to its settled case-law, even a clear, precise and unconditional provision of a directive intended to confer rights or impose obligations on individuals cannot in itself apply to a dispute between individuals alone (CJEU, C-383/21 and C-384/21, *Sambre & Biesme and Commune de Farciennes,* 2022). However, the horizontal direct effect of social rights arising from the CFREU has become possible in some instances where the Court ruled that said right constitutes a fundamental principle of EU social law. This occurred with the right to paid annual leave.

[16] Juzgado de lo Social No. 2 of Barcelona. (2013, November 19). *Judgment No. 412*; High Court of Justice of the Canaries (Las Palmas, Gran Canaria), Chamber for Social and Labour Matters. (2016, January 28) *Judgment 30/2016*, App. 581/2015; High Court of Justice of the Canaries (Las Palmas, Gran Canaria), Chamber for Social and Labour Matters. (2016, March 30). *Judgment 252/2016*, App. 989/2015; High Court of Justice of the Canaries (Las Palmas, Gran Canaria), Chamber for Social and Labour Matters. (2016, April 18). *Judgment 342/2016*, App. 110/2016.

[17] Rules of Procedure of the Court of Justice, OJ L 265, 29.9.2012, https://eur-lex.europa.eu/legal-content/EN/TXT/HTML/?uri=CELEX:32012Q0929(01). The monitoring of violations of EU social law is carried out through the procedure of request for a preliminary ruling to the Court of Justice of the European Union (CJEU). The national courts of the Member States can submit preliminary questions to the CJEU when issues of interpretation or validity of EU law arise in cases pending before them.

Furthermore, in formulating this reasoning, the CJEU also referred to the recognition of this right by the ESC (CJEU, Case C-684/16, 2018, para. 52). However, these references to the ESC fall short of attributing to it and the jurisprudence of the ECSR the role that the CJEU reserves for the ECHR. According to Article 52, paragraph 3 CFREU, the rights protected by the CFREU corresponding to those secured by the ECHR have the same meaning among themselves. Therefore, although the ESC was clearly inspired by the ECHR, the striking absence of the same reference in Article 52, paragraph 3 is noteworthy but explicable, as mentioned above.

Conclusion

The analysis reveals a lack of alignment between the European Social Charter (ESC) and the Charter of Fundamental Rights of the European Union (CFREU) in terms of social rights content. This mismatch poses sustainability concerns and may lead to conflicting obligations for EU member states, both as EU members and signatories to the European Social Charter.

Hopes for the Charter of Fundamental Rights of the European Union (CFREU) to bridge disparities with the European Social Charter (ESC) in shared rights and principles have been disappointed, as illustrated by recent examples. However, recent case law from the CJEU seems to indicate a shift in approach to the issue, as the CJEU, in order to assess whether a social right constitutes a fundamental principle of EU social law, refers, among other acts of international law, to the European Social Charter "*to which all member states are contracting parties, having acceded either to the original European Social Charter or to the revised European Social Charter or to both, and to which Article 151 of the TFEU also refers*" (CJEU, *Max-Planck-Gesellschaft zur Förderung der Wissenschaften eV κατά Tetsuji,* 2018, para. 70). This, of course, is far from accepting a generally binding nature of the ESC from EU law, but it is a very important step in this direction.

The above analysis indicates that, for different reasons, the two systems protecting social rights in Europe face significant legal constraints in terms of their effectiveness. However, it's important not to forget that this could potentially change in the near future. The process of collective complaints, which has transformed the European Committee of Social Rights into a quasi-judicial body, is relatively recent, and although limited thus far, the number of collective complaints is increasing significantly. Additionally, the ratification in 2021 of the protocol on collective complaints (Council of Europe, 1995a) by a major European country like Spain is also a positive sign in this direction. Therefore, one can expect that the impact of the collective complaints process will potentially increase within national legal systems. The example of Spanish jurisprudence, previously mentioned, clearly demonstrates such a dynamic.

The CFREU remains a relatively new institutional document. Its adoption during the economic crisis undoubtedly constrained its impact, as priority was given to austerity measures rather than social rights. However, the dialogue between these two entities is crucial for the protection of social rights. During successive crises—economic, health-related, geopolitical, among others—the need to protect workers and vulnerable groups demands a significant enhancement of social policies based on the principle of solidarity.

References

Brillat, R. (2017). Foreword: The European Committee of Social Rights and the Employment Relation: Strengths and future prospects. In N. Bruun, K. Lörcher, I. Schömann, & S. Clauwaert (Eds.), *The European social charter and the employment relation* (pp. 1–4). Hart.

Charter of Fundamental Rights of the European Union. (2007). *Charter and explanations.* OJ *C* 303/17 of 14.12.2007, https://eur-lex.europa.eu/legal-content/EN/TXT/PDF/?uri=OJ:C:2007:303:FULL

CJEU, Case C-617/10, *Åklagaren v Hans Åkerberg Fransson* [2010] ECLI:EU:C:2013:105. https://eur-lex.europa.eu/legal-content/EN/TXT/PDF/?uri=CELEX:62010CJ0617

CJEU, Case C-390/12, *Robert Pfleger* [2014]ECLI:EU:C:2014:281. https://eur-lex.europa.eu/legal-content/EN/TXT/PDF/?uri=CELEX:62012CJ0390

CJEU, Case C-650/13, Thierry Delvigne v Commune de Lesparre Médoc και Préfet de la Gironde [2015] ECLI:EU:C:2015:648. https://eur-lex.europa.eu/legal-content/EN/TXT/PDF/?uri=CELEX:62013CJ0650

CJEU, Case C-684/16, *Max-Planck-Gesellschaft zur Förderung der Wissenschaften eV κατά Tetsuji Shimizu* [2018] ECLI:EU:C:2018:874. https://eur-lex.europa.eu/legal-content/EN/TXT/?uri=CELEX:62016CJ0684

CJEU, C-383/21 and C-384/21, *Sambre & Biesme and Commune de Farciennes* [2022] ECLI:EU:C:2022:1022. https://eur-lex.europa.eu/legal-content/EN/TXT/?uri=ecli%3AECLI%3AEU%3AC%3A2022%3A1022

CJEU, Case C-370/12, *Thomas Pringle v Government of Ireland and Others,* [2012] ECLI:EU:C:2012:756

Council of Europe (1988). Additional Protocol to the European Social Charter. *European Treaty Series (ETS) No. 128,* signed in Strasbourg 05.05.1988, entry in force 04.09.1992. https://www.coe.int/en/web/conventions/full-list?module=treaty-detail&treatynum=128

Council of Europe (1995a). Additional Protocol to the European Social Charter Providing for a System of Collective Complaints, *European Treaty Series (ETS) No. 158,* Strasbourg on 09.11.1995 and entry in force 01.07.1998. https://www.coe.int/en/web/conventions/full-list?module=treaty-detail&treatynum=158

Council of Europe. (1995b). Office of Treaties for the Charter of signatures and ratifications of the Additional Protocol of 1995. https://www.coe.int/en/web/conventions/full-list?module=signatures-by-treaty&treatynum=158

Council of Europe. (1996). *Explanatory Report to the European Social Charter (Revised),* ETS, No. 163. https://rm.coe.int/16800ccde4

Council of Europe. (2021). *Signatures & ratifications.* https://www.coe.int/en/web/european-social-charter/signatures-ratifications

Council of Europe. (n.d.-a). *Charter Texts.* https://www.coe.int/en/web/european-social-charter/charter-texts.

Council of Europe. (n.d.-b). *Reporting system of the European Social Charter.* https://www.coe.int/en/web/european-social-charter/reporting-system

Council of Europe. (n.d.-c). *Accepted provisions of the European Social Charter.* https://www.coe.int/en/web/european-social-charter/provisions-of-the-charter.

De Schutter, O. (2017). The European social charter as the social constitution for Europe. In N. Bruun, K. Lörcher, I. Schömann, & S. Clauwaert (Eds.), *The European social charter and the employment relation* (p. 14). Hart.

Decision No 50/2002/EC of the European Parliament and of the Council, of 7 December 2001, *on the establishment of a community action program to encourage cooperation among Member States for the combating of social exclusion,* OJ L 010, of 12.01.2002. https://eur-lex.europa.eu/legal-content/EN/TXT/PDF/?uri=CELEX:32002D0050

Deligianni-Dimitrakou, C. (2013). The decisions of the European Committee of Social Rights on Greek austerity measures and their effectiveness. *Labor Law Review, 3*, 135. et seq. (in Greek), https://www.constitutionalism.gr/2538-oi-apofaseis-tis-eyrwpaikis-epitropis-koinwnikwn-d/

Directive No 2003/86/EC of 22 September 2003 on the right to family reunification, OJ L 251/12, of 03.10.2003. https://eur-lex.europa.eu/legal-content/EN/TXT/PDF/?uri=CELEX:32003L0086

Directive No 2014/36/EU, of the European Parliament and of the Council, of 26 February 2014, on the conditions of entry and stay of third-country nationals for the purpose of employment as seasonal workers, OJ L 94/375, of 28.03.2014. https://eur-lex.europa.eu/legal-content/EN/TXT/PDF/?uri=CELEX:32014L0036

Directive No 80/987/EEC, of the Council of the European Union, of 20 October 1980, on the approximation of the laws of the Member States relating to the protection of employees in the event of the insolvency of their employer, OJ L 283/23, of 28.10.1980. https://eur-lex.europa.eu/legal-content/EN/TXT/PDF/?uri=CELEX:31980L0987

Directive No 91/533/EEC of the Council of the European Union, of 14 October 1991, on an employer's obligation to inform employees of the conditions applicable to the contract or employment relationship, OJ L 288/32, of 18.10.1991. https://eur-lex.europa.eu/legal-content/EN/TXT/PDF/?uri=CELEX:31991L0533

Directive No 92/85/EEC, of the Council of the European Union, of 19 October 1992, on the introduction of measures to encourage improvements in the safety and health at work of pregnant workers and workers who have recently given birth or are breastfeeding (tenth individual Directive within the meaning of Article 16 (1) of Directive 89/391/EEC), OJ L 348/1, of 28.11.1994. https://eur-lex.europa.eu/legal-content/EN/TXT/PDF/?uri=CELEX:31992L0085

Directive No 94/33/EC, of the Council of the European Union, of 22 June 1994, on the protection of young people at work, OJ L 216/12, of 20.08.1994. https://eur-lex.europa.eu/legal-content/EN/TXT/PDF/?uri=CELEX:31994L0033

European Committee of Social Rights. (2010a). Complaint No. 55/2009, *Confédération Générale du Travail (CGT) v. France,* Decision on the merits of June 23, 2010. https://www.coe.int/en/web/european-social-charter/processed-complaints/-/asset_publisher/5GEFkJmH2bYG/content/no-55-2009-confederation-generale-du-travail-cgt-v-france

European Committee of Social Rights. (2010b). Complaint No. 56/2009, *French Confederation of Managers (CFE-CGC) v. France*, Decision on the merits of June 23, 2010. https://www.coe.int/en/web/european-social-charter/processed-complaints/-/asset_publisher/5GEFkJmH2bYG/content/no-56-2009-confederation-francaise-de-l-encadrement-cfe-cgc-v-france

European Committee of Social Rights. (2012a). Complaint No. 65/2011, *General Federation of employees of the national electric power corporation (GENOP-DEI) / Confederation of Greek Civil Servants' Trade Unions (ADEDY) v. Greece,* Decision on the merits of May 23, 2012. https://hudoc.esc.coe.int/eng/#{%22sort%22:[%22escpublicationdate%20descending%22],%22escdcidentifier%22:[%22cc-65-2011-dmerits-en

European Committee of Social Rights. (2012b). Complaint No. 76/2012, *Federation of Pensioners of Greece (IKA-ETAM) v. Greece*, Decision on the merits of December 7, 2012. https://www.coe.int/en/web/european-social-charter/processed-complaints/-/asset_publisher/5GEFkJmH2bYG/content/no-76-2012-federation-of-employed-pensioners-of-greece-ika-etam-v-greece

European Committee of Social Rights. (2012c). Complaint 77/2012, *Panhellenic Federation of Public Service Pensioners v. Greece,* Decision on the merits of December 7, 2012. https://www.coe.int/en/web/european-social-charter/processed-complaints/-/asset_publisher/5GEFkJmH2bYG/content/7no-77-2012-panhellenic-federation-of-public-service-pensioners-v-greece

European Committee of Social Rights. (2012d). Complaint No. 78/2012, *Union of Pensioners of Hellenic Railways (ISA.P.) v. Greece*, Decision on the merits of December 7, 2012. https://www.coe.int/

en/web/european-social-charter/processed-complaints/-/asset_publisher/5GEFkJmH2bYG/content/no-78-2012-pensioners-union-of-the-athens-piraeus-electric-railways-i-s-a-p-v-greece
European Committee of Social Rights. (2012e). Complaint No. 79/2012, *Panhellenic Federation of DEI Pensioners v. Greece*, Decision on the merits, of December 7, 2012. https://www.coe.int/en/web/european-social-charter/processed-complaints/-/asset_publisher/5GEFkJmH2bYG/content/no-79-2012-panhellenic-federation-of-pensioners-of-the-public-electricity-corporation-pos-dei-v-greece
European Committee of Social Rights. (2012f). Complaint No. 80/2012, *Union of Agricultural Bank Pensioners of Greece (ATE) v. Greece*, Decision on the merits of December 7, 2012. https://www.coe.int/en/web/european-social-charter/processed-complaints/-/asset_publisher/5GEFkJmH2bYG/content/no-80-2012-pensioner-s-union-of-the-agricultural-bank-of-greece-ate-v-greece
European Committee of Social Rights. (2013). Complaint No. 85/2012, *Swedish Trade Union Confederation (LO) and Swedish Confederation of Professional Employees (TCO) v. Sweden*, Admissibility Decision and Decision on the merits of July 3, 2013. https://www.coe.int/en/web/european-social-charter/processed-complaints/-/asset_publisher/5GEFkJmH2bYG/content/no-85-2012-swedish-trade-union-confederation-lo-and-swedish-confederation-of-professional-employees-tco-v-sweden
European Committee of Social Rights. (2020). *Statement of interpretation on the right to protection of health in times of pandemic of April 21st* 2020. https://rm.coe.int/statement-of-interpretation-on-the-right-to-protection-of-health-in-ti/16809e3640
European Committee of Social Rights. (2021a). Complaint No 173/2018, *International Commission of Jurists (ICJ) and European Council for Refugees and Exiles (ECRE) v. Greece*, Decision on the merits of January 26, 2021. https://hudoc.esc.coe.int/fre/?i=cc-173-2018-dmerits-en
European Committee of Social Rights. (2021b). *Statement on COVID-19 and social rights of March 24th* 2021. https://rm.coe.int/statement-of-the-ecsr-on-covid-19-and-social-rights/1680a230cav
European Committee of Social Rights. (2022). *Statement of March 24th 2022*. https://rm.coe.int/0900001680a5f20b
European Convention of Human Rights and Fundamental Freedoms. (1950). *European Treaty Series (ETS) No. 005*, signed in Rome on 4.11.1950 and entry in force on 03.09.1953, as amended by Protocols Nos. 11, 14 and 15, supplemented by Protocols Nos. 1, 4, 6, 7, 12, 13 and 16. https://www.echr.coe.int/documents/d/echr/convention_eng
European Social Charter (revised). (1996). *European Treaty Series (ETS) No. 163*, signed in Strasburg on 03.05.1996, entry in force 01.07.1999. https://www.coe.int/en/web/conventions/full-list?module=treaty-detail&treatynum=163
European Social Charter (ESC). (1961). *European Treaty Series (ETS) No. 35*, signed in Turin, on 18.10.1961, Entry in force 26.02.1965. https://rm.coe.int/168006b642
Garben, S. (2020). The European Pillar of Social Rights and the European Social Charter. *Europe of Rights & Liberties/Europe des Droits & Libertés, 1*, 65–78. https://www.europedeslibertes.eu/article/the-european-pillar-of-social-rights-and-the-european-social-charter/
Gavalas, N. (2011). The European Social Charter as a Mechanism for the Protection of Fundamental Labor and Social Rights: On the occasion of the two joint complaints of General Federation of Personnel/DEI and Supreme Administration of Public Employees' Unions the European Committee of Social Rights. *Labor Law Revue*, 449. (in Greek).
Gavalas, N. (2012). Departure from memorandum arrangements in Strasbourg. Decisions 65 and 66/2012 of the European Committee of Social Rights on collective complaints against Greece. *Labor Law Administration, 1561*. (in Greek).
Greek Supreme Court, *Decision No. 1512/2018*. (2018). https://www.areiospagos.gr/nomologia/apofaseis_DISPLAY.asp?cd=Q51GGQF56GTHSYB3YQMLFL980PV17N&apof=1512_2018&info=%D0%CF%CB%C9%D4%C9%CA%C5%D3%20-%20%20%C21
Greek Supreme Court, *Decision No. 366/2020*. (2020). https://www.areiospagos.gr/nomologia/apofaseis_DISPLAY.asp?cd=NENFOG7LTIZPE9ETA2WS2X2BOROCAY&apof=366_2020&info=%D0%CF%CB%C9%D4%C9%CA%C5%D3%20-%20%20%C2

Nivard, C. (2012a). Comité européen des droits sociaux (CEDS): Violation de la Charte sociale européenne par les mesures «anti-crise» grecques. In *Lettre «Actualités Droits-Libertés»*. CREDOF. https://doi.org/10.4000/revdh.19943

Nivard, C. (2012b). *L'effet direct de la Charte sociale européenne devant les juridictions suprêmes françaises* (p. 28). Revue des droits et libertés fondamentaux (RDLF).

Papadopoulos, N. (2019). The impact of the European Social Charter on the Jurisprudence of Greek Courts. *Labor Law Review*, 1351. (in Greek).

Stangos, P. (2013). Les Rapports entre la Charte Sociale Européenne et le droit de l'Union Européenne. *Cahiers de droit européen, 2013*, 319–393.

Treaty on European Union. (2009). Consolidated version. OJ C 202, 7.6.2016, pp. 1–41. https://eur-lex.europa.eu/legal-content/EL/TXT/?uri=celex%3A12016ME%2FTXT

Treaty on the Functioning of the European Union. (2009). Consolidated version. OJ C 202, 7.6.2016, pp. 42–388. https://eur-lex.europa.eu/legal-content/EL/TXT/?uri=celex%3A12016ME%2FTXT

Universal Declaration of Human Rights. (1948). UN General Assembly in Paris on 10 December 1948 during its 183rd plenary meeting. https://documents.un.org/doc/resolution/gen/nr0/043/88/pdf/nr004388.pdf

The Governance of the European Pillar of Social Rights: Open Method of Coordination or Community Method?

Alexandros Kyriakidis and Ioannis Papadopoulos

Abstract

The aim of this chapter is to analyse the issues and concerns raised in relation to the implementation of the European Pillar of Social Rights (EPSR) using the framework of governance within the European Union (EU) as a basis of analysis. We examine two methods of governance: the Open Method of Coordination (OMC) and the Community Method (CM). After an in-depth review of these two methods, an extensive analysis of the history and legal nature of the EPSR is presented. Having placed the EPSR within the wider framework of the EU's modus operandi, an evaluation of the different possibilities and issues that arise from its implementation at the supranational and national levels through either the OMC or the CM is presented, followed by a conclusion on the ways through which the EPSR could be more effectively implemented.

This research was initially funded by the University of Macedonia Research Committee as part of the "Basic Research 2019" funding programme.

A. Kyriakidis (✉)
Department of Political Science, Aristotle University of Thessaloniki, Thessaloniki, Greece

I. Papadopoulos
Department of International and European Studies, Center for Research on Democracy and Law, University of Macedonia, Thessaloniki, Greece
e-mail: ipapadopoulos@uom.edu.gr

D. Anagnostopoulou (ed.), *European Identities, Inclusion and Equality*, Diversity and Inclusion Research, https://doi.org/10.1007/978-3-031-90602-2_8

Introduction

Social policy has a long, and somewhat troublesome, history within the European Union (EU). Since the creation of the European Economic Community in 1958, various aspects of social policy have been included in the EU's operating framework. However, various factors, including the reluctance of EU member states to yield policymaking authority to the supranational level and, more recently, the Eurozone financial crisis, have adversely impacted its true Europeanization. The proclamation of the European Pillar of Social Rights (EPSR) has been portrayed as a major leap forward, presenting a change in the existing status quo of social policy within the EU.

The aim of this chapter is to evaluate the governance of the EPSR, analyse its implementation and performance, and propose possible improvements that could facilitate its more effective application. We evaluate two modes of governance, as being the most appropriate, considering the status of social policy within the EU: the classic Community Method (CM) and the relatively newer Open Method of Coordination (OMC). The chapter proceeds as follows. The following section is devoted to analysing these two modes of governance and to tracing their roots across the broader scholarship related to governance in general as well as to EU governance. A brief historical overview of social policy within the EU is, then, presented, followed by an examination of the use of the OMC in the field of EU social policy. Taking into consideration the analyses of the two aforementioned sections, the following section examines the EPSR, including its development over time, legal nature, and enforceability. The final section of the chapter concludes with an outline of possible ways through which the implementation of the EPSR could be enhanced, primarily through the combined use of CM and OMC.

Governance Within the EU

It has been argued by many scholars that the EU is a system of governance across multiple levels and actors (Verdun, 2012, p. 386; Börzel & Heard-Laureote, 2009, p. 135 and 138; Börzel, 2010, p. 192). As Verdun (2012) suggests,

> Throughout the 1990s, and indeed the 2000s, a vast body of literature emerged that sought to characterize the EU as now involved in "governance" rather than in "integration," meaning that it was no longer about transferring powers over policymaking from the national to the EU level, and, thus, giving the EU competence. Rather, it was all about how the various levels of governance jointly engage in the setting of goals and making of policies in the absence of formal transfer of powers. (p. 386)

The conceptualization of governance within the realm of EU studies is a contested subject. In their majority, scholars assume a perspective that, directly or indirectly, favours network governance[1] for the EU in one form or another (particularly lead organization-governed networks or network government), focusing on the coordination of public and private actors, either from a political or from a societal perspective (e.g. Kohler-Koch & Rittberger, 2006, pp. 28–29 and 33–34; Jachtenfuchs, 2001, pp. 253–254; Börzel & Heard-Laureote, 2009, pp. 136–138). Within such perspective, the focus of relevant literature is on either the micro-level of policy-making within the EU or on network governance itself as a policymaking structure (Jachtenfuchs, 2001, pp. 254–255; Börzel & Heard-Laureote, 2009, pp. 135–136). Accordingly, Keohane and Hoffman (1991) characterize the EU as:

> essentially organized as a network that involves pooling and sharing of sovereignty rather than the transfer of sovereignty to the higher level," suggesting that it "operates neither as a political 'market'—characterized by arm's-length transactions among independent entities, nor as a 'hierarchy,' in which the dominant mode of regulation is authoritative rule. Rather, [...] [it] exemplifies [...] a 'network form of organization'. (Keohane & Hoffman, 1991, pp. 10 and 15)

A large part of this scholarship concerns the juxtaposition and comparison between CM and OMC, with one usually pitted against the other in the form of "hard law" versus "soft law" (Trubek & Trubek, 2005, p. 349). This is especially the case with social policy, with which there is a pre-existing connection of OMC. While the EU did use primarily CM in this area, after the early 2000s, when it began to expand to areas "that have traditionally been the exclusive province of the Member States," the use of OMC has increased considerably (Trubek & Trubek, 2005, p. 347). Early implementation of OMC in relevant areas, such as the European Employment Strategy, while not introducing sweeping changes, was deemed a partial success, especially in terms of compliance with the process, increased cooperation across member states and also across different levels of policymakers within those member states, impact on policy, and introduction of issues in the EU agenda (Trubek & Trubek, 2005, p. 351). However, OMC has always seemed to be efficient under the "shadow of hierarchy," and therefore, also under the shadow of CM. As Smismans (2008) finds in relation to the social dialogue, that "the argument 'no effective agreements without shadow of hierarchy' [...] remains, to a great extent, valid" (pp. 163–164).

[1] Börzel and Heard-Laureote (2009), tracing the emergence of networks to the "declining effectiveness of hierarchy (state failure) in domestic politics and the absence of hierarchy (anarchy) in international politics" (p. 141), suggest that "Networks can be conceived as a particular form of governance, defined as institutionalized modes of coordination through which collectively binding decisions are adopted and implemented [...] They involve non-hierarchical modes of coordination constituted by mutual resource dependencies and/or informal norms of equality among the actors involved. Given their non-hierarchical nature, networks may be considered superior to hierarchy and markets with regard to both effectiveness and legitimacy in modern societies characterized by societal differentiation, sectoralization and policy growth that lead to political overload and 'governance under pressure'" (p. 137).

Community Method

Overall, CM is identified mostly as belonging to the hierarchical type of governance (Kohler-Koch & Rittberger, 2006, pp. 33–34). It is the ordinary governance procedure through which the EU produces policy and legislation and has existed since the 1950s and the European Economic Community. CM can be seen as an alternative to the post-World War II intergovernmental diplomacy, particularly as a "reaction to the failure of the Council of Europe's intergovernmental techniques" during that time, through the introduction of supranational elements to what was otherwise a largely intergovernmental process (Devuyst, 1999, p. 109; Devuyst, 2000, p. 7; Devuyst, 2008, pp. 250–251).

Various scholars have put forward multiple propositions regarding a definition of CM,[2] but a unified and widely accepted approach remains elusive (Devuyst, 1999, p. 110). The European Commission (EC) suggests that CM "provides a means to arbitrate between different interests [of member states] by passing them through two successive filters: the general interest at the level of the Commission; and democratic representation, European and national, at the level of the Council and European Parliament, together the Union's legislature" (European Commission, 2001, p. 6). In CM, the EC holds the near-exclusive legislative initiative and the role of implementing policies. In relation to the other EU institutions, the Council of the European Union, or CEU (whenever possible through Qualified Majority Voting or QMV) and the European Parliament (EP), representing the elected governments of member states and EU citizens, respectively, vote and adopt on the legislative and budgetary proposals of the EC, and the Court of Justice of the EU (CJEU) acts as the guarantor of the rule of law and the proper implementation of, and adherence to, EU legislation (European Commission, 2001, pp. 6 and 29; Devuyst, 2000, p. 2).

[2] For example, Devuyst (1999) argues that "nine ideal-type characteristics of the Community method are identified as the principles and techniques that have made the EU polity qualitatively different from the institutional set-up of traditional intergovernmental organizations: the step-by-step approach towards 'an ever closer union'; integration through solidarity; the equilibrium between the Member States' rights and obligations; a functional division of powers between the institutions; the attempt to overcome the unanimity trap; non-hegemonic decision-making; democratic decision-making; the creation of binding Community law; and rule-based policy implementation" (p. 110). Monar (2011) identifies five primary characteristics of the CM (pp. 118–119): the existence of treaty-based common objectives that aim at further deepening the cooperation between member states or at creating common policies between them; the transfer of legislative powers to the EU level in order for the above to be materialized and "the binding effect of such legislation on all member states…;" the transfer of powers relating to oversight; implementation of policies and legislative initiative to the EC; and the authority of the ECJ to penalize member states or EU institutions for non-enforcement of relevant policies or procedures.

Open Method of Coordination

OMC falls in the category of network governance, with the modes of governance included therein cumulatively termed "New Modes of Governance" or NMGs (Kohler-Koch & Rittberger, 2006, p. 36; Timo & Kelemen, 2006, pp. 108 and 115).[3] NMGs are characterized by relying on soft law that is not legally binding, by including negotiations between different actors at different levels, but with policy implementation being left to member states, by relying increasingly on informal rules, and by a non-hierarchical, yet power-sharing and equal structure of the network (Kohler-Koch & Rittberger, 2006, pp. 36–37; Timo & Kelemen, 2006, p. 110). Within EU politics, OMC has been argued to be one of the most important new modes of multilevel governance (Benz, 2007, p. 505; Eberlein & Kerwer, 2002, pp. 9–12), presenting "a 'third way' for EU governance between regulatory competition and harmonization, capable of opening a sustainable path [...] between fragmentation and a European superstate" (Zeitlin, 2011, p. 136).

OMC originated from principles outlined at the December 1997 Luxembourg European Council, mostly in relation to employment (European Council, 1997). Drawing on the above and other European Council conclusions, e.g. in June 1999 at Cologne (European Council, 1999), OMC was officially established in the March 2000 Lisbon European Council (Hodson & Maher, 2001, p. 723; Zeitlin, 2011, p. 135). There are extensive relevant references throughout the text of the conclusions (e.g. in relation to employment and social cohesion, which was to be implemented by "introducing a new open method of coordination at all levels..."), culminating in a separate subchapter devoted to "implementing a new open method of coordination [...] as the means of spreading best practice and achieving greater convergence towards the main EU goals" (European Council, 2000). In Lisbon, OMC was introduced as an official form of governance concerning not only specific policy areas, as was the case before (the Luxembourg or Cologne processes), but also EU policymaking more broadly (European Council, 2000). Four main attributes of OMC were originally identified (European Council, 2000, p. 7; Zeitlin, 2011, p. 135; Trubek & Trubek, 2005, p. 348):

- Setting guidelines and timetables for short, medium, and long-term policy implementation, towards achieving specific aims;
- Identifying best practices worldwide, and establishing indicators and benchmarks tailored to the different needs of member states in order to adopt these practices;
- Effectively translating the above indicators and benchmarks into national policies for achieving specific targets; and
- Peer-monitoring and review towards mutual learning.

[3] Other NMGs within the EU include: delegation or regulatory tasks to independent authorities or networks of regulations; delegation or regulatory tasks to the EU's comitology system; self-regulation by the private sector; arbitration in the private sector as an alternate form of dispute resolution; and "tripartite policy-making" (Héritier & Lehmkuhl, 2011, pp. 127–128).

According to the EC, in the OMC:

> Member States agree to a measure of joint development of policies without calling into question subsidiarity. It is a flexible method, allowing exchange and coordination in a way and to a degree appropriate to the policy in question. (European Commission, 2005, p. 2)

The EC also emphasized the improved accessibility of both stakeholders[4] and the general public in the OMC process, as well as the increased learning and more efficient implementation of policies within the member states that come as a result (European Commission, 2005, pp. 8–9).

The current legal basis for OMC within the context of social policy is Article 156 of the Treaty on the Functioning of the European Union (TFEU) (Title X), which stipulates that the EC encourages cooperation between member states and facilitates "the coordination of their action in all social policy fields under this chapter" (European Union, 2016, p. 117). The Article also stipulates that the EC shall conduct studies, deliver opinions, arrange consultations, take initiatives to establish indicators and guidelines, organize exchanges to promote best practices, and prepare elements necessary for periodic monitoring and evaluation, after consulting the Economic and Social Committee (European Union, 2016, p. 117). So far, the OMC has been applied to economic coordination (the Broad Economic Policy Guidelines), employment (the Luxembourg Process or European Employment Strategy), poverty and social exclusion, pensions and healthcare (Pochet, 2011, pp. 169–170), environmental policy, tax policy, and policies related to justice and home affairs (Börzel, 2010, p. 207).

Benz (2007) provides a brief description of how the OMC unfolds procedurally (p. 514): The CEU initiates the process by defining a policy, from which common guidelines and national policy targets are drawn. National or sub-national governments elaborate on plans to achieve these targets, outlining specific policy goals and programmes while including a number of different public and private stakeholders in the process. These elements are, then, evaluated by the EC or the CEU, in measuring progress towards successfully achieving the objectives set across the entire EU.

Although OMC is almost entirely intergovernmental in nature, and thus avoids any direct increase in the authority of EU institutions, it may include what has been termed as a "partial delegation of power," i.e., delegation of, primarily, monitoring authority to member states, but not to any EU institutions or authorities (Borras & Jacobsson, 2004, p. 197). Conversely, the EC may seem to have been somewhat sidestepped, but its role as a mediator between the governments of different member states and its ability to take relevant initiatives for cooperation have compensated

[4] Conversely, Cram (2011a) finds that this can be problematic as "'civil society' groups with which it [the EC] engages are largely [...] 'engineered' civil society: effectively Brussels-based NGOs with little grass-roots connection, largely instigated or funded by the Commission [...] with little interest in curbing the expansion of EU Commission competence" (p. 160).

for its loss of the power of legislative initiative otherwise held within the framework of CM (Borras & Jacobsson, 2004, p. 198).[5]

Overall, OMC has changed, albeit oftentimes indirectly, the EU's policymaking process, mainly through the aforementioned partial delegation. While the EU's mandate remains de jure unchanged, the definition of policy aims is elevated from the national to the EU policy realm (even if, still, in an intergovernmental manner). Also, the CJEU and the EP seem to have been de facto excluded from the process, in favour of an increased role of the European Council, the CEU, and the EC. Finally, OMC introduces the so-called "democratic experimentalism"[6] within the EU decision-making process, i.e., the increased role of a wide variety of stakeholders, such as Non-Governmental Organizations (NGOs), sub-national governments, etc. (Borras & Jacobsson, 2004, pp. 199–200).

Eberlein and Kerwer (2002) expand on this last aspect, by arguing that democratic experimentalism through OMC, in addition to facilitating greater stakeholder participation, can also lead to the improvement of coordination between multiple levels of policymaking without introducing a single hierarchical control structure, thus being a "theoretically plausible potential for effective and democratic governance" (p. 11). Not only that, but OMC has been argued to improve legitimacy of EU policies, an otherwise extensively contested subject, considerably (Hodson & Maher, 2001, p. 722). OMC offers "a way of networking decentralised decision-making units by a common system of benchmarking. The decision-making autonomy of the local units is not compromised by the performance standards," and as such, OMC "can be understood as a form of democratic experimentalism" that contributes to enhancing EU legitimacy (Eberlein & Kerwer, 2002, p. 11).

OMC leads to policy change, both in terms of the policy level (from the national to the EU's) and, also, within specific policies. Borras and Jacobsson (2004) propose that the former is possible by providing a middle way between transfer of competences and national autonomy, transnationalizing issues that would otherwise

[5] Borras and Jacobsson (2004) go so far as to argue that OMC has allowed the EC to circumvent the principle of subsidiarity, suggesting that it "has allowed the Commission to take initiatives and to expand cooperation to new areas belonging to the legal competencies of the memberstates" (p. 198).

[6] Democratic experimentalism was proposed as a "new form of government" by Michael Dorf and Charles Sabel during the late 1990s. Their model is founded on deliberative principles and originates from "a series of innovations by private firms that suggest institutional devices for applying the basic principles of pragmatism to the master problem of organizing decentralized, collaborative design and development under conditions of volatility and diversity" (Dorf & Sabel, 1998, pp. 283 and 286). A major element of this new system is "directly deliberative polyarchy," defined as when "citizens in each locale participate directly in determining and assessing the utility of the services local government provides, given the possibility of comparing the performance of their jurisdictions to the performance of similar settings" (Dorf & Sabel, 1998, p. 288). Because the main elements of democratic experimentalism consist of, inter alia, a local forum by citizens, a governing council transmitting information throughout the different local forums and converting information into performance standards, relevant policy networks, and performance (instead of regulatory) standards for businesses, the theory does not run against representative democracy but rather works in support of it (Eberlein & Kerwer, 2002, pp. 10–11).

be confined to the national realm, reinforcing the multi-level nature of the EU with participation from multiple stakeholders, and offering a way for engulfing diversity into the EU's integration and policy-making processes (pp. 201–202). In terms of leading to policy change within specific policies, Trubek and Trubek (2005) identified four ways through which policy change may occur (pp. 357–9):

- Shaming, which is the one closest to a "hard-law" approach and entails member states complying with guidelines "in order to avoid negative criticisms in peer reviews and Council recommendations";
- Diffusion, which involves the spread of models applied by various actors involved in the process (e.g. member states or international organizations), and their adoption by member states either through mimesis (member states copying models provided) or discursive transformation (introduction of new conceptual and cognitive frameworks for relevant policies, gradually leading to policy change);
- Policy networks, which involve multi-level networking of all public and private stakeholders, including government officials, NGOs, civil society, etc., working towards the formation of a unified policy response to a given issue;
- Networks, but not as a top-down model, but rather as a bottom-up approach, through experimentation, deliberation, and learning, which is facilitated within the EU by the ability to implement different models at the same time and receive feedback simultaneously from multiple stakeholders at different levels.

Relevant scholarship seems split in terms of the success of OMC, with the majority, including the EC itself, evaluating such success as being rather modest (e.g. European Commission, 2008, p. 2; European Commission, 2015, p. 1; Eberlein & Kerwer, 2002; Borras & Jacobsson, 2004; Timo & Kelemen, 2006; Cram, 2011a; Zeitlin, 2011; Majone, 2011).[7] Timo and Kelemen (2006) argue that, in order for OMC to be successfully implemented, certain conditions must be met: the EC must be able to identify transgressions, the EC and member states must have incentives to shame violators, and member states must be vulnerable to EC-led shaming (p. 111). However, they maintain that these conditions are unfulfilled. The EC is largely dependent upon member states for relevant data and reports, and thus may not be able to identify non-compliance effectively, the broad nature of targets set by OMC is "not conducive to individual monitoring," the EC has little capacity and incentive to shame, since most EC reports require approval by the CEU, the EC depends on member states "to pursue its ambitions for further integration" and for future cooperation, and, in any case, any relevant EC reports must be based on legal documents (which are largely lacking in OMC) and the "authority of law" (Timo &

[7] Timo and Kelemen (2006) go so far as to suggest that modes of informal governance, such as the OMC, which they argue is limited in its success and effectiveness, is promoted by the EU to mitigate the impression that it is a largely bureaucratic organization manufacturing oftentimes nonsensical or needless rules ("quite simply…the 'Community Method' has a bad reputation"), and also to indirectly increase the influence of the EU in areas outside its competence (such as social policy), potentially paving the way for a more legally binding framework in the long run (pp. 116–117).

Kelemen, 2006, pp. 111–113). In addition, considering the limited impact of OMC in networking between member states' bureaucracies, as well as the considerable amount of information available outside the OMC in relation to policy areas, and particularly in the area of social policy that is the focus of OMC, its success seems rather limited (Timo & Kelemen, 2006, p. 115).

Another major issue with the OMC has been argued to be effectiveness and implementation of relevant policies within member states (Zeitlin, 2011, p. 139; Papadopoulos, 2013, pp. 81–95). Issues relating to coordination of multiple levels of various actors across different policy areas under no central hierarchical coordination may inescapably lead to inefficient processes or ineffective policy implementation (Eberlein & Kerwer, 2002, p. 12; Majone, 2011, pp. 32–33). An additional vulnerability of OMC stems from the lack of clear decision-making procedures, which, in turn, leads to potential problems regarding both legitimacy and accountability (Borras & Jacobsson, 2004, p. 199; Timo & Kelemen, 2006, p. 119; Benz, 2007, p. 506). Neither the CJEU nor the EP/national parliaments play any part in this process, leading to deficiencies in judicial and representative political oversight, which, in turn, raises concerns in relation to both vertical[8] and horizontal[9] accountability, although the indirect vertical accountability of the elected officials that partake in the process by citizens of member states can, at least partly, compensate for the above (Huller, 2012, pp. 252–253; Dahl, 1999, p. 21; Benz, 2007, pp. 507–508 and 514; Borras & Jacobsson, 2004, p. 199). In terms of legitimacy, especially in social policy implementation, input by stakeholders, member states' parliaments and bureaucracies, civil society, etc., has been largely mediocre, and the outputs produced have been under par (Timo & Kelemen, 2006, p. 119).

Additional criticisms include the fact that it is not possible for OMC to lead to domestic substantive policy change, i.e. new legislation, or to create policy convergence among EU member states (Zeitlin, 2011, pp. 140–142). Héritier and Eckert (2008) point out that governmental actions, or forms of a "shadow of hierarchy," such as legislative or executive actions, are not only "a precondition for self-regulation to develop," but are necessary in order to "sustain the self-regulatory effort and obtain satisfactory results" after the introduction of self-regulation (pp. 114 and 134).

Conversely, it has been argued that in a number of aspects, OMC can be pronounced a comparatively successful instrument of policymaking within the EU, especially related to social policy. Zeitlin (2011) suggests that OMC has raised the salience of social policy issues in EU member states' domestic agendas (political shifts), has led to cognitive shifts in national policy thinking, has contributed to improving the relevant national policies themselves (programmatic shifts), and has led to "procedural shifts in governance and policy making arrangements"

[8] Vertical accountability, also termed democratic accountability, occurs from the citizens to the rulers, and is exercised directly or indirectly through a variety of means, such as elections.

[9] Horizontal accountability, also termed delegative accountability, is in the form of competition and oversight between the different representative structures (e.g. court oversight over governmental actions).

(pp. 142–3). These shifts include improvements in data collection mechanisms, in coordination between independent policy areas, in the establishment of formal and informal structures for coordination policy at different levels, and in the participation of non-state stakeholders in the policy process (Zeitlin, 2011, p. 142). Zeitlin (2011) finally suggests that OMC has indeed resulted in mutual learning between member states (pp. 143–144).

Social Policy Within the EU

A Brief Historic Overview of EU Social Policy

It is useful to briefly overview the historic development of social policy within the EU. It is one of the policy areas that the EU itself has developed significantly since the 1950s, and which underwent substantial reform, especially after the Eurozone crisis of 2010 (Mailand, 2013, p. 240; Pochet, 2011, p. 167). From the beginning and at least until the 1990s, ambitions towards an EU-based welfare state were substantially limited (Crespy & Menz, 2015, p. 753; Pochet, 2011, p. 167), although, as Mailand (2013) observes, "in the mid-1980s, the speed of its [social dimension of the EU] development was deliberately increased to counterbalance economic integration" (p. 240). After all, the legal basis for EU involvement in the otherwise nationally sensitive area of social policy (especially the aspects of employment, pensions, social protection, and healthcare) remains arguably quite limited (Cram, 2011a, p. 153).

Pochet (2011) suggests that "the history of European social policy is more a story of failure than of great success," initially (in the 1950s) leaving social policy within the national policy realm of member states (p. 167). He further identifies five distinct stages of its development, which included various attempts "to develop the social dimension of economic integration" (p. 168; also Pochet, 2005, pp. 40–45):

- 1958–1973, with the introduction of the free movement of workers and the creation of the European Social Fund (ESF) in order to "retrain workers affected by economic change, due in part to integration";
- 1973–1981, with the adoption of multiple directives aimed at improving working conditions and living standards of workers (equality between men and women, health and safety regulations, insolvency of employers, etc.) as well as the adoption of the first European social programme;
- 1981–1989, with the doubling of structural funds and some improvements related to health and safety (largely adopted on account of the Single European Act), but also with failure to adopt several proposals (e.g. reduction of working time) due to the neoliberal paradigm that was predominant at the time (Thatcher/Reagan);
- 1989–1997, with the introduction of an employment title in the EU Treaties (Amsterdam Treaty), the adoption of minimum standards and regulations across the EU (with the UK opting out), and the signature of the social agreement between EU social partners; and

- 1997–2003, with the OMC becoming prevalent and with a strengthening of social protection and fundamental social rights across the EU.

While there have been improvements in recent years, most notably due to CJEU decisions on EU citizens' rights, scholarship remains sceptical, highlighting the mostly neoliberal and deregulatory direction of the EC, now exacerbated following policies implemented during the Eurozone crisis (Crespy & Menz, 2015, p. 753; Kyriakidis, 2016, pp. 219–220). This tendency has been attributed to many different factors, including the reduction of social-democratic governments within the EU, the weakening of similar political parties in the EP, the liberal-based agenda of the two Barroso-led ECs, the gradual weakening of trade unions (primarily at the EU level), and the 2004 EU enlargement that inevitably led to inability of agreement on labour standards, because of the significantly lower protections offered by the Central and Eastern European countries that acceded to the EU.[10]

Currently, social policy is primarily covered by TFEU Articles 151–164[11] (European Union, 2016, pp. 114–119). It is an area of shared, and not exclusive, competence, and as such, it is subject to the limitations of the principle of subsidiarity, i.e., the EU can act only in case that it can better achieve objectives compared to the member states, and only as far as those objectives cannot be sufficiently achieved by them (European Union, 2016, pp. 18 and 50).

After the Eurozone crisis, the European Semester[12] was introduced in 2011, which included, inter alia, the overall framework for social policy within the EU through the issuance of Country-Specific Recommendations (CSRs) to member states pursuant to the targets of "Europe 2020" (the 10-year economic, social, and employment policy strategy of the EU and successor to the Lisbon Strategy; Copeland & Daly, 2018, p. 1001). Zeitlin & Vanhercke (2018) argue that between

---

[10] Crespy and Menz (2015) go so far as to argue that "the implications of the two rounds of eastward enlargement of the 2000s do not merely complicate but fundamentally preclude any prospect of major re-regulatory social policy" (p. 754).

[11] The ESF is one of the funds of the EU through which cohesion policy is conducted, along with the European Regional Development Fund, the European Social Fund Plus, the Cohesion Fund, and the Just Transition Fund (European Parliament & Council of the European Union, 2021a, 2021b).

[12] The European Semester was legally introduced through Regulation 1175/2011, which amended the Stability and Growth Pact (SGP) Regulation 1466/97 (so-called "preventive arm" of the SGP) as part of the Eurozone crisis measures. Titled the "European Semester for Economic Policy Coordination," it originally included monitoring of economic policies implemented across the member states, formulation of employment guidelines, the stability or convergence programmes, the national reform programmes on the EU's growth and jobs strategy, and surveillance in order to prevent macroeconomic imbalances. In terms of institutional input, the CEU can "address guidance to the member states" in the form of recommendations, which they "shall take due account [...] in their development of their economic, employment and budgetary policies before taking key decisions on their national budgets for the succeeding years." Failure to adhere to the above may result in further recommendations with specific measures, EC warnings, or even sanctions, while the EC is tasked with "reinforced monitoring" that "may include surveillance missions" with on-site monitoring (European Parliament & Council of the European Union, 2011, pp. 12, 15–16 and 23).

2010 and 2016 there existed a "partial but progressive socialization [...]" (p. 153). Initially, the implementation of the European semester had an overwhelming focus on fiscal consolidation that overshadowed social policy, resulting in an even divide between "promoting social retrenchment and social investment" (Zeitlin & Vanhercke, 2018, p. 156). The EC also "withdrew its support for the Social OMC as an autonomous process" to avoid conflicting with the European semester-centred implementation of Europe 2020 (Zeitlin & Vanhercke, 2018, pp. 156–157).

However, from 2012 onwards, there was increased progress: the EC launched a number of initiatives to address the increasingly deteriorating economic and employment situation in the aftermath of the Eurozone crisis,[13] and CSRs focused increasingly on social policies. There was also an overall reinvigoration of the Social OMC, with some improvements in the governance framework (e.g. broader introduction of reinforced qualified majority voting in the CEU for CSRs), coupled with the de facto enhancement of the role of the Social Protection Committee (SPC) in monitoring and reviewing the progress of member states (Zeitlin & Vanhercke, 2018, pp. 157–162). From 2014 onwards, the Juncker Commission further streamlined the process, with the most formative change being the EC's "decision to reduce drastically the number and scope of the CSRs, focusing on key priority issues of macro-economic and social relevance identified as actionable and monitorable within a twelve—eighteen month timescale," thus emphasizing policy targets and challenges more than specific policy measures (Zeitlin & Vanhercke, 2018, p. 162). Throughout 2015 and 2016, employment policy and social inclusion were maintained as priorities, with CSRs constantly featuring, directly or indirectly (e.g. educational participation), relevant policies (Zeitlin & Vanhercke, 2018, pp. 163–165).

Open Method of Coordination and EU Social Policy

It has to be noted that OMC has been closely related to social policy since the very beginning (European Commission, 2005, p. 2; European Commission, 2008, p. 2; Zeitlin, 2011, p. 142; Trubek & Trubek, 2005, p. 343)[14] and has remained such, since "developments in EU social policy over the last two decades have largely been achieved through flexible governance processes... such as the Open Method of Coordination" (Copeland & Daly, 2018, pp. 1002–1003).[15] In fact, as Trubek and

[13] Zeitlin and Vanhercke (2018) provide some examples, such as the Special Investment Package, the Compact for Growth and Jobs, and the Employment Package (p. 157).

[14] The achievement of social policy goals through flexible governance processes appears in agreement with relevant scholarship into EU social policy formation (specifically work and employment policies) that suggests that involved actors always prioritize the formation of coalitions and alliances(for a sample of them, see Mailand, 2013, p. 241), which seems more fitting towards OMC than CM.

[15] Trubek and Trubek (2005) identified in the early 2000s two types of visions in relation to social policy within the EU and its implementation (p. 352). The first, termed "euro-corporatist," involves the direct involvement of the EU in social policy, primarily through CM, i.e. a binding suprana-

Trubek (2005) point out, "the first and most developed example of the OMC was the European Employment Strategy [...] in the 1990s" (p. 348). Cram (2011b) traces its roots as far back as "the precursor [to the Employment Strategy] networks to the European Employment Observatory, established in 1982 and 1989, and even further back in the Standing Committee on Employment, established in 1970" (p. 640). As Zeitlin (2011) observes, "the OMC on Social Protection and Social Inclusion... has become the guiding framework for EU policy-making..." (p. 137). As Pochet (2011) further argues, "there are fewer and fewer social directives and those that are adopted have minimal content. As a result, the OMC was considered by many – even those not supportive of such an approach – as the possible answer to the lack of political support for EU social regulations" (p. 167).

In the original Lisbon conclusions, where the "Lisbon Strategy" was set out (2000), OMC was primarily focused towards the social aspect (European Council, 2000, p. 7; Borras & Jacobsson, 2004, pp. 188–190). More specifically, the Lisbon Strategy aimed at addressing the relative stalemate experienced by the EU in both competitiveness and social cohesion (e.g. enterprise policy, internal market, employment, combating social exclusion, etc.; Borras & Jacobsson, 2004, p. 190). At the time, there was very limited political will towards constructing economies of scale and lowering transaction costs, as well as for awarding further social rights to EU citizens (which would include an additional transfer of legal competencies to the EU; Borras & Jacobsson, 2004, p. 190). Furthermore, the constraints in monetary or fiscal policy—the latter through the restrictions imposed by the Stability and Growth Pact—limited the capacity of member states to use them as instruments towards job creation. However, interdependences between member states, especially those arising as a result of the introduction of the euro, which made a member state vulnerable to another member state's fiscal failures, presented the need for a common social policy, because social policy can have important effects on both competitiveness (the "social market economy," according to the European social model) and the budget (social costs are a considerable portion of the budget and the economy; Trubek & Trubek, 2005, pp. 344–345).[16]

Under OMC, the aforementioned issues could be placed high in the agenda and additional measures could be agreed, while at the same time national autonomy of member states could be preserved, with actions based at the national, and not the EU, level (Borras & Jacobsson, 2004, p. 190; Trubek & Trubek, 2005, p. 351). Hence, through OMC, the EU assumed the role of coordinator and facilitator, while maintaining a strong agenda-setting capacity. Social inclusion and pensions were emphasized as priorities, with OMC including agreements on common objectives, goals, and indicators, where appropriate, National Action Plans for Inclusion and

tional social legislation. The second, termed "decentralized cooperation," involves an existent but limited role for the EU in relation to social policy, primarily including support and cooperation for national level policies. This latter approach is most concurrent with OMC.

[16] Trubek and Trubek (2005) also identify fears for a race to the bottom and willingness to experiment with different social models of different member states as additional reasons leading to the "Europeanization of social policy" (p. 346).

National Strategy Reports for pensions, and joint EC/CEU evaluations of progress on the above, with mutual learning and understanding serving as top aims of the entire process (European Commission, 2005, p. 2; Trubek & Trubek, 2005, p. 349). The EC defined a set of specific objectives for OMC in social policy, such as provision of sustainable healthcare, adequate pensions, eradication of poverty, promotion of social cohesion and inclusion, as well as various reporting and evaluation arrangements for the policies implemented by member states at the national level, such as a common section on assessing the social situation of each (European Commission, 2005, pp. 5–7).

OMC has also been linked to the creation of a number of consultative committees within the EU that have been acting as a bridge between the European Council and the EC (Borras & Jacobsson, 2004, p. 198). Of particular relevance here are the Employment Committee (EMCO) and the SPC, which provide opinions to either upon their request (Borras & Jacobsson, 2004, p. 198; Zeitlin, 2011, p. 145). These Committees have played an important role in building confidence and rapport between the various member states, and between the member states and the EC, which is a necessary element for effective policymaking in sensitive areas such as those related to social policy (Borras & Jacobsson, 2004, p. 198).

All the above, including a detailed set of indicators such as early school leavers, employment, pensions, income inequality, health expenditures, etc., became an entirely separate set of OMC policies, termed "Social OMC" (European Commission, 2008, pp. 3 and 11–12). Social OMC included a 3-year cycle of reporting, with the first year being devoted to issuing Joint CEU and Commission Reports on Social Protection and Social Inclusion based on the National Strategic Reports of member states, and the second and third years "dedicated to in-depth analysis and mutual learning on priority themes" (European Commission, 2008, p. 3).

Despite the above, a large part of the relevant scholarship, similarly to OMC more generally, remains rather sceptical regarding the outcomes of OMC in social policy. Cram (2011a) finds that "despite the Commission's best efforts, the history of EU social policy is one of Commission ambition thwarted by member state resistance" (p. 156). Crespy and Menz (2015) remain yet more sceptical, arguing that "the focus on the OMC might be misplaced and that […] recognition of the political context of the Commission might be a more fruitful insight" (p. 754). Accordingly, Majone (2011) observes that "over time, this independent institution [the EC] has become a highly politicized body, taking decisions involving political judgment and a high level of discretion" (p. 25). Mailand (2013) points out that, although OMC remains rather weak in the area of EU social policy, resulting in a supplementary role to CM, the aforementioned potential for agenda-setting and coordination in areas that do not strictly fall within the remits of EU law could be argued to present some innovative and complementary benefits (p. 241).

The European Pillar of Social Rights

The idea for the EPSR was first advanced in 2015 by the then-President of the EC Jean-Claude Juncker (European Commission, 2018, p. 1). In his annual State of the EU address, Junker said:

> I will want to develop a European pillar of social rights, which takes account of the changing realities of Europe's societies and the world of work. And which can serve as a compass for the renewed convergence within the euro area. This European pillar of social rights should complement what we have already jointly achieved when it comes to the protection of workers in the EU. I will expect social partners to play a central role in this process. (European Commission, 2015, p. 8)

A broad public consultation by the EC followed throughout 2016 (March–December), involving civil society, citizens, EU institutions, and member states (European Commission, 2016a, 2017a, p. 4). The EC, in its relevant communication,[17] stated that "the purpose of the Pillar is to express a number of essential principles to support well-functioning and fair labour markets and welfare systems" (European Commission, 2016a, p. 7). The initial proposal was for the EPSR to be "developed within the euro area, while allowing other EU member states to join if they want to do so" (also in European Commission, 2017a, p. 5), and for it to serve as a "reference framework to screen the employment and social performance of participating Member states [...]" through building and complementing the existing social acquis of the EU (European Commission, 2016a, p. 7). Upon completion of the consultation,[18] the EC identified four areas that the EPSR should contribute to: consequences of the financial crisis (exclusion, poverty, etc); work and digital market; demographic developments across Europe; and economic divergence (European Commission, 2017a, p. 4).

The final version of the EPSR was adopted as a recommendation (2017/761) by the EC under Article 292 TFEU (European Commission, 2017a, p. 6; European Commission, 2017d; European Union, 2016, p. 173), and then "was jointly proclaimed by the European Parliament, the Council and the Commission on 17 November 2017 at the Gothenburg Social Summit for Fair Jobs and Growth" (European Commission, 2018, p. 1). The EPSR was endorsed by the European Council a month later, agreeing to take steps in "implementing the European Pillar of Social Rights at Union and Member State level, with due regard to their respective competences; the Commission is invited to propose appropriate monitoring" (European Council, 2017, p. 2). It also called, inter alia, for "facilitating a well-functioning social dialogue at all levels, including the 'new start for social

[17] The communication included a detailed annex presenting a "preliminary outline of the European Pillar of Social Rights for the consultation of the general public," in which the legal basis or background of each proposed principle on the EU Treaties and Charter of Fundamental Rights was included (European Commission, 2016b).

[18] Additional input was offered by the EP, the Committee of Regions, the European Economic and Social Committee, and 21 governments of member states, along with relevant discussions at ministerial level within the CEU (European Commission, 2017a, p. 4).

dialogue'[19] at EU level" (European Council, 2017, p. 2). Its aim, according to the EC, is to make "rights and principles which were set at different times, in different ways and in different forms [...] more understandable and more explicit for citizens and for actors at all levels" (European Commission, 2017a, p. 6).

The EPSR begins by referencing, inter alia, the EU's duty to advance the well-being of its people (European Parliament et al., 2017, pp. 4–9). A total of 20 rights is, then, presented (with further specifications) separated across three chapters: "Equal opportunities and access to the labour market"; "Fair working conditions"; and "Social Protection and Inclusion" (European Parliament et al., 2017, pp. 1–23). As Copeland and Daly (2018) argue, the EPSR seems to move towards a more market-correcting (rather than market-making) approach,[20] indicating an understanding among EU policymakers that EU citizens have turned to discontent over austerity policies as well as the magnitude of poverty and social exclusion across the EU[21] (p. 1014).

In terms of its legal nature, the EC states that "the Pillar takes direct inspiration from the existing wealth of good practices across Europe, and builds on the strong body of law which exists at EU and international level," particularly on the European Social Charter[22] and the Community Charter of the Fundamental Social Rights of Workers[23] (these two documents are also referenced in Article 151 TFEU; European Union, 2016, p. 114), as well as the Charter of Fundamental Rights of the EU and CJEU case law (European Commission, 2017a, p. 6). It is further emphasized that, considering the primary or exclusive competence of member states in a broad variety of areas related to the EPSR (labour law, minimum wages, healthcare, etc.) and the fact that "they also bear the bulk of the financing" in these areas, the EPSR is in full respect with, and limited by, the principles of subsidiarity and proportionality, maintaining a complementary role for the EU (European Commission, 2017a, p. 6).

[19] Negotiations and consultations between relevant stakeholders, such as employers' associations, trade unions, public authorities, etc., aimed primarily towards the conclusion of collective agreements at the European level (Smismans, 2008, pp. 163–164).

[20] This distinction is based on Wolfgang Streeck's work. Market-making social policy is geared towards integration of the EU labour market and towards increasing the efficiency of market functioning (removing regulations or barriers, deregulating employment, reducing benefits, etc.), while market-correcting measures, which may result in market distortions, "aim at ameliorating market outcomes (or negative externalities) and call for redistributive intervention in line with standards of adequate income, social protection and even social justice" (Copeland & Daly, 2018, pp. 1003–1004).

[21] In 2018, almost 22% of EU citizens were at risk of poverty or social exclusion, with the figure in some member states, such as Greece or Bulgaria, surpassing 30% (Eurostat, 2019).

[22] The European Social Charter is an international treaty signed by the members of the Council of Europe, in 1961, outlining the efforts of member states towards realizing and fully respecting a number of social rights such as safe and healthy working conditions, freedom of association, and collective bargaining (Council of Europe, 2015, pp. 9–63).

[23] The Community Charter of the Fundamental Social Rights of Workers is a declaration by the European Council in 1989, establishing the minimum rights of workers across the EU, such as free movement, remuneration, working conditions, social and health protection and safety, freedom of association, and collective bargaining (European Council, 1989).

The EC further clarified the enforceability of the EPSR in an accompanying staff document, which outlined the EU legal basis, capacity and limits of enforcement for each EPSR principle (European Commission, 2017b). As the EC highlighted in this text, "these principles and rights are not directly enforceable and will require a translation into dedicated action and/or separate pieces of legislation, at the appropriate level" (European Commission, 2017b, p. 3), concluding that "the implementation of the Pillar will be primarily the responsibility of national governments, of public authorities and of social partners at all levels" (European Commission, 2017a, p. 7; similarly in European Commission, 2018, p. 8). Actions by the EC on implementing the EPSR at the EU level are always taken "within the framework of EU competences," while the EC also supports member states and other stakeholders in terms of national, regional, and local level implementation (European Commission, 2018, p. 2).

Monitoring of the EPSR, notwithstanding the aforementioned legal limitations, is done through the European Semester, which "is based on in-depth analysis, specific to the situation of each country [...], acknowledges the diversity of challenges and the need to prioritise in the light of different starting points and available means across countries [...] [and] is [...] the way to structure collective efforts over time [...]," while also serving as an instrument "to structure peer reviews and benchmarking among Member States" (European Commission, 2018, p. 10). The semester is enhanced so as to take into account the specific elements of the EPSR. It now includes additional elements of benchmarking and exchange of good practices among all stakeholders involved in the implementation of the EPSR principles, as well as a social scoreboard (European Commission, 2018, pp. 10–11).

The social scoreboard consists of "key indicators to screen employment and social performance of participating Member States [...] [that] would allow [...] benchmarking successful outcomes to ensure overall improvement" (European Commission, 2017c, p. 2). The EC defined societal progress (the main element monitored through the scoreboard) as "the capacity to enhance and sustain wellbeing and opportunities, creating conditions for people to reach their full potential and to meet their basic needs," with three dimensions: "equal opportunities and access to the labour market [...], dynamic labour markets and fair working conditions [...], public support/social protection and inclusion" (European Commission, 2017c, p. 2). Based on these dimensions, the scoreboard includes 12 indicators of measuring societal progress, such as the impact of social transfers on poverty reduction, the employment and unemployment rates, the income inequality, etc. (European Commission, 2017c, pp. 4–6).

In terms of the EPSR's implementation, a number of initiatives were adopted throughout 2017 and 2018 at the EU level. Until 2018, out of the 22 EU legal acts proposed, covering multiple areas of the EPSR, such as gender pay gap, social dialogue, education and training, and occupational safety and health, ten were adopted, while the EC also "mainstreamed social priorities across the board," enhancing the social aspect of various EU-wide instruments, such as the European Semester, Cohesion Policy, Digital Single Market, Trade Policy, etc. (European Commission, 2018, pp. 3–6). In addition, in 2018 the EC proposed a new "Social

Fairness Package" that included three main proposals (European Commission, 2018, p. 7):

- establishment of a European Labour Authority, which is to provide access to information for all stakeholders, to facilitate inter-member state cooperation and improve cross-border enforcements of law, and to mediate in cross-border dispute cases;
- proposal of a CEU recommendation[24] aimed at ensuring that all EU workers have adequate access to social protection, such as unemployment or sickness benefits (with a focus on those working under temporary or flexible contracts);
- development of a European Social Security Number, to facilitate more efficient and quicker access to benefits of EU citizens across all member states ("facilitate the portability of rights across borders").

From the above proposals, the European Labour Authority was eventually established a year later under Regulation 2019/1149 (in which the EPSR features on the third recital), based on Articles 46 and 48 TFEU.[25] The Authority's overall tasks are assisting member states in effectively applying EU law related to labour mobility and in coordinating their social security systems within the overall EU framework, including through carrying out relevant analyses and risk assessments and coordinating joint inspections (European Parliament & Council of the European Union, 2019).[26] In the same year, the Council Recommendation "on access to social protection for workers and the self-employed" was also adopted, based on Articles 153[27] and 352[28] of the TFEU, recommending that member states provide adequate social protection to all workers and self-employed individuals, and also establish minimum standards in the field of social protection for the above (through combination of schemes—whether public or provided for by other entities—in accordance with the respective national systems). The recommendation also includes provisions for establishing a more effective monitoring framework, including improvement of data

[24] It is worth noting that, in relation to the CEU Recommendation on social protection, the EC itself acknowledged that, while initially aiming to propose the issuance of a Directive, i.e. a (more) binding piece of EU legislation, this was abandoned "given the diversity of situations and limitations of the legal framework to take action at EU level" (European Commission, 2018, p. 7).

[25] Freedom of movement of workers and measures relating to social security to ensure such freedom of movement, respectively (European Union, 2016, pp. 66–67).

[26] The specific objectives include facilitation of access to information on rights/obligations related to labour mobility and relevant services across the EU, enhancement of member states' cooperation in effectively applying relevant EU legislation, mediation towards a solution in cases of relevant cross-border disputes of member states, and supporting cooperation between member states in combating undeclared work.

[27] Supporting/complementing member states' activities by the EU on, inter alia, social security and social protection of workers, and modernization of social protection systems (European Union, 2016, pp. 114–115).

[28] Adopting appropriate measures, without harmonizing member states' laws/regulations, if action by the EU is necessary and the Treaties do not explicitly provide powers for such measures (European Union, 2016, pp. 196–197).

collection from the member states, on all the above (Council of the European Union, 2019). Improvements were also made in the coordination framework for social security systems, with the above Regulation 2019/1149 including a number of changes to the original Regulation 883/2004, and a number of other initiatives were also adopted in specific fields, such as gender equality, impact of Artificial Intelligence on employment, sustainable finances, collective bargaining frameworks, minimum income, etc. (European Commission, n.d.; European Parliament & Council of the European Union, 2004).

Following the above, and especially in light of the COVID-19 pandemic, the implementation of the EPSR was further advanced through the EC's EPSR Action Plan and the political agreement in the Social Summit in Porto (May 2021). The focus was on the importance of the European Semester process in implementing the EPSR, as well as on specific quantitative targets for EPSR's implementation to be achieved by 2030: 78% of employment rate (20–64-year-olds); 60% adult (20–64-year-olds) participation in learning in the last 12 months; reduction of number of people at risk of poverty or social exclusion from over 100 million in 2016 to approximately 77 million in 2050 (Hacker, 2023, pp. 9–11).

The Porto declaration of the European Council was particularly important, indicating a strong political commitment at the highest level for implementing the EPSR. The European Council emphasized the need to achieve social cohesion and prosperity, and committed to "deepening the implementation of the European Pillar of Social Rights at the EU and national level," recognizing that the EPSR "is a fundamental element of the recovery [from the COVID-19 pandemic]," albeit still highlighting that this should be achieved "with due regard for respective competences and the principles of subsidiarity and proportionality" (European Council, 2021). The European Council also committed to creating more jobs with fairer wages, fighting inequalities, social exclusion, poverty, and discrimination, enhancing education and skills, facilitating the green and digital transition, and supporting youth, through close monitoring and effective implementation, "including at the highest level" within the framework of the EPSR (European Council, 2021).

Open Method of Coordination or Community Method for the EPSR?

As discussed throughout the chapter, the EPSR has constituted a considerable advancement in the field of social policy within the EU. Despite the fact that social policy belongs to the shared, and not exclusive, competences of the EU, the adoption of the EPSR, its inclusion in the monitoring and feedback process of the European Semester, as well as the adoption of a number of legislative initiatives related to it, seem to have promoted a wide variety of measures related to social policy. But has this been a success story so far, and what can be done from a governance perspective to improve it?

From the overview of CM and OMC presented above, the idea that these two are exclusionary may actually be a false dilemma in functionalist terms; an original and targeted combination of both may well be the optimal solution. CM is the basic mode of governance used within the EU to produce regulatory and legislative texts. As such, it is invaluable; without it there can be no legally binding acts. However, CM by itself is not enough, especially when policy areas of shared, not exclusive, competence are concerned, like social policy. CM is a very structured and hierarchical mode of governance, with limited and well-established institutional actors participating in most of the process, which, in itself, is legally confined within the limits of the EU Treaties (and relevant EU legislation). While its use is effective in adopting specific legal measures within the EU, when there is a need to tackle a broader area of policy, which may include a wide variety of different specific policy aspects and which falls outside the exclusive competence of the EU, CM cannot be the option used. It is there where OMC can give the necessary impetus for creating change. True, OMC, when examined alone against adopted legislation or strict monitoring/sanctioning mechanisms, is insufficient compared to CM. But where OMC is useful is in establishing a sound foundation of political will and honest cooperation between EU member states, upon which specific measures (adopted through CM) can then build.

A combination, then, of OMC and CM seems to be the optimal solution. This, after all, has been highlighted by the EC itself, which emphasized that OMC is mostly applied on a case-by-case basis, and is combined in different ways with existing governance approaches, underlining that OMC "should be a complement, rather than a replacement, for Community action [...] it should not be used when legislative action under the Community method is possible" (European Commission, 2001, p. 21). But it has also been highlighted by part of the relevant scholarship. The often binary-exclusionary terms under which relevant analyses take place (either CM or OMC) exclude not only much empirical depth, but also the possibility of a hybrid governance mode, which has seemed to work quite well in some policy areas, such as EU environmental law (Trubek & Trubek, 2005, pp. 344 and 362). Zeitlin (2011) also argues that in reality OMC is not exclusionary to CM, but rather works to reinforce it and, in fact, EU hard law (e.g. EU Directives) now often includes "provisions for implementation, monitoring, evaluation, peer review, and periodic revision through 'soft law' OMC-style procedures" (p. 138).

In relation to the EPSR, which has become the primary vehicle through which the EU is now pursuing complementary action in the area of social policy, this exact combination of CM and OMC seems to have been implemented. As outlined in the analysis above, OMC was the main method of EU action in the field of social policy even prior to the EPSR, and the EPSR itself is, primarily, based on OMC (e.g. not directly enforceable; progress is evaluated primarily by willing provision of data by member states to the EC). However, using the impetus of the EPSR, and based on its principles that cover a wide area of specific policies, the EU then began adopting legislative texts that implemented specific policy aspects of it, excellent examples of which are the creation of an entirely new (though mostly advisory in nature) authority (European Labour Authority), enhancing the regulatory framework for the coordination of member states' social security systems, and issuing recommendations in relation to social protection of workers.

Considering the above, in terms of whether the implementation of the EPSR through the utilization of OMC (for the broad policies) and CM (for legislative measures on specific policy areas) has been effective, the answer is largely positive, although with significant delay compared to potential implementation through CM alone. However, given the nature of the EU's competence in this area and its sensitiveness for the national level polity of member states, this has, perhaps, been the optimal way through which measures could be adopted, even if with delay. As far as the drawbacks of OMC are concerned, primarily the fact that it is an unofficial process with a large number of potentially unidentifiable stakeholders participating, which sidelines the EP and the CJEU, this does not seem to be the case with the EPSR in relation to the specific measures implemented so far, most of which have been adopted through CM and so are official legislative or regulatory acts. One possible adverse effect of this approach is the fragmented nature of the specific measures (as opposed to the unified and more straightforward approach of the OMC-based broad policy aims), which may lead to overlaps and overcomplicated structures, ultimately causing confusion and making actual monitoring difficult. Hence, a more cohesive approach to the CM-based stage would be advantageous and lead towards a more effective implementation (and monitoring thereof) of the EPSR.

References

Benz, A. (2007). Accountable multilevel governance by the open method of coordination? *European Law Journal, 13*(4), 505–522.

Borras, S., & Jacobsson, K. (2004). The open method of co-ordination and new governance patterns in the EU. *Journal of European Public Policy, 11*(2), 185–208.

Börzel, T. (2010). European governance: Negotiation and competition in the shadow of hierarchy. *Journal of Common Market Studies, 48*(2), 191–219.

Börzel, T. A., & Heard-Laureote, K. (2009). Networks in EU multi-level governance: Concepts and contributions. *Journal of Public Policy, 29*(2), 135–151.

Copeland, P., & Daly, M. (2018). The European semester and EU social policy. *Journal of Common Market Studies, 56*(5), 1001–1018.

Council of Europe. (2015, January 1). European social charter. https://rm.coe.int/CoERMPublicCommonSearchServices/DisplayDCTMContent?documentId=090000168048b059

Council of the European Union. (2019, November 8). Council recommendation... on access to social protection for workers and the self-employed. *Official Journal of the European Union, L 387*, 1–8.

Cram, L. (2011a). In the shadow of hierarchy: Governance as a tool of government. In D. Renaud (Ed.), *The 'community method': Obstinate or obsolete?* (pp. 151–165). Palgrave Macmillan.

Cram, L. (2011b). The importance of the temporal dimension: New modes of governance as a tool of government. *Journal of European Public Policy, 18*(5), 636–653.

Crespy, A., & Menz, G. (2015). Commission entrepreneurship and the debasing of social Europe before and after the Eurocrisis. *Journal of Common Market Studies, 53*(4), 753–768.

Dahl, R. (1999). Can international organizations be democratic? A skeptic's view. In I. Shapiro & C. Hacker-Cordon (Eds.), *Democracy's edges*. Cambridge University Press.

Devuyst, Y. (1999). The community-method after Amsterdam. *Journal of Common Market Studies, 37*(1), 109–120.

Devuyst, Y. (2000). The European Union's constitutional order - Between community method and ad hoc compromise. *Berkeley Journal of International Law, 18*(1), 1–52.

Devuyst, Y. (2008). The European Union's institutional balance after the treaty of Lisbon: 'Community method' and 'democratic deficit' reassessed. *Georgetown Journal of International Law, 39*, 247–325.

Dorf, M. C., & Sabel, C. F. (1998). A constitution of democratic experimentalism. *Columbia Law Review, 98*(2), 267–473.

Eberlein, B. E., & Kerwer, D. (2002). Theorising the new modes of European Union governance. *European Integration Online Papers (EIoP), 6*(5) https://ideas.repec.org/a/erp/eiopxx/p0078.html

European Commission. (2001). *European Governance: A White Paper*, COM (2001) 428, Brussels, 25 July, 2001. https://ec.europa.eu/commission/presscorner/detail/en/DOC_01_10

European Commission. (2005). *Communication from the Commission: Working together, working better: A new framework for the open coordination of social protection and inclusion policies in the European Union*, COM (2005) 706 final, Brussels, 22 December, 2005. https://eur-lex.europa.eu/legal-content/EN/ALL/?uri=celex:52005DC0706

European Commission. (2008). *Communication from the Commission: A renewed commitment to social Europe: Reinforcing the Open Method of Coordination for Social Protection and Social Inclusion*, COM (2008) 418 final, Brussels, 2 July, 2008. https://eur-lex.europa.eu/legal-content/EN/ALL/?uri=CELEX%3A52008DC0418

European Commission. (2015). *State of the Union 2015 by European Commission President Jean-Claude Juncker*, Strasbourg, 9 September, 2015. https://ec.europa.eu/info/publications/state-union-2015-european-commission-president-jean-claude-juncker_en.

European Commission. (2016a). *Communication from the Commission: Launching a Consultation on a European Pillar of Social Rights*, COM (2016) 127 final, Strasbourg, 8 March, 2016. https://eur-lex.europa.eu/resource.html?uri=cellar:bc4bab37-e5f2-11e5-8a50-01aa75ed71a1.0004.02/DOC_1&format=PDF

European Commission. (2016b). *Annex 1: First Preliminary Outline of a European Pillar of Social Rights...*, COM (2016) 127 final, Strasbourg, 8 March, 2016. https://eur-lex.europa.eu/resource.html?uri=cellar:bc4bab37-e5f2-11e5-8a50-01aa75ed71a1.0004.02/DOC_2&format=PDF

European Commission. (2017a). *Communication from the Commission: Establishing a European Pillar of Social Rights*, COM (2017) 250 final, Brussels, 26 April 2017. https://ec.europa.eu/transparency/regdoc/rep/1/2017/EN/COM-2017-250-F1-EN-MAIN-PART-1.PDF

European Commission. (2017b). *Commission Staff Working Document accompanying the Communication from the Commission 'Establishing a European Pillar of Social Rights'*, SWD (2017) 201 final, Brussels, 26 April, 2017. https://eur-lex.europa.eu/legal-content/EN/TXT/PDF/?uri=CELEX:52017SC0201&from=EN

European Commission. (2017c). *Commission Staff Working Document: Social Scoreboard,* SWD (2017) 200 final, Brussels, 26 April, 2017. https://eur-lex.europa.eu/legal-content/EN/TXT/PDF/?uri=CELEX:52017SC0200&from=EN

European Commission. (2017d). Commission recommendation (EU) 2017/761… on the European pillar of social rights. *Official Journal of the European Union, L 113*, 56–61.

European Commission. (2018). *Communication from the Commission: Monitoring the Implementation of the European Pillar of Social Rights*. COM (2018) 130 final, Strasbourg, 13 March 2018. https://eur-lex.europa.eu/legal-content/EN/TXT/PDF/?uri=CELEX:52018DC0130&from=EN

European Commission. (n.d.). *The European Pillar of Social Rights Action Plan*. https://ec.europa.eu/social/main.jsp?catId=1607&langId=en

European Council. (1989). *Community Charter of the Fundamental Social Rights of Workers,* 8 December, 1989. https://eur-lex.europa.eu/EN/legal-content/summary/community-charter-of-fundamental-social-rights-of-workers.html

European Council. (1997). "*Presidency conclusions: Luxembourg European Council 12 and 13 December 1997*". http://www.europarl.europa.eu/summits/lux1_en.htm

European Council. (1999). *Conclusions of the Presidency: Cologne European Council 3–4 June 1999*. http://www.europarl.europa.eu/summits/kol1_en.htm

European Council. (2000). *Presidency Conclusions: Lisbon European Council 23 and 24 March 2000*. https://www.consilium.europa.eu/media/21038/lisbon-european-council-presidency-conclusions.pdf

European Council. (2017). *European Council meeting (14 December 2017)—Conclusions*, EUCO 19/1/17, Brussels, 14 December, 2017. https://www.consilium.europa.eu/media/32204/14-final-conclusions-rev1-en.pdf

European Council. (2021). *The Porto Declaration*, 8 May, 2021. https://www.consilium.europa.eu/en/press/press-releases/2021/05/08/the-porto-declaration/

Regulation (EU) No 883/2004 of the European Parliament and the Council of the European Union. (2004). *Official Journal of the European Union, L 166*, 1–123.

Regulation (EU) No 1175/2011 of the European Parliament and the Council of the European Union. (2011). *Official Journal of the European Union, L 306*, 12–24.

Regulation (EU) No 2019/1149 of the European Parliament and the Council of the European Union. (2019). *Official Journal of the European Union, L 186*, 21–56.

Regulation (EU) No 2021/1057 of the European Parliament and the Council of the European Union. (2021a). *Official Journal of the European Union, L 231*, 21–59.

Regulation (EU) No 2021/1060 of the European Parliament and the Council of the European Union. (2021b). *Official Journal of the European Union, L 231*, 159–706.

European Parliament, Council of the European Union & European Commission. (2017). *European pillar of social rights: Building a fairer and more inclusive European Union*. Booklet. https://ec.europa.eu/info/strategy/priorities-2019-2024/economy-works-people/jobs-growth-and-investment/european-pillar-social-rights/european-pillar-social-rights-20-principles_en#documents

European Union. (2016). Consolidated versions of the Treaty on the European Union and the Treaty on the Functioning of the European Union. *Official Journal of the European Union, C 202*, 1–388.

Eurostat. (2019). Over 20% of EU population at risk of poverty or social exclusion in 2019. *Eurostat News*. https://ec.europa.eu/eurostat/web/products-eurostat-news/-/edn-20201016-2

Hacker, B. (2023, November). The European Pillar of Social Rights: Impact and Advancement. *SWP Research Paper* 14.

Héritier, A., & Eckert, S. (2008). New modes of governance in the shadow of hierarchy: Self-regulation by industry in Europe. *Journal of Public Policy, 28*(1), 113–118.

Héritier, A., & Lehmkuhl, D. (2011). New modes of governance and democratic accountability. *Government and Opposition, 46*(1), 126–144.

Hodson, D., & Maher, I. (2001). The open method as a new mode of governance: The case of soft economic policy co-ordination. *Journal of Common Market Studies, 39*(2), 719–746.

Huller, T. (2012). On infeasibilities of cosmopolitan democracy—Lesson from the European Union. *Swiss Political Science Review, 18*(2), 249–271.

Jachtenfuchs, M. (2001). The governance approach to European integration. *Journal of Common Market Studies, 39*(2), 245–264.

Keohane, R. O., & Hoffman, S. (1991). Institutional change in Europe in the 1980s. In R. O. Keohane & S. Hoffman (Eds.), *The new European community: Decision making and institutional change*. Westview Press.

Kohler-Koch, B., & Rittberger, B. (2006). Review article: The 'governance turn' in EU studies. *Journal of Common Market Studies, 44*(s1), 27–49.

Kyriakidis, A. (2016). Input or output? Evaluation of the EU democratic deficit approaches after the Eurozone crisis. In D. Anagnostopoulou, I. Papadopoulos, & L. Papadopoulou (Eds.), *The EU at a crossroads* (pp. 211–234). Cambridge Scholars Publishing.

Mailand, M. (2013). Slowing down social Europe? The struggle over work and employment regulation. *Industrial Relations Journal, 44*(3), 240–257.

Majone, G. (2011). Is the community method still viable? In R. Dehousse (Ed.), *The 'community method': Obstinate or obsolete?* (pp. 16–40). Palgrave Macmillan.

Monar, J. (2011). Deviations from and alternatives to the community method in justice and home affairs. In R. Dehousse (Ed.), *The 'community method': Obstinate or obsolete?* (pp. 118–134). Palgrave Macmillan.

Papadopoulos, I. (2013). The efficiency of debt crisis management by EU mechanisms: Lessons from the Greek case. In A. Bitzenis, I. Papadopoulos, & V. A. Vlachos (Eds.), *Reflections on the Greek sovereign debt crisis: The EU institutional framework, economic adjustment in an extensive shadow economy* (pp. 24–109). Cambridge Scholars Publishing.

Pochet, P. (2005). The open method of co-ordination and the construction of social Europe: A historical perspective. In J. Zeitlin, P. Pochet, & L. Magnusson (Eds.), *The open method of co-ordination in action: The European employment and social inclusion strategies* (pp. 37–82). Presses Interuniversitaires Européennes.

Pochet, P. (2011). Social Europe: Why hard law remains important. In R. Dehousse (Ed.), *The 'community method': Obstinate or obsolete?* (pp. 91–117). Palgrave Macmillan.

Smismans, S. (2008). The European social dialogue in the shadow of hierarchy. *Journal of Public Policy, 28*(1), 161–180.

Timo, I., & Kelemen, D. (2006). New modes of governance, the open method of co-ordination and other fashionable red herring. *Perspectives on European Politics and Society, 7*(1), 108–123.

Trubek, D. M., & Trubek, L. G. (2005). Hard and soft law in the construction of social Europe: The role of the open method of co-ordination. *European Law Journal, 11*(3), 343–364.

Verdun, A. (2012). Experimentalist governance in the European Union: A commentary. *Regulation & Governance, 6*(3), 385–393.

Zeitlin, J. (2011). Is the open method of coordination an alternative to the community method? In R. Dehousse (Ed.), *The 'community method': Obstinate or obsolete?* (pp. 135–150). Palgrave Macmillan.

Zeitlin, J., & Vanhercke, B. (2018). Socializing the European semester: EU social and economic policy co-ordination in crisis and beyond. *Journal of European Public Policy, 25*(2), 149–174.

Part III

The Role of the European Union and National Policies in Fighting Social Exclusion Based on Racial Origin and Other Characteristics

European Union Approaches to Europe's Romani People: The Potential of a Capabilities Approach to Law and Policy Making

Tawhida Ahmed and Nuno Ferreira

Abstract

This chapter critiques the European Union's efforts to support Romani people in overcoming the disadvantaged positions they hold in EU Member States (MS). It reviews current EU measures and developments and argues that these have produced limited results for the improvement of the lives of Romani people in Europe. The chapter argues that the EU should revise its approach for potentially more effective impacts, by gearing its efforts towards empowering Romani people to take up the opportunities that the EU and its MS offer in a manner which allows them to lead lives of their choosing. To this end, this chapter adopts Sen's capabilities approach as a way forward, which suggests that people need to have the freedom (capability) to choose a variety of lifestyles, and thus require empowerment to make choices and implement these in their lives. The capabilities approach goes beyond having access to goods and services and requires authorities to create the conditions to empower citizens to make effective use of

The authors wish to wholeheartedly thank Dr Julija Sardelić (Victoria University of Wellington) for all her in-depth and constructive feedback on various earlier drafts of this piece. This work was initially envisioned as a co-authorship with Dr Sardelić. This did not materialise owing to other personal and professional commitments, but the piece still benefited from extensive advice and input from Dr Sardelić, for which the authors are deeply thankful. The authors also wish to thank Dr Lilija Alijeva, Dr Stephanie Berry and Dr Elizabeth Craig for their very helpful feedback on an earlier version.

T. Ahmed
City Law School, University of London, London, UK
e-mail: tawhida.ahmed.1@city.ac.uk

N. Ferreira (✉)
University of Sussex, Brighton, UK
e-mail: n.ferreira@sussex.ac.uk

D. Anagnostopoulou (ed.), *European Identities, Inclusion and Equality*, Diversity and Inclusion Research, https://doi.org/10.1007/978-3-031-90602-2_9

those goods and services. This chapter elaborates on Sen's capabilities theory and assesses whether the EU supports it, and how it might (further) do so in the future. It concludes that to enhance the capabilities of Romani people in the EU, the EU institutions should adopt a multipronged strategy based on: greater use of Article 7 TEU and infringement procedures; the introduction of a hard law, Romani-specific measure; and the creation of a Roma Truth and Reconciliation Commission.

Introduction

"Roma are among the most deprived peoples in Europe" (UNDP, 2017). The injustices that Romani people have suffered in Europe are the subject of documentation by civil society organisations, international organisations, and academics (Ahmed, 2015; Barany, 2000; Council of Europe, 2016; Ferreira, 2019; FRA, 2018; Iusmen, 2018; McGarry, 2011; Parker, 2012; Sardelić, 2017; Sardelić, 2021; Sigona & Vermeersch, 2012; UNDP, 2015; Vermeersch, 2012).[1] This chapter critiques the efforts of the European Union (EU) to support Romani people in overcoming their disadvantaged place in EU Member States. It reviews EU measures and developments and argues that these have had limited effectiveness in improving the lives of Romani people in Europe. In fact, according to some data, standards of living for Romani people have deteriorated in EU Member States and Romani people continue to face abject poverty, systematic discrimination, antigypsyism, and lack of respect for their human rights across the EU (Amnesty International UK, 2023; FRA, 2018; UNDP, 2015). This is despite the EU addressing Romani people formally since 1990 both in its enlargement policy (Appel, 2023; Ram, 2022; Simhandl, 2009), and internal policies, both of which have reflected weak attempts to support Romani people in Europe (Fischer, 2018). The EU's human rights approach is readily achieved through formal equality, and superficial and soft law measures of economic and social inclusion, ignoring the deeper measures needed to address the specific and complex contexts relevant to the Romani people. This also overlooks the antigypsyism difficulties they experience in using this legal framework to vindicate their rights. Moreover, the implementation of objectives to support Romani people is carried out at the national level, leaving the EU with very limited opportunities for monitoring and progressing support for Romani people at the national level. Indeed, the EU's efforts have been widely held as ineffective (Findor et al., 2023; Guy, 2009; Ram, 2022).

[1] Terminology in this field varies considerably and possesses a range of connotations. We have opted for the expression "Romani people" as the most encompassing and neutral possible alternative available, following the increasing preference for this term by a range of scholars as well as the European Parliament's terminological choice: "whereas the new definition, Romani people, better includes even those stigmatised as gypsies without having a corresponding ethnic background, such as Egyptians, Ashkali, or Travellers" (European Parliament, 2020, point C). However, the term "Roma" in the title of official documents or references is kept.

This chapter argues that EU efforts need an overhaul, through a reflection on the tools and approaches utilised in the EU to support the Romani people. To this end, the chapter adopts Sen's capabilities approach as a way forward, which suggests that people need to have the freedom (capability) to choose a variety of lifestyles and, thus, require empowerment to make choices and implement these in their lives (further elaborated in section "Sen's Capabilities Approach and Ethnic Minorities"). The capabilities approach goes beyond having access to goods and services, and requires authorities to create the conditions to empower citizens to make effective use of those goods and services. The use of Sen's capabilities approach to Romani matters has so far been very limited, topic-specific, and disengaged with formal law and policy making mechanisms, especially at EU level (New & Kyuchukov, 2018; Ryder et al., 2021).[2] Aside from these limited efforts, scholarship has not yet truly explored the potential of Sen's capabilities approach to Romani law and policy making, including at the EU level. Instead, academic efforts have so far mainly considered the root causes of why Romani people are not successfully taking up the opportunities that human rights and programmes of social inclusion provide to them (Andor, 2018; La Parra-Casado et al., 2023; Moschovidis, 2022; Rostas, 2020; Szilvasi & Saitovic-Jovanovic, 2023). This chapter thus elaborates on Sen's capabilities theory and assesses whether the EU supports the approach advocated within it, and how it might (further) do so in the future across its law and policy making activities. It concludes that to enhance the capabilities of Romani people in the EU, the EU institutions should adopt a multipronged strategy based on: greater use of the suspension mechanism in Article 7 of the Treaty on European Union (TEU) and other EU law infringement procedures; the introduction of Romani-specific hard law measures; and the creation of a Romani Truth and Reconciliation Commission.

To make these points, in section "The Framework of EU Action Relevant to the Romani People" of the chapter we provide an overview of EU competences and actions that are relevant to the issues faced by Romani people in the EU. Section "Sen's Capabilities Approach and Ethnic Minorities" analyses the theoretical approach that we propose as *suitable* for addressing the concerns of Romani people. We then *assess* in section "Assessing EU Law and Policy on Romani People through a Capabilities Approach" whether the arrangements promoted by the body of EU law and policy have been appropriate and effective in enhancing Romani people's capabilities. In section "The Way Forward: A Multipronged Strategy", we then examine what additional measures the EU can and should take to help eliminate sources of *unfreedom* that prevent Romani people from exercising their agency and expanding their capabilities.

[2] William New and Hristo Kyuchukov have considered this framework within the specific topic of language education for Romani people (New & Kyuchukov, 2018); Andrew Ryder, Marius Taba, and Nidhi Trehan have also used Sen's capabilities approach as a central theme to an edited collection on Romani communities and social change (Ryder et al., 2021).

The Framework of EU Action Relevant to the Romani People

This section of the chapter is contextual. It sets out the overarching framework of EU action applicable to or available for supporting the Romani people in the EU, before introducing the specificities of Sen's capability approach. The EU's framework consists of a mixture of policy and strategy level initiatives, funding mechanisms, and legal instruments of protection or enforcement. Among these, only some are Romani-specific initiatives, while the majority are generic instruments of EU law. There is no legally binding initiative in the EU specifically supporting Romani people and no specific obligation on Member States to take action to address discrimination towards them.

The EU's engagement with Romani issues commenced in the 1990s, during the time of the EU's Eastern Enlargement, under which the EU assessed minority protection in candidate countries. Since 2000, addressing Romani discrimination and impoverishment began to emerge as a specific internal priority of the EU, under the EU Lisbon Strategy to combat social exclusion (European Council, 2000). Within this strategy, Member States could set targets regarding Romani people in national action plans (NAPs) regarding education, employment, healthcare, housing, and pensions, with progress reported to the European Commission. Following the lack of improvement in addressing discrimination against Romani people,[3] the Commission—in a renewed social agenda—advocated for the use of existing EU structures (European Commission, 2008, p. 56), and positioned the EU as a facilitator and coordinator of Member State actions on Romani matters (Guy, 2009, p. 27). This led to the Commission holding "Roma summits" (2008, 2010 and 2014) bringing together national and regional governments to discuss best practices and joint ideas. Since 2009, the European Platform for Roma Inclusion has fulfilled a similar function, with specific reference to issues of inclusion (European Commission, 2022). A more targeted Romani policy was adopted in 2011 under the European Commission's Framework for National Roma Integration Strategies up to 2020, offering a set of policy guidelines for Member State actions at the domestic level (European Commission, 2011), in the areas of access to education, employment, healthcare and housing. Under the framework, Member States developed national action plans, which were monitored by the Commission. The Framework was coupled with the 2013 Council's guidelines on how Member States could achieve these aims (Council of the European Union, 2013). This was the first time a substantial effort towards Romani people had been adopted at the EU level. As with the social

[3] The reasons included lack of innovative approaches, poor planning, and the inability to enforce plans at the local level (Guy, 2009, p. 39). In addition, the enlargement process failed to bring changes to Romani people for multiple reasons, including lack of political will from candidate Member States and low levels of public support, but from the EU level, they included lack of legal competence, lack of sufficient funding, lack of input from Romani communities, and ineffective strategising from the European Commission. For instance, employment and life expectancy were two of the most prominent concerns for Romani people, yet less than 10% and 3% of EU funding, respectively, were targeted at these (Guy, 2009, p. 32).

inclusion policy, progress was driven by Member States, with the Commission adopting an oversight role.

However, in the lead up to 2020, the conditions of Romani people in Europe remained poor, and the EU's approach to Romani people, particularly its 2011 Framework, was criticised for lack of data, unclear goals in national plans, ineffective use of national and EU funds, and lack of political will (European Commission, 2018; European Commission, 2020a, p. 2; Fischer, 2018). Further, with a hands-off role, there was little possibility for the EU to influence progress on Romani rights at the national level. Acknowledging deficiencies, the Commission produced its post-2020 strategic framework for Romani inclusion (European Commission, 2020a). This framework offers, inter alia, four strategies. First, it broadens the scope of action towards Romani people, which is now to include "promoting effective equality, socio-economic inclusion and meaningful participation of Roma" (European Commission, 2020a, p. 2). Second, it requires further focus on utilising EU mechanisms for protection, with the EU taking responsibility for doing its part "by enforcing equality legislation, mainstreaming Roma equality, inclusion and participation in EU policy initiatives, mobilising EU funds for Roma and combating antigypsyism" (European Commission, 2020a, p. 6). Third, it calls for better engagement and participation of a multiplicity of actors, including the Romani communities (European Commission, 2020a, p. 3). Finally, it sets out seven objectives and quantitative EU headline targets in order to monitor achievements (European Commission, 2020a, pp. 4–5). Underlying all of this, the Commission states that it recognises antigypsyism as the root cause of the persistent discrimination against Romani people in Europe.

The EU's strategy level initiatives are supported by EU funds (Vermeersch, 2014). European Commission funding can support schemes relating to national integration strategies for Romani people (European Commission, 2020a). Romani-related initiatives could also seek financial support from the EU funding schemes related to human rights or culture, such as the EU Enlargement budget, the Culture programmes, and the Rights, Equality and Citizenship funding programme, or from the EU's general funding schemes, which include the European Social Fund, the European Regional Development Fund, and the European Agricultural Fund for Rural Development.

Aside from the Commission initiatives thus far discussed, there are no other Romani-specific initiatives at the EU level. Romani people can, of course, avail themselves of generic EU legal instruments and rights. One such key right is that of non-discrimination. EU primary law prohibits discrimination on grounds of sex, racial or ethnic origin, religion or belief, disability, age or sexual orientation, as well as colour, ethnic or social origin, genetic features, language, political or any other opinion, membership of a national minority, property, or birth (Charter of Fundamental Rights of the EU, 2012, Article 21; Treaty on the Functioning of the European Union, 2008, Articles 18–19). This right applies, to varying extents, to areas such as employment, education, housing, access to goods and services, and so on. Under the EU Race Directive 2000/43, where discrimination occurs, Romani people can bring cases before national courts and seek the support of national equality bodies (Directive 2000/43/EC, 2000, Articles 7 and 13). In addition, through the Framework Decision 2008/913 on combating racism and xenophobia, the EU requires Member States to impose criminal penalties for racist expressions (Framework Decision 2008/913/JHA, 2008). Other relevant human rights include voting rights and other civil and political rights under the EU Charter of Fundamental Rights. There is no human right to minority protection declared in EU law to protect Romani people as a vulnerable minority in the EU. However, Article 2 TEU describes the EU as founded on the value of respecting minority rights (Treaty on European Union, 2012, Article 2).

From this brief overview of relevant EU law and policy, it can be deduced that the EU has no Romani-specific competence, and does not impose any Romani-specific obligations on Member States as part of an explicit, binding legal framework. Romani concerns have been singled out at policy and strategy level, but only soft law measures have been taken while the competence and responsibility to take action rest on Member States. The EU's human rights and anti-discrimination legal framework provide rights for Romani people but, as discussed below, are not so readily enforced. Sen's capabilities approach—to which we now turn—can offer a solid analytical framework to design more effective EU measures in this field.

Sen's Capabilities Approach and Ethnic Minorities

Amartya Sen, being an economist by training, may not seem the most obvious source of inspiration for a framework that aims to offer the benchmark against which EU law and policy affecting Romani people should be assessed. Yet, Sen's work has gradually, throughout the decades, proven to be of immense value to broader analyses of law and policy on a range of matters. In the 1980s, Sen started working on the notion of "capabilities" (Sen, 1980, 1984). "Capabilities" should be understood as the ability to function in ways that people value, or the substantive freedom "to choose a life one has reason to value": the focus is on what people can actually do, not just on how they "*desire or react to* their ability or disability to do these things" (Sen, 1984, pp. 309–10; Sen, 2001, pp. 36–7, 74). Sen elaborates on this notion by specifying that the "capability" of an individual consists of the "alternative combinations that are feasible for her to achieve (…) thus a kind of freedom: the substantive freedom to achieve alternative functioning combinations (or less formally put, the freedom to achieve various lifestyles)" (Sen, 2001, p. 75; Sen, 2010, p. 233). This may include the possibility to exercise freedom that people may not yet want to exercise but have an interest in possessing (e.g. the freedom to participate in public debates) (Sen, 2001, pp. 36–7).

A capabilities approach differs from a rights approach, because rights-based approaches tend to focus reductively on negative and procedural rights, whilst a capabilities approach focuses on individuals' actual capabilities and how others (individuals and institutions) may be under an obligation to facilitate the exercise of rights (Sen, 1984, p. 313). So far, this would seem to fit well within a (positive) rights approach, but Sen goes further and insists on characterising "positive freedoms in the form of capabilities of persons" (Sen, 1984, p. 315). This shifts the focus from access to goods and services (and what their characteristics are) to the actual capability to make effective use of certain goods and services, thus to function. This capability to function should be valued, insofar as it comes very close to the notion of positive freedom (Sen, 1984, p. 316).

Sen is keen on not only adding a moral dimension to economics but also adopting a highly personalised approach to it. As Sen puts it, "[t]o insist on the mechanical comfort of having just one homogeneous 'good thing' would be to deny our humanity as reasoning creatures" (Sen, 2001, p. 77). The capabilities approach thus "focuses on human life" and represents a "serious departure from concentrating on the *means* of living, to the *actual opportunities* of living" (Sen, 2010, p. 233). Consequently, a focus on equality of resources does not suffice, as:

> (...) depending on our body size, metabolism, temperament, social conditions, etc., the translation of resources into the ability to do things does vary substantially from person to person and community to community, and to ignore that is to miss out on an important general dimension of moral concern. (Sen, 1984, p. 323)

Sen concludes that if we value positive freedoms, then we also need to value peoples' capabilities and whatever may enhance those capabilities. Although related to the notion of quality of life, the notion of capabilities is richer than that, insofar as it also entails the idea of responsibility. Indeed, promoting capabilities does not mean being responsible for others' lives and interests, which would be counterproductive at so many levels (including motivation, involvement, and self-knowledge) (Sen, 2001, p. 283). Instead, the capabilities approach combines social responsibility for making available social just arrangements with individual responsibility (Sen, 2001, pp. 283–4). That individual responsibility, however, is contingent on our substantive freedoms, which are contingent on personal, social, and environmental circumstances (Sen, 2001, p. 284). To enhance individual responsibility (e.g. obtaining employment and an income), we also need to enhance peoples' capabilities (e.g. provide education and health services) (Sen, 2001, p. 284). As "[r]esponsibility *requires* freedom", social support to expand people's freedom is essential to promote individual responsibility (Sen, 2001, p. 84). Freedom, capabilities, and responsibility go hand in hand in Sen's capabilities approach. This does not translate into advocating for a "nanny state", but instead calls for the existence of a range of institutions—political and social organisations, NGOs, media, civil society and market actors—to facilitate individuals' "opportunity for choice and for substantive decisions" (Sen, 2001, p. 284).

By replacing a focus on income levels with a focus on capabilities deprivation, we gain a broader informational basis that allows us to "better understand the poverty of human lives and freedoms" (Sen, 2001, p. 20). Sen's proposals have, unsurprisingly, encountered some resistance from academic and political circles, but Sen has addressed those critiques himself very effectively (Sen, 1993, 2010, pp. 264–8), including by ensuring that the capabilities approach is understood within the context of broader demands for justice, fairness, equity, equality, and multiple perspectives on capabilities (Sen, 2010, pp. 295–8). Consequently, we can confidently use his work in the context of law and policy making related to Romani people.

Indeed, the capabilities approach has been applied to a range of different contexts and issues (Chiappero-Martinetti et al., 2020). Crucially, Sen's work is directly relevant to ethnic minorities, as his own writing highlights. Sen points to the remarkably high extent of capability deprivation that can be observed even in the most affluent countries (e.g. in relation to health care, education, employment, or social security) and illustrates this with studies that demonstrate that African-American men have much lower life expectancy than men in much poorer countries and white people in the USA (Sen, 1993, pp. 114–115; Sen, 2001, pp. 15 and 21–23). This difference cannot be explained by differences in outcome, but rather by problems with healthcare, prevalence of urban crime, standards of social care, less access to food owing to its cost, and other characteristics of the social environment—all factors that affect the capabilities of African-American men. This range of factors may render certain ethnic minorities not only relatively deprived in relation to other ethnic groups within the same country, but also absolutely more deprived than people with low incomes in much poorer countries (Sen, 2001, p. 22). Furthermore, ethnic background (including "race" and skin colour) not only may have positive statistical correlation with social class, but also may relate in particular ways to the deprivation suffered by individuals who are visibly members of an ethnic minority (Sen, 1993, p. 121). That visibility can act as a "barrier to functioning possibilities" in a range of daily contexts, including in employment, medical care, and access to justice, which makes inequality of income distribution only one element of a broader picture (Sen, 1993, pp. 121–22). Crucially, Sen also points out that capabilities can be understood not only as individual but also as collective. As such, capabilities can be attributes of collectivities, such as communities and ethnic groups, so one can talk about "group capabilities" (Sen, 2010, pp. 244). Both the notions of capability deprivation and group capabilities are patently relevant for the context of Romani people, as section "The Framework of EU Action Relevant to the Romani People" already suggested and section "Assessing EU Law and Policy on Romani People through a Capabilities Approach" will further evidence.

Also directly relevant to Romani people is Sen's insistence that both the majority rule and the protection of minority rights are integral parts of democratic practice, as well as his emphasis on the need to form "tolerant values and priorities" (Sen, 2010, p. 337). This not only requires liberal rights, but may also entail unanimous decision making over certain matters (Sen, 2010, p. 337). A richer understanding of democracy thus requires accommodating minority rights: majority votes go hand in hand with tolerant values, "inclusive and interactive political processes", the "recognition of the multiple identities of each person", and an "active and energetic media" that highlight the "problems, predicaments and humanity of certain groups" (Sen, 2010, pp. 352–4).

What Sen's capabilities approach means in practice is that social arrangements will only be just if they are sensitive to the impact they have on people's actual freedoms and capabilities (Sen, 1993, p. 147). This means addressing, amongst others, deprivation, destitution, and oppression, all signs of lack of development that affect individual agency, in other words, people's capabilities (Sen, 2001, p. xi). To enact a vision of development as the expansion of real freedoms, Sen proposes focusing on: (1) political freedoms (including civil rights, such as free speech and right to vote), (2) economic facilities (i.e. opportunities to use economic resources), (3) social opportunities (which influence individuals' substantive freedoms, such as education and health), (4) transparency guarantees (dealing with the need for openness to ensure trust), and (5) protective security (providing a social safety net when the economic system does not prevent deprivation and vulnerability) (Sen, 2001 pp. xii, 10–11 and 38–40). Greater development thus entails making advancements in all these freedoms, which are not discrete or optional, but rather the main end of development, the constituent components and principal means of development, empirically and causally linked, and mutually reinforcing (Sen, 2001, pp. xii, 4, 5 and 36–7).

A focus on development might seem misplaced in the context of Romani issues, as all EU Member States are generally considered developed countries in official and public discourses. Nonetheless, we argue that such assessment is relative and development is simply a matter of degree; hence, there is scope for further development within the EU geographical space in relation to a range of aspects affecting Romani people's capabilities. How one measures that, however, is not straightforward. To address this, Sen adopts a very pragmatic solution: the "affirmation of the importance of capabilities can go with various strategies of actual evaluation involving practical compromises" (Sen, 2001, p. 85). There is, therefore, no "specific formula for policy decisions" (Sen, 2010, p. 232). More important than adopting a set of reductive or impoverishing indicators is to concentrate on poverty, inequality, and social performance from the perspective of freedom (Sen, 2001, p. 286). We will not, therefore, propose or espouse a rigid set of benchmarks but rather adopt a loose set of broad key principles, namely advancing the five key abovementioned freedoms identified by Sen: political freedoms, economic facilities, social opportunities, transparency guarantees, and protective security. This exercise will also lead us to consider whether the injustices suffered by Romani people in the EU can be reasonably and rationally prevented and addressed (Sen, 2010, p. 4). This is not a mere normative or institutional design exercise, because justice depends on "actual realizations and accomplishments" and "the kind of lives that people can actually lead", not just "getting the basic institutions and general rules right" (Sen, 2010, p. 10).

The question we thus need to ask ourselves is whether the EU enhances Romani people's freedom and agency, and, if not, what can and should the EU do to help remove sources of *unfreedom* preventing Romani people from exercising their agency and expanding their capabilities. The next sections consider these questions.

Assessing EU Law and Policy on Romani People Through a Capabilities Approach

This section analyses law and policy that the EU has elaborated to address Romani people's interests, needs and rights, as well as the situation on the ground in Member States, through a capabilities lens. It also examines those freedoms that, according to Sen, are essential to enhance people's capabilities. In this process, we will also highlight tensions between, on the one hand, the current situation and the meagre results of EU law and policy in this field, and on the other hand, the international human rights norms that should inform policy making but are far from being fulfilled. This will bring to the fore the rights dimensions of Sen's capabilities approach.

Let us recall that the first freedoms on which Sen focuses are political freedoms, including civil rights, such as free speech and the right to vote. The pervasive and continuous violations of Romani people's civil rights make it apparent that EU action in this field has not influenced improvements on the ground. To use the language most familiar to the European audiences in light of the European Convention on Human Rights (ECHR) and its protocols, this translates into recurrent violations of Romani people's rights to life, prohibition of torture, liberty and security, fair trial, respect for private and family life, freedom of expression, assembly and association, prohibition of discrimination, and prohibition of collective expulsion of foreigners, amongst others (Möschel, 2012). Across Europe, Romani people continue to face intolerable levels of racist abuse, attacks, and unlawful killings, and exclusion from settlements and property, both nationally and internationally, such as the targeted killings and displacement that occurred in France and Italy in 2007 and 2008 (Carrera, 2013; Duez, 2010; Guy, 2009, p. 24; Sigona & Monasta, 2006), as well as police brutality in Slovakia in 2020 (Koslerova, 2021), and in the Czech Republic in June 2021 (Rorke, 2021). Moreover, Romani women are sterilised against their will to prevent further births.[4] The "othering" of Romani people that occurred in the context of Brexit, since 2015, is another example, with Romani people being blamed for strains on UK resources, and its migration "problem" (Richardson & Codona, 2018). The rise of right-wing politics across Europe has spurred on such treatment and attitudes, across the EU as a whole.

Furthermore, Romani people are very often arbitrarily deprived of their right to a nationality—enshrined in Article 15 of the Universal Declaration of Human Rights (UDHR)[5]—by public authorities with impunity, while access to citizenship, residency, and official documentation is a recurrent challenge (Sardelić, 2021). Both research and NGO advocacy have shown that many Romani people around Europe, both in the EU Member States and in candidate countries, are more vulnerable to statelessness than the majority population (European Roma Rights Centre, 2017). This means that they are often deprived of what Hannah Arendt has called the "the

[4] For example, ECtHR, 2011, *V.C. v. Slovakia*.

[5] Proclaimed by the United Nations General Assembly in Paris on 10 December 1948 (General Assembly Resolution 217 A, https://www.un.org/en/development/desa/population/migration/generalassembly/docs/globalcompact/A_RES_217(III).pdf).

right to have rights" (Arendt, 1968). As the European Roma Rights Centre has asserted, some state officials "blame" Romani people for their lack of documents and hence for having no citizenship, commenting that their state is not responsible if marginalized minorities are not using the rights they are given (European Roma Rights Centre, 2017). However, such comments in fact show a complete misunderstanding of how centuries of exclusion, discrimination, and segregation have contributed to Romani people not "using" the rights that are given to them. Many Romani people are actually very well aware that even though they officially have the right not to be discriminated against, that does not in practice mean that they will be able to be offered a job on the same conditions as non-Romani fellow citizens, have the same quality education as the majority of the population, or be able to speak in public without being judged on the basis of their skin colour (European Roma Rights Centre, 2017). The fact that they manifestly do have certain rights does not prevent latent discrimination and ignorance about these rights from the majority population, as the responsibility to enforce such rights is not placed on the majority population. Although they have a range of rights associated with their status as nationals of a certain Member State, due to multi-layered exclusion, segregation, and often isolation, their rights remain invisible to them or they are prevented from exercising them. This is also evident in the case of Romani people who want to exercise their EU citizenship rights: the fact they have been granted EU citizenship has not necessarily led to access to the rights they should have as EU citizens (Sardelić, 2017).

A distinct limitation of EU law in this context is that Romani people often do not know their EU law rights or have the confidence to challenge discrimination under the Race Directive, for instance. Options for institutional action as an alternative to Romani people taking personal action are also not effective. The first option is the infringement procedure when the European Commission may take action against Member States based on Article 258 of the Treaty on the Functioning of the EU (TFEU) for breaches of EU law, including in relation to obligations owed to EU citizens. Under the Race Directive, the European Commission has initiated proceedings against three states for segregation of Romani people in schools (Beger, 2014; European Commission, 2023; Pollák, 2022).[6] However, the relevant infringement procedures have not yet been concluded, suggesting that this legal action is not an effective enforcement means, but rather initiates a slow process for change and action. Another option is based on Article 7 TEU, through which Member States can be investigated and sanctioned for breaches of EU values under Article 2 TEU (including minority rights and human rights). However, this provision has been scarcely invoked at EU level at all, most likely on account of the requirement of unanimity voting and mutual support from like-minded Member States, despite

[6] See European Commission's infringement proceedings against the Czech Republic in 2014 in respect of school segregation, INFR(2014)2174 25/09/2014 (listed as an active case); Slovakia in 2015, INFR(2015)2025 29/04/2015 (listed as active); Hungary in 2016, INFR(2015)2206 26/05/2016 (listed as active).

instances of clear violations of EU values in some Member States (Scheppele et al., 2020).[7]

Sen's second group of freedoms relates to access to economic facilities. Here we would like to highlight the shortcomings of EU policy in fostering Romani people's access to the labour market. Romani people's situation in the field of employment is extremely worrying, with a growing gap between the percentage of Romani and non-Romani individuals registered unemployed (European Parliament, 2020, Point N). In 2020, it was reported that a large proportion of Romani people in Western Europe were unemployed (FRA, 2020). This is compounded by an increasing proportion of young Romani people "not in employment, education or training" (NEETs) (European Commission, 2020b, p. 3). This state of affairs is in clear tension with Article 23 UDHR and Article 6 of the International Covenant on Economic, Social and Cultural Rights (ICESCR),[8] which enshrines the right to work, to free choice of employment, to just and favourable conditions of work, and to protection against unemployment. This is even more the case if we read Article 6 ICESCR in conjunction with Article 2(2) of the same Covenant, on the principle of non-discrimination.

As for Sen's third group of freedoms related to social opportunities, education provision for Romani children and youth is still inadequate, in particular in subsisting cases of segregation (euphemistically called "special education" by some Member State authorities), but also more generally in terms of completion of schooling. According to the 2019 Fundamental Rights Report of the EU Fundamental Rights Agency (FRA), segregated education of Romani children has increased 50% in 5 years (from 10% in 2011 to 15% in 2016) (FRA, 2019). Moreover, as underscored by the COVID-19 pandemic, there is also a dire inadequacy in healthcare provision, with Romani people being disproportionately affected by poor health (European Commission, 2020b, p. 3).[9] High gaps remain in terms of affordability of healthcare for Romani as compared with non-Romani people. In general, the prosperity of Romani people has stagnated (Chopin et al., 2017, p. 10), and in some instances even declined (Amnesty International, 2018, 2023; Chopin et al., 2017, p. 10; Ram, 2012), across Europe. This is particularly disappointing in the EU, which is one of the world's richest regions. Against this background, both letter and spirit of Article 21 UDHR (on the right to equal access to

[7] Article 7 TEU has only been used twice by the European Commission and the European Parliament—in relation to Hungary and Poland—and after several years of the violations in question, showing that it lacks effectiveness. In the case of Hungary, 7 years after breaches of EU law; and in the case of Poland, 2 years after breaches of EU law (Scheppele et al., 2020).

[8] Adopted and opened for signature, ratification and accession by General Assembly resolution 2200A (XXI) of 16 December 1966.

[9] In Slovakia, a lack of access to clean water and proper sanitation was exacerbated by the COVID-19 pandemic for the Romani community; in Hungary, a Romani community feared hunger over contracting the virus; while lockdown measures prevented Romani access to employment (Rorke & Lee, 2020); malnutrition was already a significant problem before the pandemic, and life expectancy is now, on average, 10 years lower compared to that of the general population of the countries where they live (Lecerf, 2021).

public service), Article 25 UDHR and Article 11 ICESCR (right to a standard of adequate living, including food, clothing, housing and medical care, and necessary social services), and Article 26 UDHR and Article 13 ICESCR (on the right to education) are severely called into question.

Sen's transparency guarantees are no better safeguarded by EU law and policy. Romani people's right to participation in policy and decision making that affect them is patently insufficiently implemented, as illustrated by the fact that only 13% of EU funding is directed at the two top priorities of Romani people, namely employment and life expectancy (Guy, 2009, p. 32). A 2015 study commissioned by the European Parliament, evaluating the National Roma Integration Strategies of EU Member States, suggested four areas of reform: design, funding, implementation, and monitoring and data collection (Bartlett et al., 2015). The suggested reforms entailed ideas such as involving stakeholders, better resources, combining mainstreaming and targeted approaches, reducing bureaucratic complexity in funding, and better monitoring processes. An important aim was better stakeholder involvement; however, it should be implemented effectively and on a large-scale manner. The abovementioned 2015 study also emphasised the "dearth" of national and sub-national political will on Romani issues (Bartlett et al., 2015, p. 9), which also suggests a lack of influence of Romani people in decision making at the national level. The above findings provide additional argumentation for advocating a capabilities approach: policies affecting Romani people must involve strategies of self-empowerment so that Romani people's hopes are not reliant on governments and changes in government that do not serve their needs. One key tool in this process of increasing transparency and self-empowerment is the creation of a Romani Truth and Reconciliation Commission at EU level—a recommendation to which we will return in section "The Way Forward: A Multipronged Strategy".

Finally, Sen's protective security freedoms have not been sufficiently secured and promoted by EU law and policy either. In terms of (social) housing, a substantial proportion of Romani people still lives in inadequate conditions (European Parliament, 2020, point J), and, as noted by the European Commission in 2020, housing is still one of the biggest challenges for Romani people (European Commission, 2020b, p. 3). Romani communities also tend to have a lower life expectancy from birth and more limited access to health insurance than the general population (Roma Health Network, 2022). A large proportion of Romani people in Western Europe are excluded from the welfare safety net, living in extreme poverty, deprived of basic needs such as access to food, water, and toilet facilities (FRA, 2020). Up to 30% of Romani people live in households with no tap water or sanitary facilities (European Commission, 2020c). In many Member States, nearly 80% of Romani communities reside in overcrowded neighbourhoods (European Commission, 2020c). This stands in stark contrast with what is prescribed by Articles 22 and 25 UDHR and Article 9 ICESCR (on the right to social security).

Transversal to all of these freedoms, the right to equality and non-discrimination of Romani people is violated in a widespread manner. EU law and policy addressing

Romani people have done very little to significantly reduce the amount of racist abuse, violence, and discrimination against them, from both private and public actors. The EU has placed a greater focus on socio-economic issues, rather than on Romani-specific anti-discrimination strategies (Iusmen, 2018, p. 430). Many Romani people experience antigypsyism on a daily basis and in all spheres of life, which stands in direct contrast with Article 7 UDHR, Article 26 of the International Covenant on Civil and Political Rights (ICCPR),[10] and Article 2 ICESCR. Antigypsyism is widely prevalent in the EU, with 45% of EU citizens expressing discomfort when having Romani or Traveller neighbours (FRA, 2020, p. 14). Tackling antigypsyism is fundamental to improve Romani lives, as the distinct and specific type of prejudice against Romani people means that laws and policies cannot perform optimally (Iusmen, 2018, p. 430).

Indeed, antigypsyism constitutes a "specific form of racism, an ideology founded on racial superiority, a form of dehumanisation and institutional racism nurtured by historical discrimination, which is expressed, among others, by violence, hate speech, exploitation, stigmatisation and the most blatant kind of discrimination" (ECRI, 2011). Amongst other definitions (Alliance against Antigypsyism, 2022; Cortés Gómez, 2019, p. 368), Carrera et al. (2017) argue for an extended understanding of antigypsyism that "refers to the historical role, everyday behaviour, and prejudices/stereotypes of institutions that co-produce and reproduce the fear or hatred of Roma in laws, policies and practices that are contrary to fundamental human rights and citizenship freedoms of Roma communities". As commonly known, the consequences of antigypsyism are of such a scale as to make access to rights and opportunities futile. Indeed, "as long as strategies for inclusion fail to also explicitly address conscious or unconscious negative stereotypes and biases against the Roma by the majority population, they are likely to only produce limited, if any, real inclusion" (Van Hout et al., 2019). An example of this negative impact is that while Romani people may have the right to vote, they are often disempowered and unable to exercise this right, due to shortcomings in education and a lack of awareness of their rights, among other factors. As New and Kyuchukov (2018) have argued, this is explained because human rights concern the provision of formal rights, but this alone is not sufficient to make them effective or to achieve justice. In fact, a human rights approach to supporting Romani people can only be effective in combating antigypsyism if it is implemented properly and grounded on truth and reconciliation (Van Hout et al., 2019). Components of truth and reconciliation approaches necessitate that society tackle stigma heads-on in order to secure a changed future.

Despite the EU Race Directive having been adopted more than two decades ago, it has brought minimal change to Romani people's lives, considering the majority is not fully aware of the rights they derive from this EU legal act and the respective implementing national rules. European Commission proceedings against Member States infringing the Race Directive against Romani people are welcome, but too

[10] Adopted and opened for signature, ratification, and accession by General Assembly resolution 2200A (XXI) of 16 December 1966.

lengthy and yet without any clear improvement in practice. Moreover, a mainly formal equality approach to the Race Directive is unlikely to achieve the desired outcomes.

Another transversal matter is that EU law and policy funding tools have also proven to be insufficient due to a combination of factors such as lack of funding, absorption capacity, technical capacity, and stakeholders' coordination, as well as excessive procedural bureaucracy and poor alignment between funding and Romani priorities. The complexity of these funding schemes, along with their reliance on the application and management by the Member States, has hindered effective support for Romani people. There has also been an inadequate strategy regarding how EU funds should benefit Romani people (Vermeersch, 2014, p. 201). As a result, even though the EU allocates funds towards Romani inclusion projects,[11] these schemes have often proven futile.

The analysis so far can lead to two conclusions. First, the position of Romani people in the EU is comparable to that of African-Americans, as discussed by Sen (2001, p. 96). Similarly to African-Americans, Romani people also suffer from capabilities deprivation in their own countries, including issues regarding relative poverty and lower life expectancy. Although their rights are usually guaranteed in the national legislation, this fact does not provide them the opportunity to enjoy these rights in practice. Second, these findings, coupled with other contemporary pressing issues (such as rising xenophobia and popular extremism), urgently call for a new approach to Romani integration within the European context.

We, therefore, need to rethink the root causes of capabilities deprivation of Romani people, such as insufficient "hard law' tools, monitoring, and enforcement. Simply making use of broadly defined EU strategies, European summit conclusions, platforms, and national action plans—even if positive to some extent—has not translated into any substantial improvements in Romani people's capabilities. The addition of quantitative targets in the latest European Commission's EU Roma Strategic Framework for equality, inclusion, and participation, adopted in October 2020, constitutes a positive step towards the right direction (European Commission, 2020a). However, the Framework still lacks any enforcement mechanism, justifying its description as a "toothless tiger" (Franz, 2020) and supporting the warning issued by VoRAE (2020) that this tool remains hostage to domestic political will. Moreover, rights that do not specifically go beyond formal equality are unlikely to make the desired impact in improving the situation for Romani people.

So, what should the way forward be?

[11] Between 2000 and 2006, the EU spent over 275 million euros on projects geared towards Romani inclusion (Popova, 2014, p. 7); the EU designated 1.5 billion euros towards Romani integration strategies for the period of 2014–2020 (European Court of Auditors, 2016).

The Way Forward: A Multipronged Strategy

In this section, we propose a multipronged strategy that would meet the requirements of a capabilities approach to Romani-specific law and policy, aimed at empowering Romani communities to overcome the various unfreedoms that affect them. Many different strategies have been advocated so far in this field. For example, Ingi Iusmen (2018) argues that the EU should focus on policy quality over the quantity of policies aimed at facilitating Romani integration (Iusmen, 2018, p. 438). Peter Vermeersch cautions that the extensive focus on Romani people at the EU level could have detrimental effects at the local level: in some cases, nationalist extremist parties and narratives have reinterpreted the EU's attention on Romani people as proof that they are European outsiders rather than a national minority (Vermeersch, 2012). A more holistic and integrated approach has also been advocated for by one of the authors of this chapter (Ferreira, 2019). Our multipronged strategy described below builds on and complements these various proposals. Before outlining our multipronged strategy, it is essential to recall that the key underlying cause for fundamental rights' violations and socio-economic deprivation of Romani communities is antigypsyism (European Parliament, 2017; Iusmen, 2018: 436). We adopt a broad definition of antigypsyism (section "Assessing EU Law and Policy on Romani People through a Capabilities Approach") and share the opinion that fighting antigypsyism needs to be at the centre of the EU strategy for Romani inclusion. The multipronged strategy that we propose is based on the following three key measures: (1) greater use of Article 7 TEU and European Commission infringement procedures (Treaty on the Functioning of the EU, Article 258), (2) the introduction of a hard law, Romani-specific measure, and (3) the creation of a Romani Truth and Reconciliation Commission. Each one of these measures corresponds particularly, but not exclusively, to specific requirements of Sen's capabilities approach, and—together—they are to complement (not replace) the current measures.

First, we advocate in favour of the greater and more effective use of Article 7 TEU and of infringement procedures, rather than creating new tools. This measure corresponds specifically to Sen's political freedoms, economic facilities, and social opportunities. So far, Article 7 TEU has been used too rarely and only following long-lasting violations of EU values. Similarly, Article 258 TFEU has not been used adequately or effectively to carry out infringement procedures against Member States where Romani rights are blatantly violated. Although it may be considered politically unrealistic or unadvisable to rely more extensively on these legal tools, their increasing use in recent years—including in relation to Romani matters—indicates that the European Commission has finally understood the need to maximise the use of these tools to uphold the values of the EU, including the rule of law and fundamental rights. We thus believe the European Commission should proceed with an increasingly dynamic use of Article 7 TEU and infringement procedures in relation to all violations of rights of Romani communities that fall within the scope of EU law. This means not only more effectively carrying out the ongoing procedures against Slovakia and the Czech Republic, but also initiating infringement procedures more frequently against other Member States that violate the rights of Romani communities as well (as has been the case, e.g. with Italy and France in relation to forced evictions and fingerprinting) (Ferreira & Kostakopoulou, 2016, pp. 210–3).

Second, we advocate in favour of a hard law, Romani-specific legal tool—a Directive or a Regulation on combating antigypsyism and promoting substantial Romani inclusion. Depending on its exact scope, this legal act could address all of Sen's freedom categories, with specific emphasis on economic facilities, social opportunities, and protective security. This is an idea that had already been advanced by the European Union Network of Experts in Fundamental Rights (2004), and has more recently also been put forward by the European Parliament, which called on the Commission to submit a legislative proposal to protect the equality, inclusion and participation of Romani people, and combat antigypsyism, using Article 19(2) TFEU as a legal basis (European Parliament, 2020). As mentioned above, EU law and policy need to directly address antigypsyism as the root cause of the exclusion of Romani people in all EU Member States. While there have been a number of European Parliament resolutions, no form of binding legislation has been adopted to specifically address Romani rights and socio-economic well-being. A Romani-specific tool could avoid the dilution of Romani issues, which risks happening even if one uses mainstreaming as a policy tool. It is thus important to explore if and under what conditions could capabilities deprivation be addressed in a form of EU hard law. We argue that addressing antigypsyism requires new policies on Romani integration that not only engage Romani populations, but also tackle the prejudice that affects the majority population. Moreover, while anti-discrimination legislation protecting Romani communities is already in place, and the EU Race Directive has made efforts to address instances of antigypsyism,[12] there is a need for more effective legislation and policy that could incentivize the non-Romani population to recognize and tackle antigypsyism. To introduce a more effective legal tool, a potential EU Regulation or Directive should make it clear that antigypsyism is damaging not only to the Romani populations in Europe, but also to all EU citizens and residents. The next few paragraphs will describe how such legislation could look like considering Sen's capabilities approach.

The European Parliament's, 2020 proposal is framed quite broadly, including equal participation in all domains of public life and specific reference to language, arts, culture, and history of Romani people, in addition to the four main priority areas of education, employment, housing, and healthcare (European Parliament, 2020). We suggest going even further than this proposal in several respects. A new, Romani-specific binding legal tool could, for example, introduce a reward system that would not only punish antigypsyism but also promote long-term practices that successfully tackle antigypsyism and promote Romani inclusion (e.g. through tax incentives as will be illustrated below). This new legal tool should also render it

[12] See, for example, how the Court of Justice of the EU interpreted the Race Directive in CJEU, 2010, *CHEZ Razpredelenie Bulgaria AD v Komisia za zashtita ot diskriminatsia.*

compulsory that Member States report on their obligations deriving from the 2020 EU Roma Strategic Framework. Denmark, Luxembourg, and the Netherlands did not report to the European Commission on relevant measures in the context of the 2016 report, and apparently they did not face any consequences (European Commission, 2016). Legally binding extensive obligations need to be imposed on Member States to overcome the current shortcomings and enhance Romani capabilities. Relying on yet further "soft law" tools—like the Council has done in 2020—is clearly unsuitable to tackle the breadth and depth of the issues in question (Council of the European Union, 2021).

We also suggest using this new legal tool to broaden the scope of application of the Race Directive to protect Romani people in further spheres of life (beyond employment, education, social protection, social advantages, and access to goods and services) and possibly even introduce relevant positive discrimination measures. Indeed, mere non-discrimination is often insufficient: for example, if an employer has two equally qualified applicants, the employer does not need to justify the employment of a non-Romani over a Romani individual. Instead of simply relying on the right to access to employment, this new piece of legislation should create incentives for the employment of Romani individuals. For example, employers who employ Romani people with permanent contracts or develop long-term, sustainable employment strategies that benefit Romani people should be offered an incentive (e.g. more favourable tax provisions).

A piece of EU Romani-specific legislation could also engage with Sen's political freedoms. Besides being entitled to a Member State nationality, Romani people should be able to effectively use the rights attached to that nationality, such as freedom of speech, freedom of assembly, and right to vote. While these rights are already to a large extent protected by the ECHR and related jurisprudence, a binding EU piece of legislation tailored to the needs of the Romani people could help highlight specific concerns, enhance their protection, and increase penalties applicable for violations of these rights. In addition, the current Council Framework Decision 2008/913 on combating certain forms and expressions of racism and xenophobia by means of criminal law should also prohibit any crime committed with a discriminatory motive and include an obligation on states to investigate any allegation of discriminatory motive (Amnesty International, 2014, p. 31). Moreover, Romani people should enjoy the right to vote not just in theory but also in practice. The practice of political parties buying votes—a problem that exists in poorer Romani communities across the EU (Francelová, 2020; Jovanovic, 2014)—should be deemed as a serious criminal offence, where none currently exists and should attract more severe penalties than currently exist where certain ethnicities of voters are targeted. In addition, Romani individuals should be provided with training on how to effectively participate in democratic processes, since many are early leavers from school education.

This proposal for a new piece of hard law could be criticised on the basis that all other minorities could equally demand legislation addressing their particular concerns. The response to such an argument is that Romani people are unique as the only European non-territorial trans-border minority, and have suffered centuries of socio-economic deprivation and discrimination, which continue until this day. These characteristics render them more vulnerable and in need of a tailored legislative tool.

Our third and final point, targeted at Sen's transparency guarantees, is that there is an urgent need for tangible results, which can only be achieved with evaluation and monitoring undertaken by representatives of Romani communities themselves, as well as by experts on human rights with specific expertise on the position of Romani people (with such experts not outnumbering Romani stakeholders in such evaluation and monitoring processes). First and foremost amongst such processes, we recommend the evaluation of past conducts towards Romani people through a Romani Truth and Reconciliation Commission.

The European Parliament has made a similar recommendation, to be enacted both at an EU and Member State level (European Parliament, 2017, para 3–4). Subsequently, various Third Sector efforts have explored this proposal, especially in the context of the CHACHIPEN Project—"Paving the way for Truth and Reconciliation Process to address antigypsyism in Europe"—based on German, Swedish, Romanian, and Spanish case studies (Carballo-Mesa et al., 2023; Matache & Bhabha, 2021; Rostas et al., 2022). Although failing to provide details, the EU's post-2020 strategic framework for Romani inclusion indicates the Commission's intention to promote truth and reconciliation approaches under its citizens, equality, rights, and values programmes (European Commission, 2020a, p. 15). Similarly to various Truth and Reconciliation commissions around the world (e.g. Canada, South Africa), a Romani Truth and Reconciliation Commission in the EU could investigate the past and present occurrences of antigypsyism in different sectors and offer recommendations for new instruments, based on input from Romani communities themselves, laying the ground for better community relationships and diminishing antigypsyism. Truth and reconciliation approaches are suitable for expanding the capabilities of Romani in Europe because they recognise that future progress is hindered by a lack of remediation of past injustices. They involve "breaking of culture of suspicion, opening spaces in which people hear and can be heard" (Van Hout, 2021). For such efforts to be successful, however, lessons need to be learned from past experiences, namely by ensuring that such commission(s) are: operationally independent; embedded in Romani advocacy, representation, and ownership; approached as a long-lasting political process; aligned to international transitional justice standards; carefully planned and timed; sufficiently resourced and administratively supported; and capable of enforcing their recommendations (Carballo-Mesa et al., 2023). A Romani Truth and Reconciliation Commission designed and resourced according to the abovementioned principles could make significant strides in fostering openness and building trust between Romani and non-Romani communities, thus serving as a crucial foundation without which many other aspects of Romani people's capabilities are unlikely to successfully increase.

Conclusion

There has undoubtedly been some concerted effort at the EU level to improve the position of Romani people in the EU. Yet, studies have indicated that not much has changed, nor has the way in which Romani people are perceived by the majority population. At a general level, the EU's approach to improving the situation of Romani people employs weak tools of action. Since the 2000s, the combination of all EU efforts at policy and strategy level, and in particular those of the European Commission, has been argued to focus on four fronts: enhancing Romani representation; promoting better domestic policies; promoting the use of existing EU instruments for Romani inclusion; and inspiring societal change through awareness-raising (Vermeersch, 2012, p. 1202). However, these efforts have yielded little to no results in terms of effectuating significant improvements in the lives of Romani people (Bartlett et al., 2015; European Commission, 2018). Consequently, it would not be unfair to state that the EU has become no more than a platform to bring together civil society and government institutions, to debate and exchange best practices. The monitoring of Member State action plans has not made a difference on the ground, and the targets are superficial, lacking a foundational vision or direction, and provide no intrinsic motivation on the part of Member States to make a real effort towards Romani people. These policies have not offered the skills or the expertise to break through the deadlock that has been present in Europe on how to improve Romani people's lives. The European Commission's post-2020 strategy for Romani people is an improved strategy towards Romani empowerment. It entails a renewed emphasis on enforcing discrimination legislation, as well as a commitment to promoting effective equality, social inclusion, and participation of Romani people. It recognises the need to tackle antigypsyism. However, the strategy is not legally binding, and the EU remains in a monitoring role, which has thus far proved ineffective.

We trust that the multipronged strategy that we propose—based on greater use of Article 7 TEU and infringement procedures, the introduction of a hard law, Romani-specific measure, and the creation of a Romani Truth and Reconciliation Commission—has the potential to enhance the capabilities of Romani people in the EU. Each one of these measures corresponds to one or more of the capabilities as envisaged by Sen, namely political freedoms, economic facilities, social opportunities, transparency guarantees, and protective security. In combination with the EU Romani law and policy that already exist, we can achieve a powerful—even if far from perfect—legal and social network that empowers Romani people. As Heaney (1990, p. 77) notes:

> History says, *Don't hope*
> *On this side of the grave,*
> But then, once in a lifetime
> The longed-for tidal wave
> Of justice can rise up,
> And hope and history rhyme.

We are confident hope and history can rhyme for Romani people in the EU.

References

Ahmed, T. (2015). The many vulnerabilities of the Roma and the European Legal Framework. In F. Ippolito & S. Iglesias (Eds.), *Conceptualizing vulnerability in European law* (pp. 142–158). Hart Publishing.

Alliance against Antigypsyism. (2022). Working definition on antigypsyism. Alliance against Antigypsyism. Retrieved December 15, 2023, from https://antigypsyism.eu/reference-paper/#referencepaper-workingdefinition

Amnesty International. (2014). "We ask for justice": Europe's failure to protect Roma from racist violence. Retrieved December 15, 2023, from https://www.amnesty.org/en/documents/eur01/007/2014/en/

Amnesty International. (2018, July 26). Italy: Authorities defy European Court's ruling and render dozens of Roma homeless. Retrieved December 15, 2023, from https://www.amnesty.org/en/latest/news/2018/07/italy-authorities-defy-european-courts-ruling-and-render-dozens-of-roma-homeless/

Amnesty International. (2023). Hungary 2022. Retrieved December 15, 2023, from https://www.amnesty.org/en/countries/europe-and-central-asia/hungary/report-hungary/

Amnesty International UK. (2023). Briefing: Human rights on the margins—Roma in Europe, 2020. Retrieved December 15, 2023, from https://www.amnesty.org.uk/resources/demand-dignity-campaign-briefing-roma-europe

Andor, L. (2018). EU policy and Roma integration. *Journal of Poverty and Social Justice, 26*(1), 113–126.

Appel, H. (2023). Minority rights, the Roma, and neoliberal reform in EU accession. *Eastern European Politics, 40*, 21–42. https://doi.org/10.1080/21599165.2023.2180731

Arendt, H. (1968). *The origins of totalitarianism*. Houghton Mifflin Harcourt.

Barany, Z. (2000). The socio-economic impact of regime change in Eastern Europe: Gypsy marginality in the 1990s. *Eastern European Politics and Societies, 15*(1), 64.

Bartlett, W., Gordon, C., & Kamphuis, B. (2015). *Evaluation of the EU Framework for National Roma Integration Strategies*. European Parliament. Retrieved December 15, 2023, from http://www.lse.ac.uk/business-and-consultancy/consulting/assets/documents/evaluation-of-the-eu-framework-for-national-roma-integration-strategies.pdf

Beger, N. (2014, November 13). *Racism, segregation, and rejection: The reality for Romani children in The Czech Republic*. Amnesty International. Retrieved December 15, 2023, from https://www.amnesty.org/en/latest/campaigns/2014/11/racism-segregation-and-rejection-the-reality-for-romani-children-in-the-czech-republic/.

Carballo-Mesa, A., Carrera, S., Casermeiro Cortes, P., Rostas, I., Selling, J., & Stan, L. (2023). *Paving the way for truth and reconciliation process to address antigypsyism in Europe: Remembrance, recognition, justice and trust-building*. CEPS. Retrieved December 15, 2023, from https://antigypsyism.eu/wp-content/uploads/2023/07/Truth-and-Reconciliation-Process-to-Address-Antigypsyism-in-Europe.pdf

Carrera, S. (2013, June). *Shifting Responsibilities for EU Roma Citizens: The 2010 French affair on Roma evictions and expulsions continued*. CEPS Paper in Liberty and Security in Europe No. 55.

Carrera, S., Rostas, I., & Vosyliūtė, L. (2017). *Combating institutional anti-gypsyism: Responses and promising practices in the EU and selected member states*. CEPS. Retrieved December 15, 2023, from https://www.ceps.eu/ceps-publications/combating-institutional-anti-gypsyism-responses-and-promising-practices-eu-and-selected/

Charter of Fundamental Rights in the European Union. (2012). OJ C 326, p. 391. https://publications.europa.eu/resource/cellar/20e2519e-c2d9-4b23-86ed-7b65a7dd81ec.0007.03/DOC_1

Chiappero-Martinetti, E., Osmani, S., & Qizilbash, M. (Eds.). (2020). *The Cambridge handbook of the capability approach*. Cambridge University Press.

Chopin, I., Germaine, C. and Tanczos, J. (2017, September 5). *Roma and the enforcement of anti-discrimination law*. European Commission. Retrieved December 15, 2023, from https://publica-

tions.europa.eu/en/publication-detail/-/publication/cd62f9fe-92ae-11e7-b92d-01aa75ed71a1/language-en
CJEU. (2010). Court of Justice of the European Union, Case C-83/14, CHEZ Razpredelenie Bulgaria AD v Komisia za zashtita ot diskriminatsia, Judgment (Grand Chamber) of 16 July 2015 https://curia.europa.eu/juris/liste.jsf?num=C-83/14
Cortés Gómez, I. (2019). Escaping the labyrinth of Roma political representation: Reflections on common citizenship. In I. C. Gómez & M. End (Eds.), *Dimensions of Antigypsyism in Europe* (pp. 366–386). ENAR Anti-Racism in Focus 3, Central Council of German Sinti & Roma. Retrieved December 15, 2023, from https://eriac.org/wp-content/uploads/2021/01/CORTSG1.pdf
Council of Europe. (2016, October 20). The situation of roma and travellers in the context of rising extremism, xenophobia and the refugee crisis in Europe. CPL31 (2016)03final. Retrieved December 15, 2023, from https://rm.coe.int/168071 8bfd
Council of the European Union. (2013). Council Recommendation of 9 December 2013 on effective Roma integration measures in the Member States. 2013/C 378/01, OJ C 378, 24.12.2013, pp. 1–7.
Council of the European Union. (2021). Council recommendation of 12 March 2021 on Roma equality, inclusion and participation. 2021/C 93/01 (ST/6070/2021/INIT), OJ C 93, 19.3.2021, p. 1–14.
Directive 2000/43/EC. Council Directive 2000/43/EC of 29 June 2000 implementing the principle of equal treatment between persons irrespective of racial or ethnic origin [2000] OJ L 180, p. 22 ('Race Directive'), https://eur-lex.europa.eu/legal-content/EL/ALL/?uri=celex%3A32000L0043
Duez, J.-B. (2010). Europe is Afraid of its Roma. Retrieved 15 December 2023 from https://booksandideas.net/Europe-Is-Afraid-of-Its-Roma
ECRI – European Commission against Racism and Intolerance. (2011). ECRI General Policy Recommendation No 13 on Combating Anti-Gypsyism and Discrimination against Roma, CRI(2011)37rev, adopted on 24 June 2011 and amended on 1 December 2020, Strasbourg, December 2020. Retrieved December 15, 2023, from https://rm.coe.int/ecri-general-policy-recommendation-no-13-on-combating-anti-gypsyism-an/16808b5aee
ECtHR. (2011). European Court of Human Rights, *V.C. v. Slovakia*, Application no. 18968/07, Judgment of 8 November 2011, https://hudoc.echr.coe.int/fre#{%22itemid%22:[%22001-107364%22]}
European Commission. (2008). Communication from the Commission to the European Parliament, the Council, the European Economic and Social Committee and the Committee of the Regions—Renewed social agenda: Opportunities, access and solidarity in 21st century Europe, Brussels, 2.7.2008 COM(2008)412 final. Retrieved December 15, 2023, from https://eur-lex.europa.eu/legal-content/EN/TXT/PDF/?uri=CELEX:52008DC0412
European Commission. (2011). Communication from the Commission to the European Parliament, the Council, the European Economic and Social Committee and the Committee of the Regions: An EU Framework for National Roma Integration Strategies up to 2020, Brussels, 5.4.2011 COM(2011) 173 final.
European Commission. (2016). Communication from the Commission to the European Parliament, the Council, the European Economic and Social Committee and the Committee of the Regions: Assessing the implementation of the EU Framework for National Roma Integration Strategies and the Council Recommendation on effective Roma integration measures in the Member States — 2016 (COM (2016) 424, 27 June 2016.
European Commission. (2018). Communication from the Commission to the European Parliament and the Council Report on the evaluation of the EU Framework for National Roma Integration Strategies up to 2020, COM/2018/785 final.
European Commission. (2020a). Communication from the Commission to the European Parliament and the Council—A Union of Equality: EU Roma strategic framework for equality, inclusion and participation for 2002–2030 {SWD(2020) 530 final} Brussels, 7.10.2020 COM(2020) 620 final.

European Commission. (2020b). Proposal for a Council Recommendation on Roma equality, inclusion and participation {SWD(2020) 530} COM(2020) 621 final, Brussels, 7.10.2020.

European Commission. (2020c). Overview of the impact of coronavirus measures on the marginalised Roma communities in the EU. Retrieved December 15, 2023, from https://commission.europa.eu/system/files/2020-05/overview_of_covid19_and_roma_-_impact_-_measures_-_priorities_for_funding_-_23_04_2020.docx.pdf

European Commission. (2022, December 15). European Roma Platform & Roma Summits. Retrieved December 15, 2023, from https://commission.europa.eu/strategy-and-policy/policies/justice-and-fundamental-rights/combatting-discrimination/roma-eu/european-roma-platform-roma-summits

European Commission. (2023, April 19). The European Commission decides to refer Slovakia to the Court of Justice of the European Union for not sufficiently addressing discrimination against Roma children at school. Retrieved December 15, 2023, from https://ec.europa.eu/commission/presscorner/detail/EN/IP_23_2249

European Council. (2000). Lisbon European Council, 23 and 24 March 2000: Presidency Conclusions. Retrieved December 15, 2023, from https://www.europarl.europa.eu/summits/lis1_en.htm

European Court of Auditors. (2016, June 28). Special Report no 14/2016: EU policy initiatives and financial support for Roma integration: significant progress made over the last decade, but additional efforts needed on the ground. From https://www.eca.europa.eu/en/Pages/DocItem.aspx?did=36850

European Parliament. (2017). Resolution of 25 October 2017 on fundamental rights aspects in Roma integration in the EU: fighting anti-Gypsyism (2017/2038(INI)).

European Parliament. (2020). Implementation of National Roma Integration Strategies: combating negative attitudes towards people with Romani background in Europe (2020/2011(INI)), Resolution of 17 September 2020 (P9_TA(2020)0229).

European Roma Rights Centre. (2017). *Statelessness, Discrimination and Marginalisation of Roma in the Western Balkans and Ukraine*. Retrieved December 15, 2023, from http://www.errc.org/uploads/upload_en/file/roma-belong.pdf

European Union Network of Experts in Fundamental Rights. (2004). *Report on the situation of fundamental rights in the European Union for 2003*. European Commission - Directorate General of Justice and Home Affairs.

Ferreira, N. (2019). A Roma European crisis road-map: A holistic answer to a complex problem. In T. Magazzini & S. Piemontese (Eds.), *Constructing Roma migrants: European narratives and local governance* (pp. 31–49). Springer.

Ferreira, N., & Kostakopoulou, D. (2016). The Roma and European Union citizenship: In search of a humane answer from the EU. In N. Ferreira & D. Kostakopoulou (Eds.), *The human face of the European Union: Are EU law and policy humane enough?* (pp. 206–234). Cambridge University Press.

Findor, A., Hruška, M., Hlatky, R., Hrustič, T., & Bošeľová, Z. (2023). Equality, reciprocity, or need? Bolstering welfare policy support for marginalized groups with distributive fairness. *American Political Science Review, 117*(3), 805–821.

Fischer, G. (2018). Does the EU framework for Roma integration promote the human rights of Romani persons in the union? In C. Strohal, S. Kieber, W. Benedek, P. Czech, L. Heschl, K. Lukas, & M. Nowak (Eds.), *European yearbook on human rights 2018* (pp. 167–192) Intersentia.

FRA – EU Fundamental Rights Agency. (2018). Fundamental Rights Report 2018. Retrieved December 15, 2023, from https://fra.europa.eu/sites/default/files/fra_uploads/fra-2018-fundamental-rights-report-2018_en.pdf

FRA – EU Fundamental Rights Agency. (2019). Fundamental Rights Report 2019. Retrieved December 15, 2023, from https://fra.europa.eu/en/publications-and-resources/publications/annual-reports/fundamental-rights-2019

FRA – EU Fundamental Rights Agency. (2020). Roma and travellers in six countries. Retrieved December 15, 2023, from https://fra.europa.eu/sites/default/files/fra_uploads/fra-2020-roma-travellers-six-countries_en.pdf

Framework Decision 2008/913/JHA. Council Framework Decision 2008/913/JHA of 28 November 2008 on combating certain forms and expressions of racism and xenophobia by means of criminal law OJ L 328, p. 55, https://eur-lex.europa.eu/legal-content/EL/TXT/?uri=CELEX%3A32008F0913

Francelová, N.H. (2020, February 14). *2020 election sees unprecedented mobilisation of Roma*. The Slovak Spectator. Retrieved December 15, 2023, from https://spectator.sme.sk/c/22325176/roma-minority-in-slovakia-before-election-of-2020.html

Franz, R. (2020, October 8). *Why EU's new Roma strategy is welcome, but toothless*. EU Observer. Retrieved December 15, 2023, from https://euobserver.com/opinion/149677

General Assembly Resolution 217 A, https://www.un.org/en/development/desa/population/migration/generalassembly/docs/globalcompact/A_RES_217(III).pdf.

Guy, W. (2009). EU initiatives on Roma: Limitations and way forward. In N. Sigona & N. Trehan (Eds.), *Romani politics in contemporary: Europe, poverty, ethnic mobilisation and the neoliberal order* (pp. 23–50). Palgrave Macmillan.

Heaney, S. (1990). *The cure at Troy: A version of Sophocles' Philoctetes*. Faber.

Iusmen, I. (2018). 'Non multa, sed multum': EU Roma policy and the challenges of Roma inclusion. *Journal of European Integration, 40*(4), 427–441.

Jovanovic, Z. (2014, May 22). *The power of the ballot box for Roma in Europe*. Open Society Foundations. Retrieved December 15, 2023, from https://www.opensocietyfoundations.org/voices/power-ballot-box-roma-europe

Koslerova, A. (2021, May 20). *Authorities don't treat Roma like ordinary citizens*. Al Jazeera. Retrieved December 15, 2023, from https://www.aljazeera.com/news/2021/5/20/authorities-dont-treat-roma-like-ordinary-citizens

La Parra-Casado, D., Solheim, E. F., & Estévez, J. F. (2023). Health inequalities between Roma and non-Roma populations in Europe: A study of 118,834 individuals combining the UNDP Roma and the EU-SILC surveys. *Scandinavian Journal of Public Health, 51*(3), 347–356.

Lecerf, M. (2021, March). *The impact of the coronavirus crisis on Roma and travellers*. European Parliament Research Service. Retrieved December 15, 2023, from https://www.europarl.europa.eu/RegData/etudes/ATAG/2021/690524/EPRS_ATA(2021)690524_EN.pdf

Matache, M., & Bhabha, J. (2021). The Roma case for reparations. In J. Bhabha, M. Matache, & C. Elkins (Eds.), *Time for reparations (Chapter 15)*. University of Pennsylvania Press.

McGarry, A. (2011). The dilemma of the European Union's Roma policy. *Critical Social Policy, 32*(1), 126–136.

Möschel, M. (2012). Is the European Court of Human Rights' Case Law on Anti-Roma Violence "beyond reasonable doubt"? *Human Rights Law Review, 12*(3), 479–507.

Moschovidis, M. (2022). The Fundamental Right Agency's influence in reforming EU Roma policy. *International Journal of Roma Studies, 4*(2), 92–117.

New, W., & Kyuchukov, H. (2018). Language education for Romani children: Human rights and capabilities approaches. *European Education, 50*(4), 371–384. https://doi.org/10.1080/10564934.2017.1401437

Parker, O. (2012). Roma and the politics of EU citizenship in France: Everyday security and resistance. *JCMS: Journal of Common Market Studies, 50*(3), 475–491.

Pollák, P. (2022, May 31). *Progress of infringement cases against Slovakia, Czechia and Hungary concerning discrimination against Roma children in their education systems*. Parliamentary Questions. Retrieved December 15, 2023, from https://www.europarl.europa.eu/doceo/document/E-9-2022-001989_EN.html

Popova, Z. (2014, March). Roma inclusion: A feasible EU project? *EMCI Working Paper, 75*, 1–24. Retrieved December 15, 2023, from https://www.ecmi.de/fileadmin/redakteure/publications/pdf/ECMI_Working_Paper_75.pdf

Ram, M. H. (2012). Lost in transition? Europeanization and the Roma. *L'Europe en Formation, 364*(2), 417–434.

Ram, M. H. (2022). European Union Roma policy: Under construction. In T. H. Malloy & B. Vizi (Eds.), *Research handbook on minority politics in the European Union* (pp. 250–266). Edward Elgar.

Richardson, J., & Codona, J. (2018). Blame and fear: Roma in the UK in a changing Europe. *Journal of Poverty and Social Justice, 26*(1), 95.

Roma Health Network. (2022). *Roma health and housing: Filling in the gaps — A policy paper by the Roma health network.* European Public Health Alliance. Retrieved December 15, 2023, from https://epha.org/roma-health-and-housing-filling-in-the-gaps/

Rorke, B. (2021, June 24). *Outrage grows following the death of "the Romani George Floyd" in the Czech Republic.* European Roma Rights Centre. Retrieved December 15, 2023, from http://www.errc.org/news/outrage-grows-following-the-death-of-the-romani-george-floyd-in-the-czech-republic

Rorke, B., & Lee, J. (2020). *Roma rights in the time of COVID.* European Roma Rights Centre. Retrieved December 15, 2023, from http://www.errc.org/uploads/upload_en/file/5265_file1_roma-rights-in-the-time-of-covid..pdf

Rostas, I. (2020). The EU Framework and its implementation in Hungary. *Journal of Contemporary European Studies, 29*(1), 60–72.

Rostas, I., Vosyliūtė, L., & Kalotay, M. (2022). *State of the art report: Transitional justice for Roma in Europe.* CHACHIPEN. Retrieved December 15, 2023, from https://antigypsyism.eu/wp-content/uploads/2022/08/May-20_2022_Transitional-Justice-for-Roma-in-Europe_FINAL-SoA-report-formated_MODIF.pdf

Ryder, A., Taba, M., & Trehan, N. (Eds.). (2021). *Romani communities and transformative change: A new social Europe.* Bristol University Press.

Sardelić, J. (2017). The position and agency of the "irregularized": Romani migrants as European semi-citizens. *Politics, 37*(3), 332–346.

Sardelić, J. (2021). *The fringes of citizenship, Romani minorities in Europe and Civic Marginalisation.* Manchester University Press.

Scheppele, K. L., Kochenov, D. V., & Grabowska-Moroz, B. (2020). EU values are law, after all: Enforcing EU values through systemic infringement actions by the European Commission and the Member States of the European Union. *Yearbook of European Law, 39*, 3–121.

Sen, A. (1980). Equality of what? (1979 Tanner Lecture at Stanford). In S. M. McMurrin (Ed.), *Tanner lectures on human values* (pp. 197–220). University of Utah Press.

Sen, A. (1984). *Resources, values and development.* Harvard University Press.

Sen, A. (1993). Capability and well-being. In M. Nussbaum & A. Sen (Eds.), *The quality of life.* Clarendon. (Oxford Scholarship Online, 2003).

Sen, A. (2001). *Development as freedom.* Oxford University Press.

Sen, A. (2010). *The idea of justice.* Penguin Books.

Sigona, N., & Monasta, L. (2006). *Cittadinanze imperfette.* Edizioni Spartaco.

Sigona, N., & Vermeersch, P. (2012). Editors' introduction. The Roma in the New EU: Policies, frames and everyday experiences. *Journal of Ethnic and Migration Studies, 38*(8), 1189–1193.

Simhandl, K. (2009). Beyond boundaries? Comparing the construction of the political categories "Gypsies" and "Roma" before and after EU enlargement. In N. Sigona & N. Trehan (Eds.), *Romani politics in contemporary Europe* (pp. 72–93). Palgrave Macmillan.

Szilvasi, M., & Saitovic-Jovanovic, M. (2023). Social accountability and legal empowerment initiatives: Improving the health of underserved Roma communities in Eastern Europe. *Health Human Rights, 25*(1), 67–79.

Treaty on European Union, Consolidated Version. (2012). OJ C 326, p. 13, https://eur-lex.europa.eu/legal-content/EN/ALL/?uri=OJ%3AC%3A2012%3A326%3ATOC

Treaty on the Functioning of the European Union, Consolidated Version [2008] OJ C 115, p. 13, https://eur-lex.europa.eu/LexUriServ/LexUriServ.do?uri=OJ:C:2008:115:0013:0045:EN:PDF

UNDP. (2015). *Decade of Roma inclusion progress report, 2015.* Retrieved December 15, 2023, from https://www.eurasia.undp.org/content/rbec/en/home/library/roma/decade-of-roma-inclusion%2D%2Dprogress-report.html

UNDP. (2017). *Regional brief 2017: The roots of poverty among the Roma*. Retrieved December 15, 2023, from https://www.eurasia.undp.org/content/rbec/en/home/library/roma/roma-programming%2D%2Dregional-brief-2017.html

Van Hout, B. (2021, March 29), *Closing Remarks at 50th International Roma Day Towards justice and building trust*. OHCHR. Retrieved 20 December 2024, from https://europe.ohchr.org/resources/speeches/50th-international-roma-day

Van Hout, B., Hrabanova, G., Montano Pena, G., Rose, R., and Post, S. (2019, March 21). *Time for truth, recognition and reconciliation for Roma in Europe*. EURACTIV. Retrieved December 15, 2023, from https://www.euractiv.com/section/justice-home-affairs/opinion/time-for-truth-recognition-and-reconciliation-for-roma-in-europe/

Vermeersch, P. (2012). Reframing the Roma: EU initiatives and the politics of reinterpretation. *Journal of Ethnic and Migration Studies, 38*(8), 1195–1212.

Vermeersch, P. (2014). The European Union and the Roma: An analysis of recent institutional and policy developments. In T. H. Malloy & J. Marko (Eds.), *Minority governance in and beyond Europe* (pp. 199–216). Brill Nijhoff.

VoRAE – Voice of Roma, Ashkali and Egyptians in Kosovo. (2020, October 13). Will the new EU Roma strategic framework make a difference? Retrieved December 15, 2023, from https://www.vorae.org/en/a/will-the-new-eu-roma-strategic-framework-make-a-difference

Beyond Recognition? Locating "Roma Representation" in Italy and Spain

Tina Magazzini

Abstract

Identity politics are among the most compelling and criticized issues in contemporary politics as well as scholarly debates, where the recognition paradigm has been challenged, revisited, and critiqued over the past few decades. As a way of trying to look at how issues of recognition and representation play out in different settings for the same minority, this chapter offers an overview of how Roma minority participation has factored into the policies addressed at their "integration" in Italy and Spain since the establishment of the first EU Framework for National Roma Integration Strategies. By drawing upon extensive fieldwork carried out as part of my PhD thesis, this chapter looks at the role that Roma's participation played in the policies aimed to "integrate" this part of the population in two different, yet comparable contexts. What emerges is a significantly different approach in the two settings, yet in both cases, failings are political in nature. "Plugging" participation as a top-down requirement, based on an ethnic dimension that is never explicitly articulated nor is reflected in civil society organizations, seems in both cases to lead to processes of misrecognition, rather than representation.

Introduction

Minority representation, the governance of diversity, and struggles for recognition have dominated the political landscape for decades (Hobson, 2003; Malik, 2023). Contrary to some predictions, multiculturalism, identity politics, and recognition

T. Magazzini (✉)
Department of Mobility and Migration, Czech Academy of Sciences, Institute of Ethnology, Prague, Czechia
e-mail: magazzini@eu.cas.cz

D. Anagnostopoulou (ed.), *European Identities, Inclusion and Equality*, Diversity and Inclusion Research, https://doi.org/10.1007/978-3-031-90602-2_10

struggles have not only remained central to equality debates, but the backlash to the recognition paradigm has turned into its own subfield of sorts (Zambory, 2020; Sealy, 2025).

Regardless of whether the attempts to overcome the shortcomings of recognition have focused on increasing diversity as the result of migration processes—such as super-diversity (Vertovec, 2007; Magazzini, 2017)—or on structures of power and discrimination—such as intersectionality (Crenshaw, 1989; Collins & Bilge, 2020)—a widespread concern is that "*With the rise of identity politics, antagonistic groups have struggled for recognition and expanded social divisions among the people, which has led to a representation crisis*" (Guo & Hu, 2019, p. 272). In other words, one of the main criticisms to the recognition paradigm has not been to the concept itself, but rather to its implementation: if "access" to recognition relies on establishing a position of victimhood, how can we avoid competition among disadvantaged groups for it? Who gets to decide which minorities should be recognized, especially when such recognition is tied to some form of representation? Nation-states, international organizations, regional bodies? And based on which criteria?

Against this backdrop, the politics of Romani identity in Europe offers an emblematic case to explore some of the challenges of minority recognition and representation in a continent that typically shies away from positive action measures (Kostka, 2018; Rostas, 2019; Magazzini, 2021). By drawing from research conducted for my doctoral research on the National Roma Integration Strategies in Italy and Spain, which included 32 interviews with policymakers and stakeholders, and aimed at problematizing integration policies themselves and the understanding of the "Roma issue" that informs such policies, rather than the Roma (Magazzini, 2018), this chapter hopes to contribute to ongoing debates on the crisis of recognition. More specifically, it aims to explore the entanglements between recognition and representation and to speak to the Critical Romani Studies literature that over the past years has been shifting the focus from the exceptionality of Roma exclusion to the study of discriminatory policies and of inclusion/exclusion mechanisms more broadly (Kostka, 2015; Yildiz & De Genova, 2018; van Baar & Kóczé, 2020; Dolabela & Fotta, 2021). By tracing the ways in which Roma-targeted policies emerged in recent years in two Mediterranean countries (Italy and Spain) and problematizing how such processes took place from the viewpoint of policymakers (Bacchi, 2009), I look at what Nancy Fraser called the danger of political "misrecognition" of a minority. By misrecognition, Fraser identifies the social subordination of a group, in the sense of a minority being prevented from participating as a peer in social life: her suggestion to address the problem of a group not being afforded the same status as the rest of society is "a politics aimed at overcoming subordination by establishing the misrecognized party as a full member of society, capable of participating on a par with the rest," which can take different forms depending on the context (Fraser, 2000, p.113). In order to understand which participation mechanisms are at play in the two case studies and what other participation might be possible, I start by providing a brief overview of how the recognition and representation of Roma became a political issue in the EU since the early 2010s.

Roma Recognition and Representation in the European Union

In its 2011 Communication, the European Commission committed itself to help promote Roma participation and representation at regional and national levels, stating that:

> The efforts of countries to improve the social and economic inclusion of Roma through strengthening the involvement of civil society by encouraging institutionalized dialogues with Roma representatives to become involved and take responsibility for policy formulation, implementation, and monitoring on regional, national and local level (European Commission, 2011, p. 13).

The idea that Roma integration required a set of measures that explicitly (even though not exclusively) targeted this ethnic minority was justified by the acknowledgment that many of the estimated 10–12 million Roma in Europe face prejudice, discrimination, and social exclusion in their daily lives (European Commission, 2011, p. 1; Magazzini & Piemontese, 2016).

In line with the EU Framework for *National Roma Integration Strategies up to 2020*, by March 2012 all Member States had presented a National Roma Integration Strategy or a corresponding set of policy measures within their broader social inclusion policies. However, since most European countries do not include ethnicity in their census and have color-blind social policies (Magazzini, 2024), each country dealt with the issue of recognition in its own way, i.e., how to identify the Roma to be "integrated"—and that of representation and participation: who to choose as interlocutors among the Roma.

The above-mentioned Communication by the European Commission stressed that *"concerned stakeholders, especially representatives of the Roma communities, should have the possibility to play a role in the European Framework for National Roma Integration Strategies"* (European Commission, 2011, p. 9). Yet, the lack of specific mechanisms or requirements resulted in a wide-ranging diversity of processes in different countries and regions. The upcoming sections look at how Italy and Spain, respectively—two Southern European countries with a similar institutional framework and a relatively recent immigration history, diverse Roma populations (particularly in terms of nationality)—have framed the issue of Roma recognition and representation.

The Politics of Roma Recognition and Representation in Italy

In Italy, the 2012 National Roma Integration Strategy was drafted by the Office for Anti-Racial Discrimination (UNAR henceforth), a body created in 2003 when the EC Race Equality Directive 2000/43 was transposed in Italian legislation through Legislative Decree 215/2003 (Italian Government, Decreto Legislativo 9/7/, 2003 n° 215). The UNAR, which remains the National Focal Point for Roma Integration, claimed that it involved in the process *"those institutional actors and associations being the most relevant to socio-economic policies and services for the Roma, Sinti, and Caminanti communities*" (National Office on Anti-Racial Discriminations National Focus Point, 2012, p. 28).

To achieve its aims, it organized a structure in which several Ministries and Municipalities were represented (Interior, Justice, Labor and Social Policies, Education, University and Research, Health, the Conference of Regions' Presidents, the National Association of Italy's Municipalities, the Union of the Italian Provinces). An exchange with some Roma associations was initiated by posting on the UNAR website a public call "*for those relevant stakeholders interested in participating in future Tables to be set up at the regional, provincial and municipal levels*" in 2011 (National Office on Anti-Racial Discriminations National Focus Point, 2012, p. 29).

However, while 94 Roma or pro-Roma organizations registered to the open call launched by UNAR between December 2011 and March 14, 2012, many of them subsequently complained that they were not involved in shaping the Strategy and were given only a few days to read the Strategy and provide feedback before it was sent to the European Commission. On February 22, 2012, the Roma association "Federazione Romaní" published a post titled "General Observations to the draft of the national strategy for the Roma population" stating that it had only been given five days between the draft being made available to them and the meeting organized by UNAR to consult and include Roma's feedback on the Strategy. The observations made by the Federation noted that Roma participation was only included marginally in the National Roma Integration Strategy and that the main decisional bodies in charge of defining the policies and the target indicators included no Roma representatives (Federazione Romani, 2012).

How was the process of Roma recognition and representation—or of locating the relevant stakeholders—on behalf of the authorities carried out? According to the (non-Roma) policymaker in charge of creating the list of eligible associations with a consultative status for the Italian Strategy, the involvement of Roma and pro-Roma associations was encouraged to the best of UNAR's capacity, despite some administrative hurdles:

> We immediately made a call to create a list of associations interested in the subject, or representatives of the Roma themselves, but they had to have some basic requirements: thus, for example, the founder [of the association] of course had to have a clean criminal record, they had to be registered as a legal entity, etc. Between December 2011 and March 2012, 96 associations registered: 12 or 13 were national associations, and 7 or 8 were constituted by Roma people. We had to exclude 2 of the 96 associations. One of the two exclusions was Roma, but unfortunately, they submitted their application late, and we had to respect the rules[1]...the second case was excluded because the person who registered with his association had no legal entity, he had just invented an association from scratch, so it was of course excluded. So that's the context. The list of these 94 registered associations was then shared

[1] It is noteworthy that while all strategies were supposed to be submitted by Member States to the European Commission by the end of 2011, the Italian strategy was submitted with a three-month delay.

> with the then-president of the Conferenza Stato-Regioni[2] responsible for policies concerning the Roma –we are talking of 2012– and he in turn shared it with the Regions, since the Regional Tables for the Inclusion and Integration of the Roma were being created. As of today, there are 10 Regional Tables in 20 Regions (Interview with the author, August 2015, own translation).

The role, scope, structure, and composition of such Regional Tables, as well as the role of the organizations that participated in them, is, however, not clearly defined in the Strategy, where they are mentioned as both sites of "awareness raising" as well as platforms in charge of developing—in coordination with UNAR—the Local/Regional Inclusion Plans for Roma and Sinti. According to the same interviewee, who was in charge of the participatory dimension of the National Strategy, the practice of the Regional Tables seemed in hindsight to not have worked as initially envisioned:

> The thing is, with the Lazio Regional Table, for instance, when it was first constituted it started out with this approach: "We are open to all, any association who wants to join can do so!" And from a point of view of transparency, it would be ideal to allow everyone to participate: but so many organizations joined that it was simply not manageable. So, we had to put some barriers, some rules, to decide who to include and who not, otherwise it would have been a mess. (Interview with author, August 2015, own translation).

In the Emilia-Romagna region, where a Regional Plan for the Integration of Roma was approved in 2015, following the guidelines of the National Strategy, a (non-Roma) policymaker involved in the strategy described the issue of Roma recognition and representation in the following way:

> Direct involvement is not an easy thing to achieve. We are talking about communities who have never sought representation within the institutions, just as the institutions have never felt any responsibility to represent these communities. The administration has dealt with them [Roma]—if at all—as elements external to the population, either to be 'saved' through humanitarian actions or avoided altogether. (Interview with author, March 2015, own translation).

According to the Rome-based watchdog NGO Associazione 21 Luglio, which was charged by the European Commission with drafting a shadow report of the Italian NRIS, the representation and participation of Roma minorities in the policies addressed to them were also impaired by wider political and corruption issues. In the words of the (non-Roma) NGO's founder and director:

> While the bosses [of Mafia Capitale] have been removed, the system—which is a criminal system—still stands. It is the system itself that must be replaced. I am talking about a system that over the past twenty years has been invested in segregating the Roma and generating a huge revenue, both economic and in terms of political consensus. This system operates

---

[2] The Permanent Conference for relations between the state, the regions and the autonomous provinces of Trento and Bolzano (also known as the State-Regions Conference) is a collegial body created in 1983 aimed at fostering institutional collaboration and communication between the state and local governments.

> through political references, mainly city councilors and in certain cases deputies, who favor friends who in turn guarantee a certain number of votes for them. [...] What role does representation play in all this? This system is aimed at keeping the Roma segregated and relies on internal "kapo" figures, which are alleged Roma representatives, so the whole system runs smoothly. There is always one, or more than one, bosses in each camp, who are the same "representatives" that have meetings with the assessors, the mayors, and which are unscrupulous persons...above and beyond their criminal records, these are people whose job it is to oppress the Roma community inside the camps, and then give a different image to the outside. (Interview with author, July 2015, own translation).

Similarly, according to a (non-Roma) policymaker in charge of designing a Roma integration plan for the city of Rome:

> In Rome there is no such thing as 'Roma representatives'. It is well known that those who like to identify themselves in this way, represent nothing but their own personal interests, and, amazingly, it is still the very same people that were doing so ten years ago. For this reason, my proposal to the Department for Social Policies has been to do away with the Regional Roma Table altogether, since there is no Roma representation in Rome: we should work on an individual basis with each Roma family instead. [...] Of course, I was asked to square the circle, and in the end we will have to keep the Regional Table on Roma Integration because it's included in the National Strategy, but what I will make sure happens from now on is that those associations that take part to the Table will no longer be able to participate to the Municipality's tenders. Because one cannot first make policy suggestions, and then be the one to implement them, as was common practice until now: there's a huge conflict of interest. (email follow-up with an interviewee working in the Social Policies Department of the municipality of Rome, December 2016, own translation).

Even though Rome's "camps system" has been replicated elsewhere, not everywhere in Italy is the situation the same as in the capital, where the size of the population and the concentration of Ministries and political power complicate matters. Different issues are, however, often present. For instance, in Trento, an autonomous province in northern Italy, a local policymaker who had pushed for the adoption of legislation to favor the integration of Sinti and Roma residing in the province of Trento (previously to the National Strategy) did not encounter strong opposition by the main parties. In fact, the legislation was approved by a compact majority, even though the linguistic minorities (Ladin, Mocheni, Cimbro, and German speakers) all voted against it. Sadly, the legislation never translated into concrete policy actions because the responsibilities and the division of tasks remained unclear, which resulted in different administrative departments blaming each other, the political climate, administrative obstacles, and sometimes, even the Roma themselves.

In different regions, several open discussions and hearings on Roma inclusion policies were organized by public bodies after the approval of the National Strategy, but only a few Roma took part in such debates. The few Italian Roma activists who had the means to make their opinions known often expressed their frustration with the majority–minority power dynamics and with the lack of Roma representation in those forums where issues that directly impact their life take place. Radames

Gabrielli, the General Secretary of an association that was established in 2007 and comprises 28 Roma organizations ("Rom e Sinti Insieme"), posted a commentary in 2013 on the website of the association that expresses such feelings:

> On Tuesday, September 17th [2013] I participated in a congress promoted by the Italian Senate of the Republic and the association "21 luglio" at Palazzo Giustiniani, in Rome. Minister Cècile Kyenge, senator Luigi Manconi, senator Francesco Palermo, anthropologist Ulderico Daniele, Jurist Aurora Sordini, professor Paolo Bonetti, and the president of the association "21 luglio" Carlo Stasolla, were all there. These are all people I hold in high esteem, but that even though they work for the betterment of the lives of Roma and Sinti, did not think of inviting even one single Roma or Sinto as a speaker to this important event. Not only did the organizers not invite any Roma to intervene, but they did not even invite them to participate: I, an Italian Sinto, was only invited by senator Palermo because I had met him a few days before. Had that not been the case, I probably would not have even found out about the event. The issues debated at the congress were extremely important for all Roma and Sinti, but the conference room was filled with representatives of the majority culture, with only five Roma amongst the audience. I, as president of the association "Nevo Drom" and as General Secretary of the "Rom e Sinti Insieme" Federation, deplore this attitude in which the future of Roma and Sinti is debated and decided without the full participation of us directly affected. They do not call on us, they do not invite us to explain our reasons, and yet they continue to talk about us in conferences and debates... (Gabrielli, 2013).

The National Project Officer of the Italian chapter of ROMACT, Serbian-Italian Roma activist Dijana Pavlovic, expressed similar views on numerous occasions, which eventually led her to become involved in politics (coming from a career in acting) and to launch, in 2015, the campaign "If you recognize me, you respect me" in favor of the recognition of Roma as a national minority in Italy: *"They [academics and politicians] only talk about us when they talk about camps, poverty, and crime. But we are a people and want to be recognized as such. We are not here for academics to write essays on poverty."* (Strasbourg, March 2015, conversation with the author, own translation). However, the initiative did not reach the 50.000 signatures threshold necessary for it to be brought before Parliament.

This picture is rendered even more complex by the fragmentation and, at times, contradictions of the Roma organizations themselves, many of which call for more Roma recognition and participation, but often with criteria based on "expertise," which has been the keyword used in the political narrative at the European level. Nazzareno Guarnieri, the Romani president of the "Federazione Romanì" since 2009, has argued for years that what is needed is a shift from cultural mediation to participation. Yet, after years of campaigning, Roma participation in politics remains limited at best and instrumentalized at worst, as a statement on the organization's official webpage acknowledges:

> To be Roma does not automatically mean that one is an expert. In Italy, most of the projects and initiatives carried out with the active participation of Roma people or Roma associations show that the active participation model of the Roma, often backed and supported by the institutions, has not produced (or even proposed) a radical change that is beneficial to

> improve the social, cultural, and political situation of the Romani minority. (Radio interview, own translation).[3]

Overall, despite Italy's National Roma Integration Strategy having been in place for over a decade, to date the situation of Roma and Sinti's presence in Italian institutions and their political participation does not seem to have changed significantly from the one predating the National Strategy (Alietti & Riniolo, 2019), nor has the new Strategy (2021–2030) radically changed this paradigm. Moreover, the high visibility of the so-called "Gypsy problem" operates alongside, and in synergy with, the invisibility of Roma and Sinti as political subjects (Sigona & Treheran, 2009, p. 274; Magazzini, 2020). As a result, political parties in Italy tend not to engage with Roma issues, unless it means opportunities for promoting securitization policies and blame placing, such as the sensationalization of what is portrayed as "Roma crime," mainly but not exclusively by the two extreme right-wing parties Fratelli d'Italia and Lega Nord (Ivasiuc, 2022; McMahon, 2015).

The Politics of Roma Recognition and Representation in Spain

In Spain, the picture appears to be quite different. While Italy scrambled to put together a National Strategy in response to Brussels's requests, Spain had already developed a participatory methodology in its 2010–2012 Action Plan for the Development of the Roma Population, which predated and in many ways inspired the NRIS. This type of methodology involved the consultation, through meetings and shared documents, of eight Ministries, as well as of the Autonomous Communities (or regions), the Spanish Federation of Provinces and Municipalities, and "the most representative Roma entities" (Spanish Government, Ministerio de Sanidad Servicios Sociales e Igualdad de España, 2012, p. 50). Additionally, the State Council of the Roma People was a party to the process since its inception.

The Annex I of the first Spanish Strategy is quite comprehensive in listing the associations and departments involved in the process of the elaboration of the Strategy, including the names of the 20 Roma or pro-Roma organizations consulted in the process (while a similar list is not included in the Italian Strategy). Additionally, Annex III lists all the existing plans and bodies specifically targeting the Roma—at the time, five regional plans (Extremadura, Basque Country, Andalusia, Catalonia, and Navarra), the State Council of the Roma People, the Action Plan for the Development of the Roma Population 2010–2012, the Roma Development Programme, and the Roma Cultural Institute.

The issue of Roma recognition and the debate around which entities constitute "the most representative Roma entities" is, however, quite controversial in the Spanish context as well, and there has been an ongoing animosity within the Roma communities, as well as between the diverse, and differentially powerful, Roma

[3] Radio interview available (in Italian) at https://www.radioradicale.it/scheda/309762/intervista-al-presidente-della-federazione-romani-nazzareno-guarnieri-sulla-politica

organizations that compete for funding when it comes to integration projects and actions.

Despite the declaration of inclusive processes outlined in all Roma plans and in the National Strategy, all the interviewed (mostly non-Roma) Spanish policymakers agreed that Roma participation in public life, in government institutions, and even in the drafting of those policies that affect them directly is scarce and nowhere near what it should be. To the question of whether they considered the participation of Roma individuals and communities in the development of Roma-targeted policies to be satisfactory, the typical response was "*No, it is not. There are very few Roma men and women who participate in decision-making spaces*" (interview with author, October 2014, own translation). When asked for suggestions on how to improve such participation, the answers were, overall, well-intentioned but hinting at the need for socio-economic improvement, rather than one in cultural recognition or political representation. One social worker commented, for instance:

> Representation could improve through trainings for Roma mediators, involving them in the development of actions that improve and raise awareness of the situation in which they are, and of course improving the employment aspects that would facilitate their participation (Interview with author, October 2014, own translation);

while a civil servant stated:

> Roma participation is indeed weak, but so is civil society in general. On the one hand, it is crucial for the [Roma] associations to have an institutional backing with measures of control and technical support, marking clear lines of actions and demands. On the other hand, it is necessary for minorities to receive better training and higher standards of living (Interview with author, October 2014, own translation).

The issue of "better training"—just like the abovementioned issue of "expertise"—is one that was recurrent in discussions regarding the needs of the (Spanish) Roma population and the possibility of involving more Roma in social projects and programs. The local administrations seemed to distinguish starkly different "kinds" of Roma: the "trained" ones who belonged to associations and could be involved as a constructive (or acquiescent) interlocutor and those who were not "trained" or who were too highly critical of the policies designed for them, and finally the foreign Roma who were often left out of targeted measures because of linguistic and/or residential requirements.

A Romani member of the State Council of the Roma People argued that political parties did not promote the involvement of Roma among their representatives, which hampered both the image of the Roma and that of the integration measures. The result was that the presence of Roma activists or representatives involved in proposing measures, designing policies, or voting and holding decisional power over the final outcomes was meager. In the words of a (non-Roma) policymaker:

> While in other groups there are such things as participation councils where civil society has the capacity to propose and participate in the articulation of measures, in the Roma community, this presence is significantly smaller. There exists the State Council of the Roma

> People, indeed, but, at regional levels, no similar bodies have been created. The creation of specific bodies at different levels—regional, local, or even at neighborhood level would give the issue more visibility and would help make right the historical debt that the majoritarian society holds towards the Roma people. Such institutions would give a voice to the Roma community.[4] (Interview with author, October 2015, own translation).

The "Fundación Segretariado Gitano"—which is by far the most institutionalized, powerful, and well-known organization in Spain working on Roma inclusion, advocated for an intercultural approach, rather than Roma-only councils or associations. The rationale for this was the following:

> The Segretariado Gitano is an intercultural organization, which has both Roma and non-Roma in its patronage. Approximately 45% of the people who work in the organization are Roma, and this is very important. Not only for the Roma themselves, but for society as a whole… This is not to say that there shouldn't be ethnic associations. I think there should be, and they should be supported. But my understanding is that from a point of view of social intervention and social problems, an intercultural approach is both more effective and it holds the potential of being more easily accepted by society as a whole. (Interview with author, October 2014, own translation).

The fact that the composition of the most powerful pro-Roma, nongovernmental organization comprises a majority of non-Roma[5] is a sticky issue.

On the one hand, the Secretariado Gitano (FSG) has managed to get many (both Roma and non-Roma) citizens involved in actions aimed at fostering social inclusion and has achieved a significant capacity for project management, visibility, international standing, and access to resources that would have been virtually impossible to accomplish on behalf of a smaller, Roma-only organization. On the other hand, in the process of expanding its reach and personnel, the FSG has also become the main Roma-related interlocutor for both the Spanish government and European institutions. This has, in turn, generated some resentment and bitterness on behalf of some smaller, Roma-led organizations.

For instance, Augustín Vega Cortés, president of the organization "Opinión Romaní," complained that he witnessed decades of similar projects and policies in Spain, always carried out by the same Roma organizations, animated by good intentions, but with little results to show for:

[4]The statement that there are no regional Roma bodies is not completely accurate. In 2003, the "Consejo para la promoción integral y participación social del Pueblo Gitano en el País Vasco" was created in the Basque Country with the decree 289/2003 of 25 November 2003. In June 2013, the Autonomous Community of Castilla-La Mancha approved the creation of a "Consejo Regional del Pueblo Gitano" with the declared aim of fostering equality. The "Plan integral del Pueblo Gitano de Cataluña 2014–2016" instituted a "Consejo Asesor del Pueblo Gitano", composed by 21 representatives of Roma organizations. Since the interview, the Autonomous Community of Extremadura has also approved the creation of a "Consejo Regional del Pueblo Gitano de Extremadura" in May 2016.

[5]According to the 2025 data available on the official webpage of the Secretariado Gitano (FSG), its staff amounts to 1049, of which 37% are Roma. While the participation of Romani employees has diminished over the past decade, since 2021 the President of the FSG is, for the first time since its inception, a Romani lawyer and politician, Sara Giménez Giménez.

> The issue of the "poor marginalized Roma" has almost always been a business for a few know-it-all and a niche employment market for unemployed social workers and sociologists, and things keep working this way. Of course, there are many well-intentioned people, but that is beyond the point. The point is that this is a perverse system that has only served the purpose of projecting a false appearance of specific, targeted social policies to justify the fact that the State is abandoning its main obligation, which is simply to treat all people equally and to remove obstacles to equality where obstacles exist.

The same activist commented on the issue of "representation" in Roma-targeted policies:

> "I don't know what irritates me the most: those who hate us [Roma], or those who won't leave us alone. Please, stop making plans and strategies to help us. And what about the Roma of these organizations, who are always the same? Why don't you limit yourselves to speaking in the name of your families or in the name of the members of your association? Who elected you and gave you a right to speak in the name of all of us? This is neither democratic, nor is it Roma. I understand that everyone must make a living, but don't do so by speaking in my name..." (Email exchange as follow up to the workshop "Bridging the Gap between Policy Making and Social Research. Strengths and challenges of the policies for gitanos/Roma in Spain," that took place in Barcelona with scholars, policymakers, and NGOs in October 2014).

Another issue worth addressing is how representative are the "targets" or beneficiaries of these "explicit but not exclusive" policies (Magazzini & Piemontese, 2016). The Spanish Roma integration policies, led by the Secretariado Gitano, have so far been based on large projects, such as the flagship ACCEDER program, that heavily rely on EU funding. To get financed, Roma integration projects understandably require being able to show some measurable results in a relatively short timeframe from the completion of the project. Pre-assessment criteria were added in the EU programming period following the assessment of the NRIS, precisely as a means of obtaining more accountability for the money spent and more reliable data on the projects. The objective of setting up these kinds of indicators were both accountability and the creation of a database of good practices. However, Messing and Bereményi, among others, have argued that bidding for large and highly ambitious projects, at least in the past, has led to (a) a selection of those Roma beneficiaries who are not necessarily the most in need of support and (b) a conflict of interest of the Secretariado Gitano, that is, both the organization in charge of ethnic data collection on Roma in Spain (including for the National Strategy) and the one implementing many of the Roma inclusion projects (Messing & Bereményi, 2016).

The selection of the beneficiaries of the integration programs is a difficult matter that generally relies on some sort of points-based system and minimum requirements to determine eligibility. The choice of the most "worthy" Roma beneficiaries is, according to Messing and Bereményi, at least to some degree influenced by the fact that they already possess the skills to perform well in the job market. In contrast, those who lacked the basic skills requested to participate in such schemes and who were the most in need (such as non-Spanish Roma living in informal encampments on the outskirts of Madrid) remained stuck at the pre-access stage and were excluded from the programs, even though, according to the National Strategy, the most vulnerable should have been the main target group.

The PROMOCIONA project, also carried out by the Fundación Secretariado Gitano, was an important endeavor to overcome the significant existing gaps in educational attainment between Roma and non-Roma pupils. This program, however, also presented some aspects related to the framing of the Roma involved that can be seen as problematic: even though the FSG had for decades denounced segregation in schools, it did not mention structural or systemic factors in the PROMOCIONA project. It heavily focused instead on the agency of the Roma families, for which it provided detailed data in its reports. The result of this kind of approach, in which "leveling up" policies have typically been implemented by non-Roma social workers, risked therefore reinforcing the idea that the Roma students' low performance was caused mainly by the Roma families themselves, rather than a structurally discriminatory system.

In sum, while these types of redistributive policies were overall more participatory and effective than Italy's cultural mediation schemes (Bernàt, 2016; Carrasco & Poblet, 2019), they remained confined within the realm of what Fraser labeled as "affirmative policies," which do not ultimately challenge the status quo and the mechanisms that produce the injustices in the first place. The results of the evaluation of Spain's 2012–2020 Strategy have shown that the levels of Roma participation that occurred during the development of the 2010–2012 Action Plan that preceded the Strategy were not maintained in a sustainable manner during its implementation. To address this issue, the 2021–2030 stresses the importance of increasing the number of Romani associations involved in the new Strategy's implementation, yet it does not go into detail about how it intends to achieve this goal.

Representation, Recognition, or Misrecognition?

In the case of the European Union's institutional approach to Roma integration, the recognition of the Roma as a disadvantaged and discriminated group has been foundational to the creation of ad hoc policies and specific funding aimed at inclusion. Within this recognition paradigm, the requirement for Roma participation and representation in the policy process has been consistent with several internationally accepted policy principles and guidelines that deal with minority participation in decision-making processes—such as the 1995 Framework Convention for the Protection of National Minorities and the 1999 Lund Recommendation for the Participation of Minorities in Public Life. A participatory approach is also in line with scholarly work on the political struggle for representation on behalf of disempowered groups in society (Ryder et al., 2015; Williams, 1998). Following an understanding of democracy that, in order to be such, must be inclusive, particularly in multicultural societies in which majoritarian rule could numerically, permanently exclude minorities from power, representation means that minorities must be able to influence the policymaking process by which they are affected, rather than being mere policy objects (Surdu, 2016, Cianetti, 2014, pp. 86–112; Lijphart, 1999;

Young, 2000). In Young's words, "[the] normative legitimacy of a democratic decision depends on the degree to which those affected by it have been included in the decision-making process and have had the opportunity to influence the outcome" (Young, 2000, pp. 5–6).

This has been the reason for looking into how the 2011 EU Framework for National Roma Integration Strategies emerged (NRIS, since 2021 the new EU Roma strategic framework for equality, inclusion and participation) and how it has been transposed into national policies in two comparable cases, Italy and Spain. The question of how such principles have translated into practice brings up structural issues that the recognition struggles have, so far, proven unable to address successfully, when the criterion to access social programs is framed as one of ethnicity, and if the ethnic identity is conflated with the "lack" of some fundamental aspect of social inclusion:

> The overall effect is to impose a single, drastically simplified group identity which denies the complexity of people's lives, the multiplicity of their identifications, and the cross-pulls of their various affiliations. Ironically, then, the identity model serves as a vehicle for misrecognition: in reifying group identity, it ends by obscuring the politics of cultural identification, the struggles within the group for the authority—and the power—to represent it. By shielding such struggles from view, this approach masks the power of dominant fractions and reinforces intragroup domination. The identity model thus lends itself all too easily to repressive forms of communitarianism, promoting conformism, intolerance, and patriarchalism. (Fraser, 2000, p. 112).

The failure of integration schemes based on such premises has then often been attributed to the actors (as corrupted, not representative, etc.) rather than to a structure that constrains those struggling for recognition into a "victimhood competition." Such competition has tended to automatically exclude those beneficiaries who do not fit the minority's reified model. This, in turn, in the case of Roma minorities in Italy and Spain, has perpetuated a self-fulfilling prophecy of either failure or success, depending on how the beneficiaries are identified by the majority.

Acknowledgments The preparation of this chapter was supported by the Lumina Quaeruntur of the Czech Academy of Sciences (LQ300582201).

References

Bacchi, C. (2009). Introducing a 'what's the problem represented to be?' Approach to policy analysis. In *Analysing policy: What's the problem represented to be?* (pp. 1–53). Pearson.

Alietti, A., & Riniolo, V. (2019). The national strategy for Roma inclusion in Italy: Between contradictions and loss of responsibilities. *Journal of European Comtemporary Studies, 29*(1), 9–19.

Bernàt, A. (2016). Integration policies focused on Roma. Policies applied in practice in selected Eu member states through comprehensive Programmes. *Rivisteweb. The Italian Platform for the Humanities and Social Sciences, XXXIX*(1), 65–88.

Carrasco, S., & Poblet, G. (2019). *Overview of the integration of Roma citizens in Spain and some transferable lessons for the EU*. NESET ad hoc question No. 4/2019.

Cianetti, L. (2014). Granting local voting rights to non-citizens in Estonia and Latvia: The conundrum of minority representation in two divided democracies. *Journal of Ethnopolitics and Minority Issues in Europe, 13*(1), 86–112.
Collins, P. H., & Bilge, S. (2020). *Intersectionality (Key concepts)* (2nd ed.). Polity Press.
Crenshaw, K. (1989). Demarginalizing the intersection of race and sex: A black feminist critique of antidiscrimination doctrine, feminist theory and antiracist politics. *University of Chicago Legal Forum, 1*(8), 139–167.
Dolabela, H., & Fotta, M. (2021). Ciganos as a traditional people: Romanies and the politics of recognition in Brazil. *Ethnopolitics, 22*(2), 157–176.
European Commission (2011). *An EU Framework for National Roma Integration Strategies up to 2020*. https://eur-lex.europa.eu/LexUriServ/LexUriServ.do?uri=COM:2011:0173:FIN:EN:PDF
Federazione Romani. (2012). *Osservazioni generali alla bozza di strategia nazionale per la popolazione romanì*, Pubblicato da: amministratore su 22 febbraio 2012. https://federazioneromani.wordpress.com/2012/02/22/osservazioni-generali-alla-bozza-di-strategia-nazionale-per-la-popolazione-romani/
Fraser, N. (2000). Rethinking recognition. *New Left Review, 3*, 1–8.
Gabrielli, R. (2013). *Chi fa una cosa per me senza di me è contro di me* (Those who do something for me but without me are against me), Blog Post on October 10, 2013, https://comitatoromsinti.blogspot.com/2013/10/chi-fa-una-cosa-per-me-senza-di-me-e.html
Guo, D., & Hu, S. (2019). Identity politics and democratic crisis in Western Europe. *Chinese Political Science Review, 4*, 255–275.
Hobson, B. (2003). Introduction. In B. Hobson (Ed.), *Recognition struggles and social movements: Contested identities, Agency and Power*. Cambridge University Press.
Italian Government, Decreto Legislativo 9/7/2003 n° 215. Attuazione della direttiva 2000/43/CE per la parità di trattamento tra le persone indipendemente dalla razza e dall'origine etnica. *Gazzetta Ufficiale della Repub blica Italiana n° 186* del 12/8/2003.
Italian Government, National Strategy for the Inclusion of Roma, Sinti and Caminanti Communities, (2012) (European Commission Communication No. 173), 1–90. http://ec.europa.eu/justice/discrimination/files/roma_italy_strategy_en.pdf
Ivasiuc, A. (2022). Provincialising security: Materiality and sensoriality. *Critical Studies on Security, 11*(1), 50–62.
Kostka, J. (2015). Implementation of Roma inclusion policies: Why defining the problem matters. *Social Inclusion, 3*(5).
Kostka, J. (2018). *Financing Roma inclusion with European structural funds: Why good intentions fail*. Routledge.
Lijphart, A. (1999). *Patterns of democracy*. Yale University Press.
Magazzini, T. (2017). Making the Most of super-diversity. Notes on the potential of a new approach. *Policy & Politics, 45*(4), 527–545.
Magazzini, T. (2018). *Redistribution, recognition or representation? EU Roma integration policies as a test for social justice a comparative study of Italy and Spain*. PhD dissertation. Available at http://hdl.handle.net/20.500.14454/782
Magazzini, T. (2020). Integration as an essentially contested concept: Questioning the assumptions behind the National Roma Integration Strategies of Italy and Spain. In S. Hinger & R. Schweitzer (Eds.), *Politics of (dis)integration* (pp. 41–59. IMISCOE Research Series). Springer.
Magazzini, T. (2021). Antidiscrimination meets integration policies: Exploring new diversity-related challenges in Europe. *Social Sciences, 10*(6).
Magazzini, T. (2024). When ethnicity is "national": Mapping ethnic minorities in Europe's framework convention for the protection of national minorities. *Ethnic and Racial Studies, 47*(9), 1812–1833.
Magazzini, T., & Piemontese, S. (2016). 'Roma' migration in the EU: The case of Spain between 'new' and 'old' minorities. *Migration Letters, 13*(2), 228–241.

Malik, K. (2023). *Not so black and white.* A History of Race from White Supremacy to Identity Politics. Hurst.

McMahon, S. (2015). *Immigration and citizenship in an enlarged European Union. The political dynamics of intra-EU mobility.* Palgrave Macmillan.

Messing, V., & Bereményi, B. Á. (2016). Is ethnicity a meaningful category of employment policies for Roma? A comparative case study of Hungary and Spain. *Ethnic and Racial Studies, 9870*(August), 1–20.

Rostas, I. (2019). *A task for Sisyphus: Why Europe's Roma policies fail.* Central European University Press.

Ryder, A., Kocze, A., Rostas, I., Dunajeva, J.-E., Bogda, M., Taba, M., & Junghaus, T. (2015). Nothing about us without us ? Roma participation in policy making and knowledge production. *Rights Journal of the European Roma Rights Centre, 2.*

Sealy, T. (2025). *Post-multiculturalism, religion and recognition.* Bristol University Press.

Sigona, N., & Treheran, N. (Eds.). (2009). *Romani politics in contemporary Europe: Poverty, ethnic mobilisation and the new liberal order.* Palgarve Macmillan.

Spanish Government, Ministerio de Sanidad Servicios Sociales e Igualdad de España. (2012). *Estrategia Nacional para la Inclusión Social de la Población Gitana en España 2012–2020.*

Surdu, M. (2016). *Those who count. Expert practices of Roma classification.* Central European University.

van Baar, H., & Kóczé, A. (2020). *The Roma and their struggle for identity in contemporary Europe.* Berghan Books.

Vertovec, S. (2007). Super-diversity and its implications. *Ethnic and Racial Studies, 30*(6), 1024–1054.

Williams, M. S. (1998). *Voice, trust, memory: Marginalized groups and the failings of Liberal representation.* Princeton University Press.

Yildiz, C., & De Genova, N. (2018). Un/free mobility: Roma migrants in the European Union. *Social Identities, 24*(2), 1–17.

Young, I. M. (2000). *Inclusion and democracy.* Oxford University Press.

Zambory, M. (2020). Beyond recognition. Crises of politics and representation. *Intersections. East European Journal of Society and Politics, 6*(1), 4–7.

The Role of EU Accessibility Legislation in Fighting Social Exclusion of Persons with Disabilities

Delia Ferri

Abstract

In the last 25 years the European Union (EU) has developed a comprehensive disability policy. The ratification of the UN Convention on the Rights of Persons with Disabilities (CRPD) by the EU, in 2010, has been a major driver for the most recent developments. Since then, the EU has identified accessibility as a priority area of action and has used its competence related to the internal market to enact harmonising legislation. This chapter interrogates the role of EU accessibility legislation in fighting social exclusion. It recalls the core tenets of the CRPD accessibility provisions and then provides an overview of the complex network of EU accessibility legislation. Next, it focuses on the most recent directives: the Web Accessibility Directive (WAD), which provides for mandatory accessibility requirements for websites and mobile applications of public sector bodies, and the European Accessibility Act (EAA), which mandates the accessibility of a range of key products and services in the internal market, including, among others, software, banking services, payment terminals, e-books, and ticketing machines. This chapter concludes by reflecting on the role of the WAD and EAA in ensuring equal access to different goods and services and supporting the inclusion of people with disabilities in society.

*Professor of Law Maynooth University (MU) School of Law and Criminology and Co-Director of the MU Assisting Living and Learning (ALL) Institute. This chapter is based on the speech given on occasion of the conference "Social exclusion, vulnerable groups and the new EU Social Rights Pillar" held on 5–6 March 2021 and organised by the Jean Monnet Project EUVadis (University of Macedonia).

D. Ferri (✉)
Maynooth University School of Law and Criminology, Kildare, Ireland
e-mail: delia.ferri@mu.ie

D. Anagnostopoulou (ed.), *European Identities, Inclusion and Equality*, Diversity and Inclusion Research, https://doi.org/10.1007/978-3-031-90602-2_11

Introduction

Until the late nineties the then European Community (EC) addressed disability mostly by means of soft law and programmes designed to support Member States' actions (Waddington, 2005; O'Mahony & Quinlivan, 2020, pp. 12–28). In 1999, the Treaty of Amsterdam conferred upon the former EC the competence to combat discrimination on the grounds *inter alia* of disability, prompting the adoption of Directive 2000/78/EC of 27 November 2000, establishing a general framework for equal treatment in employment and occupation (Employment Equality Directive) (Directive 2000/78/EC, 2000). Notably, the Treaty of Amsterdam also included a Declaration stating that the European institutions must take into account the needs of persons with disabilities in adopting harmonisation measures under former Article 95 EC (now art. 114 of the Treaty on the Functioning of the European Union-TFEU).[1] In 2000, the EU Charter of Fundamental Rights (CFR or "the Charter") introduced an all-embracing prohibition on discrimination (art. 21) and a provision on the integration of persons with disabilities (art. 26). In 2009, the Treaty of Lisbon granted to the Charter constitutional status and, while recasting former Article 13 EC as Article 19 TFEU, included two cross-cutting clauses: Article 9 TFEU and Article 10 TFEU. The former states that "*[i]n defining and implementing its policies and activities, the Union shall take into account requirements linked to […] the fight against social exclusion*", while the latter provides for the mainstreaming of non-discrimination within all European Union (EU) actions.

Those constitutional innovations furthered the advancement of EU disability law (Ferri & Broderick, 2020, pp. 1–10). However, it is commonly acknowledged that the ratification of the UN Convention on the Rights of Persons with Disabilities (2006) (CRPD or "the Convention"), which occurred in 2010 (Decision 2010/48/EC, 2009), represents the most significant driver of recent developments. It stimulated the adoption of the "European Disability Strategy 2010–2020" (EDS) (Commission Communication, 2010; Hosking, 2013), which set out a 10-year-long disability policy framework, and of the subsequent "Union of equality: Strategy for the rights of persons with disabilities 2021-2030" (hereafter "Strategy 2021–2030") (Commission Communication, 2021). It also spurred an array of policy and legislative measures to protect and promote the rights of persons with disabilities (Ferri & Broderick, 2020, pp. 1–10). Furthermore, the CRPD itself has become an integral part of EU law, as recognised by CJEU (CJEU, *HK Danmark*, 2013; Waddington, 2018). On the whole, as discussed elsewhere (Ferri, 2021), the CRPD has provoked a quantitative shift in EU actions, in the sense that disability has become more visible, but has triggered a substantive change in the approach to disability, which is now informed by the social-contextual understanding purported by the Convention, i.e., by the view that disability is an interactive process between people with impairments and societal barriers (Broderick, 2015; Ferri & Broderick, 2020, pp. 1–10).

[1] Accessibility requirements are relatively widespread in the area of transport, including air, rail, road and water transport and are established in relation to certain physical facilities, such as cableway installations and lifts, or specific goods, such as medicinal products (Waddington, 2009).

Since the ratification of the CRPD, accessibility, which entails the removal of a range of environmental barriers to access, has become a priority area of action for the EU, falling within the remit of EU shared competence (Waddington, 2011). The EDS envisaged a portfolio of diverse legislative and other instruments capable of improving access for people with disabilities to a wide range of goods and services and complementing existing accessibility requirements included in EU sectorial legislation (Waddington, 2009). The Web Accessibility Directive (WAD) (Directive (EU) No 2016/2102, 2016) and the European Accessibility Act (EAA) (Directive (EU) No 2019/882, 2019) represent the most significant tools in this portfolio. In a similar vein to the EDS, the Strategy 2021–2030 places a strong emphasis on accessibility and defines it as an "enabler of rights, autonomy and equality". This hints at a conception of accessibility as a key tool to redress exclusion, remedy stigmatising experiences faced by people with disabilities in inaccessible environments (including digital environments), realise Article 26 CFR, and implement the CRPD as well as the cross-cutting clause embedded in Article 9 TFEU.

Against this background, building on relevant literature (Ferri & Favalli, 2018, pp. 40–59; Charitakis, 2018; Ferri, 2020; Charitakis, 2020, pp. 221–242), this chapter discusses the role of the WAD and the EAA in fighting social exclusion faced by persons with disabilities. After these introductory remarks, section 2 outlines the core tenets of accessibility obligations in the CRPD. Section 3 briefly recalls the marginalisation faced by persons with disabilities in the EU, and highlights the importance of accessibility in supporting the participation of people with disabilities in society. With a view of contextualising the WAD and EAA, section 4 provides a synopsis of the complex network of accessibility requirements mainstreamed in EU law. Section 5 focuses on the WAD and the EAA and examines their potential in fighting social exclusion. The chapter concludes by reflecting on how market goals have become increasingly intertwined with social objectives (Ferri, 2020) and the extent to which the WAD and the EAA can contribute to foster participation of persons with disabilities in society.

Accessibility Obligations in the UN Convention on the Rights of Persons with Disabilities: An Overview

As Perlin (2014) contends, the CRPD is 'revolutionary' because it "*sets out explicitly the many steps that States must take to create an enabling environment so that persons with disabilities can enjoy authentic equality in society*" (p. 538). Such an enabling environment is characterised by full accessibility. In fact, the Preamble to the Convention, in paragraph (v), explicitly recognises "*the importance of accessibility to the physical, social, economic and cultural environment, to health and education, and to information and communication, in enabling persons with disabilities to fully enjoy all human rights and fundamental freedoms*". Accessibility is a general principle of the CRPD and one of its keystones. Article 9 CRPD requires States Parties to "*take appropriate measures to ensure to persons with disabilities access, on an equal basis with others, to the physical environment, to transportation, to information and communications, including information and communications technologies and systems, and to other facilities and services open or provided to the public, both in urban and in rural areas*" (Lawson, 2018). It obliges States Parties to the Convention to develop and monitor the implementation of minimum standards and guidelines for the accessibility of facilities and services open or provided to the public. In that vein, the UN Committee on the Rights of Persons with Disabilities (CRPD Committee) acknowledges that accessibility is a "dynamic concept" and "*its application requires periodic regulatory and technical adjustments*" (see *inter alia* UN Committee, 2016, para. 22).

The CRPD does not differentiate between the public or private ownership of buildings, transport means, or technologies. Article 9 para. 2, lett. (b) and (d) CRPD makes it clear that States Parties must ensure that private entities and market operators provide accessible services and facilities. The obligation to provide accessible goods and services envisaged in Article 9 CRPD is an *ex ante* duty. This means that Parties to the Convention have the responsibility to ensure that accessibility is provided before an individual request to enter or use a place or service is made (UN Committee, 2014, para. 25). The CRPD Committee contends that States Parties are under the obligation to ensure access to all newly created infrastructures, goods, and services and that existing barriers to access "*shall be removed gradually in a systematic and, more importantly, continuously monitored manner, with the aim of achieving full accessibility*" (UN Committee, 2014, para. 14). According to the CRPD Committee, the obligation to implement accessibility is unconditional, and not subject to the limit of the disproportionate burden (UN Committee, 2014, para. 25).[2] Accessibility obligations are also included in several of the substantive rights spelled out in the CRPD (Broderick & Ferri, 2019, chap. 5).

As indicated by the CRPD Committee, accessibility must be "*approached in all its complexity*" (UN Committee, 2014, para. 13). Charitakis (2020), in identifying different dimensions of accessibility, suggests that accessibility has, alongside physical and information aspects, also a social or attitudinal aspect, in that it links to "the removal of stigma and other negative forms of behaviour that people with disabilities, their families and their carers experience throughout their lives" (p. 25).

In the CRPD, accessibility is conceived of as "*precondition for persons with disabilities to live independently and participate fully and equally in society*" (UN Committee, 2014, para. 1). As noted by Broderick (2019), accessibility is conceived of as "*a vital tool for ensuring the equalisation of opportunities for persons with disabilities.*" (p. 22) In that connection, the CRPD does recognise that accessibility is essential to social inclusion.

[2] In that regard, accessibility obligations can be contrasted with the duty to provide reasonable accommodation which is provided in the CRPD.

Social Exclusion, Disability, and Accessibility

Social exclusion is usually defined as "*a multidimensional phenomenon not limited to material deprivation; poverty is an important dimension of exclusion, albeit only one dimension*". In fact, while the meaning of social exclusion was initially revolving around the concept of poverty, it has then come to address more broadly social marginalisation. Rimmerman (2014) argues that "*[s]ocial exclusion is a complex concept that expresses disadvantages in relation to certain norms of social, economic or political activity related to individuals, households, spatial areas or population group*" (p. 33). Social exclusion encompasses restricted opportunities to participate in wider social and cultural activities. In that regard, Rimmerman (2014) also contends that "*[i]nclusion is viewed as a desirable outcome or as a strategy to combat social exclusion, whereas exclusion is viewed as an expression of poor social cohesion*" (p. 35).

Combatting social exclusion has become an important feature of EU social policy since the late 1980s (Rimmerman, 2014, p. 34) and was embedded in Article 3 TFEU as an objective of the EU and in Article 9 TFEU. Fighting against "poverty" and "deprivation" is a most recent policy endeavour (Garben, 2017). It is at the heart of the European Pillar of Social Rights (EPRS), a soft law document that lays down twenty principles "*essential for fair and well-functioning labour markets and welfare systems in 21st century Europe*" (European Pillar of Social Rights, 2017). Combatting social exclusion and promoting inclusion are also at the core of EU action on disability. The Strategy 2021–2030 makes inclusion a strong pivot, whereas the former EDS had suggested that social inclusion processes require going beyond mere access to economic resources.

While data reveal significant differences across the EU, people with disabilities are at a higher risk of poverty and social exclusion (Eurostat, 2023). As noted by Inclusion Europe, "poverty and disability reinforce each other, contributing to increased vulnerability and exclusion" (Inclusion Europe, 2019). It is acknowledged that there are a variety of interlinked barriers to social inclusion of persons with disabilities—engendered by lack of education, lack of employment opportunities, lack of services, and ableist attitudes. Inaccessible environments further impact people with disabilities' chances of establishing relationships and engaging socially. In that regard, as noted above in the introduction, and in line with the CRPD, both the former EDS and the Strategy 2021–2030 are underpinned by the idea that inclusion of persons with disabilities is ensured *inter alia* by means of accessible infrastructures, goods, and services. In particular, the Strategy 2021–2030 makes it clear that accessibility is crucial to achieving social and economic equality and redressing social exclusion experienced by persons with disabilities because it expands opportunities for communication, interaction, education, and employment. In a similar vein, the European Economic and Social Committee has also highlighted the role of accessibility in ensuring independent living and supporting participation in society (European Economic and Social Committee, 2019). The EPRS itself, in chap. III, comprises a provision (Principle 17) on the inclusion of people with disabilities, stating that "*[p]eople with disabilities have the right to income support that ensures living in dignity, services that enable them to participate in the labour market and in society, and a work environment adapted to their needs*". While it does not mention accessibility as such, it does refer to services that *enable* people with disabilities to participate. All those documents point to the fact that accessibility is key to addressing the interface between poverty and inequality and point to the idea that accessibility (including digital accessibility) is a gateway to ensure access to healthcare, education, employment, and transportation services for persons with disabilities, which is consistent with what is predicated by the CRPD.

Placing the Web Accessibility Directive and the European Accessibility Act in Context: Accessibility in EU Law

Even before the ratification of the CRPD and the adoption of a comprehensive policy framework, the EU embedded accessibility requirements across different strands of its legislation (Waddington, 2009; Charitakis, 2018). Since 2010, accessibility has been further mainstreamed across EU legislation.

Currently, EU transport legislation guarantees equal access to different modes of transport for persons with disabilities and includes technical prescriptions for accessible vehicles (Varney & Pearson, 2020, pp. 182–200). Furthermore, it provides accessible information for travellers with disabilities (Regulation (EU) 181/2011, 2011; Regulation (EU) 1177/2010, 2010). A number of disability-specific instruments have also been enacted, such as Regulation (EC) No. 1107/2006 that protects the rights of disabled persons and persons with reduced mobility when travelling by air (Regulation (EC) No. 1107/2006, 2006). The most recent regulations in the field further embed accessibility as a key overarching goal. For example, the Regulation on Union Guidelines for the Development of the Trans-European Transport Network (TEN-T) qualifies accessibility for elderly people, persons with reduced mobility, and disabled passengers as one of its objectives (Regulation (EU) 2024/1679 on Union guidelines for the development of the trans-European transport network, para. 11 of the Preamble and art. 4, 2024).

Although the accessibility of the physical environment is mainly regulated at the national level, the EU has adopted directives including accessibility requirements for certain types of specific physical infrastructures, such as cableway installations and lifts (Regulation (EU) 2016/424, 2016), and for workplace premises (Directive 89/654/EEC, 1989). The 2014 European Directives on Public Procurement, which replace and strengthen previous texts, have also a great potential to support accessibility of the physical environment, as well as of goods and services in general (Directive 2014/24/EU, 2014; Directive 2014/25/EU, 2014). Both Directives set out that public tenders must, except in duly justified cases, be drawn up so as to take into account accessibility criteria for persons with disabilities or design for all users.

A number of EU legislative instruments address the accessibility of information and communication, as well as the accessibility of cultural content. The Directive that harmonises laws related to radio equipment (Directive 2014/53/EU, 2014) includes references to the accessibility of telecommunications terminals for persons with disabilities. The Audiovisual Media Services Directive (AVMSD) (Directive 2010/13/EU, 2010), as most recently amended in 2018 (Directive (EU) 2018/1808, 2018), requires Member States to ensure that audiovisual media services are made accessible for persons with disabilities (Ferri, 2023, Charitakis, 2020).

On the whole, the EU legal framework includes a net of legislative provisions that address accessibility to varying degrees and complement accessibility-focused instruments, such as the WAD and the EAA, and are further reinforced by the use of standardisation (Hosking, 2013).[3]

The Web Accessibility Directive and the European Accessibility Act

The Core Tenets of the WAD

While, as outlined above, accessibility has been mainstreamed across EU legislation, to date, the WAD and the EAA are the most important legislative enactments and aim to implement the CRPD. Both these directives have the merit to ensure access to a range of goods and services and, broadly speaking, the digital environment.

The WAD was adopted in 2016 and has the aim to "*approximate the laws, regulations and administrative provisions of the Member States relating to the accessibility requirements of the websites and mobile applications of public sector bodies, thereby enabling those websites and mobile applications to be more accessible to users, in particular to persons with disabilities*" (Web Accessibility Directive, art. 1, para. 1). It provides for mandatory accessibility requirements, but, given that this is a minimum harmonisation directive, "*Member States may maintain or introduce measures in conformity with Union law which go beyond the minimum requirements*" established by this Directive (Web Accessibility Directive, art. 2).

The non-binding Preamble of the Directive includes a general definition of accessibility, which, however, is not reproduced in Article 3 (on definitions). According to this definition, "*accessibility should be understood as principles and techniques to be observed when designing, constructing, maintaining, and updating websites and mobile applications in order to make them more accessible to users, in particular persons with disabilities*". Furthermore, recital 37 of the Preamble and Article 4 link the concept of accessibility to principles laid out in the Web Content Accessibility Guidelines (WCAG).[4] Namely, Article 4 provides that Member States

[3] With regard to standardisation, Mandate M/376 addressed ICT accessibility standards for public procurement, while Mandate M/420 focused on accessibility of the built environment, but included ICT that is used in that context. Mandate M/473 aims to mainstream "design-for-all" (universal design) principles in relevant European standardisation initiatives. In April 2017, Mandate M/554 was also issued in relation to the development of a harmonised standard covering the essential requirements of the WAD.

[4] The Web Content Accessibility Guidelines (WCAG) 2.1, adopted in June 2018 within the remit of the Web Accessibility Initiative (WAI) of W3C are the most recent guidelines. Those Guidelines

shall ensure that public sector bodies' websites and mobile applications are accessible by making them perceivable, operable, understandable, and robust.[5]

The WAD also includes a provision stating that accessibility requirements should not impose a "disproportionate burden" upon public sector bodies (Web Accessibility Directive, Preamble, recital 39, art. 5). As stated in the Preamble of the WAD, this limitation entails that "*in justified cases, it might not be reasonably possible for a public sector body to make specific content fully accessible*". In order to assess the extent to which compliance with accessibility requirements imposes a disproportionate burden, the "*size, resources, and nature of the public sector body concerned" must be considered alongside "the estimated costs and benefits for the public sector body concerned in relation to the estimated benefits for persons with disabilities, taking into account the frequency and duration of use of the specific website or mobile application*". Where this disproportionate burden has arguably been established, public sector bodies must outline which parts of the accessibility requirements could not be complied with and consequently provide accessible alternatives.

Article 6 of the WAD refers to standards that make websites and mobile apps more accessible, while Article 7 requires Member States to "*ensure that public sector bodies provide and regularly update a detailed, comprehensive, and clear accessibility statement on the compliance of their websites and mobile applications*" with the WAD. Additionally, Member States must "*ensure the availability of an adequate and effective enforcement procedure to guarantee compliance*" with the WAD (Web Accessibility Directive, art. 9).

The Core Tenets of the EAA

The EAA was adopted by the EU legislators in 2019 with the explicit aim of improving the functioning of the internal market for accessible products and services by removing regulatory barriers across the EU.

Differently from the WAD, the EAA explicitly embeds a social-contextual understanding of disability. The Preamble of the Directive and Article 3 refer to persons with disabilities in line with Article 1(2) CRPD (European Accessibility Act, Preamble, recital 3, art. 3, para. 1). Furthermore, Recital 50 of the Preamble

---

update the previous version, the WCAG 2.0, released in 2008. The WCAG 2.1 extend the WCAG 2.0, but do not supersede them. In fact, both are existing standards, and websites that fulfil WCAG 2.1 requirements also conform to the WCAG 2.0. The WCAG are described by Pelzetter as a "technology-agnostic description of the requirements for accessible web pages". Jens Pelzetter, "A Declarative Model for Web Accessibility Requirements and its Implementation", (2012) 3 *Frontiers in Computer Science.*

[5] Recital 37 of the WAD Preamble states that "The four principles of accessibility are perceivability, meaning that information and user interface components must be presentable to users in ways they can perceive; operability, meaning that user interface components and navigation must be operable; understandability, meaning that information and the operation of the user interface must be understandable; and robustness, meaning that content must be robust enough to be interpreted reliably by a wide variety of user agents, including assistive technologies".

provides that accessibility should be achieved by the removal of barriers, preferably through a universal design as defined by the CRPD (European Accessibility Act, Preamble, recital 50). The link to the CRPD is reinforced by the reference to the CRPD Committee's General Comment No 2 (European Accessibility Act, Preamble, recital 50). The Preamble also makes an explicit reference to the CFR, *verbatim* linking accessibility to the inclusion of persons with disabilities in society and, specifically, to Article 26 CFR (European Accessibility Act, Preamble, recital 103).

The EAA provides for accessibility of a range of key products and services, such as computers, smartphones, tablets, TV sets, banking ATMs and services, payment terminals, e-books and e-readers, e-commerce websites and mobile applications, ticketing machines, and check-in machines. It places a range of accessibility obligations on manufacturers, authorised representatives, importers, distributors, and service providers (European Accessibility Act, art. 7 et seq.), which apply equally to economic operators from the public and private sectors (European Accessibility Act, Preamble, para. 57). However, microenterprises are exempt from complying with the accessibility requirements and any obligations relating to compliance with those requirements (European Accessibility Act, art. 4). Manufacturers, when placing their products on the market, have to ensure that the products "*have been designed and manufactured in accordance with the applicable accessibility requirements of this Directive*" and that "*procedures are in place for series production to remain in conformity with this Directive*" (European Accessibility Act, art. 7). Importers must "*place only compliant products on the market*" (European Accessibility Act, art. 9). They also have to carry out a conformity assessment before placing a product on the market (European Accessibility Act, art. 9). Distributors must "act with due care in relation to the requirements of [the] Directive" (European Accessibility Act, art. 10, para. 1), and "*ensure that, while a product is under their responsibility, storage or transport conditions do not jeopardise its compliance with the applicable accessibility requirements*" (European Accessibility Act, art. 10, para. 4). Finally, service providers must "*ensure that they design and provide services in accordance with the accessibility requirements*" of the EAA (European Accessibility Act, art. 13, para. 1).

Similarly to the WAD, Article 14 of the EAA establishes that accessibility requirements do not apply where they would impose a disproportionate burden on the economic operators concerned (European Accessibility Act, art. 14). This provision includes an additional limit by establishing that accessibility does not apply when it would imply a significant change in a product or service that results in the fundamental alteration of its basic nature. However, economic operators are required to document the reasons for which they are not subject to accessibility duties, and if they receive funding to ensure accessibility, they cannot rely on the disproportionate burden defence. Notably, these accessibility requirements will become applicable in 2025 (European Accessibility Act, art. 2).

Member States are obliged to put in place adequate enforcement measures to avoid businesses circumventing or disregarding accessibility obligations and provide clear and proportionate "*penalties applicable to infringements of national provisions adopted pursuant to [the EAA]*" (European Accessibility Act, art. 29–30).

The EAA, as does the WAD, sends a clear message to the Member States that they should avoid accessibility legislation being a "paper tiger".

The Role of the WAD and EAA in Fighting Social Exclusion: A Bitter–Sweet Picture

In 2009, Waddington predicted that the CRPD would "*breath new life into [Article 114 TFEU], thereby requiring a much more vigorous consideration of the need to incorporate disability accessibility standards in internal market harmonisation legislation*" (Waddington, 2009). The WAD and EAA are certainly the evidence of such "*new life*", although are not *per se* sufficient to comply with the obligations laid out in Article 9 CRPD. In fact, the WAD and the EAA, taken together, do apply to a broad range of services and digital goods and facilities, and their material scope mostly extends the digital environment, which is though not fully adequate to ensure equal opportunities in all fields of life, as required by the CRPD. In this respect, since the enactment of the EAA, the European Disability Forum (EDF), the major EU-wide umbrella organisation of persons with disabilities, has indicated that the EAA does not cover "*healthcare services, education, transport, housing, and household appliances*" (European Disability Forum-EDF, 2019). By contrast, full accessibility to healthcare, education, and housing would in fact be essential to end social exclusion. With regard to housing, the European Parliament, in its resolution of 21 January 2021, has stressed the importance of creating accessible, non-segregated housing and providing accessible community-based services for persons with disabilities (Resolution of European Parliament, 2021). Further, as mentioned above, the EAA excludes from its scope microenterprises, which are not subject to accessibility obligations. The most evident loophole of both the WAD and the EAA is that they are limiting accessibility obligations to situations in which these do not cause a disproportionate burden on the duty bearer. Such a limit is not compliant with the unconditional characterisation of accessibility obligations in the CRPD.

Yet, in spite of their evident drawbacks, both the WAD and the EAA are important stepping stones to achieve equality for persons with disabilities and support their social inclusion. Notably, EDF, alongside highlighting its weaknesses, has praised the strengths of both the WAD and EAA. In particular, in relation to the EAA, EDF states that it represents "*a significant step in the journey of making the EU fully accessible for persons with disabilities*" (European Disability Forum-EDF, 2019). While their material scope is somewhat limited, they do support access to a range of digital goods that are essential for participation in society. Further, the application and implementation of these directives may display knock-on effects. In 2018, Anderson already indicated that the WAD, albeit targeting only the public sector, is likely to have a significant impact on private companies that sell to the public sector, as they will need to ensure their products are compliant if they are to be used by public servants (Anderson, 2018). Similarly, the reach of the EAA can be greater than its formal material scope, ensuring accessibility of services that are connected with those falling within the remit of the Directive. In that regard, the

WAD and EAA can support and influence innovation adoption patterns and diffusion of accessibility requirements, in turn enhancing participation of persons with disabilities across all areas of life. Ensuring accessible public and commercial websites, as well as commercial services such as ATMs, has a great potential to positively impact citizens with disabilities' ability to interact socially, to travel, and to avail of services. Reinforcing the internal market for accessible products and services has also a great potential to lower prices, and give people more choices. While the EAA particularly does not address poverty per se, it is expected to enhance the purchasing power of persons with disabilities. In that regard, the WAD and the EAA do support the fight against social exclusion envisaged in Article 9 TFEU. Further, harmonised accessibility requirements for websites, digital goods, and services will arguably stimulate public operators and private companies to share research and technology.

On the whole, the WAD and the EAA have great potential to facilitate social inclusion of persons with disabilities.

Concluding Remarks

Thus far, the WAD and the EAA are probably the most important legislative enactments in the field of accessibility. They complement the accessibility measures sparse in EU legislation and must be considered in conjunction with other non-legislative tools. While the WAD only applies to the websites and apps of public organisations, the EAA applies to a range of private and commercial services. In that connection, Broderick (2019) highlights that the EAA "*represents a horizontal legal tool that can serve to complement sectoral legislation on digital accessibility in the field of audiovisual services and electronic communications and ensure new EU-wide minimum accessibility requirements for a relatively broad range of digital (and other) products, and services*" (p. 34).

Both the WAD and EAA fall short of the obligations laid down in the CRPD but, as noted elsewhere, they show how market goals have become intertwined with social objectives, evidencing the increasing social dimension of market integration (Ferri, 2020), in line with Article 9 and 10 TFEU. In that regard, we can safely affirm that the WAD and the EAA do constitute accessibility of products and services as a key tool to fight social exclusion. The Strategy 2021–2030 signals a strong commitment from the Commission to support the implementation of those pieces of legislation, ensuring that both the WAD and EAA are fully effective.

The COVID-19 pandemic pushed an unprecedented digitalisation with consumers being forced to use online channels. In the aftermath of the pandemic and in such an expanded digital environment, the WAD and the EAA have an essential role in ensuring that both the public sector and businesses make their services and digital facilities accessible to persons with disabilities and that the abandonment of embedded routines and established exclusionary practices in the physical environment leads to new inclusive digital services. Ultimately, the WAD and the EAA, by enhancing availability of accessible products and services, have a great potential to support greater participation and inclusion of people with disabilities in society.

References

Anderson, B. (2018). *Is the public sector ready for the web accessibility directive?* Public Technology.

Broderick, A., & Ferri, D. (2019). *International and European disability law and policy*. Cambridge University Press.

Broderick, A. (2015). *The long and winding road to equality and inclusion for persons with disabilities: The United Nations convention on the rights of persons with disabilities*, Intersentia, p. 77.

Broderick, A. (2019). The European accessibility act: A paradigm of inclusive digital equality for persons with disabilities? In C. Ricci (Ed.), *Building an inclusive digital society for persons with disabilities new challenges and future potentials* (pp. 19–38). Pavia University Press.

Charitakis, S. (2018). *Access denied: The role of the European Union in ensuring accessibility under the United Nations Convention on the rights of persons with disabilities*. Intersentia.

Charitakis, S. (2020). Accessibility of goods and services. In D. Ferri & A. Broderick (Eds.), *Research handbook on EU disability law* (pp. 221–242). Edward Elgar.

CJEU, Joined cases C-335/11 and C-337/11, HK Danmark. (2013, April 11). *ECLI:EU:C:2013:222*. https://curia.europa.eu/juris/liste.jsf?num=C-335/11&language=EN

Commission Communication "European Disability Strategy 2010-2020: A Renewed Commitment to a Barrier-Free Europe", COM (2010). 636 final, 15 November 2010. https://eur-lex.europa.eu/legal-content/en/ALL/?uri=CELEX%3A52010DC0636

Commission Communication "Union of equality: Strategy for the rights of persons with disabilities 2021–2030", COM (2021). 101 final, 21 March 2021. https://op.europa.eu/en/publication-detail/-/publication/3e1e2228-7c97-11eb-9ac9-01aa75ed71a1/language-en

Council Decision 2010/48/EC, of 26 November 2009, concerning the conclusion, by the European Community, of the United Nations Convention on the Rights of Persons with Disabilities (2010), OJ L23/35. https://eur-lex.europa.eu/legal-content/EN/TXT/?uri=CELEX:32010D0048

Council Directive 2000/78/EC, establishing a general framework for equal treatment in employment and occupation (2000), OJ L303/16. https://eur-lex.europa.eu/legal-content/EN/TXT/?uri=CELEX:32000L0078

Council Directive 89/654/EEC, of 30 November 1989, concerning the minimum safety and health requirements for the workplace (1989), OJ L393/1. https://eur-lex.europa.eu/eli/dir/1989/654/oj

Directive (EU) 2018/1808, of the European Parliament and the Council, of 14 November 2018, amending Directive 2010/13/EU on the coordination of certain provisions laid down by law, regulation or administration action in Member States concerning the provision of audiovisual media services (Audiovisual Media Services Directive) in view of changing market realities (2018), OJ L303/69. https://eur-lex.europa.eu/eli/dir/2018/1808/oj

Directive (EU) No 2016/2102 of the European Parliament and of the Council, on the accessibility of the websites and mobile applications of public sector bodies (2016), OJ L327/1. https://eur-lex.europa.eu/eli/dir/2016/2102/oj

Directive (EU) No 2019/882 of the European Parliament and of the Council, of 17 April 2019, on the accessibility requirements for products and services (2019), OJ L 151/70. https://eur-lex.europa.eu/eli/dir/2019/882/oj

Directive 2010/13/EU of the European Parliament and of the Council, of 10 March 2010, on the coordination of certain provisions laid down by law, regulation or administrative action in Member States concerning the provision of audiovisual media services (Audiovisual Media Services Directive), (2010), OJ L 95/1. https://eur-lex.europa.eu/eli/dir/2010/13/oj

Directive 2014/24/EU of the European Parliament and of the Council, of 26 February 2014, on public procurement and repealing Directive 2004/18/EC (2014), OJ L94/65. https://eur-lex.europa.eu/legal-content/EN/TXT/?uri=celex%3A32014L0024

Directive 2014/25/EU of the European Parliament and of the Council, of 26 February 2014, on procurement by entities operating in the water, energy, transport and postal services sectors and repealing Directive 2004/17/EC (2014), OJ L94/243. https://eurlex.europa.eu/legal-content/EN/TXT/?uri=celex%3A32014L0025

Directive 2014/53/EU of the European Parliament and of the Council, of 16 April 2014, on the harmonisation of the laws of the Member States relating to the making available on the market of radio equipment and repealing Directive 1999/5/EC (2014), OJ L153/62. https://eur-lex.europa.eu/legal-content/EN/TXT/PDF/?uri=CELEX:32014L0053

European Economic and Social Committee, "Shaping the EU agenda for disability rights 2020–2030" SOC/616—EESC-2019-01571-00-00-AC-TRA (EN). (2019, January 24).

Interinstitutional Proclamation on the European Pillar of Social Rights. (2017) OJ C 428/10. https://eur-lex.europa.eu/legal-content/EN/TXT/?uri=CELEX%3A32017C1213%2801%29&qid=1747156235461

Eurostat. (2023). *Disability statistics–poverty and income inequalities*. https://ec.europa.eu/eurostat/statistics-explained/index.php?title=Disability_statistics_-_poverty_and_income_inequalities#At_risk_of_poverty_or_social_exclusion

Ferri, D. (2023). The role of the European Union in ensuring accessibility of cultural goods and services: All about that… internal market? *European Law Review, 48*(3), 257–280.

Ferri, D., & Broderick, A. (2020). Introduction. In D. Ferri & A. Broderick (Eds.), *Research handbook on EU disability law* (pp. 1–10). Edward Elgar.

Ferri, D., & Favalli, S. (2018). Web accessibility for people with disabilities in the European Union: Paving the road to social inclusion. *Societies., 8*, 40–59.

Ferri, D. (2020). The European accessibility act and the shadow of the social market economy. *European Law Review, 5*, 660–680.

Ferri, D. (2021). The UN Convention on the rights of Persons with disabilities in the EU legal framework and the development of EU disability policies after 2020. What is coming is better than what is gone? In M. Ganner, E. Rieder, C. Voithofer, & F. Welti (Eds.), *The implementation of the UN convention on the rights of persons with disabilities in Austria and Germany*. Innsbruck University Press.

Garben, S. (2017). Social Policy. In P. J. G. Kapteyn & P. ver Loren Van Themaat (Eds.), *European Union Law*. Kluwer Law International.

Hosking, D. (2013). Staying the course: The European disability strategy 2010–2020. *European Yearbook of Disability Law, 4*, 73.

Inclusion Europe. (2019). *Poverty and intellectual disability in Europe*. https://www.inclusion-europe.eu/wp-content/uploads/2019/01/SocInc_EUPovertyRreport.pdf

Lawson, A. (2018). Article 9: Accessibility. In M. A. Stein, I. Bantekas, & D. Anastasiou (Eds.), *The UN convention on the rights of persons with disabilities: A commentary*. Oxford University Press.

European Disability Forum- EDF (2019). *Our analysis of the European accessibility act*. European Disability Forum. https://www.edf-feph.org/newsroom-news-our-analysis-european-accessibility-act/

O'Mahony, C. & Quinlivan, S. (2020). The EU disability strategy and the future of EU disability policy. In D. Ferri & A. Broderick (Eds.), *Research handbook on EU disability law* (pp. 12–28). Edward Elgar.

Perlin, M. (2014). The ladder of the law has no top and no bottom: How therapeutic jurisprudence can give life to international human rights. *International Journal of Law and Psychiatry*.

Regulation (EC) No 1107/2006 of the European Parliament and of the Council, concerning the rights of disabled persons and persons with reduced mobility when travelling by air, (2006) OJ L204/1. https://eur-lex.europa.eu/legal-content/EN/TXT/?uri=CELEX:32006R1107

Regulation (EU) No 181/2011 of the European Parliament and of the Council, concerning the rights of passengers in bus and coach transport and amending Regulation (EC) 2006/2004 (2011) OJ L55/1. https://eur-lex.europa.eu/LexUriServ/LexUriServ.do?uri=OJ:L:2011:055:0001:0012:EN:PDF

Regulation (EU) 2016/424 of the European Parliament and of the Council, of 09 March 2016, on cableway installations and repealing Directive 2000/9/EC (2016) OJ L 81/1. https://eur-lex.europa.eu/eli/reg/2016/424/oj/eng

Regulation (EU) 2024/1679 of the European Parliament and of the Council of 13 June 2024 on Union guidelines for the development of the trans-European transport network, amending Regulations (EU) 2021/1153 and (EU) No 913/2010 and repealing Regulation (EU) No 1315/2013 (2024), OJ L 2024/1679. https://eur-lex.europa.eu/eli/reg/2024/1679/oj

Regulation (EU) 1177/2010 of the European Parliament and of the Council, concerning the rights of passengers when travelling by sea and inland waterway and amending Regulation (EC) 2006/2004 (2010), OJ L334/1. https://eur-lex.europa.eu/legal-content/EN/TXT/PDF/?uri=CELEX:32010R1177

Resolution of European Parliament, on access to decent and affordable housing for all, of 21 January 2021 (2019/2187(INI)). https://oeil.secure.europarl.europa.eu/oeil/popups/ficheprocedure.do?lang=en&reference=2019/2187(INI)

Rimmerman, A. (2014). *Social Inclusion of People with Disabilities: National and International Perspectives*. Cambridge University Press.

UN Committee on the Rights of Persons with Disabilities, General Comment No. 4 on Article 24, UN Doc. CRPD/C/GC/4 (2016) https://digitallibrary.un.org/record/1313836?v=pdf

UN Committee on the Rights of Persons with Disabilities, General Comment No. 2 on Article 9, UN Doc. CRPD/C/GC/2 (2014) https://digitallibrary.un.org/record/812025?v=pdf

UN Convention on the Rights of Persons with Disabilities. (2006, December 13). in force 03 May 2008, UN Doc. A/RES/61/106.

Varney, E., & Pearson, A. (2020). Disability in EU transport legislation. In D. Ferri & A. Broderick (Eds.), *Research handbook on EU disability law* (pp. 182–200). Edward Elgar.

Waddington, L. (2005). *From Rome to Nice in a wheelchair. The development of a European disability policy*. Europa Law Publishing.

Waddington, L. (2009). A disabled market: Free movement of goods and services in the EU and disability accessibility. *European Law Journal, 5*, 575.

Waddington, L. (2011). The European Union and the United Nations convention on the rights of persons with disabilities: A story of exclusive and shared competences. *Maastricht Journal of European and Comparative Law, 18*, 431.

Waddington, L. (2018). The European Union. In L. Waddington & A. Lawson (Eds.), *The UN convention on the rights of persons with disabilities in practice* (p. 131). Oxford University Press.

From Policy to Case Law: Have the Rights of Intersex Persons and Non-Binary and Gender-Diverse Persons Finally Become Visible Across Europe?

Kalliopi Chainoglou

Abstract

The vulnerability of LGBTIQ+ persons is accelerated by the intersecting forms of discrimination they face in multiple and overlapping ways. A constellation of factors increases the vulnerability of intersex persons and non-binary and gender-diverse persons. With limited visibility, they have been subjected to historical discrimination in varying contexts (legal, policy, social, cultural, political, workplace, etc.). Recent case law before the European Court of Human Rights and the Court of Justice of the European Union opens up the space for interaction with the lived experiences of these two groups and critical thinking on the interpretation of human rights law in Europe.

Introduction

Human rights often become politicised or fall victim to populist and sensitised narratives. LGBTIQ+ rights may confuse the wider audiences; when mentioned they are mistaken for a claim of a new set of rights (Chainoglou, 2023). LGBTIQ+ rights are often viewed as a manifestation of the 'woke' culture and they face backlash from ultraconservative and ultranationalist groups (UN Independent Expert on Sexual Orientation and Gender Identity, Effective Inclusion of LGBT persons, n.d.; UN Independent Expert on Protection against Violence and Discrimination Based on Sexual Orientation and Gender Identity, 2024, para. 19). It is also noted that some countries in the West have been displaying anti-LGBTIQ+ attitudes and policies that are coinciding with an overall human rights rollback at a domestic level. In

K. Chainoglou (✉)
Department of International and European Studies, University of Macedonia, Thessaloniki, Greece
e-mail: chainoglou@uom.edu.gr

D. Anagnostopoulou (ed.), *European Identities, Inclusion and Equality*, Diversity and Inclusion Research, https://doi.org/10.1007/978-3-031-90602-2_12

particular, in the United States it is not only that we see more anti-LGBTIQ+ legislation being passed, but we get to hear more and more about threats against participation in pride events (Council of Foreign Relations, 2024). While in certain parts of Europe, we view the steady advancement of their rights, other European countries with far right-wing governments in power have been eroding LGBTIQ+ rights and LGBTIQ+ acceptance.

The 2030 Agenda for Sustainable Development contains a pledge to leave no one behind, and it aims at achieving respect for human rights, equality and non-discrimination for all. LGBTIQ+ persons face intersecting forms of discrimination and various dynamics of exclusion in different contexts (i.e. in displacement settings and refugees) that increase their vulnerability (UN Independent Expert on Protection against Violence and Discrimination Based on Sexual Orientation and Gender Identity, 2019). From a legal perspective, existing international human rights instruments already cover the human rights and fundamental freedoms of LGBTIQ+ persons. LGBTIQ+ persons have the right to live free from discrimination, violence, persecution and stigma and without being subjected to homophobic and transphobic attitudes. Yet the existence of international human rights instruments and the increasing number of policy documents and reports on LGBTIQ+ issues by regional organisations do not necessarily guarantee a fast pace of amending and/or introducing legislation at a national level that guarantees the full and meaningful inclusion of LGBTIQ+ persons. With the protection of human rights of vulnerable groups, including LGBTIQ+ persons, domestic accountability often lags behind. What is even more worrisome is that LGBTIQ+ persons are at even greater risk in geographic regions where there is the absence of a regional human rights protection system.

The vulnerability of LGBTIQ+ persons is accelerated by the intersecting forms of discrimination they face in multiple and overlapping ways; the LGBTIQ+ rights are correspondingly claimed to overcome social exclusion and persistent, structural barriers (Chainoglou, 2023, pp. 325–333). The UN has not proceeded to this day with elaborating on a human rights convention addressing per se LGBTIQ+ rights. If only the Yogyakarta Principles Plus 10 could be adopted as a binding human rights instrument (International Commission of Jurists, 2017), this would have been an effective means to bring down the structural and binary barriers that hinder the equal enjoyment of human rights by LGBTIQ+ persons. What the UN has done though is to reaffirm that the existing UN human rights instruments guarantee the rights of LGBTIQ+ persons. For the implementation of the rights of LGBTIQ+ persons, states bear five minimum core obligations to protect, fulfil and respect the human rights of LGBTIQ+ persons on the basis of the existing human rights norms and standards, including customary law (i.e. prohibition of torture) (OHCHR, 2023). Accordingly, states are under the duty to refrain from taking measures that violate the enjoyment of human rights of LGBTIQ+ persons; prevent human rights abuses conducted by state organs, public authorities and individuals; investigate human rights abuses and provide remedies to the victims in an appropriate manner. States have to comply with core obligations, including the protection of individuals from homophobic and transphobic violence; the prevention of torture and cruel, inhuman and degrading treatment; the repealing/amendment of laws criminalising homosexual activity and transgender people; the prohibition of discrimination based on sexual orientation and gender identity; the safeguarding of the freedoms of expression, association and peaceful assembly for LGBTIQ+ persons (UN Independent Expert on Protection Against Violence and Discrimination based on Sexual Orientation and Gender Identity, 2024).

In the European continent, both the EU and the Council of Europe have developed and strengthened standards on non-discrimination and equality for LGBTIQ+ people and have been working towards cementing more inclusive societies. However, this does not necessarily reflect what individual EU member states think of LGBTIQ+ equality. On a political level, the EU is currently implementing the LGBTIQ+ Equality Strategy for 2025 and has found that the strategy is having a positive impact on the situation of the LGBTIQ+ persons across Europe (EU Commission Report, 2024). Even though only 12 out of the 26 member states of the EU have developed national action plans towards LGBTIQ+ equality, the EU remains committed to promoting LGBTIQ+ equality and has prepared through the LGBTIQ+ Equality Subgroup guidelines for all member states to implement equality in a strategic and evidence-based manner (European Commission Guidelines for Strategies and Action Plans to Enhance LGBTIQ+ Equality, 2022). Within this context, the EU Commissioner for Equality is expected to deliver an updated strategy on LGBTIQ+ equality (EU Commission Political Guidelines, 2024–2029). Furthermore, the EU has been pushing forward with the advancement of the rights of LGBTIQ+ across its external actions, such as the decriminalisation of consensual same-sex sexual acts or the establishment of a rapid response mechanism, to protect LGBTIQ+ human rights defenders at risk. All these are positive steps but there are still areas of intersectional discrimination that are not fully explored, for example, LGBTIQ+ persons with disabilities being denied or having their sexual orientation or gender identity controlled and LGBTIQ+ persons with disabilities having inadequate access to healthcare or social services. Accordingly, new targeted actions have to be designed, for example, in order to align disability and other strategies with LGBTIQ+ equality strategies. The lack of access, space and visibility for LGBTIQ+ persons at the national and European levels is also acknowledged by representative organisations such as the European Disability Forum and ILGA:

> EU law does **not** prohibit discrimination based on sexual orientation or gender identity, nor discrimination based on disability outside the field of employment and vocational training. This means that discrimination based on one or a combination of these grounds is not illegal under EU law and is only prohibited where Member States adopted specific legislation, which is different from one country to another. This results in difference of treatment across the EU, which impacts the EU right to freedom of movement... The EU does not sufficiently address the intersection between disability, sexual orientation and gender identities in its laws and policies. (European Disability Forum and ILGA Europe, 2024, p. 4).

Hence, it is recommended that the EU identifies who are the most marginalised people with intersecting identities and proposes plans, services and prevention mechanisms that leave no one behind (European Disability Forum and ILGA Europe, 2024, p. 5).

The Council of Europe aims at eliminating discrimination based on gender identity and/or expression in twelve areas such as freedom of association, freedom of expression, respect for private and family life, employment, housing, health education, asylum, intersection discrimination, freedom from violence, etc. Various bodies of the Council of Europe have adopted important soft law instruments that deal with a wide array of LGBTIQ+ issues and purport to eliminate discrimination based on sexual orientation, gender identity and other sex-protected characteristics.

By moving away from socio-behavioural and medicalised definitions (i.e. treating LGBTIQ+ issues as mental health references), the bodies of the Council of Europe contribute to the recognition of how LGBTIQ+ persons have been historically left out of policies, how LGBTIQ+ persons (especially older persons) have suffered from historical discrimination and social exclusion, and how more vulnerable groups within the LGBTIQ+ community, such as intersex and non-binary persons have experienced intersectional discrimination and marginalisation. So far, the Committee of Ministers has issued three review reports on the implementation of the Recommendation (2010) 5 on measures to combat discrimination on grounds of sexual orientation or gender identity in three thematic areas:

1. Legal gender recognition (Council of Europe Steering Committee on Anti-Discrimination, Diversity and Inclusion, 2022),
2. Hate crimes and other hate-motivated incidents based on sexual orientation, gender identity, gender expression and sex characteristics in Europe (Council of Europe Steering Committee on Anti-Discrimination, Diversity and Inclusion, 2023),
3. Health and access to healthcare for LGBTIQ+ persons (Council of Europe Steering Committee on Anti-Discrimination, Diversity and Inclusion, 2024).

With regard to legal gender recognition, the Committee of Ministers has inter alia recommended the lift of restrictions to non-nationals' access to the legal gender recognition; the inclusion of non-binary, gender-diverse and intersex in the legal gender recognition framework (i.e. by removing the gender markers from official documents), and most notably, the amendment of national hate crime and hate speech legislation in order to consider motives related to the victim's gender identity or sex characteristics as 'aggravating factors'. With regard to hate crimes, the Committee of Ministers places particular emphasis on the need to address the root causes of crimes committed based on sexual orientation, gender identity, gender expression and sex characteristics (SOGIESC). For example, societal prejudice, stigmatisation and discrimination are identified as some of the root causes of such crimes. Furthermore, it is equally important to collect data on hate crimes and to train and support law enforcement, judiciary and other stakeholders in unmasking the SOGIESC elements of such crimes. With regard to access to healthcare, the Committee of Ministers has delivered a strong message about the need to restructure health, social care and equality policies by taking into consideration the intersectional grounds upon which LGBTIQ+ persons have historically been discriminated against (and effectively left out of such policies). The impact of intersectional discrimination on LGBTIQ+ persons has profound implications for their right to life and right to health, especially mental health. Furthermore, it is stressed out there in that LGBTIQ+-specific issues must be visible in national policy-making and they must be addressed in a comprehensive and unambiguous manner. What is also important is that respect for LGBTIQ+ persons and their lived experiences can only materialise if stereotypes and prejudices are eliminated. Hence, the Committee of Ministers recommends that States proceed with the amendment of school curricula to reflect LGBTIQ+ realities and respect their rights. On a similar note, it is equally important to have public officials promoting tolerance for the human rights of LGBTIQ+ persons.

Committee of Ministers Instruments
Recommendation 2024 (4) on combating hate crime
Recommendation (2022) 16 on combating hate speech
Recommendation CM/Rec(2010)5 on measures to combat discrimination on grounds of sexual orientation or gender identity Committee of Ministers
Parliamentary assembly instruments
Resolution 2418 (2022) on alleged violations of the Rights of LGBTI people in the Southern Caucasus.
Resolution 2417 (2022) on combating rising hate against LGBTI people in Europe
Resolution 2339 (2020) on upholding human rights in times of crisis and pandemics
Resolution 2239 (2018): Private and family life: achieving equality regardless of sexual orientation
Resolution 2191 (2017): Promoting the human rights of and eliminating discrimination against intersex people
Resolution 2048 (2015): Discrimination against transgender people in Europe
Resolution 2021 (2013) on tackling discrimination on the grounds of sexual orientation and gender identity
Resolution 1729 (2010) on discrimination on the basis of sexual orientation and gender identity
Resolution 1474 (2000) on the situation of lesbians and gays in Council of Europe Member States
Congress of local and regional authorities
Resolution 471 (2021) on the role of local and regional authorities with regard to the situation of LGBTI people in Poland.
Resolution 470 (2021) on protecting LGBTI people in the context of rising anti-LGBTI hate speech and discrimination: The role of local and regional authorities
Resolution 380 (2015): Guaranteeing lesbian, gay, bisexual and transgender (LGBT) people's rights: a responsibility for Europe's towns and regions
Resolution 230 (2007): Freedom of assembly and expression for lesbians, gays, bisexuals and transgendered persons;
European Commission against racism and intolerance instruments
Policy recommendation (no 17) on preventing and combating intolerance and discrimination against LGBTI persons

Source: The author

The normative work of the Council of Europe bodies contributes to creating and sustaining a European consensus (a form of comparative legal reasoning based on positions taken by the member states of the Council of Europe) on how the rights of LGBTIQ+ persons can be protected under the European Convention on Human

Rights. Sustaining a European consensus on the matter is more important than ever given the rise of anti-LGBTIQ+ and anti-woke narratives and the lack of comprehensive laws against hate speech and hate crime on the basis of sexual orientation or gender identity in particular countries in the region, i.e. Poland, Italy and the Czech Republic (Guillot & Coi, 2024; EU FRA, 2024). Despite the growing social acceptance of LGBTQI+ persons, it is noted that there is an increase in reported violence against LGBTQI+ persons while a significant number of states are stalling in enforcing policies and laws on the meaningful inclusion and protection of LGBTQI+ persons (EU FRA, 2024). For this reason, as of 2024, transgender and intersex persons in Europe report the highest rates of being victims of discrimination (EU FRA, 2024). The European Court of Human Rights has a long record of adjudicating cases concerning sexual orientation and gender identity. It has delivered landmark judgments that have been used as a point of reference by the Court of Justice of the European Union. However, both these European supranational courts have examined so far only a handful of cases whereby the applicants were either intersex or non-binary. As these two groups are characterised by the constellation of factors that increase their vulnerability and their victimisation in various (legal, social, cultural, political, etc.) contexts, this chapter examines how the rights of these two vulnerable groups are currently understood within Europe and how recent case law before the European Court of Human Rights and the Court of Justice of the European Union can open up the space for more litigation in the future.

Intersex Rights

Intersex persons are persons that have innate variations of sex characteristics (i.e. genitals, reproductive organs, chromosomal or hormonal patterns) that are different from the stereotypical definitions of male and female bodies. Such variations of sex characteristics are the grounds upon which intersex persons are subjected to discrimination and harmful medical practices and infanticides (Jorge et al., 2019). The right to life, the right to health and freedom from torture are not the only affected rights when it comes to intersex children and adults. Discrimination against intersex children and adults also manifests within the socio-economic and cultural sphere of their lives; for example, they experience discrimination in education, public spaces, sports, aspects of cultural life and employment while their access to health services is also hindered due to lack of awareness and training or because of negative stereotypes and inter-phobic attitudes that are embedded in national health and social care systems.

Intersex rights are gaining increasing recognition globally and within Europe (Council of Europe Commissioner for Human Rights, 2014). This development comes after decades of campaigning on raising awareness about the unique challenges that intersex people have faced in terms of harmful practices, discrimination and stigmatisation they have suffered either as children or adults across societies. It should be noted that without persistent advocacy and grassroots campaigning, intersex issues are likely to remain on the sideline for the years to come despite the overall progressive development and implementation of LGBTIQ+ rights at the national level around the world. Currently, there are two main issues that need urgent attention to: (1) the right of intersex persons to not be classified as 'Female' or 'Male' and (2) the criminalisation of intersex genital mutilation and any other 'correcting' or 'normalising' therapies, as intersex children and persons have historically been deprived of their right to bodily autonomy and to physical and psychological integrity.

Legal recognition of gender identities is a core claim for intersex rights, as intersex persons are usually denied legal recognition or registration at birth as 'Intersex' due to the 'Female' and 'Male' dichotomy. Furthermore, due to this binary dichotomy, intersex persons are assigned a sex at birth that does not necessarily correspond with their gender identity. Furthermore, due to the non-comprehensive legal frameworks on legal gender recognition across national jurisdictions, intersex persons have been registered as 'Female' or 'Male' and it has been legally difficult (if not impossible) for them to amend the gender marker on official documents.

Unnecessary medical interventions have historically been carried out on intersex persons and minors without their prior, informed consent. Such medical interventions are intrusive and non-reversible; they are effectively infringing human dignity, the freedom of self-determination and of bodily integrity, the right to health and the right to development of the person. Such medical interventions have often been complemented by other 'normalising' therapies aiming at changing or suppressing someone's gender identity, gender expression or sexual orientation. The latter may be carried out by educational, religious/spiritual and mental health professionals and other professionals providing care and support. Even though such therapies may not be *stricto* sensu medical interventions in nature, they are unethical and harmful and have a lifelong impact. In all of the above scenarios, whether medical interventions or other 'normalising' therapies, the psychological distress—caused by the outcomes of such medical operations—has often led intersex persons to self-harming and suicidal thoughts or acts (EU Parliament Briefing, 2022).

A wide array of such medical procedures aiming at treating intersex as a healthcare issue have been carried out without the full, informed and free consent of the victims and they are only now considered to be a textbook case of harmful practice and gender-based violence (see discussion below). For many decades, the binaried healthcare systems at a national level have contributed to intersex erasure. Medical professionals have pushed parents to consent to 'normalising' medical interventions (i.e. genital mutilation, cosmetic interventions, hormonal treatment, forced or coerced sterilisation) that would provide intersex foetuses, babies and children with a 'fixed' 'female' or 'male' body yet without such medical interventions being necessary to the well-being of the affected person. Treating intersex identity as a medical issue and allowing for medical interventions have resulted in intersex erasure. Consequently, this has led, on the one hand, to the exclusion of intersex persons from any equality and diversity national plans and social policies and, on the other hand, to the intersex persons being overlooked by national legislators, policy makers and practitioners (Monro et al., 2024) as well national human rights institutions that were not clearly mandated to examine their human rights claims. Furthermore, as such interventions start at a young age and continue through a person's life, they have significant socio-economic consequences on those persons' lives, i.e. in terms of missing out on education and employment opportunities. This lived-in reality of intersex persons has been historically overlooked at the policy level where there have been limited (if none at all) measures to offer them opportunities to maximise their skills and earning potential. The lack of full inclusion of intersex persons remains even to this day critical to elevating human capital and reducing gender inequality in labour markets. This has also been confirmed by the World Bank which has noted that the exclusion of sexual and gender minorities contributes to a loss in productivity and 'is impacting economies, including at the level of GDP' (Clifton et al., 2023, p. 1; CIDP. 2023).

International organisations are currently producing standard-setting instruments (albeit soft law ones) that are creating a roadmap for a better understanding of the human rights violations that intersex persons have been subjected to as well as raising awareness on the need to create legal guarantees and policy measures that will protect the bodily integrity and bodily autonomy of intersex persons and will ensure their full access to their own medical records (OHCHR, 2023; Zelayandia-Gonzalez, 2023; ILGA Database Conversion Therapies, 2024). A plethora of UN human rights committees have made recommendations concerning the need to abolish unnecessary medical interventions, especially during childhood (OHCHR, 2023). This is in line with Article 32 of the Yogyakarta Principles plus 10 (International Commission of Jurists, 2017), which states that:

> Everyone has the right to bodily and mental integrity, autonomy and self-determination irrespective of sexual orientation, gender identity, gender expression or sex characteristics. Everyone has the right to be free from torture and cruel, inhuman and degrading treatment or punishment on the basis of sexual orientation, gender identity, gender expression and sex characteristics. No one shall be subjected to invasive or irreversible medical procedures that modify sex characteristics without their free, prior and informed consent, unless necessary to avoid serious, urgent and irreparable harm to the concerned person.

The UN Rapporteur on Torture has called upon all States to repeal any legislation that allows intrusive and irreversible treatments, including forced genital-normalizing surgery, involuntary sterilisation, unethical experimentation, medical display, 'reparative therapies' or 'conversion therapies' when enforced or administered without the free and informed consent of the person concerned (Report of the Special Rapporteur on torture and other cruel, inhuman or degrading treatment or punishment (2013), paras. 38, 76–87). Furthermore, the UN Special Rapporteur on extrajudicial executions has called for the protection of gender-diverse and intersex persons from both State and non-State actors and has requested from States to investigate and prosecute those responsible for the killings of intersex children and adults (UN Special Rapporteur on extrajudicial executions, 2024).

Most recently, the Human Rights Council adopted a landmark resolution that is essentially the first step towards providing a remedy to all intersex victims of historical human rights abuses and creating a paradigm for states' accountability in the future (UN HRC 55/14, 8 April, 2024). The resolution aims at protecting the rights of intersex persons, especially their right to the highest attainable standard of physical and mental health. It aims to address the root causes of historical discrimination that intersex persons have faced and any misconceptions that exist with regard to intersex persons through a comprehensive approach. The resolution, which was spearheaded by Australia, Chile, Finland and South Africa, calls for the High Commissioner for Human Rights to prepare a report on all discriminatory practices (including acts of violence and harmful practices) and laws against persons with innate variations in sex characteristics and to hold a panel discussion in its 60th session with the participation of States, civil society actors and all other stakeholders.

Unfortunately, this is a resolution that was marginally adopted with 24 states voting in favour (Albania, Argentina, Belgium, Brazil, Bulgaria, Chile, Costa Rica, Cuba, Dominican Republic, Finland, France, Germany, Ghana, Honduras, India, Japan, Lithuania, Luxembourg, Montenegro, Netherlands (Kingdom of the), Romania, South Africa, United States of America, Viet Nam) and 23 states abstaining from the voting procedure (Algeria, Bangladesh, Benin, Burundi, Cameroon, China, Côte d'Ivoire, Eritrea, Gambia, Georgia, Indonesia, Kazakhstan, Kuwait, Kyrgyzstan, Malawi, Malaysia, Maldives, Morocco, Paraguay, Qatar, Somalia, Sudan, United Arab Emirates). This polarised voting suggests that there is a considerable number of States across the world that are reluctant to address intersex rights at the domestic level with the urgency required. Consequently, it is within such States that the UN and other regional organisations need to offer support to human rights defenders and intersex rights activists in order for them to be able to bring visibility to intersex issues and push for changes at the domestic level (Garland et al., 2022).

In the European continent, as early as in 2014 a report was issued aimed at alarming the states that intersex persons lack recognition in Europe despite the human rights challenges they face (Council of Europe Commissioner for Human Rights, 2015). In 2015, another more detailed report was released in order to address the various developments at the medical and legal level and request governments to work on best practices in this area with intersex activists (Council of Europe Commissioner for Human Rights, 2015). Despite the improvements that have been noted with regard to how national councils on medical ethics and national medical professional associations were treating intersex cases, it is felt that these developments have been isolated at the national level. The legal status of intersex persons (the right to a gender identity and the designation of a legal gender) is also dealt with in an ambivalent manner across national jurisdictions (Scherpe, 2018; Malta Declaration, 2013).

Intersex persons are also impacted by age discrimination. Within the European Union framework, half of the states do not recognise multiple discrimination, i.e. age and sexual orientation or gender identity, and this results in intersex people having limited—if none at all—protection against multiple discrimination (see European Disability Forum and ILGA Europe, 2024). Older intersex persons are often overlooked in the collection of data and health and social care policy-making. Consequently, intersex persons are led to an increased risk of heightened discrimination and social exclusion. In a survey conducted by FRA, it was reported that many of intersex persons reported (especially older intersex and transgender persons of an ethnic minority) concern or discrimination in accessing age-appropriate and intersex-appropriate health and social care services, i.e. nursing homes (EU FRA, 2024). Furthermore, the existing national health and social care systems have been designed without taking into consideration the needs of intersex persons or the personal medical stories of intersex persons. The emotional and psychological distress they suffer from these non-consensual normalising therapies is also overlooked (Council of Europe Steering Committee on Anti-Discrimination Diversity and Inclusion, 2024, para. 6):

> Intersex people may struggle to address their ongoing health needs because they have been lied to, or had information withheld, by HCPs. In two European studies, intersex participants reported plans to end their life before going into a care facility for older people due to fear of being disrespected, ridiculed, shamed, and bullied.

The lack of knowledge and cultural competencies concerning the needs of older intersex persons along with non-inclusive attitudes by health and social care professionals can only increase inequalities for intersex persons (Council of Europe Steering Committee on Anti-Discrimination Diversity and Inclusion, 2024, para. 63).

Redress for human rights violations of intersex persons is also another area that merits attention from States. Given the wide exclusion of intersex persons from equality and diversity as well as social, health, educational and other policies across all countries around the world, it is of utmost importance to adopt a top-down approach and design measures that challenge the historical and systemic erasure of intersex identity and provide for redress for any of the harms inflicted upon intersex persons. At the same time, a bottoms-up approach is recommended for legal reforms that are required to address the intersectional grounds upon which intersex persons have faced discrimination, i.e. age, disability and gender. Strategic litigation could be a means to establishing redress for violations of the rights of intersex persons.

Currently, there is an almost non-existent case law on the matter within the European legal order. The European Court of Human Rights (ECtHR) has examined so far only two cases concerning intersex persons' alleged violations under the ECHR. *M v France* was the first case where the ECtHR had to examine whether unnecessary medical interventions (such as bilateral castration, clitoridoplasty, vaginoplasty and vulvoplasty) on an intersex person constitute a violation of Article 3 of ECHR (European Court of Human Rights, 2022b). Additionally, the Court had to assess whether France has failed to fulfil its positive obligation under Article 3 of the Convention to take effective measures to protect vulnerable intersex persons (including children) from ill-treatment perpetrated by other individuals and to carry out a proper investigation into the matter. The Court rejected the application on inadmissibility grounds, as the claimant had not exhausted domestic remedies. While the Court's decision does not serve the applicant with the expected redress for their human rights violations, at least the Court is indirectly inviting future litigation on the matter of unnecessary medical interventions performed on intersex persons. The Court's position is that medical procedures without a therapeutic purpose and without the affected person's consent are in principle incompatible with the respect for human dignity and constitute a violation of Article 3 of ECHR. The Court is taking a firm stance on non-consensual medical interventions and their incompatibility with the ECHR by relying on its previous case law on forced sterilisations of Romani women (see European Court of Human Rights, 2011, *V.C. v Slovakia*; European Court of Human Rights, 2012, *N.B. v Slovakia*). The Court is also clear in drawing a clear line as to the necessity of any medical interventions on intersex persons; the medical necessity of any procedures must be 'convincingly demonstrated'. Furthermore, the violation of Article 3 ECHR does not require the subjective intention of the perpetrators as the prohibition of torture is absolute. In *Y v France* (European Court of Human Rights, 2023) the ECtHR examined whether the refusal of national authorities to replace the term 'male' with the term 'neutral' or 'intersex' on the applicant's birth certificate constituted a violation of Art. 8 of the ECHR). In this case, the Court of Appeal of Orleans had refused to acknowledge the applicant's claim based on a consistent approach that the French courts have displayed in other cases. Due to the principle of separation of powers, the Orleans Court of Appeals refrained from recognising a third gender, a 'neutral' or 'intersex' gender, as this would amount to an interference with the legislature's powers and would result in far-reaching implications for the French legal order. The ECtHR affirmed that there is still a lack of European consensus in the area of the rights of intersex persons; hence, it was up to every single member state of the Council of Europe to determine—at its own pace and pursuant to its society's understandings and attitudes—the extent it could accommodate the rights of intersex persons. France enjoyed a wide margin of appreciation in determining the extent of intersex rights. The Court found that there was no violation of Article of ECHR, which unfortunately translates into the maintenance of the *status quo* of the legal binarity that is already in place in the French legal order.

Are the two judgements, *M v France* and *Y v France*, capturing the momentum on intersex rights? Undoubtedly, there are legislative efforts across Europe to criminalise conversion practices and to raise awareness on intersex issues. For example, a number of European states have introduced a legal ban on sex conversion practices (Malta (2016), Norway (2023), Iceland (2024), Germany (2020), France (2022), Belgium (2023), Spain (2023), Portugal (2024), Cyprus (2023) and Greece (2022)). It would also be fair to say that these changes are much owed to the feverous commitment of the various European institutions, including the European Parliament, to ban and sanction the advertising and conduct of conversion practices aimed at changing and suppressing a person's sexual orientation, gender identity and/or gender expression (EU Parliament Briefing, 2022; Council of Europe Commissioner for Human Rights, 2024). At a domestic level, even though the Court did not find France in violation of its human rights obligations, the litigation before the European Court of Human Rights spearheaded reactions from civil society actors and coincided with the adoption of the Bioethics Act and the amendment of the Public Health Code which has been supplemented by a government decree that states

> the sole purpose of conforming the child's atypical genital organs to representations of the feminine and masculine does not constitute a medical necessity. It is appropriate to wait in this case until the minor is capable of participating in the decision (Annex, II-3, Aims) (Derave & Ouhnaoui, 2023).

This is a very welcome development for intersex children within France that could also serve as a good practice for other states in the region. At an international level, the impact of these two cases is likely to inspire hope in strategic litigation and reparations for intersex persons and—at the same time—alert national authorities on strengthening human rights standards for intersex persons.

Is the Court honest about its assessment of the lack of the European consensus in the area of the rights of intersex persons? One may disagree with the Court's assessment and point out that there is a significant number of states that have adopted bills or are currently debating draft bills on the protection of intersex persons' rights, for example, Austria, the Netherlands, Ireland, Switzerland. Eventually, unnecessary medical interventions and sex conversion therapies will be abolished across Europe in the next few years. However, it is also important to note that even existing bans on medical interventions may be deemed to be ineffectively implemented or may leave entry points for misusing them (Alaatinoglu, 2023, p. 1272). For example, in a recent case, the Oii Germany and Oii Europe protested against a German's Family Court decision to approve the unnecessary medical intervention to modify the intersex minor's sex characteristics (Oii Europe, 2024). Despite the German Court acknowledging that there was no immediate danger to the minor's life (who was only born in 2023), the Court considered the medical intervention being necessary and in the child's best interests. However, the reaction by the civil society actors was premised on their belief that the Court was effectively assigning a sex to the intersex child. This case is just an example of how there is still unclear legal territory as to how an intersex child itself has a right to self-determination and to bodily integrity and how this can be sidelined when the child is not given the possibility to form or express their own opinion. Hence, even when laws banning unnecessary medical interventions on intersex persons are in place, there is still an increased possibility that they can be bypassed or applied in a way that perpetuates the pathologisation and medicalisation of innate variations of sex characteristics.

What the Court is rightly pointing out though is that European societies are currently far away from recognising a third gender. The European Court of Human Rights has affirmed that transition towards another binary gender identity is protected under the European Convention on Human Rights but has not interpreted the right of intersex persons to not belong to one of the two binary categories as a right protected under the ECHR. The Court of Justice of the EU recently examined the case of a trans person's legal gender recognition (civil registration) as a matter of breach of the rights protected under the European Charter of Fundamental Freedoms (Arts. 7, 45) and the TFEU (Arts. 20, 21) (Court of Justice of the European Union 2024, *Mirin*). The ruling comes at a time when the EU is in the process of finalising its accession to the European Convention on Human Rights and it stands as a friendly node to the European human rights system (Plan, 2024). The *Mirin* case is essentially clarifying that even though it is within EU member states competence to regulate a person's status in relation to changing a first name and gender identity, when they do so, they need to comply with EU law, specifically, the freedom of movement and residence across the EU Member States. The *Mirin* case calls for the automatic recognition of gender markers obtained in other EU member states based on the understanding that the freedoms of movement and residence are attached to EU citizenship. Hence, the case frames legal gender recognition through the exercise of EU citizen rights:

> Thus, for a Union citizen who, like the applicant in the main proceedings, has exercised his or her freedom to move and reside in another Member State and who, during his or her period of residence in that other Member State, has changed his or her first name and gender identity in accordance with the procedures laid down for that purpose in that other Member State, there is a real risk, because he or she bears two different first names and has been given two different identities, of having to dispel doubts as to his or her identity and the authenticity of the documents submitted or the veracity of their content, which is such as to hinder the exercise of the right which flows from Article 21 TFEU [...]
>
> Therefore, national legislation, such as that at issue in the main proceedings, which does not permit a first name and gender identity, lawfully acquired in another Member State, to be registered and which obliges the person concerned to bring new judicial proceedings for a change of gender identity in the Member State of origin, which disregard the fact that the Union citizen has already lawfully acquired the change of his or first name and gender identity in his Member State of residence and has been subject to the procedures laid down for that purpose in that Member State, infringes the requirements under Article 21 TFEU.
>
> In the light of all the foregoing considerations, the answer to the questions referred is that Article 20 and Article 21(1) TFEU, read in the light of Articles 7 and 45 of the Charter, must be interpreted as precluding legislation of a Member State that does not permit recognition and entry in the birth certificate of a national of that Member State of a change of first name and gender identity lawfully acquired in another Member State, when exercising the right to free movement and residence, with the consequence that that person is obliged to initiate, before a court, new proceedings for a change of gender identity in the first Member State, which disregard the change that was previously lawfully acquired in that other Member State. In that regard, it is irrelevant that the request for recognition and entry of the change of first name and gender identity was made in that first Member State on a date on which the withdrawal from the European Union of the other Member State had already taken effect (Court of Justice of the European Union 2024, *Mirin*, paras. 56, 70-71).

The Court of Justice of the EU heavily relied on case law by the European Court of Human Rights (European Court of Human Rights, 2021, *X and Y v Romania*; European Court of Human Rights, 2022a, *A.D. and Others v Georgia*), whereby the ECtHR has affirmed that under Art. 8 of the ECHR transgender persons can exercise their right to legal gender recognition and oblige the State to correct their gender, forenames and personal digital codes corrected on their national identity papers (even in the absence of gender reassignment surgery which was required under the national law). Herein, the ECtHR once again recalled that more than 25 member states of the Council of Europe no longer made gender reassignment surgery a requirement for the legal recognition of gender identity. The Court of Justice of the EU is thus affirming the ECtHR approach to legal gender recognition and requires

EU member states to guarantee legal gender recognition in conformity with the standards set out by the ECtHR. The impact of the *Mirin* case is likely to be positive for intersex persons in the exercise of their EU citizen rights. The Court of Justice of the EU is paving the way for intersex citizens to have just as effective access to their EU rights to move across EU member states and exercise all other freedoms as any other EU citizen.

Non-Binary and Other Gender-Diverse Rights

People who identify as non-binary and/or other gender-diverse identities (for example, gender-non-conforming persons and persons who do not identify with gender) present an extremely vulnerable group in the LGBTIQ community. A historically underrepresented group, it includes persons whose gender identities fall outside the gender binary of 'male' and 'female'. The existence of non-binary and gender-diverse persons, although confirmed in certain cultural and historical contexts (see, for example, Pape & Ialongo, 2024), is attracting the attention of more and more policy-makers as well as international organisations due to the fact that they are facing a spiral of violence, social exclusion and socioeconomic marginalisation, especially across healthcare, education and employment (UN High Commissioner for Human Rights, 2015).

The rights of non-binary and gender-diverse persons are increasingly central in the public and legal debate and they are often entangled in the clash of the 'woke' and 'anti-woke' arguments that are polarising contemporary societies across the world (Özbilgin & Erbil, 2024). At the same time, as most of the contemporary legal systems still maintain gender binary categories, there is a struggle to accommodate the emerging demands of non-binary persons to enjoy their identity beyond their right to gender recognition (Osella & Rubio-Marín, 2023). This means that self-determination of non-binary persons may often be dependent on the predominantly binary understanding of self-determination. Furthermore, existing administrative and legal hurdles that are attached to gender recognition may create or increase discrimination and socio-economic marginalisation of non-binary persons.

Even where legal systems provide more than two legal genders or more, the enjoyment of the human rights of non-binary persons is firstly dependent on gender recognition and secondly dependent on interpretations that have not been shaped or informed by the non-binary or gender-fluid perspective. As human rights have developed and progressed following the societal needs of any democratic society, it is expected that non-binary rights will eventually follow this trajectory. It is inevitable that this dynamic will be met with resistance from other individuals and/or groups of the societies; it is also inevitable that the understanding and formation of non-binary rights will clash with and feed from the intersection with other identities and with human rights claims' of other mainstream or vulnerable groups. Ultimately, in human rights law, there is not a hierarchy of groups that deserve more human rights as opposed to others; to the contrary, the discourse on non-binary rights is offering a new paradigm to incorporate inter-sectional thinking.

Currently, there are ongoing efforts around the world to bring awareness as to how non-binary and gender-diverse persons may experience discrimination and face particular challenges in enjoying their human rights, especially due to the fact that they do not conform to the gendered expectation of how they express or present themselves. This strict binarism creates grounds upon which persons who self-identify outside of it (non-binary, intersex) become victims of discrimination. From intolerance to prejudices and from systemic and structural biases to legal lacunae, non-binary and gender-diverse persons are ab initio excluded from societal structures, services and legal systems that were created predominantly through the binary lens. The question that arises is whether the existing legal orders at a national and international level are flexible enough to accommodate their needs and meet the human rights obligations that arise for them under existing national legislation and international human rights instruments.

Within international organisations, there is an increasing support towards the protection of the human rights of non-binary and gender-diverse persons. At the same time, within the UN there are efforts to ensure that the UN system is a safe and inclusive workplace for all the workforce in the UN system and its peacekeeping operations (UN System-Wide Strategy on Gender Parity, 2017; UNGLOBE Resources, 2024). Critics may point to the slow or limited steps that are being taken by the UN to adjust to the changing gender landscape; however, one should also appreciate the fact that by aiming at transforming the workplace culture within the UN and its agencies, the UN becomes a gender non-conforming leader that sets by example rather than just words.

At the European level, non-binary rights are still partially understood (Kompatscher & Roßbach, 2024). In 2024, the Commissioner for Human Rights of the Council of Europe issued a Paper that presents the challenges that LGBTIQ+ persons face with regard to legal gender recognition, hate crimes, detention family life, education, sports employment, poverty, housing, healthcare, sanitation and asylum (Council of Europe, 2024). The paper identifies key issues for non-binary persons and most importantly the lack of data on the lived experiences of non-binary persons, in order to be able to form targeted policy measures in the future. The legal status of non-binary persons and their right to self-determination is currently the biggest challenge.

Within Europe, only a handful of states have adopted ‘third’ gender or ‘x’ gender marker (Tissandier-Nasom, 2023). However, even in the cases where there are legal frameworks for legal gender recognition, they usually lack non-binary-appropriate options. A few constitutional courts have examined cases concerning gender markers. The German Federal Constitutional Court held that it was unconstitutional to require a gender marker for everybody when the only available markers were ‘male’ and ‘female’. This case led to the amendment of the Civil Status Act according to which non-binary persons are allowed to identify themselves as ‘diverse’ (which is a non-binary gender option) or choose a blank entry. In 2024, the German Bundestag adopted the *Selbstbestimmungsgesetz* [‘Self-determination Act’], which replaces the previous *Transsexuellengesetz* [‘Transsexuals Act’] and essentially disentangles the technical hurdles, such as psychiatric evaluations, from the act of legal gender recognition. Pursuant to this Act, persons can declare their gender without evaluation and minors as young as 14 years old can change their gender with the consent of their guardian (Paulikas & Cobanoglu, 2024). The European Court of Human Rights has affirmed that the transition towards another binary gender identity is protected under the European Convention on Human Rights; in particular, the Court has pointed out that a person's gender identity is an 'essential aspect of individual intimate identity' and thus it is covered by Art. 8 of ECHR (European Court of Human Rights, 2023, *Y v France*). However, access to a non-binary (neutral) gender-marker is not yet covered by Art. 8 of the ECHR. It is rightly pointed out by the Commissioner for Human Rights of the Council of Europe that

> while the Court has so far not interpreted the Convention to include a right to non-binary recognition, the Convention equally does not require the recording of legal gender/sex, let alone in a binary manner. Member states can therefore choose to adopt measures that improve respect for the human rights of non-binary people. The Commissioner calls on member states to consider including a third legal gender marker in identity, social security and other documents, as well as public registries, for those who seek it. (Council of Europe, 2024, p. 24).

Furthermore, a small victory for non-binary persons was the case brought by the Mousse Association against France's national state-owned railway company with regard to their practice of making their passengers to choose between binary civil titles 'Mr.' and 'Ms.' when purchasing tickets (Court of Justice of the European Union, 2025, *Mousse*). The Advocate General of the Court of Justice of the EU found the practice not necessary under the GDPR and also recognised that the existence of such a practice could create grounds for discrimination for non-binary persons. Such cases (and future cases) can drive change and they could result in having European states officially recognise non-binary gender markers. But for the time being the progress is as slow as it is across other geographic regions where there are only a few States (i.e. India) that have extended legal gender recognition to non-binary persons.

Concluding Remarks

The overall picture as it shapes out is that we are currently living in a very polarised environment concerning the protection and enforcement of the human rights of LGBTIQ+ persons. LGBTIQ+ representation and inclusion matter more than ever in order to prevent the erosion of democratic norms and institutions and the rollback of LGBTIQ+ equality. Failing to uphold the human rights standard-setting can only result in the perpetuation of the structural drivers of inequality and the social and economic marginalisation of LGBTIQ+ persons.

The developments at legislative and policy levels are essential to guaranteeing the human rights of LGBTIQ+ persons and to creating a culture of tolerance and inclusion. However, even with these developments going on at the national level, there still is a long way before there is a comprehensive understanding of LGBTIQ+

realities. And this is what needs to be done in order to design and implement better policies for LGBTIQ+ persons. Such policies need to cover LGBTIQ+-specific themes and deal with the intersectional grounds that hinder the full and meaningful inclusion of LGBTIQ+ persons. The limited case law that exists with regard to intersex and non-binary persons, two of the most vulnerable groups within the wider vulnerable LGBTIQ+ group, is promising as it is likely to encourage further strategic litigation. It is also opening up the legal and scholarly space for further debate on and research into the matters of redress for the human rights violations that these two groups experience.

References

Alaatinoglu, D. (2023). Intersex intervention as human rights violations: The European Court of human rights sets out guiding principles in M v France. *Modern Law Review, 86*(5), 1265. https://doi.org/10.1111/1468-2230.12795

Chainoglou, K. (2023). LGBTQ+ Rights. In K. Chainoglou & Z. Aliozi (Eds.), *Human rights: A comparative approach* (pp. 325–359). Kallipos Open Academic Editions. https://repository.kallipos.gr/handle/11419/11713

CIDP. (2023). *Transgender and non-binary inclusion at work*. https://www.cipd.org/globalassets/media/knowledge/knowledge-hub/guides/2023-pdfs/2023-transgender-non-binary-edi-workplace-8363.pdf(open in a new window)

Clifton, C. et al. (2023). World Bank gender thematic policy note series: Evidence and practice note. *Sexual Orientation and Gender Identity Inclusion and Gender Equality*. https://documents1.worldbank.org/curated/en/099704309082335836/pdf/IDU0f7ae7d630cd3e04f2a0a1c70e226f1217870.pdf

Council of Europe Commissioner for Human Rights. (2024). Human Rights and Gender Identity and Expression, Issue Paper. https://rm.coe.int/issue-paper-on-human-rights-and-gender-identity-and-expression-by-dunj/1680aed541

Council of Europe Commissioner for Human Rights. (2015). Human Rights and Intersex People Issue Paper. https://rm.coe.int/16806da5d4

Council of Europe Commissioner for Human Rights, Human Rights Comment, "A boy or a girl or a person—intersex people lack recognition in Europe", 9/5/2024, https://www.coe.int/en/web/commissioner/-/a-boy-or-a-girl-or-a-person-intersex-people-lack-recognition-in-euro-1

Council of Europe, Steering Committee on Anti-Discrimination, Diversity and Inclusion, Thematic Report on Legal Gender Recognition First Thematic Implementation Review Report on Recommendation CM/Rec (2010) 5 to member states on measures to combat discrimination based on sexual orientation or gender identity. (2022). https://rm.coe.int/thematic-report-on-legal-gender-recognition-in-europe-2022/1680a729b3

Council of Europe, Steering Committee on Anti-Discrimination, Diversity and Inclusion, Hate Crimes and other Hate-motivated incidents based on Sexual Orientation, Gender Identity, Gender Expression and Sex Characteristics, Second Thematic Implementation Review Report on Recommendation CM/Rec (2010) (2023). https://rm.coe.int/gt-adi-sogi-2023-3-en-european-report-sogiesc-based-hate-crime-final-t/1680ac3c18

Council of Europe, Steering Committee on Anti-Discrimination, Diversity and Inclusion, Right to the highest attainable standard of health and access to healthcare for LGBTI people in Europe, Third Thematic Review of the Implementation of the Council of Europe Committee of Ministers Recommendation CM/Rec (2010) 5 to member states on measures to combat discrimination based on sexual orientation or gender identity. (2024). https://rm.coe.int/prems-124824-gbr-2575-right-to-the-highest-attainable-standard-of-heal/1680b1ba4d

Council on Foreign Relations, The Rise in LGBTQ+ Hate and Democratic Backsliding. (2024, June 4). https://www.cfr.org/event/rise-lgbtq-hate-and-democratic-backsliding

Court of Justice of the European Union. (2023), Case C-394/23, Mousse: Request for a preliminary ruling from the Conseil d'État (France) lodged on 28 June 2023, ECLI:EU:C:2024:610.

Court of Justice of the European Union. (2024). Case C-4/23, Mirin, 4 October 2024, ECLI:EU:C:2024:845.

Court of Justice of the European Union. (2025). Case C-394/23, Mousse, 9 January 2025, ECLI:EU:C:2024:610.

Derave, C. & Ouhnaoui, H. (2023, February 14) *M v France: Recognising the existence of intersex persons, but not (yet) their bodily integrity, Strasbourg Observers*. https://strasbourgobservers.com/2023/02/14/m-v-france-recognising-the-existence-of-intersex-persons-but-not-yet-their-bodily-integrity/

EU FRA. (2024). EU Agency for Fundamental Rights. (2024). *LGBTIQ equality at crossroads: Progress and challenges*. EU LGBTIQ Survey III. https://fra.europa.eu/sites/default/files/fra_uploads/fra-2024-lgbtiq-equality_en.pdf

EU FRA. (n.d.). EU Agency for Fundamental Rights (FRA). *EU-LGBTI II, A long way to go for LGBTI equality*, p. 34 https://fra.europa.eu/sites/default/files/fra_uploads/fra-2020-lgbti-equality-1_en.pdf

EU Commission, Communication from the Commission on Union of Equality: LGBTIQ Equality Strategy 2020–2025, 12 November 2020, COM (2020) 698.

EU Commission Guidelines for Strategies and Action Plans to Enhance LGBTIQ Equality, High-Level Group on Non-Discrimination, Equality and Diversity 2022. https://commission.europa.eu/document/download/c442d610-c462-4aaf-b341-8f5a3cde5830_en?filename=guidelines_for_strategies_and_action_plans_to_enhance_lgbtiq_equality_2022final16_05.pdf

EU Commission Political Guidelines 2024–2029, 18 July 2024. https://commission.europa.eu/document/e6cd4328-673c-4e7a-8683-f63ffb2cf648_en

EU Commission Report. (2024). Report on the Implementation of the 2020-2025 LGBTIQ Equality Strategy, https://commission.europa.eu/document/download/d9e23ccc-4032-41d0-b208-68650103ef8a_en?filename=Report%20LGBTIQ.pdf

EU FRA. (2015). EU Fundamental Rights Agency, The Fundamental Rights Situation of Intersex People, 04/2015. https://fra.europa.eu/sites/default/files/fra_uploads/fra-2015-focus-04-intersex_en.pdf

EU Parliament Briefing. (2022). Bans on Conversion Therapies: The Situation in Selected EU Member States. https://www.europarl.europa.eu/RegData/etudes/BRIE/2022/733521/EPRS_BRI(2022)733521_EN.pdf

European Commission. (2014). Joint report on the implementation of Council Directive 2000/43/EC and Council Directive 2000/78/EC, COM (2014) 2 final. http://www.europarl.europa.eu/meetdocs/2014_2019/documents/com/com_com(2014)0002_/com_com(2014)0002_el.pdf

European Court of Human Rights. (2011). V.C. v Slovakia, Application No. 18968/07, 8 November 2011, Final 08/02/2012.

European Court of Human Rights. (2012). N.B. v Slovakia, Application No. 29518/10, 12 June 2012, Final 12/09/2012.

European Court of Human Rights. (2021). X and Y v Romania, Applications Nos. 2145/16 and 2-6-7/16, 19 January 2021.

European Court of Human Rights. (2022a). A.D. and Others v Georgia, Applications Nos. 57864/17, 79087/17 and 55353/19, 1 December 2022.

European Court of Human Rights. (2022b). M. v France, Application No. 42821/18, 19 May 2022.

European Court of Human Rights. (2023). *Y v France*, Application No. 76888/17, Judgment 31 January 2023, Final 26 June 2023.

European Disability Forum and ILGA Europe, Policy recommendations on intersectionality between disability and lesbian, Gay, Bisexual, Trans and Intersex (LGBTI), 2024. https://www.edf-feph.org/publications/policy-recommendations-disability-lgbti/

Garland, F., Lalor, K. & Travis, M. (2022). Intersex activism, medical power/knowledge and the scalar limitations of the United Nations. *Human Rights Law Review, 22*, ngac020.

Guillot, L. & Coi, G. (2024, May 15). Violence against LGBTQ+ people on the rise in Europe, report says. *Politico*. https://www.politico.eu/article/violence-lgbtq-rights-rise-europe-report/

ILGA Database conversion therapies, 2024. https://database.ilga.org/conversion-therapies-lgbti

International Commission of Jurists (ICJ). (2017, November 10). *The Yogyakarta principles plus 10–additional principles and state obligation on the application of international human rights law in relation to sexual orientation, gender expression and sex characteristics to complement the Yogyakarta principles*. Accessed Nov 28, 2024, from https://www.refworld.org/legal/resolution/icjurists/2017/en/122482

Jorge, J. C., Valerio-Pérez, L., Esteban, C. & Rivera-Lassen, A. I. (2019). Intersex care in the United States and international standards of human rights. *Global Public Health, 16*(5), 679–691. https://doi.org/10.1080/17441692.2019.1706759

Kompatscher, A. & Roßbach, S. (2024, Aug 09). *Non-Binary Gender Markers in Italy?: On the Decision No. 143/2024 of the Italian Constitutional Court, VerfBlog*. https://verfassungsblog.de/non-binary-gender-markers-italy/, https://doi.org/10.59704/f6ad459f4eb39c1f.

Malta Declaration, Third international intersex forum, 2013. https://www.seksediversiteit.nl/en/basis/verklaring-van-malta/

Monro, S., Wall, S. S. & Wood, K. (2024). Intersex equality, diversity and inclusion and social policy: Silences, absences, and erasures in Ireland and the UK. *Critical Social Policy, 44*(1), 3–22. https://doi.org/10.1177/02610183231175055

OHCHR. (2023). Technical note on the human rights of intersex people. *Human Rights Standards and Good Practices*. https://www.ohchr.org/sites/default/files/2023-11/ohchr-technical-note-rights-intersex-people.pdf

Oii Europe, Oii Germnay & Oii Europe comment on deeply concerning German family Court decision authorizing an intervention on an intersex minor, 2024. https://www.oiieurope.org/wp-content/uploads/2024/07/oiide-oiieu-joint-statement_court_EN-12-06-24.pdf

Osella, S. & Rubio-Marín, R. (2023). Gender recognition at the crossroads: Four models and the compass of comparative law. *International Journal of Constitutional Law, 21*(2), 574–602. https://doi.org/10.1093/icon/moad045

Özbilgin, M. F. & Erbil, C. (2024). Non-binary individuals, visibility and legitimacy at work: Future crafting inclusive organisations in times of inclusion hysteresis. *The International Journal of Human Resource Management, 1–27*, 1. https://doi.org/10.1080/09585192.2024.2392838

Pape, E. & Ialongo, N. (2024). Error or minority? The identification of non-binary gender in prehistoric burials in Central Europe. *Cambridge Archaeological Journal, 34*(1), 43–63. https://doi.org/10.1017/S0959774323000082

Paulikas, S. & Cobanoglu, Z. (2024, June 24). Self-determination act creates new rights for transgender people in Germany. *American-German Institute*. https://americangerman.institute/2024/06/self-determination-act-creates-new-rights-for-transgender-people-in-germany/

Plan, M. A. (2024, June 05). Trans rights and gender recognition before the CJEU: Reflections on the AG'S opinion in the Mirin case (C4/23), *VerfBlog*, https://verfassungsblog.de/trans-rights-and-legal-gender-recognition/, https://doi.org/10.59704/b5c6c0a269722195.

Scherpe, J. M. (2018). Lessons from the legal development of the legal status of transsexual and transgender persons. In J. M. Scherpe, A. Dutta & T. Helms (Eds.), *The legal status of intersex persons* (pp. 203–216). Intersentia.

Tissandier-Nasom, E. (2023). Effective recognition and protection of non-binary gender identities in the Council of Europe Framework: A critical analysis of third gender marker options from a human rights law standpoint. *University of Bologna Law Review, 8*(2), 101–168. https://doi.org/10.6092/issn.2531-6133/18945

UN High Commissioner for Human Rights. (2015). Report on Discrimination and Violence against Individuals Based on their Sexual Orientation and Gender Identity. (2015, May 4). *A/HRC/29/23*.

UN Human Rights Council, Resolution adopted on 4 April 2024, Combating discrimination, violence and harmful practices against intersex persons, A/HRC/RES/55/14.

UN Independent Expert on Protection Against Violence and Discrimination based on Sexual Orientation and Gender Identity in relation to the human rights to freedom of expression, peaceful assembly and association, Report. (2024, April 18). *A/HRC/56/49.*

UN Independent Expert on Protection against Violence and Discrimination Based on Sexual Orientation and Gender Identity, Report. (2019, July 17). *A/74/181.*

UN Independent Expert on Sexual Orientation and Gender Identity, Effective Inclusion of LGBT persons. (n.d.). https://www.ohchr.org/en/special-procedures/ie-sexual-orientation-and-gender-identity/effective-inclusion-lgbt-persons

UN Independent Expert on Sexual Orientation and Gender Identity, Issues in Focus: The Struggle of Trans and Gender-Diverse Persons. (n.d.). https://www.ohchr.org/en/special-procedures/ie-sexual-orientation-and-gender-identity/struggle-trans-and-gender-diverse-persons

UN Special Rapporteur on Extrajudicial, Summary and Arbitrary Executions, (2024, July 17). *A/79/172.*

UN Special Rapporteur on torture and other cruel, inhuman or degrading treatment or punishment, 2013. (2013, February 1). *A/HRC/22/53.*

UN System-Wide Strategy on Gender Parity. (2017). https://www.un.org/gender/sites/www.un.org.gender/files/gender_parity_strategy_october_2017.pdf

UNGLOBE, Resources. (2024). https://www.unglobe.org/resources

Zelayandia-Gonzalez, E. (2023). The growing visibility of intersex demands at the United Nations: A review of the treaty bodies' concluding observations. *Social Sciences., 12*(2), 73. https://doi.org/10.3390/socsci12020073

Positive Discrimination: How it Can be Achieved in Directive 2000/78/EC?

Philippa Watson

Abstract

The purpose of this paper is to examine how positive discrimination can be implemented within Directive 2000/78, establishing a general framework for equal treatment in employment and occupation (Framework Equality Directive—FED) (Council Directive (EU) No. 2000/78, 2000, art. 7 and art. 15). The paper is structured into five parts. Part 1 discusses the concept of positive discrimination. Part 2 outlines the legislative instruments governing positive discrimination in EU employment law, along with the relevant interpretive case law of the Court of Justice of the European Union (CJEU). Part 3 focuses on the specific provisions of the Directive addressing positive discrimination, namely Articles 7 and 15. Part 4 explores how positive discrimination can be achieved using provisions within the Directive beyond Articles 7 and 15. Part 5 presents the chapter's conclusions.

The Concept of Positive Discrimination

The concept of positive discrimination[1] has been present in EU employment law for almost half a century. It first appeared in Directive 76/207/EEC, known as the Equal Treatment Directive (Council Directive (EEC) No 76/207, 1976, art. 2, para. 4). It has since been developed by the CJEU in its case law on equality between men and

[1] Also referred to (particularly in the US) as "affirmative action".

P. Watson (✉)
City Law School, City St Georges, University of London, London, UK

Barrister Essex Court Chambers, London, UK
e-mail: philippa.watson.1@city.ac.uk

D. Anagnostopoulou (ed.), *European Identities, Inclusion and Equality*, Diversity and Inclusion Research, https://doi.org/10.1007/978-3-031-90602-2_13

women in the workplace and with respect to measures in favor of women, achieving Treaty status in 1997 (Treaty of Amsterdam) with the insertion of paragraph 4 into Article 141 EC (now Article 157 TFEU) and Article 23 of the Charter of Fundamental Rights.[2] The scope of the concept of positive discrimination has been further extended to other grounds of discrimination by the FED and the Directive 2000/43 (the Race Directive), implementing the principle of equal treatment between persons irrespective of racial or ethnic origin (Council Directive (EU) No 2000/43, 2000a, art. 5), both adopted in 2000.

The mechanism of positive discrimination requires that the preferential treatment may be given to *certain* persons in order to ensure that persons of their profile, their characteristics, or their beliefs may achieve true equality. There are certain patterns of discriminatory conduct that antidiscrimination legislation alone cannot rectify. These traditional patterns of discrimination have existed for a long time and are embedded in society, the discriminatory practices toward women in the workplace having been acknowledged first, followed more recently by the recognition of the existence of long-standing discrimination on other grounds. A simple prohibition of antidiscrimination in employment policies going forward will not rectify such situations. What is needed is a root and branch change in the workplace and that requires more than the occasional hiring here and there of an employee with suitable qualifications but whose profile has been traditionally discriminated against. True equality requires that everyone be placed on an equal footing in the employment market. Positive discrimination can be a means of achieving that.

The Legislative Landscape

The various instruments providing for positive discrimination will be considered below.

Chronologically, the first of these is the Equal Opportunities Directive which provided in Article 2 para. 4 for positive discrimination with respect to access to employment and employment conditions.[3] This predated the provision for positive discrimination in the Treaty, which first appeared when Article 119 of the Treaty of Rome was amended (and renumbered) by the Treaty of Amsterdam to become Article 141 (now Article 157 TFEU).[4] Its original wording has not changed.

Article 157 para. 4 TFEU provides:

---

[2] Article 23 of the Charter on Fundamental Rights states: "*The principle of equality shall not prevent the maintenance or adoption of measures providing for specific advantages in favor of the under—represented sex.*"

[3] Article 2 para. 4 of Directive 76/207/EEC reads: "*This Directive shall be without prejudice to measures to promote equal opportunity for men and women, by removing existing inequalities which affect women's opportunities in the areas referred to in Article 1 para. 1.*" Article 1 para. 1 of the same Directive refers to "access to employment" and "working conditions."

[4] Positive discrimination in the context of equal pay was provided for in the Agreement on Social Policy (from which the UK obtained an opt-out) annexed by the Treaty of Maastricht to the Treaty of the European Community.

> With a view to ensuring full equality in practice between men and women in working life, the principle of equal treatment shall not prevent any Member State from maintaining or adopting measures providing for specific advantages in order to make it easier for the underrepresented sex to pursue a vocational activity or to prevent or to compensate for disadvantages in professional life.

Article 157 TFEU is concerned with equality of treatment between men and women in pay and employment. It permits positive discrimination only in that context and solely for the purposes of pursuing a vocational activity or to compensate for disadvantages in professional life. Thus, in *Griesmar* (CJEU, Joseph Griesmar v. et al., 2001), the CJEU refused to accept its application to a pension scheme in which an extra year of service was credited to the pension record of female employees in respect of each of their children. The scheme did nothing to further the vocational training opportunities for women, nor did it assist them in their professional lives.

In a Declaration annexed to the Treaty of Amsterdam (Treaty of Amsterdam, 1997, Declaration no 28 on Article 141 para. 4) the Member States declared that the purpose of Article 141 *"should, in the first instance, aim at improving the situation of women in working life."*

Article 19 TFEU empowers the Council to "take appropriate action to combat discrimination based on sex, racial or ethnic origin, religion or belief, disability, age or sexual orientation." There is no further provision along the lines of Article 157 para. 4 TFEU that provides for positive discrimination in the case of the unequal treatment of men and women in the workplace. Article 19 TFEU speaks of *combatting discrimination*. Article 157 refers to the *principle of equal treatment*. There is a difference here. Combatting discrimination is not the same as implementing the principle of equality. The latter may require more than the elimination of non-discriminatory measures. This may explain the presence of paragraph 4 in Article 157 TFEU and the absence of a similar provision in Article 19 TFEU. While combatting discrimination might be viewed as confined to eliminating discriminatory measures, achieving equality of treatment could require more than that to reduce the inequalities that may exist in the reality of working life (CJEU, Commission of the European Communities v. French Republic, 1988, para. 15).

Both sets of Treaty provisions have been implemented by secondary legislation in which positive discriminatory measures in national law are permitted.

The Equal Opportunities Directive was repealed and replaced in 2006 by Directive 2006/54 commonly referred to as the Recast Directive (Directive (EC) No 2006/54, 2006). Article 3 of that Directive provides for positive discrimination in the following terms:

> Member States may maintain or adopt measures within the meaning of Article 141para. 4 of the Treaty with a view to ensuring full equality in practice between men and women in working life.

For the sake of completeness, we should mention Council Recommendation 84/635 on the promotion of positive action for women, which urged Member States to adopt a positive action policy designed to eliminate existing inequalities affecting women in working life and to promote a better balance between the sexes in employment as well as to engage in such positive action in both the public and private employment sectors (Council Recommendation (EEC) No 84/635, 1984). This Recommendation and the fact that the Council considered it necessary to address the issue may indicate that the Member States were not making sufficient use of the opportunity afforded to them under the Equal Opportunities Directive of adopting or maintaining positive discriminatory measures.

Two Directives have been adopted on the basis of Article 13 TEC, now Article 19 TFEU: The Race Directive (Directive 2000/43, 2000a) and the Framework Employment Directive (Directive 2000/78, 2000b). Both provide for measures of positive action.

Article 5 of the Race Directive stipulates:

> With a view to ensuring full equality in practice, the principle of equal treatment shall not prevent any Member State from maintaining or adopting specific measures to prevent or compensate for disadvantages linked to racial or ethnic origin.

The Framework Employment Directive 2000/78 contains two provisions, specifically providing for positive action. Article 7 para. 1 is drafted in terms similar to Article 5 in the Race Directive (Directive 2000/43, 2000a). Article 15 is a more specific provision concerned with tackling the under-representation of the Catholic community in the police service and the teaching profession in Northern Ireland.

Turning now to the case law of the CJEU on positive discrimination, we see that in the context of a series of preliminary rulings on Article 2 para. 4 of the Equal Opportunities Directive, the CJEU, developed a set of rules in the 1990s which govern the application of the principle of positive discrimination as articulated in that provision.

Let us see how this case law interpreted positive discrimination. Could Member States enact measures providing for positive discrimination at their discretion? Or are there limitations on how such national positive discriminatory measures could apply, even if seemingly permissible under Article 2 para. 4 of the Equal Opportunities Directive?

The short answer is that such measures, being an exception to the principle of equal treatment, are required to be interpreted and applied restrictively (CJEU, Marguerite Johnston v Chief Constable of the Royal Ulster Constabulary, 1986 para. 36 & CJEU, Eckhard Kalanke v Freie Hansestadt Bremen, 1995, para. 21). In other words, in spite of the apparent wide discretion given to the Member States in the matter of positive discrimination, their actions are circumscribed by a number of principles which constrain the level of their discretion. The Member States are entitled to set out what objectives positive discriminatory measures seek to achieve but the application of those measures is subject to limitations.

The first case in which the CJEU considered a measure permitting positive discrimination was *Kalanke* (CJEC, Eckhard Kalanke v Freie Hansestadt Bremen, 1995, para. 15). This case concerned a dispute between Mr. Kalanke and the City of Bremen. Mr. Kalanke and Ms. Glismann had applied for the post of Section Manager in the Bremen Parks Department. Para. 4 of the Bremen law on Equal Treatment for Men and Women in the Public Service provided that women who have the same qualifications as men applying for the same post are to be given priority in sectors where they are under-represented. Under-representation was deemed to exist when women do not make up at least half of the staff in the individual pay brackets in the relevant personnel group or in the function levels provided for in the organization chart. Basing its decision on this provision, Bremen City Council appointed Ms. Glismann to the post. In a reference for a preliminary ruling to the CJEU, it was held that although Article 2 para. 4 of the Equal Opportunities Directive permitted national measures relating to access to employment, including promotion, which give a specific advantage to women with a view to improving their ability to compete in the labor market and to pursue a career on an equal footing with men, such measures had to be interpreted strictly. This meant that national measures which guaranteed women an absolute and conditional priority for appointment or promotion went beyond what was permitted under Article 2 para. 4 to achieve equality of opportunity.

Two years later, in the *Marschall* case (CJEC, Hellmut Marschall v Land Nordrhein-Westfalen, 1997), the Court found that the particular provision in issue in that case was compatible with Article 2 para. 4 of the Directive, in that it contained a "saving clause" to the effect that women are not to be given priority in promotion if "reasons specific to an individual male tilted the balance in his favor" (CJEU, Hellmut Marschall v Land Nordrhein-Westfalen, 1997, para. 26). Such a clause guarantees that candidates will be the subject of an objective assessment, which takes into account all criteria specific to the individual candidates. The Court distinguished the *Kalanke* case on the grounds that the provision in issue in that case did not contain such a "saving clause." Thus, although positive discrimination in favor of female candidates may be permissible when recruiting for posts where women are under-represented, it does not confer an absolute right to preferential treatment. The qualifications of the entire group of candidates must be examined to determine who is the most suitably qualified: in cases where a female and a male candidate have equal merits, the female candidate may be preferred, but automatic, unconditional priority to women candidates was not permitted. In simple terms—you do not get the job simply because you are a woman.

The *Badeck* case (CJEU, Georg Badeck, and Others, interveners: Hessische Ministerpräsident and Landesanwalt beim Staatsgerichtshof des Landes Hessen, 2000a) concerned a number of provisions requiring the adoption of "advancement plans" for women in public service, the objective of which was to secure equality of access to public service employment for both sexes. Although some of the schemes operated with a system of quotas that guaranteed a fixed number of appointments for women, the CJEU found that, in practice, these schemes were flexible and allowed for the objective assessment of each applicant and were therefore deemed legitimate (see also CJEC, H. Lommers v Minister van Landbouw, Natuurbeheer en Visserij, 2002). In para. 23 of its judgment, the CJEU held that a measure that is intended to give priority in promotion to women in sectors of the public service where they are under-represented must be regarded as compatible with EU law:

- Where it does not automatically and unconditionally give priority to women when men and women are equally qualified, and
- Where the candidates' applications are the subject of an objective assessment which takes account of their specific circumstances.

In *Abrahamsson* (CJEU, Katarina Abrahamsson and Leif Anderson v Elisabet Fogelqvist, 2000b), the Court considered the compatibility of the Swedish legislation with Article 2 para. 4 of the Equal Opportunities Directive, under which a candidate for a public post belonging to the under-represented sex and possessing sufficient qualifications for that post must be preferred over a candidate of the opposite sex who would otherwise have been appointed, provided this is necessary to secure the appointment of a candidate of the under-represented sex. This preference is allowed only when "the difference between the respective merits of the candidates is not so great as to give rise to a breach of the requirement of objectivity in making appointments." The Court found that the scope and effect of that condition could not be precisely defined. As a consequence, the selection of a candidate from among those who were sufficiently qualified "is ultimately based on the mere fact of belonging to the under-represented sex, and this is so even if the merits of the candidate so selected are inferior to those of a candidate of the opposite sex" (CJEU, Katarina Abrahamsson, and Leif Anderson v Elisabet Fogelqvist, 2000b, para. 53). Such a method of selection was not compatible with Article 2 para. 4 of the Directive. Neither was it compatible with Article 141 para. 4 TEC as that provision could not be read as allowing a selection method of the kind at issue in the main proceedings, which appeared to be disproportionate to the aim pursued. However, where the candidates are subjected to an objective assessment that takes account of their specific personal situations, such a selection process would not be incompatible with Article 2 paras 1 and 4 of the Directive. The Court also found that EU law did not in any way make the application of the principle of equal treatment for men and women concerning access to employment conditional upon the level of the posts to be filled. On the contrary, the principle applies to all levels of employment.

It can be assumed that the Court would apply this case law in any case involving the positive discrimination provisions in the Race Directive and the FED in the same way as it has applied the principles governing gender discrimination to other forms of discrimination prohibited under EU law.

The Framework Equality Directive (FED) and Positive Discrimination

Although as we have stated above, Article 19 TFEU, the legal basis of the FED, is silent on the question of positive discrimination, positive discrimination is expressly provided for in Articles 7 and 15 of the FED (Directive (EC) 2000/78).

The first paragraph of Article 7 FED permits Member States to maintain or adopt specific measures to prevent or compensate for disadvantages linked to any of the grounds set out in Article 1 of the Directive, which is religion, belief, disability, age, or sexual orientation. This wording is broadly similar to that used in paragraph 4 of Article 157 TFEU and Article 3 of the Recast Directive (Directive (EC) No 2006/54, 2006). It appears to envisage a wide range of circumstances. Member States are permitted to adopt specific measures to prevent or compensate for disadvantages linked to the protected grounds set out in Article 1, with a view to achieving real equality in practice. It is notable that the provision leaves a large discretion to each Member State as to which objectives it wishes to pursue by means of positive measures of discrimination but as we have seen from the discussion of the case law of the CJEU law above, subjects the application of those measures to certain constraints.

Article 7 of the FED, therefore, recognizes that a requirement to combat discrimination is not enough to bring about equality in real terms because of historically ingrained prejudice and stereotyping. Because of those factors, two individuals may not have the same opportunities in the workplace. And that matter needs to be addressed, otherwise, how can one speak of equality in the workplace? All employees should be on an equal footing in the labor market unhampered by historic discriminatory practices and attitudes.

The second paragraph of Article 7 FED is more specific. It enables Member States to maintain or adopt provisions on the protection of health and safety at work of the disabled and to adopt measures aimed at creating or maintaining provisions or facilities for safeguarding or promoting their integration into the working environment. This reflects the policy of inclusion of the disabled into both the social and work environment, which we see on many levels: international, EU, and national. Article 7 para. 2 FED is concerned with positive action for the disabled.[5]

Article 15 of the FED also provides for positive discrimination but on a more limited level—it is confined to specific types of employment in Northern Ireland, namely the police service and the teaching profession in Northern Ireland. Article 15 para. 1 FED provides that differences in treatment regarding recruitment into the police service, including its support staff, "shall not constitute discrimination, insofar as those differences in treatment are expressly authorized by national legislation." Article 15 para. 2 FED states that the provisions on religion or belief in the Directive do not apply to the recruitment of teachers in schools in Northern Ireland provided this is expressly provided for in national legislation. This exception is designed to maintain a balance of opportunity in the teaching profession while at the same time reconciling the historical differences between the major communities in Northern Ireland.

Neither provision has been the subject of a judgment of the CJEU to date.

Article 7 FED has been raised in the case of *Abercrombie and Finch* and Advocate General *Bobek* addressed the issue (CJEU, Abercrombie, & Fitch Italia Srl v

[5] See D. Ferri, The Role of EU Accessibility Legislation in Fighting Social Exclusion of Persons with Disabilities, in this book.

Antonino Bordonaro, 2017). However, he was of the view that the particular measure in that case was not one of positive discrimination. In that he followed the argument presented by the Italian Government during the oral proceedings in that case, asserting that Italy did not consider the measure in question to be one of positive discrimination. This seems to imply that national measures of positive discrimination must be explicitly identified as positive discrimination to be recognized as such. In the absence of a clear indication of their purpose, their status as positive discrimination measures cannot be presumed. This requirement has been confirmed in the *Georgiev* case (CJEU, Vasil Ivanov Georgiev v Tehnicheski universitet—Sofia, filial Plovdiv, 2010d).

However, in ascertaining the aim of particular measures a wide range of sources may be relied upon.

So, the question now is, in the apparent absence of reliance on Article 7 FED, whether there is in fact scope for positive discrimination, through other provisions of that Directive?

If we look, for example, at the provisions in the Directive 2000/78 providing for exceptions and derogations to the principle of equality, can it be concluded that they may be used by a Member State to justify favorable treatment, either in the recruitment process or at the workplace, to a particular employee or group of employees, in order to further the objectives of the Directive as set out in Article 1 FED?

The FED contains a large number of exceptions to the principle of equality—five exceptions in all. Additionally, Member States are permitted to make a number of derogations from some of its provisions. A perusal of these provisions indicates that some permit a degree of positive discrimination in the sense that they enable an employer to favor access to employment by a candidate with particular characteristics over and above another candidate with similar qualifications but who does not possess those characteristics. In other words, posts can be reserved for candidates of a particular profile. Two sets of provisions appear to provide (although not expressly) for such positive discrimination in three sets of circumstances: Article 4 FED and Article 6 FED. Article 4 para. 1 permits the favoring of a candidate with a specific characteristic where "such a characteristic constitutes a genuine and determining occupational requirement, providing that the objective is legitimate, and the requirement is proportionate." Article 4 para. 2 FED grants churches and other public or private organizations the ethos of which is based on religion or belief the right, subject to certain conditions, to depart from the principle of equal treatment. Article 6 para. 1 FED permits, subject to certain conditions, age-related differences in treatment on the grounds of age. Thus, candidates of a certain age may be preferred over other candidates not of that age even though the qualifications of both may be the same and both may be equally capable of performing the work in question.

The cases of *Wolf* (CJEU, Colin Wolf v Stadt Frankfurt am Main, 2010a) and *Prigge* (CJEU, Reinhard Prigge and Others v Deutsche Lufthansa AG, 2011) considered discriminatory provisions relating to the young and the not-so-young under Article 4 para. 1 FED. Mr. Wolf applied for a position in the fire services of the City of Frankfurt. His application was rejected on the grounds that he was over the age of 30 years. There was an age limit on the recruitment for the particular position within the fire service to which his application was related. That position required carrying out such tasks as fighting fires, rescuing persons, and dealing with dangerous animals. The Court found that such tasks required exceptional physical strength and could only be performed by young persons: "the need to possess full physical capacity to carry out [those tasks] is related to the age of the persons in that career" (CJEU, Colin Wolf v Stadt Frankfurt am Main, 2010a, para. 41). The statutory age limit for access to the position for which Mr. Wolf had applied was, therefore, a "genuine and determining occupational requirement" within the meaning of Article 4 para. 1. In *Prigge* the Court adopted a more nuanced view of an age limitation laid down in a collective agreement requiring airline pilots employed by Lufthansa to retire at the age of 60 years in the interest of safety. The Court deemed such age requirement disproportionate, noting that while international law and practice and, in many cases, national laws set the retirement age for pilots at 60 years, pilots aged 60 to 64 years were permitted to work as part of a multi-pilot crew, provided that the other crew members were under 60 years of age.

Article 6 paragraph 1 of the Directive 2000/78 states in broad terms that a Member State can provide differences in treatment on grounds of age, but this will not constitute discrimination if they are objectively and reasonably justified by a "legitimate aim". A legitimate aim may include an employment policy objective.

Article 6 paragraph 2 gives examples of acceptable differences in treatment but any measure permitting such disparate treatment is required to be appropriate and necessary.

There are three means by which candidates of a certain age profile can be favored in the workplace.

First, recruitment conditions can specify that only candidates of a specific age need to apply for particular posts. In general, these conditions are aimed at ensuring the candidates have appropriate attributes for the employment for which they applied. These attributes are usually related to required physical fitness levels, the general assumption being that younger candidates will be more agile and physically more fit than older candidates. Some types of employment may require a certain degree of physical fitness. Is an employer therefore entitled to limit recruitment to persons of a given age? In certain cases, they may if it is reasonable to assume that they have the required levels of physical fitness.

However, the CJEU has adopted a cautious approach toward favoring youth. If alternative methods exist to ascertain the required suitable profile of candidates for a specific job without relying on age-based assumptions, such age-based criteria may not be permissible.

This would be the case when an employer imposed a requirement on candidates to pass a strict physical test. Such a physical fitness test would be sufficient to determine the suitability of a candidate for a particular post making an age-based assumption unnecessary.

In the second type of case, favoring candidates of a certain age may be necessary to ensure an age balance in the workplace so that younger workers can gain access to employment or that the workforce may be composed of employees of all ages. The experience of the older employee can be passed on to the younger employee and the younger employee can bring dynamism, new ideas, and, increasingly, a familiarity with technological advances. This objective can be achieved: a) by favoring younger candidates over older candidates in the recruitment process or b) through retirement policy, by requiring employees of a certain age to take retirement and therefore free up jobs for younger employees.

In the case of *Palacios* (CJEU, Félix Palacios de la Villa v Cortefiel Servicios SA, 2007), a compulsory retirement clause in a collective agreement, authorized by legislation, was viewed by the CJEU as being a measure which imposed less favorable treatment for workers who have reached the compulsory retirement age as compared with other persons in the labor force. The relevant measure was introduced in Spain at a time of very high unemployment in that country, particularly high youth unemployment, which at the time had reached almost 50%. It was adopted as part of a national policy seeking to improve access to employment by means of a better distribution of work between the generations. It could therefore be regarded as justifiable as being a legitimate employment objective given the extraordinarily high level of unemployment amongst young people and the fact that persons who were compulsorily retired had the right to retirement pension.

The case of *Rosenbladt* (CJEU, Gisela Rosenbladt v Oellerking Gebäudereinigungsges mbH., 2010c) concerned a mandatory retirement provision for employees upon reaching the age at which they could claim a retirement pension or the age of 65 years within the cleaning sector was again accepted as being necessary to spread employment opportunities across generations. But in that case, the Court, in contrast to Palacios, did not consider whether Mrs. Rosenbladt had entitlement to a retirement pension adequate enough to enable her to meet her needs beyond retirement. Ms. Rosenbladt in fact was very poor. She had worked as a cleaner in an army barracks all her life and had little pension entitlement. Her pension was in fact only EUR 253.19. She needed to remain in employment in order to meet her needs. The German government did not see this as a relevant issue arguing she could always get another job. She was not forced to retire definitively from the labor market. The Court accepted this argument. This seems a little harsh as it may not be that obvious for a 65-year-old to seek a new job, given the general societal attitudes to the employment of the elderly.

The *Petersen* case (CJEU, Domnica Petersen v Berufungsausschuss für Zahnärzte für den Bezirk Westfalen-Lippe, 2010b) is interesting. It concerned the practice of dentistry by panel dentists in Germany within the statutory social security system. German law sets a maximum age of 68 years for the practice of dental services within the panel system in order to protect the health of patients, as it was believed that the performance of dentists beyond that age declines. Additionally, the age limit for panel dentists to remain in practice seems to have been prompted by other considerations, namely the distribution of employment among the generations and the limitation of the number of panel dentists to contain public health expenditure. The CJEU accepted that the objective of maintaining a high-quality medical service and preventing serious harm to the financial balance of the social security system was covered by the objective of public health. Therefore a compulsory retirement age of 68 years in a sector of the dental profession—public dental services—that accounted for 90% of the dental services in Germany could be legitimate in principle, if its aim was to protect the health of patients and to promote access of young people to that sector of the dental services market. Relying on Article 2 para. 5 of the FED, which states that the Directive shall be without prejudice to measures laid down by national law for the protection of health, the Court accepted that a Member State may find it necessary to set an age limit for the practice of a medical profession such as that of a dentist in order to preserve the health of patients. As to whether the age limit on dentists practicing in the public sector was justified to share out among the generations employment opportunities for panel dentists, the Court found that it might not be appropriate or necessary if the number of dentists practicing in that sector of the profession was not excessive with the result that it was usually possible for younger people to enter that market. The position would be otherwise if there was an excessive number of dentists or the risk that such a situation would occur. In other words, the legitimacy of a discriminatory measure designed to encourage youth to enter a particular employment market depends on market forces: to what extent is the market closed or largely inaccessible to new entrants? Finally, it is to be noted that the Court referred to the requirement of consistency in the application of what were in principle legitimate objectives pointing to the fact that in the private sector for dental services in Germany there was no compulsory retirement for dentists aged 68 years. This raised the question of whether a compulsory retirement age for dentists in the public sector was necessary in the interests of the health of patients if they could be treated privately by dentists over the age of 68 years.

Georgiev (CJEU, Vasil Ivanov Georgiev v Tehnicheski universitet—Sofia, filial Plovdiv, 2010d) concerned a dispute between Professor Georgiev and his university employer in Sofia, Bulgaria. Bulgarian law provided that university professors who had reached the age of 68 years were compulsorily retired and after the age of 65 years could continue working only by means of fixed-term contracts. The CJEU found that both of these practices amounted to a difference in treatment on the grounds of age. The national legislation in issue did not state the aim it pursued. However, from the submissions of the Bulgarian government and Professor Georgiev's employer university (and those of intervening governments and the European Commission), it appeared that they were consonant with the intention of allocating the posts for professors in the best possible way between the generations, in particular by appointing young professors. That policy could be considered to be a legitimate aim within the meaning of Article 6 para. 1 of the FED. A Member State could therefore set an age limit for the termination of a contract of employment provided it did not exceed what was necessary to achieve its employment policy objectives and that national legislation setting those objectives is consistent and systematic. Equally, the Court accepted that the conclusion of fixed-term contracts in circumstances such as those in issue in the national proceedings were capable of reconciling both the needs of the professors concerned and the universities and could therefore be considered as appropriate and necessary for achieving the objectives of Bulgarian government policy on university employment conditions.

We turn now to Article 4 para. 2 of the FED and religious discrimination. Under what circumstances can an employer require an employee to have a religion or a belief, or practice the tenets of a particular religion? Article 4 paragraph 2 of the FED provides:

> Member States may maintain national legislation in force at the date of adoption of this Directive or provide for future legislation incorporating national practices existing at the date of the adoption of this Directive pursuant to which in the case of occupational activities within churches and other public or private organisations, the ethos of which is based on religion or belief, a difference of treatment based on a person's religion or belief shall not constitute discrimination where, by reason of the nature of these activities or the context in which they're carried out, a person's religion or belief constitutes a genuine, legitimate and justified occupational requirement.

This provision says that national rules can permit religious organizations to require candidates to be of a particular religious persuasion. This is a very broadly drafted but imprecise provision. The first question that arises is what exactly is a religious organization? There's no definition of this concept in the Directive. Who determines what is a religious organization for the purposes of Article 4 para. 2 FED? Is it for the organization itself to declare itself to be a religious body, or to have a particular ethos, and therefore to be able to determine its own employment policy? Or can its perception be challenged?

Two cases (CJEU, *Vera Egenberger v Evangelisches Werk für Diakonie und Entwicklung e.V.*, 2018a & CJEU, *IR v. JQ*, 2018b), both requests for preliminary rulings made to the CJEU from courts in Germany, dealt with this issue and in both cases the Court held that the employment policy of religious and similar organization cannot remain immune from challenge. Where the application of a candidate is rejected on the grounds that the practice of a particular religion or belief constitutes a necessary, genuine, legitimate, and justified occupational requirement having regard to the ethos of the church or organization, it must be possible for that assertion to be the subject of effective judicial review. The applicability of Article 4 para. 2 depends on two factors: (i) the nature of the organization seeking to rely on Article 4 para. 2 and (ii) the actual job in issue.

If there is a job for a gardener within, for example, a church, is it necessary for the gardener should be a member of that church in order to do his gardening job? I rather think not. In *Egenberger* and *IR v. IQ,* the CJEU held that the nature of the occupational activity in issue and the circumstances in which it is to be carried out are determinative of whether the practice of a particular religion is necessary and objectively dictated.

Mrs. Egenberger (CJEU, Vera Egenberger v Evangelisches Werk für Diakonie und Entwicklung e.V., 2018a) applied for a position to work on a research project related to the United Nations International Convention on the Elimination of All Forms of Racial Discrimination. She was an extremely experienced researcher in this area. She was asked to declare in her application form that she was a member of a Protestant church, a church belonging to the working group of Christian churches in Germany.

She could not do this. She was not a member of any church. She basically did not practice any particular religion. She did not get the job. The successful candidate who was eventually appointed had stated with respect to his church membership that he was a "Protestant Christian active in the Berlin regional church." On a reference from the Bundesarbeitsgericht, the CJEU held that Article 4 para. 2 requires that each particular post within a religious of similar organization needs to be looked at to see if it, and the circumstances in which the work relating to that post, required the practice of a particular religion or the possession of particular belief or ethos. This approach followed that which it had adopted in the much earlier cases relating to the employment of women in the armed services. Moreover, the Court found that where a church or other organization whose ethos is based on religion or belief asserts that religion or belief constitutes a genuine, legitimate, and justified occupational requirement, that assertion must be, if need be, to effective judicial review to ensure that the criteria set out in Article 4 para. 2 are satisfied.

Likewise in *IR v. JQ*, the CJEU found that adherence to a particular aspect of the ethos of the Catholic Church, namely the sacred and indissoluble nature of religious marriage, did not appear to be necessary for the occupational activities carried out by JQ, namely the provision of medical advice and care in a hospital setting and the management of the internal medicine department, which he headed. It was not, therefore, a genuine requirement of that occupational activity within the meaning of Article 4 para. 2 FED.[6] The Court also pointed out that comparable duties were being performed by non-Catholic doctors.

Conclusions

Article 19 TFEU, the legal basis of the FED, is silent on the issue of positive discrimination. Articles 7 and 15 of the FED provide for positive discrimination. Article 7 para. 1 is a generally worded provision permitting Member States, with a view to achieving full equality in practice, to maintain or adopt specific measures to prevent or compensate for disadvantages linked to any of the grounds of discrimination referred to in Article 1—religion, belief, disability, age, or sexual orientation. Article 7 para. 2 and Article 15 FED are more specific in their scope of application.

At the time of writing neither Article 7 para. 1 nor Article 15 have been the subject of a judgment of the CJEU. This may mean that there are no issues regarding the application of positive discriminatory measures at the Member State level or it may mean that Member States are not engaging in positive discrimination as permitted by those provisions. Alternatively, can it be argued that positive discrimination can be, is being, achieved by means of other provisions in the FED not specifically labeled as measures permitting positive discrimination but in effect permitting it? The FED provides for many derogations to the principle of equal treatment in specifically defined circumstances. If we interpret positive discrimination as meaning the favoring of candidates of a certain profile over others in the recruitment

[6] It is interesting to note that these cases arose in Germany where the church is actually very powerful and is in some regions, the major employer, if not the monopoly employer. So these cases were extremely important in containing the discretion of the church and opening up opportunities to people who might have otherwise been denied.

process it does seem as if those provisions are engaging in positive discrimination. The provisions in the issue discussed above are Articles 4 and Article 6. These set out the circumstances in which the principle of equal treatment, required by the Directive, may be departed from. Article 4 para. 1 allows disparity of treatment where a characteristic related to any one of the grounds set out in Article 1 constitutes a "genuine and determining occupational requirement provided that the objective is legitimate and the requirement is proportionate." Article 4 para. 2 is concerned with occupational activities within churches and other public or private organizations the ethos of which is based on religion or belief. Article 6 para. 1 allows discrimination on the grounds of age in the pursuit of legitimate employment policy, labor market, or vocational training objectives provided that the measures in question are appropriate and necessary. Some examples of permissible differences in treatment are set out. These provisions differ from Article 7 para. 1, which allows positive discrimination only to prevent or compensate for disadvantages linked to the prohibited grounds of discrimination specified in Article 1. Articles 4 and 6 are couched in broader terms allowing Member States to achieve objectives other than the prevention or compensation for disadvantages linked to the prohibited grounds of discrimination. For example, Member States are permitted wide discretion in determining what is their "legitimate employment policy." This may have nothing to do with the prevention or compensation of disadvantages experienced by those having the characteristics specified in Article 1. Article 4 para. 2 is concerned with balancing the interests of churches and other similar religious organizations with the right of individuals to equal treatment. In contrast to Articles 4 and 6, Article 7 does not articulate that measures adopted by Member States are subject to the principle of proportionality but that can be assumed, it being a general principle of EU law and in the light of dicta of the CJEU in *Abrahamsson* (CJEU, Katarina Abrahamsson and Leif Anderson v Elisabet Fogelqvist, 2000b, para. 55). Interestingly the favoring of one candidate with a particular profile over another on the basis of Articles 4 or 6 does not appear at first sight to require an objective assessment of all candidates for a particular position as required by *Badeck* and *Abrahamsson*: once a candidate has the profile required by the employer they can be appointed without any reference to the suitability of their qualifications and other relevant criteria. Profile is determinative in the recruitment process. Employees of a particular profile, say youth, or of a particular religious persuasion, can be preferred to others without that profile without an exact comparison being made between them from the standpoint of their qualifications and other related attributes. This appears to depart from the principles governing equality between men and women.

From the above discussion, it seems that we can conclude that positive discrimination in the FED can be achieved, and is being achieved, by provisions other than Articles 7 and 15, but in all cases, the practical application of measures of positive discrimination is governed by the principles set out by the CJEU, namely the principle of proportionality and, most importantly, the requirement that any exception to the principle of equality must be interpreted restrictively so as not to undermine the essence of that principle.

References

Charter on Fundamental Rights, art. 23. https://fra.europa.eu/en/eu-charter/article/23-equality-between-women-and-men

CJEC, Case 222/84, *Johnson v. Chief Constable of the Royal Ulster Constabulary* (1986). ECLI:EU:C:1986:206. https://eur-lex.europa.eu/legal-content/EN/TXT/PDF/?uri=CELEX:61984CJ0222

CJEC, Case 312/86, *Commission of the European Communities v French Republic* (1988). ECLI:EU:C:1988:485. https://eur-lex.europa.eu/resource.html?uri=cellar:be18ec45-d47e-4557-9e33-cfb510c6a337.0002.06/DOC_1&format=PDF https://eur-lex.europa.eu/resource.html?uri=cellar:be18ec45-d47e-4557-9e33-cfb510c6a337.0002.06/DOC_2&format=PDF

CJEC, Case C-450/93, *Eckhard Kalanke v Freie Hansestadt Bremen* (1995). ECLI:EU:C:1995:322. https://eur-lex.europa.eu/legal-content/EN/TXT/PDF/?uri=CELEX:61993CJ0450

CJEC, Case 409/95, *Hellmut Marschall v Land Nordrhein-Westfalen* (1997). ECLI:EU:C:1997:533. https://eur-lex.europa.eu/legal-content/EN/TXT/PDF/?uri=CELEX:61995CJ0409

CJEC, Case C-158/97, *Georg Badeck and Others, interveners: Hessische Ministerpräsident and Landesanwalt beim Staatsgerichtshof des Landes Hessen* (2000a). ECLI:EU:C:2000:163. https://eur-lex.europa.eu/legal-content/EN/TXT/PDF/?uri=CELEX:61997CJ0158

CJEC, Case C-407/98, *Katarina Abrahamsson and Leif Anderson v Elisabet Fogelqvist* (2000b). ECLI:EU:C:2000:367. https://eur-lex.europa.eu/legal-content/EN/TXT/PDF/?uri=CELEX:61998CJ0407

CJEC, Case C-366/99, *Joseph Griesmar v. Ministre de l''Économie, des Finances et de l'Industrie & Ministre de la Fonction publique, de la Réforme de l'État et de la Décentralisation*, (2001). ECLI:EU:C:2001:648

CJEC, Case C-476/99, *H. Lommers v Minister van Landbouw, Natuurbeheer en Visserij* (2002). ECLI:EU:C:2002:183. https://eur-lex.europa.eu/legal-content/EN/TXT/PDF/?uri=CELEX:61999CJ0476

CJEC, Case C-411/05, *Félix Palacios de la Villa v Cortefiel Servicios SA* (2007). ECLI:EU:C:2007:604. https://eur-lex.europa.eu/legal-content/EN/TXT/PDF/?uri=CELEX:62005CJ0411

CJEU, Case C-229/08, *Colin Wolf v Stadt Frankfurt am Main* (2010a). ECLI:EU:C:2009:509. https://eur-lex.europa.eu/legal-content/EN/TXT/PDF/?uri=CELEX:62008CC0229

CJEU, Case C-341/08, *Domnica Petersen v Berufungsausschuss für Zahnärzte für den Bezirk Westfalen-Lippe* (2010b). ECLI:EU:C:2010:4, https://eur-lex.europa.eu/legal-content/EN/TXT/?uri=CELEX%3A62008CA0341

CJEU, Case C-45/09, *Gisela Rosenbladt v Oellerking Gebäudereinigungsges mbH.* (2010c). ECLI:EU:C:2010:601. https://eur-lex.europa.eu/legal-content/EN/TXT/PDF/?uri=CELEX:62009CJ0045

CJEU, Joined Cases C-250/09 & 268/09, *Vasil Ivanov Georgiev v Tehnicheski universitet - Sofia, filial Plovdiv* (2010d). ECLI:EU:C:2010:699. https://eur-lex.europa.eu/legal-content/EN/ALL/?uri=CELEX%3A62009CJ0250

CJEU, Case C-447/09, *Reinhard Prigge and Others v Deutsche Lufthansa AG* (2011). ECLI:EU:C:2011:573. https://eur-lex.europa.eu/legal-content/SL-EN/ALL/?uri=CELEX:62009CJ0447&from=SL

CJEU, Case C-143/16, *Abercrombie & Fitch Italia Srl v Antonino Bordonaro* (2017). ECLI:EU:C:2017:235. https://eur-lex.europa.eu/legal-content/EN/TXT/?uri=CELEX%3A62016CC0143

CJEU, Case C-414/16, *Vera Egenberger v Evangelisches Werk für Diakonie und Entwicklung e.V.* (2018a). ECLI:EU:C:2018:257. https://curia.europa.eu/juris/document/document.jsf?text=&docid=201148&pageIndex=0&doclang=el&mode=lst&dir=&occ=first&part=1&cid=13409865

CJEU, Case C-68/17, IR v. JQ (2018b). ECLI: EU:C:2018:696. https://eur-lex.europa.eu/legal-content/EN/TXT/?uri=CELEX%3A62017CJ0068
Council Directive (EC) 2000/43, of 29 June 2000, on the implementing the principle of equal treatment between persons irrespective of racial or ethnic origin, OJ L 180/22, of 19.07.2000a. https://eur-lex.europa.eu/legal-content/EN/TXT/PDF/?uri=CELEX:32000L0043
Council Directive (EC) 2000/78, of 27 November 2000, on the establishing a general framework for equal treatment in employment and occupation, OJ L 303/16, of 2.12.2000b. https://eur-lex.europa.eu/legal-content/EN/TXT/PDF/?uri=CELEX:32000L0078
Council Directive (EC) 2006/54, of 05.07.2006, on the implementation of the principle of equal opportunities and equal treatment of men and women in matters of employment and occupation (recast), OJ L 204/23, of 26.07.2006. https://eur-lex.europa.eu/legal-content/EN/TXT/PDF/?uri=CELEX:32006L0054
Council Directive (EEC) 76/207, of 9 February 1976, on the implementation of the principle of equal treatment for men and women as regards access to employment, vocational training and promotion, and working conditions, OJ L 39, of 14.2.1976, pp. 40–42 https://eur-lex.europa.eu/legal-content/EN/TXT/PDF/?uri=CELEX:31976L0207
Council Recommendation 84/635/EC, of 13.12.1984, on the promotion of positive action for women, OJ L 331/34, of 19.12.1984. https://eur-lex.europa.eu/legal-content/EN/TXT/PDF/?uri=CELEX:31984H0635
Treaty of Amsterdam amending the Treaty on European Union, the Treaties establishing the European Communities and certain related acts, 2 October 1997 [entry in force 1999], OJ C 340, of 10.11.1997. https://eur-lex.europa.eu/legal-content/EN/TXT/?uri=CELEX:11997D/TXT

The Role of the Ombudsman as National Equality Body: The Case of Greece

Kalliopi Lykovardi

Abstract

This contribution provides a concise overview of the institutional framework governing the principles of equal treatment and non-discrimination, established at European, and national level, tracing briefly the developments and their evolution over the past two decades. It emphasises the crucial role of national equality bodies, both in addressing discrimination (through preventive, mediating, deterrent, and repressive measures) and in providing essential feedback to enhance the tools and strategies used to achieve meaningful results. With regard to practical implementation of equal treatment legislation the contribution focuses on discrimination issues as drawn on the experience and practice of the national equality body in Greece, i.e. the Ombudsman. The discrimination issues presented are categorised according to the grounds covered by national legislation, namely: gender, ethnic or racial origin, religious or other beliefs, disability or chronic illness, age, social or family status, sexual orientation, gender identity, gender expression, or gender characteristics. Within these specific thematic areas, trends in reporting for each ground of discrimination are highlighted, along with gaps in protection, as well as structural or procedural challenges that arise in addressing violations. The chapter also identifies weaknesses in institutional safeguards, highlights the significance of prevention policies and social dialogue, and emphasises the importance of coordination in achieving meaningful progress in combatting the complexity of the ways and forms in which discrimination manifests itself.

K. Lykovardi (✉)
Deputy Ombudsperson for Equal Treatment in Greece, Athens, Greece

D. Anagnostopoulou (ed.), *European Identities, Inclusion and Equality*, Diversity and Inclusion Research, https://doi.org/10.1007/978-3-031-90602-2_14

Introductory Remarks

Achieving substantive equality remains a challenging goal that extends beyond the realm of legislative frameworks. While the existence of a robust legislative framework and its effective and consistent implementation are crucial, equally essential are fostering ideological discourse, challenging stereotypes, and promoting the intrinsic value of human diversity.

Discrimination, deeply rooted in long-standing societal assumptions and prejudices, is particularly resistant to change. Its persistence often appears justified and even natural, making its reduction—and eventual elimination—especially challenging. Thus, any anti-discrimination framework is insufficient if it does not target the root causes of inequality and encourage critical engagement with the perceptions and biases that sustain it.

Ensuring equal treatment as a cornerstone of human rights is a complex, multidimensional task. Although legislation is vital in driving tangible progress, the varied forms and manifestations of discrimination highlight the limitations of relying solely on legal instruments. Achieving meaningful societal advancement requires more comprehensive and coordinated efforts.

Anti-discrimination legislation is designed to uphold the principle of equal treatment, addressing and remedying individual violations, while also extending its scope beyond individual cases. Effective enforcement necessitates proactive measures such as preventive vigilance and deterrence, all aimed at transforming societal and workplace norms.

The European Union has pioneered a dynamic and evolving framework for combating discrimination, positioning national equality bodies as central to these efforts. Member States are mandated to establish and sufficiently support these bodies, which play a pivotal role in implementing anti-discrimination policies and fostering equality.

This contribution explores legislative developments at both European and national levels, briefly tracing their evolution over the past two decades. It also provides an overview of the practical application of the equal treatment legislation by the Greek Ombudsman, which functions as the national equality body in Greece.

Equal Treatment and EU Law

Legislation and initiatives at the EU level have significantly influenced the development of anti-discrimination laws in Greece. Until 2000, these initiatives primarily addressed gender discrimination in employment and labour, (Directive 76/207/EEC, 1976), equal pay (Directive 75/117/EEC, 1975), equality in social security (Directive 86/378/EEC, 1986, amended by Directive 96/97/EC, 1996), and the burden of proof in discrimination cases (Directive 97/80/EC, 1997).

The year 2000 marked a turning point in equal treatment and anti-discrimination EU law with the adoption of two landmark directives, aimed at establishing a unified legislative framework for promoting equal treatment. These include Directive

2000/43/EC (Directive 2000/43/EC, 2000), which addresses discrimination based on racial or ethnic origin,[1] and Directive 2000/78/EC (Directive 2000/78/EC, 2000), which focuses on discrimination in employment and occupation based on religion or belief, disability, age, or sexual orientation. The framework for gender equality has been shaped by additional directives, including Directive 2006/54/EC (Directive 2006/54/EC, 2006) on employment and occupation, Directive 2004/113/EC (Directive 2004/113/EC, 2004) on goods and services, and Directive 2010/41/EU (Directive 2010/41/EU, 2010) on self-employment.

These directives define the concept of discrimination and its various forms, including direct and indirect discrimination, harassment (including sexual harassment), and instruction to discriminate, drawing on the jurisprudence of the Court of Justice of the European Union (CJEU). For the first time, discrimination and its manifestations received specific normative content within binding frameworks for Member States.

Thus, although the focus is on redressing the individual offence and providing remedies, the directives outline mechanisms for enforcing equal treatment, which extend beyond traditional individual-based approach and include: (a) mediation and promotional activities; (b) engagement with civil society to raise awareness and represent victims; (c) encouragement of social dialogue; and (d) adoption of positive measures to address systemic inequality and (e) litigation. These approaches aim to provide not only independent support and remedies to victims of discrimination but also systemic interventions that address structural inequality and promote broad societal collaboration in order to respond sufficiently to (a) the needs for protection of "vulnerable groups"; (b) the structural nature of unequal treatment practices; and (c) the need for broader social coordination to combat effectively discrimination and the prejudices that fuel it.

However, disparities remained in the level of protection provided and the sectors covered by these directives. In 2008, the European Commission proposed extending the scope of Directives 2000/43/EC and 2000/78/EC (Directive 2000/43/EC, 2000; Directive 2000/78/EC, 2000) to encompass additional areas beyond employment and labour. Unfortunately, consensus could not be reached, and the proposal was not finally adopted (European Commission, 2008).

Equality Bodies in EU Law

Equality bodies were first established by the Racial Equality Directive (Directive 2000/43, 2000).[2] Article 13 of Directive 2000/43/EC outlines the competences of these bodies to (a) provide independent assistance to victims of discrimination; (b)

[1] The Directive 2000/43/EC applies to employment and labour but also to social protection, including social benefits and health care, education, and the provision of goods and services which are commercially available to the public, including housing.

[2] In the Employment Directive (2000/78/EC), there is no explicit obligation to designate equality bodies, but it is a discretionary power of the Member States, which they have mostly used.

conduct independent surveys; (c) publish independent reports; and (d) cooperate with competent national bodies and services. The EU Gender Equality Directives (Directive 2004/113/EC, 2004; Directive 2006/54/EC, 2006; Directive 2010/41/EU, 2010) provide for the same competences for equality bodies, only adding the competence to cooperate and exchange information with relevant European bodies.

The role of equality bodies in the scope of the Directives appears to be crucial (European Commission, 2006) and, in principle, twofold. It concerns not only the monitoring of implementation but also the promotion of the principle of equal treatment. Regarding the monitoring and mediation role of equality bodies, this primarily involves the handling of individual complaints of discrimination. At the same time, however, beyond investigating individual cases, these bodies conduct surveys, publish reports, and collect data, which highlight the systemic problems and enable interventions of a broader nature that extend beyond individual cases. In this context, the national equality bodies are in the position to document violations of the principle of equal treatment, to identify their trends, to report obstacles to their prevention, and to monitor the progress made over time.

Although no specific guarantees of independence are explicitly provided for, the provision for the assignment of competences to rights protection bodies, along with the wording of the tasks outlined, such as providing independent assistance to victims of discrimination, conducting surveys, and publishing independent reports, clearly implies that the organisational and functional independence of these bodies is a prerequisite for effectively carrying out their mandate. Moreover, the examination of the bodies´ mandate in conjunction with the effectiveness of the work produced has been the subject of periodic monitoring by the European Commission (European Commission, 2014, p. 14).

In this light, the absence of specific provisions and standardisation of the operation and exercise of the competences of the bodies leaves scope for creative adaptation to the national legal context and reality. However, identified shortcomings or variations (Crowley, 2018) highlight the need for corrective and more specific interventions. Since 2000, the evaluation and assessment of experience and practice also allow conclusions to be drawn on the conditions necessary for the independent and effective exercise of the duties of equality bodies.

Responding to this need the European Network of Equality Bodies (European Network of Equality Bodies, Equinet, 2016) has undertaken an initiative to standardise the operating models of equality bodies. The European Commission against Racism and Intolerance (ECRI) has issued its revised Recommendation on equality bodies in 2017 (General Policy Recommendation GPR N°2 revised, 2017) and in December 2022, the European Commission took the initiative (European Commission, 2022a, 2022b) to submit two proposals establishing minimum common standards for equality bodies (European Commission, 2022a, 2022b). The aim of the two parallel proposals of the European Commission was to strengthen the effectiveness and independence of equality bodies in the context of all the Directives adopted in the field of equal treatment, namely Directives: 79/7/EEC, 2000/43/EC, 2000/78/EC, 2004/113/EC, 2006/54/EC, and 2010/41/EU. Due to the fact that the six Directives were adopted on two different legal bases[3] and under two different legislative procedures, the initiative consisted of two essentially identical proposals that were adopted by the European Council in June 2023 (Council of the EU, 2023) and by the Parliament in May 2024.

The Directives (Directive (EU) 2024/1499, 2024; Directive (EU) 2024/1500, 2024) are a milestone in the development of EU equality law. They replace the previous provisions on equality bodies in the EU Framework Directives on Equality with a strengthened and more detailed normative framework. They set out the minimum standards for their operation in order to empower their effectiveness and ensure their independence, strengthening at the same time the implementation of EU equal treatment legislation. The 2024 EU Directives focus in particular on the organisational and operational autonomy and independence of equality bodies, and their accessibility, ensuring that they have all the necessary institutional tools and resources (human, financial, and technical). They also establish guarantees and preconditions for the exercise of all their tasks, including monitoring, promotion, prevention, assistance to victims, and access to justice. Furthermore, they directly link the provision of the necessary institutional tools to the achievement of tangible and measurable results. Article 18 (monitoring of implementation) of Directives 2024/1499 and 2024/1500 provides for the establishment of specific indicators for measuring results, a task which has been entrusted to the European Commission. These indicators will relate to *"human, technical and financial resources, the independent functioning, accessibility and effectiveness of equality bodies, as well as developments in their mission, competences and structure"* (Directive (EU) 2024/1500, 2024, art. 18, para. 1).

The EU institutions have taken the initiative to give concrete and binding normative content to the way equality bodies operate, strengthening equal treatment legislation. The Member States are now called upon to meet the standards that have been set.

The Ombudsman as the Equality Body in the Greek Legal Order

The law that incorporated Directive 2000/43 and Directive 2000/78 into the Greek legal order was Law 3304/2005, *"implementing the principle of equal treatment irrespective of racial or ethnic origin, religious or other beliefs, disability, age or sexual orientation"*. The competent bodies that have been designated as equality bodies in Greece were the following: In the public sector, the Ombudsman (Law 3304/2005, art. 19 para. 1) and in the private sector the Labour Inspectorate (Law 3304/2005, art. 19 para. 3). For other types of discrimination that do not fall within the competence of the aforementioned bodies, the designated competent body was

[3] Article 157(3) of the Treaty on the Functioning of the European Union (TFEU) is the legal basis for equal treatment between men and women and Article 19(1) of the TFEU for equal treatment irrespective of national or racial origin, religion or belief, disability, age, or sexual orientation.

the Equal Treatment Committee of the Ministry of Justice (Law 3304/2005, art. 19 para. 2).

Despite the positive elements of the law, particularly its incorporation of the innovative provisions of the Directives (2000/43/EC; 2000/78/EC), the Greek legislator did not use the discretion provided in the Directives to extend the scope of protection or the grounds of discrimination beyond those provided in the Directives. Thus, the law was criticised because of its limited regulatory scope, the almost identical transposition of the text of the Directives and the organisational choice of fragmenting the competence and assigning it to three bodies, two of which were not independent authorities but units within ministries (Ministry of Employment/ Ministry of Justice).[4]

In practice, given the limitations of the regulatory scope of Law 3304/2005, the general mandate of the Greek Ombudsman as a human rights institution was often invoked in cases where the provisions of the anti-discrimination law were not applicable (Greek Ombudsman, 2015). The normative relevance of the general provisions of Law 3304/2005 with other fundamental rules of national law (in particular with the principle of equality proclaimed in Article 4 of the Constitution), allowed their use in areas beyond the scope of the specific law. In these cases, however, it would not be possible to use the institutional tools provided by Law 3304/2005, such as the reversal of the burden of proof, while at the same time, it would be difficult to ensure comprehensive and consistent supervision and monitoring of discrimination cases in the broad range of administrative action and practice.

Initially operating only in the public sector, the Greek Ombudsman[5] used its general competence (Greek Law 3094/2003) in order to intervene in cases of discrimination that did not fall within the scope of the specific law (goods and services, social benefits, education, healthcare, police abuse, etc.) At the same time, the Ombudsman, responding to its promotional duties, sought to create networks of cooperation with civil society organisations in order to fill in the identified institutional gap in contact with victims of discrimination, especially those belonging to vulnerable population groups.

In 2007, it created a pilot network of organisations and agencies for refugees and Roma (Greek Ombudsman, 2007). The aim was to communicate and coordinate actions with central and especially regional civil society organisations active in the field of protection and support of the rights of these vulnerable" population groups.

[4] However, in addition to the competent national bodies (in particular the ESC, Economic and Social Committee) and the European Commission, other international monitoring bodies with competence in the fight against racism and discrimination have repeatedly criticised the organisational choice to delegate responsibilities to three separate bodies, combining it in particular with the non-independent character of the two bodies and the ineffective exercise of their competences (United Nations Committee on the Elimination of Racial Discrimination (CERD), 2009; United Nations Committee on the Elimination of Racial Discrimination (CERD) 2016; European Commission against Racism and Intolerance (ECRI); European Commission against Racism and Intolerance (ECRI), 2015.

[5] The Ombudsman is a constitutionally enshrined independent authority, operating since 1998, with the mission to protect citizens' rights, uphold the rule of law, and combat maladministration.

These actions were gradually extended from 2013 onwards to the creation of a network with organisations and bodies across the spectrum of protected characteristics (disability, age, religious beliefs, sexual orientation) (Greek Ombudsman, 2013a).

In 2006, the competence of the Ombudsman on issues of discrimination on the grounds of national or racial origin, religious or other beliefs, disability, age, and sexual orientation was further strengthened with the designation of the Ombudsman as a body for gender equality in the public and private sector (Law 3844/2006).[6] The assignment of this competence, according to the law applied uniformly to both the public and private sectors on gender issues. Two years after, in 2008 gender equality became a specific thematic unit in the internal structure of the institution and its supervision was assigned to a separate Deputy Ombudsman for Gender Equality.

In 2016, a new legislative and organisational change was introduced. Law 4443/2016 revised and repealed Law 3304/2005. This law, together with Law 3896/2010 on equal treatment between men and women, assigns the Ombudsman with the exclusive competence to monitor and promote the implementation of equal treatment legislation in the public and private sector.[7] The grounds for discrimination are broadened and, chronic illness, gender identity, family, and social status, are added as protected grounds in the area of employment and work. Moreover, multiple discrimination, discrimination on the basis of perceived characteristics, discrimination by association, and reasonable accommodation, as provided for in the International Convention on the Rights of Persons with Disabilities (CRPD), are also included as forms of discrimination. In addition, this law provides, albeit in a vague manner as regards their competences, for a number of bodies and services that make up the mesh of an institutional cooperation mechanism for the achievement of the objectives of the law (Law 4443/2016, art. 13, 15, 16).

The explicit requirement of the law for specific justification for any derogation from the principle of equal treatment is of particular practical importance and is repeated in individual provisions of the law. The obvious aim is to reinforce the value of justification and to remind institutions and services of this legal obligation, so that the reason for the possible discrimination becomes practically verifiable. Of particular importance is also the implicit requirement of full and detailed reasoning in cases where there is a deviation from the part of the Ombudsman's final findings in discrimination cases.

Apart from the strengthening of the ways of exerting influence in the context of the Ombudsman's mediation intervention, the law does not provide for any other type of intervention or escalation of intervention, even of a mildly punitive nature. Nor does it provide for any type of representation or in any form its participation before the courts.[8] The acts of the Ombudsman continue to be non-enforceable with

[6] In 2010, this law was repealed by the current Law 3896/2010, which incorporated the recast Directive 2006/54/EC.

[7] Law 3769/2009, which transposed the Directive on gender equality in the provision of goods and services (2004/113/EC), maintains the Consumer Ombudsman as an equality body in this area.

[8] Reliance or use of the findings of the equality body is often made when the cases it has examined reach the courts. This is, however, at the initiative of the parties, and in some cases, the equality

its role primarily focused on mediation—an approach deeply rooted in the institution's character and traditional function. While this type of intervention has long been established and widely practiced in the public sector, its application in the private sector has been more limited, only extending to cases of gender discrimination in employment since 2006. For this reason, after the assignment of the competences in the private sector to the Ombudsman, the institution established a close cooperation with the Labour Inspectorate (SEPE). Similar cooperation, albeit in a vague manner, is provided in the law for all public services with the competence to control and impose sanctions on private disputes (NGOs, professional associations, chambers of commerce, etc.), as well as the obligation to forward all relevant complaints of these services to the Ombudsman in the context of filing complaints on discrimination issues falling within the scope of the relevant law.

This legislative development at the end of 2016 (Law 4443/2016) was accompanied by the internal organisational choice of the Ombudsman to establish a distinct thematic unit for the protection and promotion of equal treatment on all protected grounds. This internal change practically meant that complaints of discrimination received by the Ombudsman within the scope of the law would be allocated to the "Equal Treatment unit". Moreover, this unit has the overall supervision of issues directly or indirectly related to discrimination. At the same time, communication and promotional activities of the new unit led to a significant increase in the number of relevant complaints lodged and allowed for analysis, documentation, and further strengthening of the implementation of the legislation.

However, Law 4443/2016 failed to horizontally extend the scope of Directive 2000/78 to the fields covered by Directive 2000/43. That has in practice weakened both the scope of the protection afforded, its consistency, the structural adequacy of the legislation but also the means of intervention of the competent supervisory body. This regulatory deficit was subsequently partly addressed by Law 5023/2023, which extended the scope of equal treatment to areas beyond employment and work in cases of discrimination on the grounds of disability, and the recently adopted Law 5089/2024 on equality in civil marriage, with a corresponding extension to cases of discrimination on the grounds of religion or other beliefs, sexual orientation, gender identity, characteristics or expression. So far, however, this significant legislative change has yet to be accompanied by the provision of additional institutional means of intervention and the necessary resources to carry out the new competences.

body's views have been sought by the courts themselves, as in the case of indirect discrimination against women through the introduction of a single height limit for female and male candidates (1.70)

The Application of the Framework in the Practice of the National Equality Body

Discrimination between Men and Women

Equal treatment of men and women in employment and occupation, equal participation in decision-making bodies and professional development, equal opportunities, and effective measures against gender-based violence, sexual harassment, or moral harassment are indicators of the extent to which real gender equality has been achieved. In this area, however, the data is not positive for Greece.[9] Inequalities in employment and work are not, of course, exclusively related to discrimination on the basis of gender or discrimination on the basis of any other protected characteristic or status. A number of other factors affect the conditions of access to employment and work, but also the conditions of provision of work, and highlight serious inequalities, particularly in terms of equal opportunities. It is undeniable, however, that inequalities in employment disproportionately affect women. Whether it is the proportion of women in the labour market, the form and sector of employment (e.g. temporary, part-time in low-paid occupations, etc.) or their pay, the occupation of positions of responsibility (managerial tasks and positions) or the risk of losing their job (dismissal due to pregnancy or maternity), the position of women workers, as reflected in relevant complaints, appears to be consistently worse. This disadvantage is further compounded by the disproportionate burden of caregiving responsibilities for children, the elderly, and other dependent relatives, which continues to fall largely on women. As a result, women face multiple challenges, both in the workplace and in broader social contexts.

In particular, complaints submitted to the Ombudsman highlight violations of maternity protection and child-rearing leave provisions, as well as workplace treatment and accommodations related to balancing family and professional obligations. More specifically, they concern difficulties or unfair conditions in the granting of leave, unfavourable employment treatment following return from maternity leave or loss of positions of responsibility following maternity leave, dismissal of pregnant women or mothers, gender-based harassment, and in particular sexual harassment mainly against women[10] but also indirect gender discrimination in terms of recruitment notices.[11]

A key issue that the Ombudsman has identified is the wide variation in the provisions for the protection of maternity and family life, and the difficulties in reconciliation of private and professional life depending on the employment status

[9] Greece, with 58.0 points out of 100, ranks 24th in the EU on the Gender Equality Index in 2023 (European Institute for Gender Equality (EIGE), 2023, while in the index of 2022, Greece with 53.4 out of 100 points, ranks last in the EU on the Gender Equality Index 2022 (European Institute for Gender Equality, (EIGE), 2022).

[10] Almost all of sexual harassment complaints at the expense of women (Greek Ombudsman, 2022).

[11] A typical example is the height requirement (1.70) in a uniform way for men and women in a Fire Brigade notice or the participation in competitive procedures with uniform performance thresholds.

(permanent, or fixed-term employees, contract workers, etc.) and the sector of employment (public, wider public or private).[12] The central aim[13] for the equality body was to reveal the gaps and to make interventions in order to unify the relevant framework and to establish at least a minimum but common protection for all working parents regardless of the type of contract they have or their sector of employment (public or private). An important development in this field was brought about by Law 4808/2021, which transposed the EU Directive on the work-life balance (Directive 2019/1158, 2019).

Although the vast majority of cases of violations of the principle of equal treatment involve women, men are also subject to the adverse effects of discrimination. It is indicative that deeply entrenched stereotypes regarding the distribution of gender roles in the family are still maintained and reproduced, resulting in working fathers being excluded from exercising rights related to child-rearing or subjected to unfair restrictions (e.g. Greek Ombudsman, 2018, pp. 41–42) or even harassment in the exercise of their rights. Discriminatory provisions against men also exist in the provision of pension rights (e.g. Greek Ombudsman, 2018, p. 42). The maintenance of this situation, however, undermines the efforts for reconciliation of work and family life and the necessary change in perceptions of gender roles in child-rearing.

It is worth pointing out that gender discrimination cases are an area where the confluence of an additional protected ground of discrimination can often lead to multiple discrimination. The common grounds of discrimination that combine to aggravate discrimination, particularly against women, are age, disability, marital status, national or racial origin, both of the persons themselves and sometimes of their spouses/partners.[14]

Discrimination Based on Racial or Ethnic Origin

The issues of racial discrimination mainly concern cases of discrimination against the Roma. The central finding with regard to Roma discrimination is the systematic failure of the competent state authorities to recognise the extent and consequences of their social and labour exclusion, and the reluctance to take a decisive central

[12] Indicative of this distortion is a series of cases that have been before the Ombudsman for many years, in which employees with private law contracts in entities of the wider public sector were deprived of both the rights of the Civil Service Code, on the grounds that they are not civil servants, and the rights of labour law, on the grounds that they are employed in the wider public sector and not in enterprises or holdings. (Greek Ombudsman, 2018, pp. 48–49).

[13] Already in November 2019, with a central intervention to the then General Secretariat for Family Policy and Gender Equality, the Greek Ombudsman, on the occasion of Directive 2019/1158, had recommended specific proposals to address the problems and the establishment of uniform protection for all workers regardless of the type of contract they have or their employment in the public or private sector.

[14] See case of refusal to pay child benefit to a Greek mother due to the foreign nationality of her husband (Greek Ombudsman, 2017, p. 103).

initiative both for their urban registration to official registers and for addressing their acute housing problem. Maintaining the existing situation—particularly regarding registration and settlement—directly impacts equal access to fundamental rights, including education, employment, healthcare, social protection, and access to goods and services. Registration and settlement serve as essential prerequisites for securing and exercising these rights, making them a critical foundation for further progress in equality.

In addition, this fact undermines social cohesion and peace, but also any effort for effective social integration. It is indicative that the lack of identity documents, the almost complete exclusion from work and formal economy, the resort to noxious and polluting livelihood activities of the informal economy, and the living under inappropriate sanitary conditions in makeshift camps have consequences not only for the Roma themselves but also for the enjoyment of the rights of citizens living near arbitrary Roma settlements. The issues that the Ombudsman has addressed include obstacles in obtaining identification cards, preventing arbitrary demolitions of shacks, assistance for relocations to suitable sites, as well as mediation for adequate policing and interventions to stop polluting activities.[15]

Similarly, migrants and refugees who are long-term residents are discriminated against in a wide range of areas, which indicates that the realisation of equal access to rights, as well as goods and services, remains a constant aspiration and need. The issues raised by the cases examined by the Ombudsman relate to procedural obstacles that hinder the exercise of rights and impede their social integration, as well as unfair exclusions from the provision of goods and services on racially motivated grounds (Greek Ombudsman, 2017, pp. 46–49). The pervasive wariness towards the "ethnically or ethnically different" is also highlighted in cases that impose unfair restrictions even on European Union (EU) citizens (Greek Ombudsman, 2017, pp. 49–51) despite the increased protection[16] afforded by the legislation to European citizens and their family members. Finally, this attitude appears to maintain discrimination with a legislative basis[17] even against Greek citizens of foreign origin in their access to public functions, based on the way they acquired Greek citizenship or the time that has elapsed since their naturalisation. However, even if the specific nature of certain functions may, in principle, permit the exclusion of foreign nationals from exercising them, differentiations between Greek citizens on the basis of their national origin cannot constitute a legitimate criterion of discrimination (Greek Ombudsman, 2015, p. 102; Greek Ombudsman, 2020a, pp. 56–57).

[15] Since 2005 a relevant chapter is contained in each annual report on the Authority's equal treatment mandate.

[16] As it has already been pointed out, Directive 2014/54, which specifically concerns the free movement and rights of EU citizens and their family members, was incorporated into Greek law, in addition to other Directives with Law 4443/2016.

[17] See requirement of 5 years from the naturalisation of article 36 paragraph 3 of the Code of the Organization of Courts and the Status of Judicial Officers, Law 1756/1988, or in the past, article 3 paragraph 1 subparagraph b of the previous Code of Lawyers, Law 3026/1954.

In cases of discrimination on the grounds of racial or ethnic origin, the Ombudsman also examines the dimension of gender or other possible grounds of discrimination (disability, age, sexual orientation, gender identity, or gender characteristics), in order to highlight the need to take into account this parameter in the policies and practices applied regarding the provision of appropriate protection to vulnerable population groups[18] and in ensuring appropriate living conditions in accommodation facilities or settlements. Accordingly, the intersectional nature of discrimination in multiple areas of activity (housing, education, employment, health, goods and services) and the interconnectedness of such discrimination are often highlighted and emphasised.

However, a key feature, affecting both Roma and refugees or foreigners is the increasing number of complaints filed with the Ombudsman by local residents living near their camps. These complaints often stem from the impact of living conditions and social exclusion on the surrounding communities. This growing trend is consistently documented in the Ombudsman's Annual Reports, underscoring the risk of escalating social tensions that may lead to intolerance, xenophobia, and broader threats to social cohesion.

The persistence and intensification of these tensions are largely fuelled by the lack of effective mediation and social reconciliation mechanisms, as well as the reluctance to implement coordinated social support measures. This absence of intervention affects not only the vulnerable populations themselves but also the surrounding residents, who experience the consequences of poor living conditions and inadequate reintegration solutions.

Discrimination on the Basis of Religious or Other Beliefs

Complaints submitted to the Ombudsman concerning discrimination on the grounds of religious or other beliefs often fall outside the scope covered by anti-discrimination legislation. Specifically, the majority of them do not concern discrimination on the grounds of religion or other beliefs in the field of employment and work. In this context, the cases investigated do not differ in their qualitative characteristics from those received by the Ombudsman in the past and in the context of its general competence as a body for the protection of citizens' rights. They basically concern either normative provisions on issues sensitive to religious or other beliefs minorities (licensing of places of worship, conscientious objectors, teaching of religious education in schools) or problems that reflect the administration's ingrained perception of the separation of the secular and religious character of certain administrative functions (burial, registration of children's names, teaching of religious education). The misunderstanding of the function of religious acts at the administrative level sometimes leads to the impression that they substitute or can substitute for formal institutionalised administrative procedures. This in turn may create a suspicion

[18] See relevant interventions of the Authority, especially during the period of the migration, but then also the health crisis.

among citizens that they are or may be discriminated against on the basis of their religious beliefs when they are asked directly or indirectly to declare their religion.[19]

In the field of employment, the specific complaints lodged with the Ombudsman concerned the use of a religious symbol (headscarf) by a Muslim employee during an internship in a public hospital,[20] the requirement of a declaration of religion on an application form for employment in a food marketing shop (Greek Ombudsman, 2020b)[21] and the indirect impact on access to employment of the indication of "alternative service" on military certificates (Greek Ombudsman, 2021, pp. 52–53).

Discrimination on the Grounds of Disability or Chronic Disease

The prohibition of discrimination on the grounds of disability and the promotion of the principle of equal treatment in this field is part of a broader process of transition[22] from the medical-welfare to the social model of approach to disability (Greek Ombudsman, 2013a, 2013b, 2013c, 2013d, pp. 107–108). In the medical-welfare model, disability was seen as an individual problem and the resulting inability to find work or to participate in social or economic life was seen as natural and inevitable. Under this model, the options available to the State were limited to medical rehabilitation and the provision of welfare benefits. The social model, on the other hand, focuses on the interaction between the individual and their environment, with disability viewed as the result of the latter's inability to respond to the specific conditions created for certain individuals by the existence of a long-term physical, mental, intellectual, or sensory condition. In this light, the social, legal, economic, or

[19] An indicative case of the above misunderstanding is the reference in the form of application for granting the child support allowance or the allowance for families with three or more children, as "unbaptized" with regard to child for whom the first name has not yet been declared.

[20] In this case, the Ombudsman found that the prohibition of the use of headscarves during the practical practice of nursing in clinics does not constitute direct discrimination, according to Law 4443/2016, as the prohibition is not linked and not differentiated on the basis of religious beliefs, but concerns the observance of the prescribed uniform dress of nurses, based on provisions of a regulatory nature, which apply to nursing staff indiscriminately.

[21] See Greek Ombudsman. (2020a, 2020b). *Mediation Summary: Indicating religion in candidates' online applications for jobs in a company*.

[22] This transition on an international scale is unfolding gradually, with the first important milestone being the adoption in 1993 by the General Assembly of the United Nations of standard rules (United Nations (UN) Standard Rules for the Equalisation of Opportunities for Persons with Disabilities 1993) which were adopted by Greece through Article 3 of Law 2430/1996. This was followed, at the European Union (EU) level, by the revision of Article 13 of the European Communities by the Treaty of Amsterdam, which included disability among the prohibited criteria of discrimination and provided the basis for the adoption of the EU Directive 2000/78 on employment and occupation. The transition to the new model received a further strong impetus with the entry into force in 2008 of the United Nations Convention on the Rights of Persons with Disabilities (UNCRPD) and its Optional Protocol, not only because it lays down obligations for States Parties to respect, protect and ensure the conditions for the effective exercise of the rights of persons with disabilities, but also because it sets out definitions and general principles compatible with the new model that permeate the entire legal order and are now firmly established in the relevant case law.

environmental factors that hinder the full exercise of the rights of people with disabilities need to be identified and eliminated. In order to achieve this and to make a practical transition from the medical to the social model, a change in approach and perceptions is needed in the relevant State actors and in the socially active subjects in general, so that disability is seen as a manifestation of human diversity and difference, and people with disabilities are no longer seen as recipients of benefits or as dependent on third-party decisions, but as independent rights holders themselves.

According to Law 4443/2016, any discrimination based on disability or chronic illness is prohibited. According to Article 2(c) of the United Nations Convention, the term "discrimination on grounds of disability" means any discrimination, exclusion, or restriction based on disability that prevents persons from exercising or enjoying their rights and fundamental freedoms on an equal basis. However, a precise definition of what constitutes a disability or chronic condition is not included in the Convention, nor are there specific diseases that are specifically protected against discrimination. Directive 2000/78/EC uses the term "special need", which is defined as a handicap resulting in particular from a long-term physical, mental, or psychological condition which, in combination with various obstacles, may prevent a person from participating fully and effectively in working life on an equal basis with other workers.

Given the fact that disability or chronic disease are broad concepts, the Ombudsman investigates any case in which a health issue prevents a person from enjoying the equal benefit of work. It is often found, however, that management attitudes towards people with disabilities (e.g. Greek Ombudsman, 2021, pp. 54–57) continue to reflect stereotypical perceptions[23] of their abilities, while issues of reasonable accommodation, whether in terms of ensuring accessibility to the buildings of the services where they work or providing service facilities, often become difficult to resolve. In investigating cases of disability or chronic disease, factors such as the ability or capacity for employment of the worker, the reasonable adjustments made or required to be made by the employer, and any disproportionate burden on the service or undertaking of the measures or reasonable adjustments it is required to adopt, are weighed in the investigation. Cases of discrimination on the grounds of disability or chronic disease in employment and occupation are a significant number of cases received by the Ombudsman, as an equality body, and show a steadily increasing trend. The extension of the protection to fields beyond employment, as resulting from Law 5023/2022, is expected to further strengthen the relevant protection and contribute to the effective removal of discrimination in fields such as education, social protection, and access to goods and services. However, the wide intersectional nature of disability discrimination should be always taken into account and addressed.

[23] The Ombudsman has held that the refusal of public sector bodies to complete the recruitment of persons who have initially been deemed eligible for appointment, considering them to be unsuitable from the outset because of their disability, constitutes direct discrimination (Greek Ombudsman, 2021, pp. 56–57),

Age Discrimination

Over time, the Ombudsman has sought to shake the pervasive belief that age is an inherently legitimate criterion in recruitment. According to Law 4443/2016, any form of direct or indirect age discrimination in the field of employment is, in principle, prohibited. The most frequent violations of the law in this area are found in the setting of a maximum age limit as a condition for access to employment, which is allowed only exceptionally and under certain strict conditions. In order for the age criterion to be considered justified, it must (a) constitute a demonstrable characteristic of substantial importance in relation to the ability to perform a particular professional activity; (b) serve a legitimate aim; and (c) be reasonable and strictly necessary. Indeed, it is imperative that all regulatory provisions setting an upper age limit for access to specific sectors or specialisations should be accompanied by a specific justification that substantiates the above, since, in the absence of such a justification, the legality of the relevant selection procedure is called into question.

The Ombudsman has examined numerous complaints concerning the arbitrary and abusive setting of maximum age limits for access to professional activities, without specific justification for the use of age as a criterion. In the majority of cases, the required justification is (a) completely absent and (b) vague, inadequate, and not based on objective evidence. In most cases, the employer demonstrates difficulty or even complete inability to provide a justification for the age limits that have been set. On the other hand, the Ombudsman's experience is that age is strongly connected with stereotypes and perceptions that are taken for granted. In this regard, the requirement of providing specific justification when setting age limits is in itself an effective way to challenge existing perceptions and limit arbitrary use.

An indicative case handled by the Ombudsman was the Hellenic Post's (ELTA) introduction of a maximum age limit of 40 years in the call for the recruitment of "post distributors" (Greek Ombudsman, 2016, pp. 118–119). Responding to the Ombudsman's request for a specific justification for this age limit, the Hellenic Post just insisted on its necessity. It argued that performing the duties associated with this position requires specific physical capabilities, which, according to their opinion, are generally absent in individuals over the age of 40 years (Greek Ombudsman, 2016, pp. 118–119). The Ombudsman pointed out the obligation of the employer to provide specific data, including the type of offered contract, list of the exact tasks for the post, and the way and means of performing them, as well as the number of workers per age group already employed in the post, in order to fulfil the justification requirements to set age limits, as outlined in anti-discrimination legislation.

The Ombudsman also often receives complaints regarding recruitment calls for the security forces, where it is common and, in principle, legitimate to set age limits.[24] Indicative is the case in a 2021 recruitment call for special guards, where an

[24] For example, in the case law of the CJEU, see paras. 41, 43 in Case C-229/2008, *Wolf* (on the exercise of the profession of firefighter), paras. 42, 43, and 46 in Case C-258/2015, *Sorondo* (on the exercise of the profession of police officer) and paras. 39, 40 in Case C-416/2013, *VitalPerez* (local police officers).

age limit of 28 years was set without providing adequate justification.[25] The Ombudsman considered the introduction of an age limit to be legitimate in principle, for reasons of public interest relating to the safeguarding of public order and security; however, it requested justification for the specific age limit of 28 years. It called for a reassessment of this age limit, asking to take into consideration the recent developments concerning physical fitness by age, the existing ability of those already in service to perform the duties in relation to their age, the length of time spent in the duties of the post in question and the average age of retirement from the service in question. The threshold was finally amended by legislation and is now 30 years.

Discrimination Based on Sexual Orientation

Sexual orientation is an element of the individual's personality and is protected independently both by the national and international legislation binding the country and by the constitutional legal order itself, in the context of the free development of personality (Art. 5 para. of the Greek Constitution) and respect for the value of the human person (Art. 2 of the Greek Constitution). Cases filed with the Ombudsman concerning discrimination on the grounds of sexual orientation in the field of employment and work are limited, although this is obviously not an indication of the absence of discrimination in the field. On the contrary, it indicates the reluctance of victims to disclose sensitive elements of their private lives, but also their fear that the working climate will deteriorate after they have brought their case to the attention of the competent institutions. The Ombudsman, in these cases (Greek Ombudsman, 2020a, p. 79), as well as in other cases related to sensitive aspects of private and social life (e.g. discrimination on the grounds of religious belief, sexual harassment, etc.), seeks to intervene in consultation with the complainants, with the maximum possible guarantee of confidentiality and secrecy in its interventions and in the contacts carried out in the context of the examination of the cases concerned. Issues of discrimination based on sexual orientation are also raised in cases of same-sex couples entering into a civil partnership (Greek Ombudsman, 2017, p. 103) or same-sex couples marrying abroad (Greek Ombudsman, 2020a, 2020b, pp. 80–81), where the equal exercise of rights related to family was multiply discriminatory, taking into account that until 2024[26] for heterosexual couples marriage or civil partnership was an option, while for same-sex couples only a limited form of civil partnerships was recognised.

[25] The maximum age limit of 28 years is provided for in Art. 9 para. 5 of Law 2734/1999, as amended and in force, and in the decision of the Minister of Citizen Protection No. 7002/12/1-kst (Government Gazette B 3010/25.07.2019) issued on its authority, as in force (art. 1 para. 1 point b of the ministerial decision). For the purpose of calculating the age of the candidates, the date of birth is considered to be the 31 December of the year of birth.

[26] Equality in civil marriage was established in Greece by Law No. 5089/2024.

Discrimination Based on Gender Identity, Expression, or Characteristics

Regarding issues of discrimination based on gender identity, expression, or characteristics, these cases are systematically included in the scope of cases investigated by the Ombudsman in the context of its specific competence as a promoter of the principle of equal treatment. This fact is largely related to the networking and constant cooperation that the Ombudsman has sought with civil society organisations active in the field of protecting the rights of trans people, but also to the fact that some victims have come forward and lodged complaints. The complaints received relate in particular to police treatment, employment, the provision of goods and services, education and the provision of medical care in public hospitals.

In 2013, the Ombudsman investigated an individual complaint by a trans student, which made it possible to systematise and propose specific guidelines to the Ministry of Education in order to promote respect of the rights of trans students (Greek Ombudsman, 2013b). In particular, in the context of this intervention, the importance of becoming familiar not only with the institutional framework for the protection of trans people but also with the medical, social, and psychological dimensions of the issue was stressed. At the same time, specific recommendations were made, as steps of informal but practical support for trans students. Specifically, the Ombudsman proposed with regard to trans students the acceptance of (a) the use of the name of their choice by classmates and teachers, irrespective of the registered name in official documents, (b) their external appearance and clothing choices, respecting the school rules applicable to all students, and (c) the use of a toilet in which they feel safe and which corresponds to their gender identity. Similarly important was a complaint lodged by the Association for the Support of Trans People (SYD) concerning the equal access of trans candidates in the admission process for Police Academies (Greek Ombudsman, 2018, p. 61), where the application of the admission requirements is governed by the Law 11/2014, which refers to the physical fitness of soldiers and refers to "gender identity disorder" as a "disease", despite the developments that have occurred in this field, as recognised by the World Health Organization.

Discrimination Based on Family Status

The protection of family status had already been provided for by the provisions of Law 3896/2010, not independently but in connection with gender discrimination. With Law 4443/2016, family status is established as an independent ground for discrimination. The concept of this form of discrimination includes any type of relationship that creates strong family and life ties and, in particular, the ties that develop between spouses/partners (marriage, cohabitation), children and their parent(s) (birth, adoption, fostering), as well as siblings between them. The cases investigated by the Ombudsman in this field concern in particular different treatment of persons on the basis of type of union (religious or civil marriage, civil partnership,[27] same-sex or heterosexual couples), or the dissolution of the union (divorcees), as well as discriminatory treatment of parents or children of single-parent families and divorced persons or their children. Unfair treatment of employees in the public and wider public sector related to marital status is also found in cases where there is no direct question of the existence or otherwise of a particular type of partnership (marriage, civil partnership), but implicitly unfair restrictions linked, for example, to the requirement in the legislation in force that a certain period of time must have elapsed since the marriage in order for the possibility of secondment or co-service to be activated, or restrictions on the granting of parental leave. A significant number of cases concern the protection of single parents in their treatment at work with regard to secondments, transfers to other services, and the status of leaves, as well as the rights of adoptive or foster parents.

Discrimination Based on Social Status

Regarding discrimination on the grounds of social status, the introduction of this ground of discrimination is novel in national legislation. The explanatory memorandum of Law 4443/2016 defines this concept in the context of the social stigmatisation of a person due to their distinctiveness as a member of a particular social subset. Indicatively, such a situation may include former addicts, former prisoners, persons in exile, or homeless persons. Furthermore, according to the explanatory memorandum to the Act, a particular social subset may also be defined as "[...] a group of persons who are linked by a common characteristic which is often inherent, invariable and fundamental to the identity, conscience or exercise of human rights of its members". In this sense, groups linked to particular characteristics of race, colour, national or ethnic origin, disability, or chronic illness—for example, HIV-positive people, who are entitled to special protection in the context of discrimination on the grounds of chronic disease—may also be subject to discrimination on the grounds of social status. In any case, they belong to a particular social subset, against whom stereotypical perceptions prevail and are reproduced, exacerbating their social and occupational exclusion and the difficulty of enjoying rights on an equal footing.

Discrimination on grounds of social status can therefore run horizontally across almost all other grounds of discrimination. This combined approach is useful in highlighting the link between rights and equality and the influence of social status on both the level of protection of citizens' rights and the achievement of real equality. Although cases of discrimination based on social status concern, according to Law 4443/2016, exclusively the field of employment and work, the Ombudsman, in addition to cases of discrimination in this field, analyses and often records cases where the established discrimination on the basis of one of the protected grounds, including social status, appears to exert an influence in fields beyond employment and work.

[27] As it follows from the explanatory memorandum of Greek Law 4443/2016, the main objective of the addition of marital status as an independently protected ground of discrimination is the proportional equalisation of the rights arising from the types of marriage and civil partnership provided for in the Greek Civil Code and the civil partnership agreement of Greek Law 4356/2015.

Concluding Observations

Specific legislation to combat discrimination and promote the principle of equal treatment has its basis in European anti-discrimination law and, in particular, in the framework provided by Directives 79/7/EEC, 2000/43/EC, 2000/78/EC, 2004/113/EC, 2006/54/EC and 2010/41/EU. Until recently, this framework in Greece did not comprehensively address all grounds and areas of discrimination, resulting in a fragmented and complex legal landscape.

The use of the general competence of the Ombudsman as a body for the protection of citizens' rights and the observance of legality has allowed the exercise of its powers as national equality body even in areas not covered by this specific legislation. The organisational choice of autonomy in the thematic scope of equality and discrimination and the assignment of the competence to a distinct Deputy Ombudsman, since 2008 in gender equality issues and since 2016 for all discrimination and equal treatment issues-, has brought about an increase in the number of complaints, a change in the scope of the thematic subject, in its monitoring and data analysis and in the consistency of the relevant interventions and supervision.

The legislative changes introduced by Law 4443/2016 only partially addressed weaknesses and ambiguities identified from the implementation of the previous Law 3304/2003, both in terms of the normative scope of the law and in terms of ensuring means of effective intervention by the national equality body. The recent Laws 5023/23 and 5089/24 extended protection for all grounds of discrimination to areas beyond employment and work and in line with the provisions of the Ethnic and Racial Equality Directive. This is an important step in strengthening the scope and coherence of the legislation concerned, but now shifts the focus to ensure the means for its effective implementation.

In this area, clear and binding guidance is provided by the two recent Directives 2024/1499/EC and 2000/1500/EC, on minimum common standards for equality bodies. The EU institutions have responded to their duty and commitment to strengthen the legislation and functioning of equality bodies. Member States now have until July 2006 to transpose these Directives, adapting them creatively and effectively to specific national requirements. Similarly, equality bodies are required to prepare themselves and respond innovatively to the new perspectives and the dynamic of recent developments.

References

Council of the EU. (2023). *Standards for equality bodies: Council agrees its positions, 12 June 2023*, https://www.consilium.europa.eu/en/press/press-releases/2023/06/12/standards-for-equality-bodies-council-agrees-its-positions

Crowley, N. (2018). *Equality bodies making a difference*. European Commission. Directorate-General for Justice and Consumers: Publications Office of the EU, https://op.europa.eu/en/publication-detail/-/publication/408e82f7-4930-11e9-a8ed-01aa75ed71a1

Directive No 75/117/EEC, of 10 February 1975 on the approximation of the laws of the Member States relating to the application of the principle of equal pay for men and women, OJ L 45/19, of 19.02.1975, https://eur-lex.europa.eu/legal-content/EN/TXT/PDF/?uri=CELEX:31975L0117

Directive No 76/207/EEC, of 9 February 1976, on the implementation of the principle of equal treatment for men and women as regards access to employment, vocational training and promotion, and working conditions, OJ L 39/40, of 14.02.1976, https://eur-lex.europa.eu/legal-content/EN/TXT/PDF/?uri=CELEX:31976L0207

Directive No 86/378/EEC, of 24 July 1986 on the implementation of the principle of equal treatment for men and women in occupational social security schemes, OJ L 225/40, of 12.08.1986 [amended by Directive 96/97/EC], https://eur-lex.europa.eu/legal-content/EN/TXT/PDF/?uri=CELEX:31986L0378

Directive No 97/80/EC, of 15 December 1997, on the burden of proof in cases of discrimination based on sex, OJ L 14/6, 20.1.1998, [no longer in force], https://eur-lex.europa.eu/eli/dir/1997/80/oj/eng

Directive No 2000/43/EC, Council Directive 2000/43/EC, of 29 June 2000, implementing the principle of equal treatment between persons irrespective of racial or ethnic origin, OJ L 180/22, of 19.7.2000, https://eur-lex.europa.eu/legal-content/EN/TXT/PDF/?uri=CELEX:32000L0043

Directive No 2000/78/EC, Council Directive 2000/78/EC, of 27 November 2000, establishing a general framework for equal treatment in employment and occupation, OJ L 303/16, of 2.12.2000, https://eur-lex.europa.eu/legal-content/EN/TXT/PDF/?uri=CELEX:32000L0078

Directive No 2004/113/EC, Council Directive 2004/113/EC, of 13 December 2004, implementing the principle of equal treatment between men and women in the access to and supply of goods and services, OJ L 373/37, of 21.12.2004, https://eur-lex.europa.eu/legal-content/EN/TXT/PDF/?uri=CELEX:32004L0113

Directive No 2006/54/EC of the European Parliament and of the Council, of 5 July 2006, on the implementation of the principle of equal opportunities and equal treatment of men and women in matters of employment and occupation (recast), OJ L 204/23, of 26.7.2006, https://eur-lex.europa.eu/legal-content/EN/TXT/PDF/?uri=CELEX:32006L0054

Directive No 2010/41/EU of the European Parliament and of the Council, of 7 July 2010, on the application of the principle of equal treatment between men and women engaged in an activity in a self-employed capacity and repealing Council Directive 86/613/EEC, OJ L 180/1, of 15.7.2010, https://eur-lex.europa.eu/legal-content/EN/TXT/PDF/?uri=CELEX:32010L0041

Directive No 2024/1499/EU, of the Council of European Union, of 7 May 2024, on standards for equality bodies in the field of equal treatment between persons irrespective of their racial or ethnic origin, equal treatment in matters of employment and occupation between persons irrespective of their religion or belief, disability, age or sexual orientation, equal treatment between women and men in matters of social security and in the access to and supply of goods and services, and amending Directives 2000/43/EC and 2004/113/EC, OJ L 29.5.2024, https://eur-lex.europa.eu/legal-content/EN/TXT/?uri=OJ:L_202401499

Directive No 2024/1500/EU of the European Parliament and of the Council, of 14 May 2024, on standards for equality bodies in the field of equal treatment and equal opportunities between women and men in matters of employment and occupation, and amending Directives 2006/54/EC and 2010/41/EU, OJ L 29.5.2024,https://eur-lex.europa.eu/legal-content/EN/TXT/?uri=OJ:L_202401500

General Policy Recommendation N°2 revised. European Commission Against Racism and Intolerance (ECRI). (2017). *General Policy Recommendation N°2 revised of the* European Commission Against Racism and Intolerance (ECRI), *of 7 December 2017, on Equality Bodies to combat racism and intolerance at national level*, https://www.coe.int/en/web/european-commission-against-racism-and-intolerance/recommendation-no.2

European Commission against Racism and Intolerance (ECRI). (2009). *Report on Greece*, https://www.coe.int/t/dghl/monitoring/ecri/Country-by-country/Greece/GRC-CbC-IV-2009-031-GRC.pdf

European Commission against Racism and Intolerance (ECRI). (2015). *Report on Greece*, http://www.coe.int/t/dghl/monitoring/ecri/Country-by-country/Greece/GRC-CbC-V-2015-001-GRC.pdf

European Commission. (2007). Catalysts for change? Equality bodies according to Directive 2000/43/EC: existence, independence and effectiveness, https://op.europa.eu/en/publication-detail/-/publication/afd6e2fd-7893-4cd0-9fa7-1a7e678d8a2d/language-en

European Commission. (2008). *Proposal for a Council Directive on implementing the principle of equal treatment between persons irrespective of religion or belief, disability, age or sexual orientation*, SEC (2008) 2180, SEC (2008) 2181, available at: https://eur-lex.europa.eu/legal-content/en/ALL/?uri=CELEX%3A52008PC0426.

European Commission. (2014). *Joint report on the implementation of council directive 2000/43/EC and council directive 2000/78/EC*, COM (2014) 2 final. http://www.europarl.europa.eu/meetdocs/2014_2019/documents/com/com_com(2014)0002_/com_com(2014)0002_el.pdf

European Commission. (2022a). *Proposal for a Directive 2022/0400 of the European Parliament and of the Council, of 7 December 2022, on standards for equality bodies in the field of equal treatment and equal opportunities between women and men in matters of employment and occupation, and deleting Article 20 of Directive 2006/54/EC and Article 11 of Directive 2010/41/EU*, COM(2022) 688, https://eur-lex.europa.eu/legal-content/EN/TXT/?uri=CELEX%3A52022PC0688

European Commission. (2022b). *Proposal for a Directive 2022/0401 of the Council, of 7 December 2022, on standards for equality bodies in the field of equal treatment between persons irrespective of their racial or ethnic origin, equal treatment in the field of employment and occupation between persons irrespective of their religion or belief, disability, age or sexual orientation, equal treatment between women and men in matters of social security and in the access to and supply of goods and services, and deleting Article 13 of Directive 2000/43/EC and Article 12 of Directive 2004/113/EC*, COM(2022) 689 final, https://eur-lex.europa.eu/legal-content/EN/TXT/?uri=CELEX%3A52022PC0689

European Network of Equality Bodies (Equinet). (2016). (n.d.). *Standards for Equality Bodies*, https://equineteurope.org/wp-content/uploads/2019/07/equinet_workingpaper_standardsnebs.pdf

European Institute for Gender Equality (EIGE). (2023). *Gender equality index 2023*, https://eige.europa.eu/modules/custom/eige_gei/app/content/downloads/factsheets/EL_2023_factsheet.pdf

European Institute for Gender Equality (EIGE). (2022). *Gender equality index 2022*, https://eige.europa.eu/gender-equality-index/2022/EL

Greek Ombudsman. (2007). *Network of organizations cooperating with the Ombudsman on Roma Issues* https://old.synigoros.gr/?i=maps.el.lista

Greek Ombudsman. (2013a). *Meeting of the Ombudsman's cooperation network with civil society on discrimination issues* https://old.synigoros.gr/?i=equality.el.nea.145308

Greek Ombudsman. (2013b). *Mediation by the Ombudsman for the support of a transgender person's attendance in a public school* https://old.synigoros.gr/?i=equality.el.imidedu.132282

Greek Ombudsman. (2013c). *Special report* https://old.synigoros.gr/resources/docs/10-diakriseis%2D%2D2.pdf

Greek Ombudsman. (2013d). *Annual report* https://old.synigoros.gr/resources/docs/stp_ethsia_2013.pdf

Greek Ombudsman. (2015). *Special report on the prohibition of discrimination* https://old.synigoros.gr/resources/ee2015-12-diakriseis.pdf Executive summary in English : https://old.synigoros.gr/resources/docs/promoting-equal-treatment-special-report-2015%2D%2D2.pdf

Greek Ombudsman. (2016). *Annual report.* https://old.synigoros.gr/resources/synhgoros-2016_final_all-web_eng.pdf

Greek Ombudsman. (2017). *Special report on equal treatment, on the registration of foreign civil partnerships.* p. 103, https://old.synigoros.gr/resources/docs/internet_metax_2017_eng.pdf

Greek Ombudsman. (2018). *Special report on equal treatment.* https://old.synigoros.gr/resources/docs/ee_im_2018_en.pdf

Greek Ombudsman. (2020a). *Special report on equal treatment.* https://old.synigoros.gr/resources/docs/ish-metaxeirhsh-2020_english_site-1.pdf

Greek Ombudsman. (2020b). *Mediation summary: Indicating religion in candidates' online applications for jobs in a company* https://old.synigoros.gr/?i=equality.el.imbeliefsworkprivate.717390

Greek Ombudsman. (2021). *Special report on equal treatment.* https://www.synigoros.gr/en/category/eidikes-ek8eseis/post/special-report-2021-or-equal-treatment

Greek Ombudsman. (2022). *Special report: Harassment and sexual harassment at work,* https://www.synigoros.gr/en/category/eidikes-ek8eseis/post/press-release-or-equal-treatment-special-report-2022

United Nations Committee on the Elimination of Racial Discrimination (CERD), Reports on Greece, (2009). https://documents.un.org/doc/undoc/gen/g09/462/80/pdf/g0946280.pdf

United Nations Committee on the Elimination of Racial Discrimination (CERD), Reports on Greece, (2016) https://documents.un.org/doc/undoc/gen/g16/222/00/pdf/g1622200.pdf

United Nations (UN) Standard Rules for the Equalisation of Opportunities for Persons with Disabilities. (1993). https://www.ohchr.org/en/instruments-mechanisms/instruments/standard-rules-equalization-opportunities-persons-disabilities

Part IV

Contemporary Challenges and Solutions Proposed

Minimum Guaranteed Income in a Multilevel Constitutional Universe: Scope and Implementation in the Greek and EU Legal Order

Stella Christoforidou

Abstract

Following the 2019 amendment to the Greek Constitution, the Greek State is obligated to ensure decent living conditions for all citizens through a system of minimum guaranteed income (Greek Constitution, Art. 21, para. 1b). This income functions as a cornerstone of the social welfare system, designed to secure decent living standards. Moreover, the minimum guaranteed income plays a pivotal role in European Union policies aimed at poverty prevention, aligning with the Union's objectives as outlined in primary EU law.

The chapter aims to explore and evaluate the ways of the implementation of the minimum guaranteed income in the Greek legal system, during the financial crisis of the past decade and the recent immigration crisis, while taking into consideration the scope of the new constitutional provision and its convergences and deviations from the EU context and obligations.

The System of Minimum Guaranteed Income and Its Foundations in the Greek Legal Order

The Strong Debate about the Objective Scope of the System during the Constitutional Amendment of 2019

The constitutional amendment process of the Greek Constitution, completed in 2019 (Greek Constitution, 2019), was not the first to discuss constitutional protection of decent living conditions. However, it was the first to successfully incorporate this concept in the Greek Constitution. The introduction of the concept of "decent

S. Christoforidou (✉)
Dr. Juris, Post-doc Researcher, Law School of the Aristotle University of Thessaloniki, Thessaloniki, Greece

D. Anagnostopoulou (ed.), *European Identities, Inclusion and Equality*, Diversity and Inclusion Research, https://doi.org/10.1007/978-3-031-90602-2_15

living" in the Greek Constitution was initially proposed by the Greek party "Panhellenic Socialist Movement" (PASOK) during the constitutional revision of 2006–2008 (Alivizatos & Venizelos, 2006, pp. 139–147; Chrysogonos, 2011, pp. 269–278). At that time, the proposal focused on recognizing the state's obligation to ensure a minimum guaranteed standard of living (Hellenic Parliament, 2007). The proposal included a horizontal supplementary allowance, named "minimum guaranteed income" (Hellenic Parliament, 2006, p. 2). The then-ruling party of "New Democracy" did not vote in favor of this proposal because the concept of "decent living" was considered broader than an additional cash benefit. This additional cash benefit could be granted by law without the need of a previous constitutional amendment (Hellenic Parliament, 2007, p. 4; Hellenic Parliament, 2006, p. 10).

In the 2019 constitutional revision, the proposal to introduce the concept of "decent living" in the constitutional text came from three political parties in three different ways. The party of "New Democracy", being the official opposition party at the first stage of the revisionary process, and then as the ruling party, proposed the amendment of Article 25 Greek Constitution[1] and the introduction of the decent living standard as follows.[2]

> The state cares for ensuring decent living conditions for all citizens through a system of guaranteed minimum income. The state encourages volunteering with positive actions.

The combination, in the same provision, of the guaranteed minimum income with voluntary work—which is equivalent to unpaid work[3]—implies the influence of libertarian economic theories in the introduction of a basic income system to achieve deregulation of the labor market's protective legal framework, that is, the abolition of the basic wage, labor hours, and so on (Groot, 2004, p. 52). It must be noted, though, that during the procedure of constitutional revision, the General Rapporteur of the party "New Democracy" denied any connection with libertarian perspectives[4]

[1] Article 25 Greek Constitution (before its 2019 revision) "(1) The rights of the human being as an individual and as a member of the society and the principle of the welfare state rule of law are guaranteed by the State. All agents of the State shall be obliged to ensure the unhindered and effective exercise thereof. These rights also apply to the relations between individuals to which they are appropriate. Restrictions of any kind which, according to the Constitution, may be imposed upon these rights, should be provided either directly by the Constitution or by statute, should a reservation exist in the latter's favor, and should respect the principle of proportionality. (2) The recognition and protection of the fundamental and inalienable rights of man by the State aims at the achievement of social progress in freedom and justice. (3) The abusive exercise of rights is not permitted. (4) The State has the right to claim of all citizens to fulfill the duty of social and national solidarity."

[2] Explanatory Memorandum on the proposal of the President and the Members of the parliamentary group of New Democracy for the amendment of constitutional provisions in accordance with articles 110 of the Constitution and 119 of the Rules of Procedure of the Parliament, 4854/14.11.2018, p. 11.

[3] As for volunteering in a constitutional perspective, see Mitas, 2016, p. 176.

[4] Presentation by the General Rapporteur of the New Democracy, Mr. Konstantinos Tassoulas, "Report of the Committee for the Amendment of the Constitution, Period XVII—Session D," Athens 2019, p. 47.

and adopted the same approach as in the constitutional revision of 2008 (Hellenic Parliament, 2007, p. 4; Hellenic Parliament, 2006, p. 10). Nonetheless, it must be taken into consideration that, when the same party was elected, it took legislative initiatives that do follow the libertarian approach, such as the legislative regulation of the minimum wage (Greek Law 4172/2013, Art. 103), the deregulation of the opening hours of the market, [5] as well as the measures taken during the last years amid the pandemic, such as overtime work without payment.[6]

On the other hand, the Greek party of "SYRIZA" (as the governing party and, after the 2019 elections, as the official opposition) aimed to establish a constitutional guarantee of a general welfare right, which would be protected through judicial review, including the legislator's compliance with the aforementioned guarantee and with the obligation to take into consideration the current objective conditions regarding the determination of the standard of living through scientific methods.[7] Furthermore, SYRIZA sought to introduce a constitutional provision obliging the state's obligation to operate social structures and services with universal access. This proposal, which was rejected, was intended to act as a barrier against the general tendency of liquidation of social rights and state obligations.[8]

Finally, KINAL, [9] in an in-between direction, proposed the quote.[10]

> The state ensures a minimum decent standard of living for all citizens in need, as well as their free and unrestrained access to social goods.

It is worth noting that the debate, during the constitutional revision of 2019, was focused mainly on the scope of the minimum guaranteed income system, that is, on a comparison between this particular welfare system (basic income), which is based on cash benefits, to other social systems, like social insurance (which also refers to cash allowances) or public health and education (which require structures and real

---

[5] See, for example, Greek Council of State [GC], Judgment no 100/2017, which found a constitutional violation because of the opening of the market on Sundays. See comment by Lazaratos, P. & Vlachopoulos, S. (2017).

[6] See, for example, Greek Act of Legislative Content dated 14.3.2020 according to which due to COVID-19 employers who have exhausted the legally prescribed overtime ceilings of their employees may continue to work overtime, which may not exceed the daily ceilings, without the approval of the Minister of Labor and Social Affairs.

[7] Explanatory Memorandum on the proposal of the President and the parliamentary Members of the parliamentary group of SYRIZA for the amendment of constitutional provisions in accordance with articles 110 of the Constitution and 119 of the Rules of Procedure of the Parliament, 4636/2.11.2018, p. 8.

[8] For the term "liquidation," see Moyn, 2018, p. 93.

[9] The Panhellenic Socialist Movement (PASOK) in 2017, became a part of the political alliance and later political party "Movement for Change" (Kinima Allagis/KINAL). By 2019, two out of the three founding parties of the "Movement for Change" left the coalition and PASOK carried its political activity under the name "KINAL." In a recent internal election (May 2022), it was decided for the name to change to "PASOK-KINAL."

[10] Hellenic Parliament, "Proceedings of Constitutional Amendment, XVIII Period, Session A," 19.11.2019, p. 37.

and effective services). Although a clause that would explicitly oblige the state to run social services for all citizens was rejected, it is undeniable—regarding the opinions of the political parties—that the right to decent living has a broader meaning, content, and range than the notion of the minimum guaranteed income. Indeed, a mere cash benefit does not guarantee a decent living, especially when social services are lacking, as proved during the pandemic.

The New Constitutional Provision and the Functional Purpose of Decent Living

In 2019, Article 21 para. 1 of the Greek constitution was revised to include the following:

> 1. The family, being the cornerstone of the preservation and the advancement of the Nation, as well as marriage, motherhood and childhood, shall be under the protection of the State. *The State shall take care to ensure that all citizens enjoy a decent standard of living by means of a system of minimum guaranteed income, as specified by law.*

However, the system of minimum guaranteed income and the constitutional protection of decent living do not share the same content or range. "Decent living" is a notion with a broad meaning, in accordance with the human dignity principle (Greek Constitution, Art. 2, para. 1; Häberle, 2018, pp. 167–228), with multiple applications. The system of minimum guaranteed income is a way to specialize the constitutional protection of decent living in the social welfare field and is based on cash benefits. The implementation range of this system depends upon other constitutional provisions that provide other forms of protection or obligations of the state. For example, it was first the Council of State [GC] in its decision no. 2287/2015 that highlighted the distinction between the social welfare system and the public system of social insurance:

> The above situations [i.e. age, illness, disability], however, unrelated to work and payment contributions', are, among other things, cases that, according to article 21 paras. 1, 2, 3, and 6 of the Constitution, impose on the State the obligation of a distinct form of social protection, in the form of benefits in cash or in-kind, to specific groups of the population, in order to ensure a basic level of decent living, according to article 2 para. 1 of the Constitution ("social welfare").

It is important to highlight a growing tendency in both academic literature and politics to treat any amount paid by the state to citizens uniformly if it is linked to the purpose of ensuring decent living conditions. However, this approach risks overlooking the fact that each payment arises from a distinct cause, falls within a different legal framework, and is governed by separate constitutional provisions. These differences can be crucial, particularly for calculating the amount or determining its legal protection. To address this issue, the Court emphasized a clear distinction between the social welfare system and the social insurance system, noting the latter's foundation on employees' own contributions to their insurance.

Another key distinction lies between the cash benefit provided under the minimum guaranteed income system—specifically when paid to the unemployed—and the minimum wage. Wages are remuneration for work performed and fall outside the scope of the social welfare system.[11] From a teleological perspective, one might argue that since both the minimum guaranteed income and the minimum wage aim to ensure decent living conditions, the two systems could potentially converge or absorb one another. However, Article 22 of the Greek Constitution safeguards collective bargaining, ensuring that wages remain distinct from social benefits and are determined independently (Koukiadaki & Kokkinou, 2016, pp. 135–203).

The concept of "decent living" can be implemented through various approaches, particularly when defining a specific monetary amount deemed sufficient. Thus far, the Greek legislator has adopted a less generous approach, equating the decent living threshold with the poverty threshold. However, it is evident that the amount corresponding to the poverty line is insufficient to meet even basic needs. Notably, poverty statistics fail to account for the cost of living, including the prices of goods, services, rent, and indirect taxes—all of which are central to the notion of decent living, especially when cash is the primary means of securing it. This underscores the critical distinction between decent living and the poverty threshold, as the two should not be conflated.

Thus, although wages, pensions, cash, or benefits can be considered as means that contribute to decent living, this doesn't mean that they can be substituted by the system of minimum guaranteed income.

After all, as already mentioned, the notion of decent living is not confined to strictly material aspects. From that perspective, the system of minimum guaranteed income could borrow these multiple functionalities/could adopt a multifaced role supporting the balance between constitutionally protected goods. Under the light of Article 24 of the Greek Constitution, which safeguards the protection of the environment, a new ecological interpretative approach emerges. According to this approach, any activity with a severe negative impact on the environment should be discontinued given that the job opportunities that such activity might create, could be directly compensated/offset by the system of minimum guaranteed income. In other words, the ever-increasing pressure for economic growth and job creation, which leads to the approval and licensing of environmentally harmful projects, could be effectively countered by this system in order to ensure the efficient protection of both the environment and decent living conditions for the residents of the areas affected by such activities. Last but not least, one must admit that cash benefits under the social welfare system in Greece were granted for decades, [12] even before the 2019 constitutional amendment. From that point of view, one could argue that this new constitutional provision hardly changes anything in the field of social welfare. The system of minimum guaranteed income falls within the state's obligation to provide financial support to everybody in need. The Greek Courts have already

[11] For example, Article 4 of (Revised) European Social Charter protects the right to fair remuneration that guarantees decent living for oneself and its family.

[12] For an analytical catalog, see Amitsis, 2001, p. 162.

accepted that a basic prohibition rule derives from the Constitution, according to which the state cannot lessen this form of protection. However, this does not mean that the state is obliged/obligated to maintain a system of benefits without any changes (Greek Council of State, Judgment no 719/2018). The system of a minimum guaranteed income falls exactly within the scope of this appreciation margin. Nonetheless, the same constitutional provision sets the criteria of evaluation, that is, the notion of "decent living." Thus, every cash benefit, at least in light of the system of a minimum guaranteed income, should safeguard a real and effective standard of decent living.

The EU Framework, Policies, and Severe Tensions Between Multiple Levels of Protection

Labor rights, particularly the right to fair remuneration, must confront a severe threat from basic income systems that could lead to the deregulation of the labor market. Both the European Social Charter, under the framework of the Council of Europe, and the Universal Declaration of Human Rights (1948) emphasize the importance of fair remuneration and explicitly differentiate this form of protection from social welfare protection. In the Universal Declaration of Human Rights, labor protection is addressed in Article 23, while social welfare protection is covered separately under Article 25.

On the other hand, primary EU Law and, in particular, the EU Charter of Fundamental Rights doesn't include the protection of fair remuneration in Article 31. The protection of decent living is reserved in the field of the social welfare system in Article 34, para. 3, EUCFR[13] and in Article 25, which also concerns social welfare protection. This is a serious deficit for the EU primary law regarding the protection of labor rights.[14] It is doubtful if the European Pillar of Social Rights could fill this gap of protection.[15] However, the European Commission's proposal for an EU Directive on adequate minimum wages in the EU (2020) could represent a semantically significant step toward this direction, enhanced by the reservation that minimum wages should not be just "adequate" but "decent" according to the constitutional culture of the Member States. For example, in the German legal order, the content of the human dignity principle requires the safeguarding of the

[13] Following the libertarian approaches for disengagement of remuneration from work, see Groot, 2004, p. 27.

[14] For the problem of working poor, in general, see Jennings, 2004, pp. 149–154; Metzgar, 2010, pp. 398–416; Blank et al., 2006.

[15] According to the sixth Principle of the Pillar, "Workers have the right to fair wages that provide for a decent standard of living. Adequate minimum wages shall be ensured, in a way that provides for the satisfaction of the needs of the worker and his/her family in the light of national economic and social conditions, whilst safeguarding access to employment and incentives to seek work. In-work poverty shall be prevented. All wages shall be set transparently and predictably according to national practices and respecting the autonomy of the social partners."

possibility of multiple perspectives regarding social participation, and not only the prevention of material deprivation (Gruner, 2009, pp. 202–213).

Minimum guaranteed income in EU policies emerges as a means against poverty. Poverty poses a crucial hurdle that the Greek society has faced since the outbreak of the financial crisis, given that the multiple measures taken compromised citizens' quality of life. Although the minimum guaranteed income is only supplementary and even though a mere cash benefit cannot safeguard decent living conditions, at the EU political level, it was abused and overused as a solution for all the problems that the Greek society went through.

It is worth noting that the European Committee of Social Rights[16] issued a series of decisions regarding the austerity measures imposed on Greece by the ECOFIN[17] and the European Commission—measures that worsen working conditions and cut workers' remuneration and pensions—and found that these measures violate the European Social Charter (ECSR, 2013, GENOP DEH and ADEDY v. Greece; ECSR 2017, GSEE v. Greece). In a question put by Members of the European Parliament to the European Commission on monitoring the compliance of Greece with the decisions of the European Committee of Social Rights, [18] the European Commission answered that:

> The European Commission is committed to ensuring that, when implementing EU law, Member States respect the rights enshrined in the EU Charter of Fundamental Rights. However, the Program documents are not EU law, but instruments agreed between Greece and its lenders. It is for Greece to ensure that its obligations on fundamental rights are respected. [...] The program keeps very much in mind the need to ensure the fairness of the adjustment process, protecting the low-income groups. It puts great emphasis on reforms to create sustainable growth and jobs, and includes policies aiming to increase the effectiveness of social safety nets and to widen the scope of unemployment benefits to the long-term unemployed and the access of the uninsured to health services. In addition, a minimum income guarantee scheme is being launched on a pilot basis. This scheme will be rolled out across the country in a phased manner, starting in 2015. Concerning unemployment, schemes financed with EU structural funds are already in place to recruit young and long-term unemployed.[19]

---

[16] ECSR is the Council of Europe's body responsible for supervising compliance with the European Social Charter under two complementary mechanisms: a) through collective complaints lodged by the social partners and other nongovernmental organizations (Collective Complaints Procedure), and b) through national reports drawn up by Contracting Parties (Reporting System).

[17] ECOFIN is the abbreviation used for the Economic and Financial Affairs Council of the European Union, where the EU Member States Ministers of Economics and Finance meet. It is responsible for EU policy in three main areas: economic policy, taxation issues, and the regulation of financial services.

[18] Question for written answer E-005672-14 to the Commission, Rule 130, Kostas Chrysogonos (GUE/NGL), Dimitrios Papadimoulis (GUE/NGL), Georgios Katrougkalos (GUE/NGL), Kostadina Kuneva (GUE/NGL), Emmanouil Glezos (GUE/NGL), Sofia Sakorafa (GUE/NGL), 8.7.2014.

[19] The answer was given by Mr. Katainen on behalf of the Commission, Question reference: E-005672/2014, 17.9.2014. See also the answer given by Mr. Katainen on behalf of the Commission, Question reference: E-006153/2014, 22.9.2014.

Indeed, the minimum guaranteed income scheme launched in 2015 on a pilot basis is already broadened, but the real problem is that conditions of poverty had been exacerbated because of the austerity measures adopted in the previous years. It was these austerity measures that brought the need to manage these conditions of poverty.[20] Hence, the minimum guaranteed income is not an adequate solution to remuneration cuts. Another answer was given by the President of the European Council, the Council, and the Commission, to a similar question, [21] according to which

> the Council of Europe is not an institution of the European Union and its competences fall outside the scope of the Treaties. The Council, therefore, has no competence regarding monitoring the compliance of a Member State with the judgments of the European Committee of Social Rights.[22]

So, both the deterioration of the living conditions, from an empirical point of view, and the violation of social rights were not deemed to fall within the scope of the Charter. After all, it was the system of the minimum guaranteed income that gave the promise of fairness in such a complex situation.

According to the Greek Statistical Authority's Report of July 4, 2014, entitled "Living Conditions in Greece," the number of people in Greece suffering from material deprivation, that is, absolute poverty (unable to afford or deprived for financial reasons of at least three out of nine staple products and services), rose *during the first 2 years in which the Memorandum was being implemented, from 24.1% of the total population in 2010 to 33.7% in 2012.*[23] Given the above statistical data, another question was raised regarding fiscal "consolidation" under the light of Article 3, TEU (the EU aims to "*promote... the well-being of its peoples*").[24] The Commission, once again, based its answer on the minimum guaranteed income.[25]

At this point, it must be highlighted that beyond cash benefits, the taxation system also has a social impact. The VAT was astonishingly increased in Greece, even for basic goods such as food, at levels possibly violating even the human dignity

[20] For a thorough analysis of the austerity measures in Greece, see Kaidatzis, 2020.

[21] Question for written answer E-005671-14 to the Council Rule 130, Kostas Chrysogonos (GUE/NGL), 8.7.2014.

[22] Question reference: E-005671/2014, 6.10.2014.

[23] Question for written answer E-006153-14 to the Commission, Kostas Chrysogonos (GUE/NGL), 28.7.2014.

[24] Question for written answer E-006325-14 to the Commission, Kostas Chrysogonos, (GUE/NGL), 22.8.2014.

[25] "The Commission is fully aware of the difficult social situation in Greece. The reform program puts great emphasis on reforms to create sustainable growth and jobs and has a strong focus on employment and social policies, aiming to increase the effectiveness of social safety nets, including government transfers and services catering for the poor, to support the vulnerable and to facilitate the transition to new jobs. The criteria for providing unemployment benefits to the long-term unemployed have been expanded and access of the uninsured to health services improved through health passports. A minimum income guarantee scheme is being launched on a pilot basis. It will be rolled out across the country in a phased manner, starting in 2015 [...]". Answer given by Mr. Katainen on behalf of the Commission, Question reference: E-006325/2014, 9.10.2014.

principle (Article 2 TEU).[26] Regarding the tax increases and the augmentation of the number of people in need, the European Commission stated that efforts had been made to create a modern welfare system in Greece to reduce poverty and support the most vulnerable people. As stated, "*the guaranteed minimum income (GMI) scheme will be at the core of the new system.*"[27]

The EU failed to comprehend the redistribution purpose at the core of national–constitutional systems. When social groups have no access to basic needs due to tax increases, cash benefits are inadequate as a cure from the point of view of tax justice (Greek Constitution, Art. 4, para. 5). The broadening of inequality due to austerity measures during 2008–2012 had no historical precedent. The tax burden of the low-income groups increased by 337.8%, in contrast to the upper classes that were burdened by only a 9% increase.[28] So, the initiatives "*included in the adjustment program, such as the Guaranteed Minimum Income, more targeted benefits, or the introduction of the universal healthcare insurance coverage, were important steps to support vulnerable groups, including children,*" according to the European Commission, [29] but not adequate according to the Greek Constitution. These groups became vulnerable because of the unfair taxation and, for that reason, a minimum guaranteed income was, and still is, not enough.

The Subjective Scope of the System and the Risk of Exclusion through its Implementation

The Impoverished and the Framework of Greek Constitution, Article 4, Para. 5

Under the light of EU policies, the minimum guaranteed income introduces a social divide between the impoverished (low-income groups) and the nonimpoverished. The statistics of poverty contribute to this approach. From the point of view of the rule of law, it is of high significance to define the impoverished, as well as the non-impoverished, given that the subjective scope of the implementation of the system of minimum guaranteed income is delimited through this definition.

Measuring poverty requires the determination of the level of the poverty divide between poverished and nonpoverished (Zheng, 2001, pp. 337–356; Sung-Geun, 2015, pp. 635–667). Setting the poverty line in any percentage of the median or average equivalent disposable household income (Zheng, 2001, pp. 337–356), 50% or 60%, creates a dichotomy between the members of society in a conventional way

[26] Question for written answer P-009684-14 to the Commission, Kostas Chrysogonos (GUE/NGL), 26.11.2014.

[27] The answer was given by Mr. Moscovici on behalf of the Commission, Question reference: P-009684/2014, 8.1.2015.

[28] Question reference: e-004855/15, 27.3.2015.

[29] This is a part of the answer that was given by Mr. Moscovici on behalf of the European Commission, Written questions: E-004858/15, E-004855/15, 1.10.2015.

(Subramanian, 2019, p. 19; Qizilbash, 2006, p. 9; Asselin, 2009, p. 29) and does not guarantee that all persons in need have been categorized as impoverished (Subramanian, 2019, p. 47). In fact, even if democratically legitimized policymakers set the poverty line and the quantitative criteria for the classification into the two groups of impoverished and nonimpoverished, [30] the problem refers to the protection of the decent living of every citizen without distinctions that could lead to the deprivation of the enjoyment of this right. There is no other constitutional right that may be exercised based on the dependence on classification through quantitative techniques. "Poor" is a fuzzy concept for applied social sciences (Sung-Geun, 2015, pp. 635–667). For that reason, the concept of "poor" brings tremendous insecurity concerning the constitutional protection of rights.

Another dimension that must be taken into consideration is that the measurement of relative poverty is based on income, whereas critical indicators, such as product prices or indirect taxes, are not included (Lelkes & Gasior, 2018, p. 77), meaning that the cost of living is not taken into consideration. So, people above the poverty threshold may also suffer from any form of material deprivation or consumption incapability, [31] even if they have a higher income, because this income is not evaluated regarding its purchasing power.[32]

Nevertheless, the Greek legislator relies on these quantitative methods to provide social protection. For example, the amount of national pension is calculated through the relative poverty measurement techniques[33]. Moreover, the dichotomy between the impoverished and nonimpoverished is adopted for deciding upon the tuition fees exemption of postgraduate students[34] and also for the definition of eligibility for the minimum guaranteed income benefit. In particular, by now, Ministerial Decision 1935/2018 is crucial for the minimum guaranteed income to people in absolute poverty. As far as the eligibility for the allowance is concerned, one person cannot gain more than 1200 euros every semester. This definition of the impoverished could be questioned from an empirical point of view as inadequate regarding the real cost of living in Greece, but the main problem is that it absolutely lacks the necessary gradation into the same category, [35] an approach that could soften the sharp division of people to rich and poor. Indeed, the law provides more than one classification where the amount is increased (parents with one child, with two children, etc.), but that practice should not be considered as a form of gradation, because

[30] For the democratic deficit of technical approaches, see Supiot, 2017, pp. 89–105.

[31] For different techniques of measurement, such as income poverty or consumption poverty, see Luo, 2014, pp. 363–393.

[32] For the problem of purchasing power, see Dauderstädt, 2018, p. 14.

[33] According to the explanatory memorandum of the law of social insurance, the level of the national pension at 384 euros was determined based on 60% of the median income according to the [statistical] rules of the European Union.

[34] According to Greek Ministerial Decision 131,758/Z1/10.8.2018 FEK B' 3387, exemption from tuition fees for postgraduate programs is granted to the students whose total median equivalent income does not exceed the national total median equivalent income.

[35] For the notion of gradation, see Sartori, 1970.

within the same category (i.e., parents with one child) the dichotomy between the poor and nonpoor, continues to exist.

As it is widely accepted, every constitutional provision must be interpreted together with other provisions and principles that form the context. Income is not only a means to secure decent living conditions, according to Article 21 of the Greek Constitution but it is also a means for the fulfillment of tax obligations. According to Article 4, para. 5, Greek Constitution, "*Greek citizens contribute without distinction to public charges in proportion to their means.*"[36] This provision sets the constitutional tax framework, which comprises the principles of tax justice and tax equality. The main economic yardstick is income and the way to achieve equal treatment is to take into consideration the declining marginal utility of income that suggests different treatment of different incomes.[37] In this context, the term proportion has the meaning of gradation, given that in this specific constitutional provision, the term "proportion" has a predominantly economic significance. As for the tax system, the tax must be progressive and therefore more than two tax scales (poor and nonpoor) are required. In fact, two scales where the first one sets the tax exemption (poor) and the second one treats, in the same way, all the other incomes, without any differentiation between low, medium, and higher incomes, are not even close to the concept of tax progressivity and the specific form of tax equality provided by Article 4 para. 5 of the Greek Constitution.

The aforementioned constitutional framework must be applied to the system of minimum guaranteed income in order to safeguard that no one in need is excluded from this form of social protection and that everyone receives protection in proportion to their own means. The division between the impoverished and the nonimpoverished that is adopted by the system of minimum guaranteed income and other social forms of protection that rely on income are not in accordance with Article 4, para. 5 of the Greek Constitution because it lacks the necessary gradation. Furthermore, the system of the minimum guaranteed income according to Article 21 of the Greek Constitution, serves the purpose of protecting everyone's decent living, not just confronting absolute poverty. So, the new constitutional provision of Article 21, para. 1b of the Greek Constitution interpreted together with Article 4, para. 5 of the Greek Constitution requires gradation. Therefore, more than one scale where the amount of cash benefit will decrease as the income increases, until the point that there would be no need for allowance to maintain a decent standard of living. This is the only way to smooth the fuzzy concept of "poor" and to safeguard that no one is excluded from this social form of protection by implementing a sound redistribution system according to our constitutional culture.

The constitutional protection of decent living through a system of minimum guaranteed income is a field where statistical techniques, European policies, and the Constitution are applicable, and for that reason, there is a need to reconcile them.

---

[36] According to the Greek Court of Auditors [GCA], Decision no 244/2017, public charges of this constitutional provision have the meaning of cash or material transactions from citizens to the state which are obligatory, permanent, and without special return to the groups that are burdened.

[37] For the declining marginal utility of income, see Karagiorgas, 1981, p. 278.

The initiation of poverty prevention is consequential. The allowances to the poor were always a means of protection for this category of the population, but we must consider all dimensions, including the constitutional framework. The minimum guaranteed income needs to be expanded to more beneficiaries for the sake of the effective protection of decent living conditions.

Citizens and the EU Obligations: The Case of Asylum Seekers and Refugees

The subjective scope of the minimum guaranteed income is broadening through the application of qualitative criteria. First, human dignity implies that noncitizens should not be excluded from this social form of protection.[38] This means that everyone who resides in the country in a permanent way should be eligible for this benefit. In other words, it is not so crucial whether someone has a Greek passport or the right to vote in the Greek national elections, that is, if they are a citizen. The crucial point should be the permanency of their residence and the actual interaction within the Greek society.

The inclusion of noncitizens in the social welfare system is supported by the secondary law of the EU, mostly regarding asylum seekers. The living conditions for asylum seekers are protected under the EU Directive 2013/33 on standards for the reception of applicants for international protection.[39] Para. 5 of Article 17 of this EU directive explicitly provides:

> that where the Member-States provide material reception conditions in the form of financial allowances or vouchers, the amount thereof shall be determined based on the level(s) established by the Member-State concerned either by law or by the practice to ensure adequate standards of living for nationals. That means that the minimum guaranteed income system also applies to asylum seekers.

In reality, the above-mentioned Directive, together with Article 21 of the Greek Constitution, establishes the State's obligation to safeguard the decent living conditions of asylum seekers. Although hard to believe, the major problem in the Greek legal order for those persons comes up when their application has been accepted. According to Article 114 of Law 4636/2019, at the time of recognition of international or subsidiary protection status, the material conditions of reception in the form of money and in-kind are terminated. The above beneficiaries are obliged to leave accommodation structures within 30 days after delivering the recognition decision.

Consequently, the protection of living conditions halts and there is no other provision explicitly linked with the protection of the minimum guaranteed income as provided by law. This does not mean that the refugees are excluded from the protection, but that they must apply, in a very short time, for that protection and they are

[38] For the obligations arising from the principle of human dignity, see Arendt, 1958, p. 187.

[39] Implemented in the Greek legal order by Law 4636/2019.

in danger of spending time without any protection, contrary to the provisions of Article 21 Greek Const. Given that the application for the minimum guaranteed income requires residency, refugees who are forced to abandon the accommodation structures, according to the provision mentioned above, are eligible to apply as homeless provided that, according to the Ministerial Decision of the minimum guaranteed income eligibility, they have been registered by the social services of the Municipalities, or Community Centers, or they use Dormitories that operate in the Municipalities. So, the existing legal framework for the protection of the decent living of the refugees is extremely weak and forces people to live in severe conditions, a fact that could be considered a violation of both the Greek Constitution and the ECHR.[40] For those persons, there is a need for a legal provision to link the gap between the protection of asylum seekers and poor refugees.

Conclusions

The recent inclusion of the minimum guaranteed income into the Greek Constitution has reinvigorated the debate on how best to ensure decent living conditions for all residents within the Greek legal order and in alignment with broader European Union objectives. This amendment, now placed under Article 21, reflects longstanding political and scholarly efforts to guarantee a baseline of material support for the economically vulnerable and recognizes that mere constitutional acknowledgment needs to be followed by robust legislative and administrative measures. While the constitutional revision introduces a specific system of minimum guaranteed income, the concept of "decent living" remains broader, entailing access not only to adequate financial resources but also to essential social services and societal participation. As both case law and academic scholarship suggest, a monetary benefit alone cannot avert the deeper risks of social exclusion and material deprivation, particularly in times of crisis such as the recent financial downturn and the influx of refugees.

At the same time, the Greek experience underscores the complicated interplay between national social welfare initiatives and the prevailing framework of EU law. European policies have identified the minimum guaranteed income as a central pillar in the fight against poverty across Member States, but this perspective has often overlooked parallel problems of wage devaluation, the erosion of workers' collective bargaining rights, and regressive taxation measures. Throughout the austerity period, the EU's emphasis on fiscal consolidation placed heavy burdens on lower-income groups, effectively exacerbating social disparities. The promise of a minimum guaranteed income, while symbolically powerful, did little in practice to offset the systemic challenges created by wage cuts and rapidly rising indirect taxes. Indeed, national courts and international bodies, including the European Committee of Social Rights, have criticized such austerity measures for undermining core

[40] ECHR is the abbreviation used for the European Convention of Human Rights, an international convention protecting human rights that was adopted by the Council of Europe in 1950.

social rights. The tension between national constitutional protections of decent living, on the one hand, and EU-led austerity policies, on the other, has yet to be fully resolved.

Furthermore, distinctions drawn between impoverished and nonimpoverished populations, often measured through narrowly conceived statistical thresholds, risk excluding individuals who do not neatly fit within formalized definitions of poverty. Constitutional principles of equality and proportionality in taxation, found in Article 4, para. 5 of the Greek Constitution, demand a more nuanced, gradated approach to social welfare eligibility. As these principles require varied levels of taxation to reflect varied levels of income, the logical extension in social policy should be a more flexible system of benefits that adjusts to the real cost of living. Relying on rigid cutoffs can inadvertently trap people above the poverty threshold in precarious living conditions, further challenging the ambition to secure decent living for all. By mandating merely a bifurcated category of "poor" and "nonpoor," existing laws can perpetuate marginalization rather than combat it, undermining the spirit of the constitutional provision meant to safeguard dignity.

Beyond the citizenry, human dignity mandates that permanent residents, asylum seekers, and refugees be integrated into the minimum guaranteed income framework. Current legislation, however, reveals practical gaps. While asylum seekers receive certain financial and in-kind benefits tied to their status during the application process, they can find themselves abruptly excluded once they transition into recognized beneficiaries of international protection. Consequently, these individuals face periods with no assistance at all, even though the Greek Constitution obliges the state to ensure that every person in need has the means to maintain a decent standard of living. Such gaps illustrate the necessity of a coherent legal framework that seamlessly extends the right to basic welfare from the moment an individual arrives until they are fully integrated into society.

In conclusion, minimum guaranteed income in Greece, underpinned by the revised Article 21 of the Constitution, emerges as a critical but not singular tool in safeguarding decent living standards. Its success depends on a multifaceted strategy that includes progressive taxation, robust public services, and adequate minimum wage protections. This strategy must align with human dignity principles, ensuring that all residents, citizens and noncitizens alike, can fulfill their basic needs without discrimination. Only by recognizing the interconnectedness of welfare benefits, labor protections, and broader constitutional commitments can Greece, in harmony with the European Union, effectively champion the right to a truly decent standard of living and uphold its long-established social ideals in practice.

References

Alivizatos, N., & Venizelos, E. (2006). Towards a new constitutional amendment. *Administrative Law Journal*, 139–147. (in Greek).

Amitsis, G. (2001). *The protection of minimum standard of living in Greek and international legal order* (in Greek).

Arendt, H. (1958). *The human condition*. University of Chicago Press.
Asselin, L. (2009). *Economic studies in inequality, social exclusion, and well-being, theory and case studies*. Springer.
Blank, R. M., Danziger, S. H., & Schoeni, R. F. (2006). *Working and poor: How economic and policy changes are affecting low-wage workers*. Sage.
Chrysogonos, K. (2011). Democratization plan. Twelve thoughts on another constitutional amendment. *Administrative Law Journal*, 269–278. (in Greek).
Dauderstädt, M. (2018). Disposable income inequality, cohesion and crisis in Europe. In R. M. Carmo, C. Rio, & M. Medgyesi (Eds.), *Reducing inequalities: A challenge for the European Union?* (pp. 13–30). Palgrave Macmillan.
ECSR. (2013). European Committee of Social Rights, Case Complaint no. 66/2011, General Federation of employees of the national electric power corporation (GENOP-DEI) / Confederation of Greek Civil Servants' Trade Unions (ADEDY) v. Greece.
ECSR. (2017). European Committee of Social Rights, Complaint no. 111/2014, Greek General Confederation of Labour (GSEE) v. Greece.
Greek Constitution. (2019). The constitution of Greece, Revised by Resolution of November 25, 2019 of the IXth Revisionary Parliament. https://www.hellenicparliament.gr/UserFiles/f3c70a23-7696-49db-9148-f24dce6a27c8/THE%20CONSTITUTION%20OF%20GREECE.pdf
Groot, L. F. M. (2004). *Basic income, unemployment, and compensatory justice*. Springer.
Gruner, A. (2009). Der verfassungsrechtliche Anspruch auf Gewährleistung des Existenzminimums. *Journal für Rechtspolitik, 17*, 202–213.
Häberle, P. (2018). Human dignity as a foundation of the constitutional state and the political community. In M. Kotzur (Ed.), *Peter Häberle on constitutional theory* (pp. 167–228). Constitution as Culture and the Open Society of Constitutional Interpreters.
Hellenic Parliament, Proceedings of Constitutional Amendment of the Greek Constitution, XI Period, Session C, 5.10.2006 (in Greek).
Hellenic Parliament, Proceedings of Constitutional Amendment of the Greek Constitution, XI Period, Session B, 26.9.2007 (in Greek).
Jennings, J. (2004). Urban poverty, social welfare, and human rights. In L. Simmons (Ed.), *Welfare, the working poor, and labor* (pp. 149–154).
Kaidatzis, A. (2020). *Socio-economic rights enforcement and resource allocation in times of austerity: The case of Greece 2015-2018*. Populist Constitutionalism Working Papers No. 2.
Karagiorgas, D. (1981). *Public finance II, The fiscal institutions*. Papazisis Publishers (in Greek).
Koukiadaki, A., & Kokkinou, C. (2016). The Greek system of collective bargaining in the crisis. In A. Koukiadaki, I. Távora, & L. M. Martínez (Eds.), *Joint regulation and labor market policy in Europe during the crisis*. ETUI-The European Trade Union Institute. https://www.etui.org/publications/books/joint-regulation-and-labour-market-policy-in-europe-during-the-crisis
Lazaratos, P., & Vlachopoulos, S. (2017). Comment. *Theoria kai Praxi Dioikitikou Dikaiou*, 2017, 302. (in Greek).
Lelkes, O., & Gasior, K. (2018). Income poverty in the EU: What do we actually measure? Empirical evidence on choices, underlying assumptions and implications (based on EU-SILC 2005–2014). In R. M. Carmo, C. Rio, & M. Medgyesi (Eds.), *Reducing inequalities a challenge for the European Union?* Palgrave Macmillan.
Luo, F. (2014). Consumption-based poverty in the United States: New evidence and a test for robustness, studies on economic Well-being: Essays in the honor of John P. Formby. *Research on Economic Inequality*, 363–393.
Metzgar, J. (2010). Are "the poor" part of the working class or in a class by themselves? *Labor Studies, Journal, 35*(3), 398–416.
Mitas, S., (2016). *Solidarity as a fundamental principle of law*. Sakis Karagiorgas foundation. (in Greek).
Moyn, S. (2018). *Not enough, human rights in an unequal world*. Harvard University Press.

Qizilbash, M. (2006). Philosophical accounts of vagueness, fuzzy poverty measures and multidimensionality. In A. Lemmi & G. Betti (Eds.), *Fuzzy set approach to multidimensional poverty measurement* (pp. 9–28). Springer.

Sartori, G. (1970). Concept Misformation in comparative politics. *American Political Science Review, 64*(4), 1033–1053. https://doi.org/10.2307/1958356

Subramanian, S. (2019). *Inequality and poverty, A short critical introduction*. Springer.

Sung-Geun, K. (2015). Fuzzy multidimensional poverty measurement. *Springer*, 635–667.

Supiot, A. (2017). *Governance by numbers- the making of a legal model of allegiance* (pp. 89–105). Saskia Brown.

Zheng, B. (2001). Statistical inference for poverty measures with relative poverty lines. *Journal of Econometrics, 101*, 337–356. https://doi.org/10.1016/S0304-4076(00)00088-9

Can Courts Safeguard Europe's Social Acquis? Evidence from National and Supranational Jurisprudence

Anastasia Poulou

Abstract

Social policy has always been regarded as the "stepchild" of European integration. The economic freedoms of EU citizens had been legally enforceable through treaty provisions already from 1958, whereas social and labor rights became legally binding only in 2009 through the Treaty of Lisbon. The last biggest challenge to Europe's social acquis has been the Eurozone crisis and the measures introduced in response to it, which have been described as a constitutional mutation. While formally regulating economic policies, the measures adopted in the context of the financial crisis entailed detailed prescriptions that related to wage moderation, decentralization of collective bargaining, cuts in pensions and social security benefits, and reforms in public healthcare and education. Given the strong impact of those measures on the social rights of individuals, many court cases were launched at national but also supranational levels. This contribution aims at heeding the challenge faced by Europe's social acquis and the role of courts following three steps. Firstly, it assesses the crisis-driven case-law of the CJEU with regard to social rights and economic rights. Secondly, it presents the case-law of the Greek courts related to austerity measures, especially analyzing the legal grounds and arguments on the basis of which restrictions on social rights were assessed. Thirdly, it approaches social rights adjudication as a question of legitimacy, suggesting that a procedural model of social rights adjudication would mitigate the tension between decision-making over social welfare decisions and the protection of particular social rights.

A. Poulou (✉)
Administrative Court of First Instance, Athens, Greece

School of Law, National and Kapodistrian University of Athens, Athens, Greece
e-mail: anastasia.g.poulou@gmail.com

D. Anagnostopoulou (ed.), *European Identities, Inclusion and Equality*, Diversity and Inclusion Research, https://doi.org/10.1007/978-3-031-90602-2_16

Introduction

Social policy has always been regarded as the "stepchild" of European integration. While economic freedoms had been legally enforceable through Treaty provisions since 1958, social and labor rights became legally binding only in 2009 through the Treaty of Lisbon. Indeed, the Treaty of Lisbon marks the last formal change of the EU Treaties, which stressed the Union's social commitments. It elaborated the Union's values and objectives in Articles 2 and 3 of the TEU, adding social justice, social protection, and solidarity as new Treaty aims. In addition, the EU aims at sustainable development, based on a competitive social market economy, full employment, and social progress. Thus, the Lisbon Treaty introduced an integrated approach to economic and social policies targeting socioeconomic integration as a holistic overarching aim. Most importantly though, in Article 6 of the TEU, the Lisbon Treaty declared the Charter of Fundamental Rights of the EU (CFREU), the main document guaranteeing social and labor rights within the EU legal order, as having the same value as the Treaties.

In this context, the last formal change of EU constitutional law through the Lisbon Treaty gives the promise of a civilized internal market through the mainstreaming of social policy objectives. But is this an accurate picture of the reality in EU social policy? In fact, the challenges posed to social rights in European constitutional law are not to be found in the formal text of the Treaties. One of the biggest challenges to the social dimension of the EU has been the Eurozone crisis and the measures introduced in response to it. Eurozone countries in need of financial assistance received loans, which were made dependent on their compliance with economic policy conditions of extremely broad scope. While formally regulating economic policies, these conditions entailed detailed prescriptions that related to wage moderation, decentralization of collective bargaining, cuts in pensions and social security benefits, and reforms in public healthcare and education. For example, the Portuguese and Greek adjustment programs prescribed the reduction of the minimum wage and the suspension of collective bargaining agreements.[1]

Given the strong impact of those measures on the social rights of individuals, many cases were brought before courts at national but also supranational levels. Against this background, this chapter aims at heeding the role of the courts in protecting Europe's social acquis and the social rights of vulnerable groups in the following three steps. Firstly, it assesses the crisis-driven case-law of the CJEU with regard to social and economic rights. Secondly, it presents the case-law of the Greek courts related to austerity measures, focusing on the legal grounds and arguments used to assess restrictions on social rights. Thirdly, it approaches social rights adjudication as a question of legitimacy, suggesting that a procedural model of social rights adjudication would mitigate the tension between decision-making over social welfare decisions and the protection of social rights, especially those of vulnerable groups.

[1] See Memorandum of Understanding on Specific Economic Policy Conditionality, The Economic Adjustment Programme for Portugal, June 2011, Occasional Papers 79, 147.

The Crisis-driven Jurisprudence of the CJEU on Social Rights

In order to access financial assistance, Eurozone countries facing severe financial difficulties had to abide by conditions that related to wage moderation, decentralization of collective bargaining, cuts in pensions and social security benefits, and reforms in public healthcare and education.[2] Given the strong impact of those conditions on the social rights of individuals, many court cases were launched at national but also supranational levels. The jurisprudence of the CJEU with regard to crisis-driven measures, which represent a potential infringement of social rights, can be divided into two phases: the first phase of reluctance, in which the court dismissed the relevant legal complaints as inadmissible and thus abstained from judging them upon the merits, and the second phase, in which the court took a decision on the substance of the cases, though ruling against the plaintiffs.

In the first phase of its jurisprudence, the CJEU was confronted with the substantive assessment of crisis-related measures in two sets of cases. The first set of cases were brought before the court by the Greek Civil Servants' Confederation (ADEDY), which launched actions of annulment according to Article 263, para. 4 TFEU against Council Decisions 2010/320/EU, 2010/486/EU, and 2011/57/EU containing financial assistance conditionality. More precisely the legality of Decision 2010/320/EU was questioned, on the one hand, due to the reduction of Easter, holiday, and Christmas bonuses (Decision 2010/320/EU, 2010, Art. 2, para. 1, lit. f) and, on the other hand, due to the increase in the retirement age and the reduction of the pensions of civil servants (Decision 2010/320/EU, 2010, Art. 2, para. 2, lit. b). Council Decision 2011/57/EU was challenged on the basis of its provision improving the management of public assets (Decision 2011/57/EU, 2010, Art. 1, para. 4, lit. k), introducing means-testing of family allowances (Decision 2011/57/EU, 2010, Art. 1, para. 8, lit. s), and limiting recruitment in the whole general government to a ratio of a maximum of one recruitment every five retirements or dismissals, without sectoral exceptions (Decision 2011/57/EU, 2010, Art. 1, para. 8, lit. gg).

In support of their pleas, the applicants advanced the following grounds. First, the applicants submitted that the powers of the European Commission and the Council conferred by the Treaties were exceeded in the adoption of the contested decisions. More specifically, Articles 4 and 5 of the TFEU introduce the principles of subsidiarity and proportionality. In addition, under Article 5(2) of the TFEU, it is expressly provided that any competence not conferred by the Member States on the European Union remains with the Member States. Pursuant to Article 126 et seq. of the TFEU, the measures which may be decided upon by the Council under the excessive deficit procedure and included in its decisions cannot be prescribed specifically, explicitly, and without room for deviation, since that competence is not conferred upon the Council by the Treaties. Second, the applicants maintained that the contested decisions are, in their content, contrary to the Treaties. More specifically, the legal basis relied upon for the adoption of the contested decisions is Articles 126, para. 9 and 136 of the TFEU. However, they were adopted in a manner

[2] See further Becker and Poulou (2020).

that exceeded the powers of the European Commission and the Council conferred by those Articles, simply as a measure implementing a bilateral agreement between the 15 Member States of the Eurozone, which decided to grant the bilateral loans, and Greece. Such a competence for the adoption of a measure on the part of the Council is neither recognized nor prescribed by the Treaties. Third, the applicants maintained that, in introducing salary payment and pension reductions, as well as reductions to family allowances and means-testing of them, the contested decisions affected the acquired property rights of the applicants and were accordingly adopted in breach of Article 1 of the First Protocol to the European Convention for the Protection of Human Rights.

The actions of annulment brought before the General Court by the Greek Civil Servants' Confederation against Council Decisions containing financial assistance conditionality fell under the special admissibility requirements laid down in Article 263, para. 4 TFEU. The General Court examined whether the complainants were directly and individually affected by the contested measures (CJEU, 2012, *ADEDY and Others v. Council,* para. 62; CJEU, 2012, *ADEDY and Others v. Council,* para. 64). An individual is considered to be directly concerned if the Union measure requires and fully determines its implementation through national law, so that the harmful effect derives already from the EU measure without the application of other intermediate rules (Schima, 2019, p. 1803). In addition, the applicant must be individually affected by the EU act. According to the *Plaumann* test of the CJEU, "[P]ersons other than those to whom a decision is addressed may only claim to be individually concerned, if that decision affects them by reason of certain attributes which are peculiar to them or by reason of circumstances in which they are differentiated from all other persons, and by virtue of these factors distinguishes them individually just as in the case of the person addressed." (CJEC, 1963, *Plaumann & Co. v. Commission of the European Economic Community,* para. 4) In the cases at stake, the General Court held that the challenged provisions were indeterminate and left a margin to the Greek state as to the way of their implementation and thus could not themselves directly affect the applicants (CJEU, 2012, *ADEDY and Others v. Council,* paras. 70, 72, 73; CJEU, 2012, *ADEDY and Others v. Council,* paras. 81, 84, 90). It is only the content of the national implementing measures, which determine to what extent the applicants will suffer reductions, that might directly affect their legal situation. As a result, both actions were rejected as inadmissible.

As far as some of the contested measures are concerned, the arguments of the General Court are persuasive. Indeed, some of the provisions, such as the provision that provided for "better management of public assets, with the aim of raising at least EUR 7 billion during the period 2011-2013" (Decision 2011/57/EU, 2010, Art. 1, para. 4, lit. k) and the provision on means-testing of family allowances, which stipulated "means-testing of family allowances from January 2011 on yielding savings of at least EUR 150 million (net of the respective administrative costs)" (Decision 2011/57/EU, 2010, Art. 1, para. 8, lit. s) were vague and left it to the discretion of national authorities to specify the details of their implementation. As a result, the General Court convincingly held that those provisions were not of direct concern to the applicants within the meaning of Article 263, para. 4 TFEU.

In contrast, less convincing is the outcome in relation to other contested measures. The "reduction of the Easter, summer and Christmas bonuses and allowances paid to civil servants with the aim of saving EUR 1 500 million for a full year (EUR 1 100 million in 2010)" (Decision 2010/320/EU, 2010, Art. 2, para. 1, lit. f) and the provision on "an act that limits recruitment in the whole general government to a ratio of not more than one recruitment for/against? five retirements or dismissals, without sectoral exceptions, and including staff transferred from public enterprises under restructuring to government entities" (Decision 2011/57/EU, 2010, Art. 1, para. 8, lit. gg) are detailed provisions, which specified the way in which they were to be implemented by the Member State concerned. Hence, in this case, the requirement of direct and individual concern of the applicants within the meaning of Article 263, para. 4 TFEU should have been regarded as met. In view of the above, it is obvious that in this first set of cases, what the CJEU did was to deny the applicants' legal standing, approaching the cases on cuts in wages, pensions, and social benefits only in a procedural manner without assessing their compatibility with social rights.

This first phase of reluctance includes a second set of cases, which were brought before the CJEU through preliminary references on national law implementing EU conditionality. More precisely, the labor court of Porto in Portugal (Tribunal do Trabalho do Porto) made two references to the CJEU, asking whether radical reforms in domestic labor law, such as salary and allowance cuts, were compatible with Article 31(1) of the CFREU, which protects every worker's right to working conditions that respect his or her health, safety, and dignity. The CJEU declined to analyze the merits of the cases on the grounds that the orders for reference did not contain any specific evidence to support the view that the challenged laws were intended to implement EU law (CJEU, 2013, *Sindicato dos Bancários do Norte and Others,* para. 12; CJEU, 2014, *Sindicato Nacional dos Profissionals de Seguros e Afins,* para. 21; CJEU, 2011, *Cozman v. Teatrul Municipal Tärgoviste,* para. 15; CJEU, 2012, *Corpul Național al Polițiștilor,* para. 13; CJEU, 2012, *Corpul Național al Polițiștilor,* para. 15).[3] In fact, the inadequately drafted orders for reference failed to express the links between national reforms and European financial assistance conditionality. The CJEU could take this opportunity, without further ado, to escape a verdict over a complex and highly political issue. Thus, the CJEU denied the application of the social rights of the CFREU on the basis that the alleged infringement was based on domestic law and was outside the scope of Article 51, para. 1 CFREU. However, many Portuguese labor law reforms were the result of the implementation of lending conditionality into national law (Poulou, 2017a, p. 179 et seq.). The Court's refusal, for formal reasons, to take a clear stance on the conformity of austerity measures with the social acquis of the Union is not convincing, especially since, in the past, the CJEU has repeatedly helped national courts to spell out

[3] The CJEU had reached the same conclusion with regard to public-sector wage cuts in Romania, which were carried out in return for financial assistance from the EU and IMF, see (CJEU, 2011, *Corpul Național al Polițiștilor*, para. 16).

imperfectly formulated questions for a preliminary reference (Kilpatrick, 2015).[4] As a result, in both sets of cases, the CJEU declined to go into the merits shying away from the task of providing an adequate counterweight to the democratically questionable intrusion of European crisis management to sensitive fields of social policy.

In the second phase of its crisis-driven jurisprudence, the CJEU finally took a decision on the substance of the cases, though ruling against the plaintiffs. In *Ledra Advertising and Others v. Commission and ECB,* the Grand Chamber of the CJEU placed the haircut undertaken in Cyprus under substantial judicial scrutiny and finally spelled out the obligation of EU institutions to respect the CFREU when formulating financial assistance conditionality (CJEU, 2016, *Ledra Advertising and Others v. Commission and ECB*). Even though the case was decided on the basis of the right to property and not on social rights, the clear reference to the pertinence of the Charter to actions of EU institutions has to be welcomed, since the question of the applicability of the Charter in the framework of financial assistance is anything but clear. Nevertheless, the Court concluded that the bail-in implemented in the Cypriot banking sector did not constitute a disproportionate and intolerable interference with the substance of the appellants' right to property. The reason is the imminent risk of financial losses to which depositors with the two banks concerned would have been exposed if the latter had failed. Having found no unlawful conduct on behalf of the Commission, when permitting the adoption of the bail-in, the Court dismissed the appellants' claims for compensation (TFEU Art. 268, 340) as lacking any foundation in law (Dermine, 2017, p. 369; Poulou, 2017b, p. 127).

Furthermore, in *Sotiropoulou and Others v. Council* (2017), the EU General Court dealt with an action for compensation under Article 268 TFEU in respect of the loss and harm, which the applicants had allegedly sustained, as a result of the reduction of their main pensions due to the adoption of a series of Council decisions under Articles 126, para. 9 and 136 TFEU on pension reform in Greece.[5] In support of their action, the applicants relied on two pleas in law. First, the applicants claimed that, in adopting the contested decisions, which concern inter alia the laying down of detailed measures in the social security and pension system, the Council exceeded the powers conferred by the Treaty and infringed the principles of conferral and

[4] See, for example, (CJEC, 1964, *Costa v. ENEL*), where the Court stated that it "has power to extract from a question imperfectly formulated by the national court those questions which alone pertain to the interpretation of the Treaty". The willingness of the Court to tease out the real question from a reference that has not been adequately Articulated is also exemplified by (CJEC, 1997, *Krüger v. Hauptzollamt Hamburg-Jonas*, para. 23; CJEC, 2000, *Roquette Frères*, para. 18). See also (CJEU, 2017, *Farkas*, para. 58), where the Court generously reformulates what the referring court asks "in essence". In the same vein, Kilpatrick points to (CJEU, 2013, *Radu*, para. 22), in which the Court affirmed that questions on the interpretation of EU law referred by a national court "enjoy a presumption of relevance"; see Kilpatrick, C. (2015). On the rule of law and economic emergency: The degradation of basic legal values in Europe's bailouts. *Oxford Journal of Legal Studies*, 25, fn. 107.

[5] The Decisions of the Council concerned are the following: Decision 2010/320/EU, 2010; Decision 2010/486/EU, 2010; Decision 2011/57/EU, 2010; Decision 2011/257/EU, 2011; Decision 2011/734/EU, 2011; Decision 2011/791/EU, 2011; Decision 2012/211/EU, 2012; Decision 2013/6/EU, 2012.

subsidiarity as laid down in Articles 4 and 5 TEU in conjunction with Articles 2 to 6 TFEU. Second, the applicants contended that the contested decisions of the Council required the introduction of drastic pension cuts that fundamentally disturbed the applicants' financial situation and resulted in the reversal of situations that they had sought in good faith. As a result, the applicants claimed that the enactment and implementation of the reductions at issue resulted in direct infringement of their right to human dignity, their right as elderly persons to lead a life of dignity and independence, and their right to social security benefits and social services providing protection in cases such as old age, laid down in Articles 1, 25 and 34 CFREU, respectively.

As to the first plea in law, the General Court held that the principles of conferral and subsidiarity concern the division of responsibilities between the Member States and the EU and cannot be regarded as conferred rights on individuals. Consequently, any breach of these principles is not in itself sufficient to establish the noncontractual liability of the Union (CJEU, 2017, *Sotiropoulou and Others v. Council*, para. 72). In any case, the contested decisions do not infringe the principles of conferral and subsidiarity, as they were issued with a view to reinforcing and deepening the fiscal surveillance and giving notice to Greece to take measures for the deficit reduction judged necessary to remedy the situation of excessive deficit. As a result, the General Court held that the contested decisions were adopted in the context of the exercise of powers expressly conferred on the Council by Article 126, para. 9 and Article 136 TFEU (CJEU, 2017, *Sotiropoulou and Others v. Council*, para. 73).

By their second plea in law, the applicants claimed that the sum of the pension cuts appears excessive and disproportionate and does not strike a fair balance between the requirements of the general interest and the protection of their fundamental rights enshrined in Articles 1, 25, and 34 CFREU, namely the right to human dignity, the rights of the elderly and the entitlements to social security benefits and social services respectively. As to this complaint, the General Court held that, to the extent that the allegedly violated provisions of the Charter constitute rules of law intended to confer rights on individuals, it must be considered whether any breach of them could substantiate the Union's liability in this case (CJEU, 2017, *Sotiropoulou and Others v. Council*, para. 76). Furthermore, the Court stated that, according to settled case-law, when assessing the noncontractual liability of the Union, the Court has to take into account, inter alia, the complexity of the situations to be regulated, the difficulties in the application or interpretation of the legislation and, more particularly, the margin of discretion available to the author of the act in question (CJEU, 2017, *Sotiropoulou and Others v. Council*, para. 77). More precisely, the decisive criterion for establishing a sufficiently serious breach of a rule of law intended to confer rights on individuals is whether there has been a manifest and grave disregard by the institution concerned of the limits of its discretion (CJEU, 2017, *Sotiropoulou and Others v. Council*, para. 78). In the case at stake, the contested decisions constitute an exercise of the powers conferred on the Council by Articles 126 (9) and 136 TFEU in the context of the excessive deficit procedure of a Eurozone Member State. This competence mainly involves economic policy choices for which it is justified to provide a wide margin of discretion. Hence, those provisions specify only the type of measures to be taken, which may be included in the recommendations from the Council to a Member State for the attainment of a specific objective (CJEU, 2017, *Sotiropoulou and Others v. Council*, para. 81). Against this background, the General Court stated that it was necessary to assess whether the Council adopted the decisions at stake in a manifest and serious breach of the limits of its discretion (CJEU, 2017, *Sotiropoulou and Others v. Council*, para. 82). As reminded by the Court, the contested decisions were issued following the conclusion of the Council that an excessive deficit exists in Greece (Decision 2009/415/EC, 2009) and the budgetary measures included had been extensively discussed with the Greek government and commonly agreed by the European Commission, the ECB, and the IMF (CJEU, 2017, *Sotiropoulou and Others v. Council*, paras. 83–85). In light of the above, the General Court held that it was not manifestly unreasonable to envisage various cost-saving measures, including pension cuts. Therefore, in adopting the contested decisions, the Council did not exceed the limits of its wide discretion (CJEU, 2017, *Sotiropoulou and Others v. Council*, paras. 86–87).

Moreover, the Court underlined that even if the contested decisions were in fact capable of causing the alleged damage to the applicants, the rights to access social security benefits and social services are not absolute, since their exercise may be subject to restrictions justified by objectives of general interest pursued by the Union, as provided for in Article 52, para. 1 CFREU (CJEU, 2017, *Sotiropoulou and Others v. Council*, para. 88). In this vein, measures to reduce the size of pensions meet objectives of general interest, namely the ensuring of fiscal consolidation, the reduction of public expenditure, and the support of the pension system of the Member State concerned (CJEU, 2017, *Sotiropoulou and Others v. Council*, para. 89). Consequently, the General Court held that these measures also met objectives of general interest pursued by the Union, namely the ensuring of budgetary discipline of the/those Member States whose currency is the euro and the ensuring of the financial stability of the euro area (CJEU, 2017, *Sotiropoulou and Others v. Council*, para. 89). In view of those objectives and the imminent risk of insolvency of the Member State concerned, the General Court came to the conclusion that the contested measures, which were specified in Greek national laws (Law 3845/2010, 2010, Art. 3; Law 3863/2010, 2011, Art. 11; Law 3986/2011, 2011, Art. 12, 44; Law 4024/2011, 2011, Art. 2; Law 4051/2012, 2012, Art. 6; Law 4093/2012, 2012), cannot be regarded as unjustified restrictions of the rights claimed by the applicants since they do not constitute a disproportionate and intolerable interference impairing the very substance of these rights (CJEU, 2017, *Sotiropoulou and Others v. Council*, para. 90).[6] In light of the above considerations, the General Court held that the applicants did not establish that the Council had committed a serious breach of a rule of law which confers rights on individuals. Hence in absence of one of the

[6] At this point, the General Court referenced the similar outcome of the case *Ledra Advertising v. Commission and ECB*, in which the CJEU held that the restructuring of the Cypriot banks did not constitute an unjustified restriction of the depositors' right to property guaranteed by CFREU, 2009, Art. 17, para. 1.

cumulative conditions for establishing the noncontractual liability of the Union provided for in Article 340, para. 2 TFEU, the action was dismissed in its entirety (CJEU, 2017, *Sotiropoulou and Others v. Council*, paras. 92–93).

The Crisis-driven Jurisprudence of the Greek Courts on Social Rights

Domestic courts have obviously dealt more often than the CJEU with the legal assessment of austerity measures. In particular, Greece has been the biggest bailout in the Eurozone and had to implement the most intrusive austerity measures. As a result, a significant number of national laws implementing financial assistance conditions were brought before the Greek courts. This section presents the Greek jurisprudence during the crisis in an indicative and not exhaustive manner, aiming to show its gradual evolution (Bakavou, 2020, p. 148). Against this background, the relevant case-law of the Greek courts with regard to social rights can be divided into three phases: a first phase of judicial self-restraint, in which the majority of measures were declared as compatible with the Greek constitution, a second phase, in which the Greek courts adopted a more active stance and repealed austerity measures, and a third phase, in which the reorganization of the Greek social security system as a whole, led to the acceptance of restrictive measures on pensions.

In the first phase of their jurisprudence, Greek courts were confronted with questions on the constitutionality of the measures introduced by the first financial assistance package to Greece, namely reductions in salaries and pensions, and the abolition of extra pay in the public sector. The Greek Council of State assessed the compatibility of the cuts in pensions and salaries with the right to property as protected in Article 17 of the Greek constitution and Article 1 of the Additional Protocol to the ECHR, with the protection of human dignity and with the principle of equality in sharing public burdens. The Court found no disproportionate interference with these constitutional norms, emphasizing that the legislator's assessment of the reasonableness of the measures was subject only to a marginal judicial review, due to the acute financial crisis and the need to combat the risk of state insolvency (Greek Council of State, 668/2012, 2012, para. 38; Judgement 1283/2012, 2012, para. 31; Judgement 1284/2012, 2012, para. 28). In two other decisions, the abolition of holiday allowances for retired persons was assessed on the basis of the right to social security under the Greek constitution. Also in these cases, the Council of State considered the interference with the right to be proportionate, since it had been undertaken on grounds of public interest (Greek Council of State, Judgement 1285/2012, 2012, para. 13; Judgement 1286/2012, 2012, para. 13).

The only measure included in the first financial assistance package that was declared unconstitutional was the introduction in the public sector of the newly introduced labor reserve, according to which the employees would be paid 60% of their basic salary for 1 year and would then be dismissed. The Council of State underlined that although the legislator could legitimately introduce an administrative reform for financial reasons, this had to be in accordance with the principles of the welfare state and the constitutional guarantees for civil servants (Greek Council of State, Judgement 3354/2013, 2013, para. 6). However, the labor reserve led to the automatic dismissal of civil servants, without a prior estimation of the labor force required. Furthermore, the Court held that dismissals were decided randomly, since civil servants were removed only by criteria of age or seniority (Greek Council of State, Judgement 3354/2013, 2013, para. 11). The Court concluded that those criteria were not linked to the objective of public saving and thus declared the automatic dismissal of civil servants as a violation of Article 103 (4) of the Greek constitution, which guarantees the legal position of civil servants (Greek Council of State, Judgement 3354/2013, 2013, para. 11).

In the second phase of their jurisprudence, the Greek Supreme courts declared a significant number of austerity measures as incompatible with the Greek constitution. However, it should be noted that in the beginning this outcome was based on constitutional provisions which protect the status of specific social groups; only a final decision adopted a more general approach, which could be applicable to a larger part of the population. The first social group, which benefited from the declaration of unconstitutionality, were people working for the military and the police. The Council of State found that their salary cuts were against the Constitution. The main justification was that these social groups belong to the "core of the state" and are subject to important restrictions of, for example, their right to strike or their political activity. For those reasons, the Court held that these groups of public officials deserve special treatment with regard to their wages, and the government needs to take the circumstances of their profession into account when reducing their salaries (Greek Council of State, Judgement 2192/2014, 2014, para. 20; Judgement 2193/2014, 2014, para. 21; Judgement 2194/2014, 2014, para. 19; Judgement 2195/2014. 2014, para. 19; Judgement 2196/2014, 2014, para. 20). Since the law passed did not mention any of those criteria, the Court declared the cuts in wages for military and police employees as unconstitutional.

The second social group, which enjoyed judicial protection, comprised judges themselves. The Special Tribunal of Article 88 of the Greek constitution, which is responsible for the salary of the judges, ruled that the third reduction of judges' wages was incompatible with the Greek constitution. The Court deducted from the separation of powers doctrine and the independence of judges, the duty of the State to offer judges equal pay with officials of the other two powers of the State and to ensure their impartiality (Judgement 88/2013, 2013, para. 9). Against this background, the third reduction in judges' wages within a period of 3 years, without an assessment of less intrusive measures was declared unconstitutional (Decision 88/2013, 2013, para. 15). The third social group, whose cuts in salaries were declared unconstitutional, were university professors. In this case, the Court noted that, as a result of the crisis-induced austerity measures, university professors were subjected to multiple burdens which, due to the cumulative effect of the austerity measures, constituted a clear violation of the principle of proportionality, the principle of equality and the constitutional guarantees of the profession of university professors, according to Article 16 of the Greek constitution (Greek Council of State, Judgement 4741/2014, 2014, para. 23).

Besides those decisions that recognized the rights of specific social groups, the shift to a more active stance of the Greek Council of Stance was marked by a decision in 2015 concerning additional cuts in pensions.[7] In this case, the Greek Council of State found that the reductions to pensions introduced in 2012 were not compatible with the protection of human dignity, with the principle of equality in sharing public burdens, with the right to social security as protected in Article 22 (5) of the Greek Constitution and the right to property under Article 1 of the Additional Protocol to the ECHR (Greek Council of State, Judgement 2287/2015, 2015, para. 24; Judgement 2288/2015, 2015, para. 23).

This decision is remarkable for a number of reasons. First, the Greek Council of State clearly distinguished between two chronological phases of the Greek crisis: on the one hand, the years 2010–2012, when Greece was in the midst of its worst economic downturn and pension reductions could be legally justified due to the state of an economic emergency. On the other hand, the years from 2012 onward were assessed by the Court as financially more stable, since the first measures to combat the crisis were already taken. For this reason, pension cuts introduced in this year were placed under much stricter judicial scrutiny and found unconstitutional. Another reason that makes this court ruling remarkable is that for the first time in its crisis-related jurisprudence, the Court decided the case on the basis of a social right protected in the Greek constitution, namely the right to social security. The Court interpreted the right as a milestone of the welfare state and underlined that cuts in pensions cannot interfere with the constitutionally protected core of the right, which guarantees that pensioners can lead a dignified life. This includes not only the fulfillment of basic living conditions but also the capacities for a meaningful participation in public and social life, similar to the ones they had in their working life (Greek Council of State, Judgement 2287/2015, 2015, para. 7; Judgement 2288/2015, 2015, para. 7). Furthermore, the Court held that since the contested cuts in pensions were not backed up by actuarial reports reflecting the actual financial picture of the pension funds, they were violating the constitution.

Nevertheless, in the third phase of the Greek jurisprudence, the outcome of the aforementioned judgment was to a great extent mitigated. In its judgment of 2019, the Greek Council of State held that cuts in the main pensions introduced by Law 4387/2016 were not incompatible with the Greek constitution, since they were the result of the recalculation of pensions in the framework of a newly created, unified social security system, even if the final sum of the main pension was the same as with the prior law that was declared unconstitutional in 2015 (Council of State, Judgement 1890/2019, 2019, para. 20). The judgment repeated that the legislator enjoys a wide margin of appreciation for the organization, funding, and function of the social security system, as long as it is provided by the state. Only supplementary pension cuts were found to violate the Greek constitution, since they were not supported by actuarial reports explaining their financial background (Greek Council of State, Judgement 1890/2019, 2019, para. 26).

[7] The contested cuts were introduced through Greek Law 4051/2012; Greek Law 4093/2012.

Social Rights Adjudication as a Question of Legitimacy

The overview of the supranational and Greek jurisprudence shows, with some minor differentiations, that during the Eurozone crisis, courts generally shied away from the difficult task of overruling conditionality-driven decisions over complex social policy issues. In the majority of cases, the courts deferred to the legislator, leaving the final say on choices regarding social policy and resource allocation to them. The application of this general rule of task distribution between courts and parliaments relies on the assumption that the non-neutral choices of political bodies were made after the consultation and participation of all affected individuals and vulnerable groups.

However, during the current Eurozone crisis, the constitutional balance between the different institutions has been significantly altered. Decision-making was concentrated in supranational and national executives, accompanied by the input of expert bodies. The big shift toward executive politics is reflected by the simultaneous decrease in the power of both the European Parliament and national parliaments, which traditionally serve as checks on executive power (Dawson & De Witte, 2013, p. 817). Indeed, all phases of the adjustment program drafting were lacking in transparency and democratic oversight. From the preparatory phase of negotiations to the development of mandates and the formulation of specific measures, the European Parliament was until 2013 completely marginalized.[8] Negotiations were held behind closed doors, without the presence of social partners, a deficiency explicitly criticized by the International Labor Organization (International Labor Organization, Case No. 2820, Conclusions, para. 1002). In fact, the absence of prior consultation with trade union organizations has been officially admitted by the Greek government and has been ascribed to the complexity of economic and political issues and the conditions under which the European support mechanism for Greece has been formulated (International Labor Organization, Case No. 2820, Conclusions, para. 967). In sum, the institutional framework for awarding financial assistance showed profound structural shortcomings in terms of democratic legitimacy and representation of vulnerable groups.

Under these circumstances, the application of the general rule that courts should not interfere with non-neutral choices of political bodies regarding social policy and resource allocation would mean that the exclusion of the affected vulnerable groups and the eventual violation of their social rights would be left without any effective remedy. In a situation where the conduits of democratic participation are blocked, courts should thus actively undertake the task to review the procedural conditions of the decisions that, originating from financial assistance conditionality, drastically interfere with social rights. The assessment of nonadequate compliance with procedural requirements would entitle the court to proceed with the stricter substantial review of the financial assistance conditions. The courts should have asked the decision-maker responsible for a tolerable justification of the measures adopted and of

[8] This observation is reaffirmed by the EP itself. See European Parliament, 2014, para. 2. Generally on the EP's position in the new economic governance, see Fasone (2014).

the discarding of less intrusive options. In this way, non-neutral decisions on substantive social issues would in principle remain at the disposal of the respective political institution, which would bear the weight of defending them before the judiciary.

Furthermore, the relevance for the legal assessment of the participation or not of the affected actors is reflected in Regulation 472/2013 (Regulation (EU) 472/2013, 2013), which explicitly requires the involvement of social partners and relevant civil society organizations in the preparation of the adjustment programs, with a view to contributing to building consensus over its content (Regulation (EU) 472/2013, 2013, Art. 8). Moreover, in its decisions concerning pension schemes in Greece mentioned, the European Committee of Social Rights (ECSR) included the democratically questionable procedures to a factor that contributed to the violation of the Social Charter, noting that the Greek government has not discussed the pension reforms with the organizations concerned, despite the fact that they represent the interests of many of the majority of groups most affected by the measures at issue. Thus, the ECSR ruled that even though the controversial restrictions would, under certain conditions, not breach the Charter, "due to the cumulative effect of the restrictive measures and the procedures adopted to put them into place," they do amount to a violation of the right to social security (Art. 12, para. 3 ESC).[9]

Conclusion

The Eurozone crisis undoubtedly resulted in the introduction of measures that reduced Europe's social acquis. Under the rubric of economic governance, the social rights of individuals were restricted, leading to the emergence of national and supranational jurisprudence. During the European financial crisis, the CJEU did not decide, in the first phase of its case-law, on the substance of cases that challenged the conformity of crisis-related measures with social rights, and later on, when taking a decision on the substance, the Court held that restrictions on social rights were justified due to the objectives pursued and the nonviolation of the principle of proportionality. Moreover, the Greek jurisprudence fluctuated from a phase of judicial self-restraint to the repeal of austerity measures and finally to the acceptance of a series of crisis-driven restrictive measures. Nevertheless, judicial self-restraint does not always take proper account of the weakening of parliamentary controls and public scrutiny that very often comes as a side effect of the crisis. In this new

[9] ECSR, Decision on the Merits, 7.12.2012, *Federation of employed pensioners of Greece (IKA-ETAM) v. Greece*, Complaint No. 76/2012, para. 83; ECSR, Decision on the Merits, 7.12.2012, *Panhellenic Federation of Public Service Pensioners (POPS) v. Greece*, Complaint No. 77/2012, para. 79; ECSR, Decision on the Merits, 7.12.2012, *Pensioners' Union of the Athens-Piraeus Electric Railways (I.S.A.P.) v. Greece*, Complaint No. 78/2012, para. 79; ECSR, Decision on the Merits, 7.12.2012, *Panhellenic Federation of pensioners of the Public Electricity Corporation (POS-DEI) v. Greece*, Complaint No. 79/2012, para. 79; ECSR, Decision on the Merits, 7.12.2012, *Pensioners' Union of the Agricultural Bank of Greece (ATE) v. Greece*, Complaint No. 80/2012, para. 79.

context, it is argued here that courts should embrace a more protective role that makes a connection between the doubtful democratic credentials of restrictive measures and more intrusive control on the basis of social rights and the European social acquis.

References

Bakavou, M. (2020). Salus Rei Publicae Suprema Lex Esto? Welfare state reforms before the Greek courts. In Becker, U., & Poulou, A. (Eds.), *European welfare state constitutions after the financial crisis*. Oxford University Press, p. 148 https://doi.org/10.1093/oso/9780198851776.003.0006

Becker, U., & Poulou, A. (Eds.), (2020). *European welfare state constitutions after the financial crisis*. Oxford University Press.

CFREU. *Charter of fundamental rights of the EU, Art. 17, para. 1*. https://curia.europa.eu/juris/liste.jsf?num=T-531/14&language=EN

CJEC, Case 25/62, *Plaumann & Co. v Commission of the European Economic Community* [1963] ECLI:EU:C:1963:17, https://eur-lex.europa.eu/legal-content/EN/TXT/?uri=CELEX:61962CJ0025

CJEC, Case C-334/95, *Krüger v. Hauptzollamt Hamburg-Jonas* [1997] ECLI:EU:C:1997:378. https://curia.europa.eu/juris/liste.jsf?language=en&num=C-334/95

CJEC, Case C-6/64, *Costa v. ENEL* [1964] ECLI:EU:C:1964:66. https://curia.europa.eu/juris/liste.jsf?language=en&jur=C,T,F&num=6-64&td=ALL

CJEC, Case C-88/99, *Roquette Frères* [2000] EU:C:2000:652. https://curia.europa.eu/juris/liste.jsf?language=en&num=C-88/99

CJEU, Case C-128/12, *Sindicato dos Bancários do Norte and Others* [2013] ECLI:EU:C:2013:149. https://eur-lex.europa.eu/legal-content/el/TXT/?uri=CELEX:62012CO0128

CJEU, Case C-134/12, *Corpul Naţional al Poliţiştilor* [2012] ECLI:EU:C:2012:288. https://eur-lex.europa.eu/legal-content/EN/TXT/?uri=CELEX%3A62012CO0134

CJEU, Case C-264/12, *Sindicato Nacional dos Profissionals de Seguros e Afins* [2014] ECLI:EU:C:2014:2036. https://curia.europa.eu/juris/liste.jsf?num=C-264/12&language=GA

CJEU, Case C-369/12, *Corpul Naţional al Poliţiştilor* [2012] ECLI:EU:C:2012:725. https://curia.europa.eu/juris/liste.jsf?num=C-369/12&language=EL

CJEU, Case C-396/11, *Radu* [2013] ECLI:EU:C:2013:39. https://curia.europa.eu/juris/liste.jsf?num=C-396/11&language=EN

CJEU, Case C-434/11, *Corpul Naţional al Poliţiştilor* [2011] ECLI:EU:C:2011:830. https://curia.europa.eu/juris/liste.jsf?language=en&num=C-434/11

CJEU, Case C-462/11, *Cozman v. Teatrul Municipal Tärgoviste* [2011] ECLI:EU:C:2011:831. https://curia.europa.eu/juris/liste.jsf?lgrec=fr&td=%3BALL&language=en&num=C-462/11&jur=C

CJEU, Case C-564/15, *Farkas* [2017] ECLI:EU:C:2017:302. https://curia.europa.eu/juris/liste.jsf?num=C-564/15&language=EN

CJEU, Case T-215/11, *ADEDY and Others v Council* [2012] EU:T:2012:627. https://curia.europa.eu/juris/liste.jsf?num=T-215/11&language=EN

CJEU, Case T-531/14, *Sotiropoulou and others v council* [2017] EU:T:2017:297. https://curia.europa.eu/juris/liste.jsf?num=T-531/14&language=EN

CJEU, Case T-541/10, *ADEDY and Others v Council* [2012] EU:T:2012:626. https://curia.europa.eu/juris/document/document.jsf;jsessionid=CDE104A106ADC192FFDB314996FF9A90?text=&docid=131603&pageIndex=0&doclang=EN&mode=lst&dir=&occ=first&part=1&cid=4521781

CJEU, Joined cases C-8/15 P to C-10/15 P, *Ledra advertising and others v. commission and ECB* [2016] ECLI:EU:C:2016:701. https://curia.europa.eu/juris/documents.jsf?language=EN&critereEcli=ECLI:EU:C:2016:701

Dawson, M., & De Witte, F. (2013). Constitutional balance in the EU after the euro-crisis. *Modern Law Review, 76*(5), 817. https://ael.eui.eu/wp-content/uploads/sites/18/2014/05/Smulders-05-Dawson-De-Wittee.pdf

Decision 2009/415/EC of the Council, of 27 April 2009, on the existence of an excessive deficit in Greece, OJ L135/21. https://www.eumonitor.eu/9353000/1/j4nvk6yhcbpeywk_j9vvik7m1c3gyxp/vi8rm300rwzr

Decision 2010/320/EU of the Council, of 10 May 2010, addressed to Greece with a view to reinforcing and deepening fiscal surveillance and giving notice to Greece to take measures for the deficit reduction judged necessary to remedy the situation of excessive deficit, OJ L145/6. https://eur-lex.europa.eu/legal-content/EN/TXT/PDF/?uri=CELEX:32010D0320

Decision 2010/486/EU of the Council, of 7 September 2010, amending Decision 2010/320/EU addressed to Greece with a view to reinforcing and deepening fiscal surveillance and giving notice to Greece to take measures for the deficit reduction judged necessary to remedy the situation of excessive deficit, OJ L241/12. https://eur-lex.europa.eu/legal-content/EN/ALL/?uri=CELEX%3A32010D0486

Decision 2011/257/EU of the Council, of 7 March 2011, amending Decision 2010/320/EU addressed to Greece with a view to reinforcing and deepening the fiscal surveillance and giving notice to Greece to take measures for the deficit reduction judged necessary to remedy the situation of excessive deficit, OJ L110/26. https://www.eumonitor.eu/9353000/1/j9vvik7m1c3gyxp/vin58mpg24wu

Decision 2011/57/EU of the Council, of 20 December 2010, amending Decision 2010/320/EU addressed to Greece with a view to reinforcing and deepening fiscal surveillance and giving notice to Greece to take measures for the deficit reduction judged necessary to remedy the situation of excessive deficit, OJ L26/15. https://eur-lex.europa.eu/legal-content/EN/TXT/PDF/?uri=CELEX:32011D0057

Decision 2011/734/EU of the Council, of 12 July 2011, addressed to Greece with a view to reinforcing and deepening fiscal surveillance and giving notice to Greece to take measures for the deficit reduction judged necessary to remedy the situation of excessive deficit, OJ L296/38. https://eur-lex.europa.eu/legal-content/EN/TXT/?uri=CELEX%3A32011D0734

Decision 2011/791/EU of the Council, of 8 November 2011, amending Decision 2011/734/EU addressed to Greece with a view to reinforcing and deepening fiscal surveillance and giving notice to Greece to take measures for the deficit reduction judged necessary to remedy the situation of excessive deficit, OJ L320/28. https://www.eumonitor.eu/9353000/1/j9vvik7m1c3gyxp/vj3ebyoxyuz6

Decision 2012/211/EU of the Council, of 13 March 2012, amending Decision 2011/734/EU addressed to Greece with a view to reinforcing and deepening fiscal surveillance and giving notice to Greece to take measures for the deficit reduction judged necessary to remedy the situation of excessive deficit, OJ L113/8. https://eur-lex.europa.eu/legal-content/EN/TXT/?uri=CELEX:32012D0211

Decision 2013/6/EU of the Council, of 4 December 2012, amending Decision 2011/734/EU addressed to Greece with a view to reinforcing and deepening fiscal surveillance and giving notice to Greece to take measures for the deficit reduction judged necessary to remedy the situation of excessive deficit, OJ L4/40. https://eur-lex.europa.eu/eli/dec/2013/6(1)/oj

Decision 88/2013 of the Special Tribunal of Article 88 of the Greek constitution, judgement of 30 December 2013. https://www.dsanet.gr/Epikairothta/Nomologia/misthodikeio88_2013.htm

Dermine, P. (2017). The end of impunity? The legal duties of "Borrowed" EU institutions under the European stability mechanism framework: ECJ 20 September 2016, case C-8/15 to C-10/15, Ledra Advertising et al v European Commission and European Central Bank. *European Constitutional Law Review, 13*(2), 369. https://doi.org/10.1017/S1574019617000074

ECSR, Decision on the Merits, 7.12.2012, *Federation of employed pensioners of Greece (IKA-ETAM) v. Greece*, Complaint no. 76/2012.

ECSR, Decision on the Merits, 7.12.2012, *Panhellenic Federation of Public Service Pensioners (POPS) v. Greece*, Complaint no. 77/2012.

ECSR, Decision on the Merits, 7.12.2012, *Panhellenic Federation of pensioners of the Public Electricity Corporation (POS-DEI) v. Greece*, Complaint no. 79/2012.
ECSR, Decision on the Merits, 7.12.2012, *Pensioners' Union of the Athens-Piraeus Electric Railways (I.S.A.P.) v. Greece,* Complaint no. 78/2012.
ECSR, Decision on the Merits, 7.12.2012, *Pensioners' Union of the Agricultural Bank of Greece (ATE) v. Greece,* Complaint no. 80/2012.
Fasone, C. (2014). European economic governance and parliamentary representation. What place for the European Parliament? *European Law Journal*, 164. https://ael.eui.eu/wp-content/uploads/sites/18/2014/05/Smulders-09-Fasone.pdf
Greek Council of State, Judgement 1283/2012 of the Council of State, of 2 April 2012.
Greek Council of State, Judgement 1284/2012 of the Council of State, of 2 April 2012.
Greek Council of State, Judgement 1285/2012 of the Council of State, of 2 April 2012.
Greek Council of State, Judgement 1286/2012 of the Council of the State, of 2 April 2012.
Greek Council of State, Judgement 1890/2019 of the Council of State, of 4 October 2019. https://www.dsanet.gr/Epikairothta/Nomologia/steol%201890_2019.htm
Greek Council of State, Judgement 2192/2014 of the Council of State, of 13 July 2014. https://www.dsanet.gr/Epikairothta/Nomologia/steol%202192.htm
Greek Council of State, Judgement 2193/2014 of the Council of State, of 13 July 2014. https://www.dsanet.gr/Epikairothta/Nomologia/steol2193.htm
Greek Council of State, Judgement 2194/2014 of the Council of State, of 13 July 2014. https://www.taxheaven.gr/circulars/19058/ste-2194-2014
Greek Council of State, Judgement 2195/2014 of the Council of State, of 13 July 2014. https://www.taxheaven.gr/circulars/19057/ste-2195-2014
Greek Council of State, Judgement 2196/2014 of the Council of State, of 13 July 2014. https://www.taxheaven.gr/circulars/19056/ste-2196-2014
Greek Council of State, Judgement 2287/2015 of the Council of State, of 10 June 2015. https://www.dsanet.gr/Epikairothta/Nomologia/steol2287_15.htm
Greek Council of State, Judgement 2288/2015 of the Council of State, of 10 June 2015. https://www.taxheaven.gr/circulars/21151/ste-2288-2015
Greek Council of State, Judgement 3354/2013 of the Council of State, of 27 September 2013. https://www.taxheaven.gr/circulars/17401/ste-3354-2013
Greek Council of State, Judgement 4741/2014 of the Council of State, of 29 December 2014.
Greek Council of State, Judgement 668/2012 of the Council of State, of 20 February 2012. https://www.constitutionalism.gr/2316-symboylio-tis-epikrateias-668-2012-olomeleia-mnimo/
Greek Law 3845/2010, 2010. https://www.taxheaven.gr/law/3845/2010
Greek Law 3863/2010, 2011. https://www.taxheaven.gr/law/3863/2010
Greek Law 3986/2011. https://www.taxheaven.gr/law/3986/2011
Greek Law 4024/2011. https://www.taxheaven.gr/law/4024/2011
Greek Law 4051/2012. https://www.kodiko.gr/nomothesia/document/64993/nomos-4051-2012#google_vignette
Greek Law 4093/2012. https://www.taxheaven.gr/law/4093/2012
https://curia.europa.eu/juris/liste.jsf?language=el&num=C-8/15
International Labor Organisation, 365th report of the committee on Freedom of Association of the International Labor Organization, case no. 2820 (Greece).
Kilpatrick, C. (2015) On the rule of law and economic emergency: The degradation of basic legal values in Europe's bailouts. *Oxford Journal of Legal Studies, 35*(2), 325–353.
Memorandum of Understanding on Specific Economic Policy Conditionality, The Economic Adjustment Programme for Portugal, June 2011, Occasional Papers 79, 147.
Poulou, A. (2017a). *Soziale Grundrechte und europäische Finanzhilfe.* Mohr Siebeck, p.179 et seq.
Poulou, A. (2017b). The liability of the EU in the ESM framework. *Maastricht Journal of European and Comparative Law, 24*(1), 127. https://doi.org/10.1177/1023263X17693198
Regulation (EU) 472/2013 of the European Parliament and of the Council, of 21 May 2013, on the strengthening of economic and budgetary surveillance of Member States in the euro area experiencing or threatened with serious difficulties with respect to their financial stability

(Two-Pack Regulation), OJ L 140/1. https://eur-lex.europa.eu/legal-content/EN/ALL/?uri=celex%3A32013R0472

Resolution of the European Parliament, of 13 March 2014, on employment and social aspects of the role and operations of the Troika (ECB, Commission and IMF) with regard to euro-area programme countries (2014/2007(INI)). https://eur-lex.europa.eu/legal-content/EN/TXT/?uri=CELEX%3A52014IP0240

Schima, B. (2019). Article 263 TFEU. In M. Kellerbauer et al. (Eds.), *The EU Treaties and the Charter of Fundamental Rights: A commentary* (p. 1803). Oxford University Press.

Social Solidarity Economy and Social Inclusion in Greece: Radicalism Does Not Meet Vulnerability on the Ground and in Policy-making

Sofia Adam

Abstract

The chapter deals with the relative underdevelopment of social inclusion cooperative enterprises in Greece in comparison with the total number of Social Solidarity Economy Actors. A similar picture is also depicted by relevant studies exploring the participation and engagement of socially excluded groups in the foundation and management of grassroots initiatives during the period of the crisis in Greece. The chapter develops a working hypothesis as a potential explanation for this reality following the distinction between redistribution and recognition elaborated by critical thinkers in social policy. This working hypothesis highlights the development trajectory of the Greek welfare state and the associated institutional fragmentation manifested in Greek social policy-making as well as the lack of new social movements from social services' users.

Introduction

The proliferation of Social Solidarity Economy (SSE) initiatives in crisis-ridden Greece attracted international academic and policy interest leading to the development of a relevant body of research. Despite widely documented associations between the emergence of these grassroots initiatives and various facets of the socioeconomic crisis, scattered empirical evidence does not sustain the active participation of those most in need in the radical initiatives of the era. In a similar vein, the more institutionalized Social Cooperative Enterprises (SCEs) addressing the social exclusion of vulnerable social groups form the minority of the total SCEs for the relevant period of time.

S. Adam (✉)
Department of Social Policy, Democritus University of Thrace, Komotini, Greece
e-mail: sadam@sp.duth.gr

D. Anagnostopoulou (ed.), *European Identities, Inclusion and Equality*, Diversity and Inclusion Research, https://doi.org/10.1007/978-3-031-90602-2_17

This chapter intends to provide a working hypothesis as a potential explanation for this reality, drawing on critical social theory and policy. In effect, the main argument stresses the significance of the relative underdevelopment of vibrant social movements on behalf of social services' users. The lack of such social movements did not allow for the active engagement of socially vulnerable groups into grassroots initiatives despite the benevolent aspirations of their founding members. In turn, policy-making by following a logic of institutional fragmentation blocks the prospects of collective action and social participation in the future.

The first section critically discusses the discourses around the concept of social exclusion in conjunction with the aspiration held in relevant strategies for social economy organizations. The second section presents the main findings of relevant empirical studies on SSE initiatives during the period of the crisis with a special focus on those social groups most in need. The third section presents some descriptive data about the development course of SCEs for social inclusion derived from the relevant Registrar of the Ministry of Labour during the same period. The fourth section provides a working hypothesis as a potential explanation for the underrepresentation of socially excluded groups both in grassroots solidarity initiatives and institutionalized SCEs. The final section concludes with policy and research suggestions for the future.

Social Exclusion and Social Economy: Revisiting an Old Debate

Social exclusion has a long and interesting history in the field of social policy (Pierson, 2002; Marlier et al., 2007). Adam (2014) has elaborated a typology of social exclusion discourses by revisiting similar efforts by accredited scholars in the field (Levitas, 2005; Byrne, 2005; Gough et al., 2006). The main contribution of the proposed typology is the synthetic examination of the diverse social exclusion discourses in liaison with the aspirations they accommodate for third sector organizations. Thus, the focus of interest lies on the role attributed to third sector organizations in each social exclusion discourse and re-assesses all former typologies in this light. In this framework, we include within the moral underclass discourse both the individualist tradition, which treats social exclusion as a problem attributed to the norms and values of the poor as well as the new communitarianism that emphasizes the obligations of the poor toward the community while disregarding the proportional obligations of the rich. Within the social integration discourse, we locate approaches that emphasize the centrality of paid work as the royal road to social inclusion. Within the redistributionist discourse, social exclusion is associated with poverty and inequality, which are seen as inherent problems of capitalism. From this perspective, collective responses are required in order to confront the problem of social exclusion. Differences among the approaches included in this discourse have to do with the degree of necessary state involvement and the ability to overcome social exclusion within the existing capitalist socioeconomic organization.

Having depicted the main tenets of the three discourses, third sector organizations are assigned a different role in each framework. For example, in the social integration discourse, they are expected to facilitate the move from passive to active labor market policies along the lines of Third Way thinking. Within the redistribution discourse, different roles are also assigned: developing a democratic ethos through collective associations, advocating for new social rights, and developing alternative solidarity economy practices surpassing capitalist socioeconomic organization. As such, the exact role third sector organizations are expected to fulfill in relation to social exclusion depends on how the underlying framing of social exclusion itself, as well as the particular context in which third sector organizations develop in their interaction with social movements, and public institutions/policies.

The analytical framework proposed by Nancy Fraser with other but relevant concerns in mind (1989, 1995, 1997) deserves critical attention in order to further elucidate the differences among the various discourses. According to this analytical framework, two types of injustices may be detected. The first type stems from the socioeconomic order and is mainly attributed to unjust political economy structures. The second type stems from the symbolic and cultural order and reflects a lack of recognition of specific social groups. As such, injustices of the socioeconomic order are better served by redistributionist strategies, whereas cultural injustices are better served by strategies fostering the recognition of the excluded social groups. More importantly, the strategies adopted for the confrontation of both injustices may be evaluated against certain criteria. In this light, transformative strategies are preferable to affirmative ones when confronting injustices related to political economy structures. Examples of transformative practices include universal rights and access to social services. Examples of affirmative practices include targeted policies and benefits (mainly means-tested). The latter are considered less effective because they tend to stigmatize and eventually lead to political backlash. In a similar vein, deconstructing approaches (i.e., queer) are preferable in confronting cultural injustices because they tend to destabilize social stereotypes instead of reinforcing them (i.e., identity politics).

At this point, we will deal neither with the very interesting debate concerning the demarcation line between the socioeconomic and the cultural spheres nor with the articulation of certain social struggles with one sphere or the other (Butler, 1997; Young, 1997). We will simply keep the following points for the needs of our analysis:

(a) a theoretical framework which allows for the conceptualization of different types of injustices,
(b) the social inclusion of certain groups may require a combination of redistribution and recognition strategies,
(c) strategies targeting social exclusion can be evaluated against their premises and expected outcomes according to a spectrum ranging from social transformation to assimilation within the existing socioeconomic and cultural order.

Solidarity Economy in Crisis-ridden Greece: What Role for the Socially Excluded?

Emerging practices within the broader field of Solidarity Economy during the period of the crisis in Greece have renewed the academic and policy interest. Most approaches emphasized the link between these new practices and new forms of political action. In sum, new solidarity and alternative economic practices stem from a reconfiguration of political action and in turn effect changes in the course of future political action.

Many contributions highlight the antiausterity stance and engagement with solidarity as a political project of the initiatives emerging within the turmoil of the multifaceted crisis (Adam & Teloni, 2015; Adam & Kavoulakos, 2020; Andritsos & Velegrakis, 2014; Arampatzi, 2017; Bekridaki & Broumas, 2016; Daskalaki & Kokkinidis, 2017; Daskalaki et al., 2018; Kantzara, 2014; Kavoulakos, 2018; Loukakis, 2018; Papadaki & Kalogeraki, 2018; Petropoulou, 2013; Rakopoulos, 2015; Varvarousis & Kallis, 2021). It is important to note that empirical research suffers from a number of limitations inherent in the field and/or associated with the infancy of the relevant academic interest: definition battles given the proliferation of overlapping concepts and terms (Social Economy, Solidarity Economy, Social Solidarity Economy, Commons, Solidarity Initiatives, Alternative Action Organizations), the lack of a solid database of existing initiatives, the inclusion of both formal and informal initiatives, and the instability of structures and their membership base.

With these caveats in mind, the relevant research has verified that these initiatives emerged in diverse fields of activity (indicatively food, health, education, alternative/ethical/fair trade) addressing the immediate social reproduction needs as well as creating employment opportunities for those adversely affected by the austerity measures. The emerging initiatives, and mainly the informal ones explicitly addressing the social exclusion of certain social groups, were triggered by the crisis and its neoliberal management: that is, solidarity clinics addressing the primary health care needs of natives without social insurance and migrants without legal documentation; food banks addressing the immediate subsistence needs of homeless and destitute people regardless of ethnic origin (in opposition with the few but much-publicized solidarity actions of the far-right explicitly addressing only Greeks).

It is important to note that the very term of social vulnerability lost its analytical vigor in the context of the crisis and its particular management leading to a widespread perception that we are all potentially vulnerable. Indicatively, solidarity structures which were initially formed in order to address the usual suspects of social exclusion (i.e., solidarity clinics addressing the needs of migrants) were soon found serving a broader citizen base including persons previously placed on the safe side of social inclusion in mainstream society (i.e., freelancers, owners of small enterprises, etc., Adam & Teloni, 2015).

In terms of political aspirations, a significant part of solidarity initiatives had a radical political disposition as manifested in goals, values, and organizational structures (Arampatzi, 2017; Bekridaki & Broumas, 2016; Broumas et al., 2018; Daskalaki et al., 2018; Loukakis, 2018; Papadaki & Kalogeraki, 2018; Rakopoulos, 2015; Varvarousis & Kallis, 2021). This radical political disposition can be detected along the following lines: members define themselves on the left to the center part of the political spectrum, and some of these structures stem from and/or are strongly affiliated with social movements (i.e., the squares movement). Solidarity is framed as a political project and as a bottom-up strategy, in opposition to philanthropy and charity expressed by traditional institutions of the state and the church. Horizontal decision-making procedures are adopted mostly based on general assemblies and consensus-building.

However, the nascent but burgeoning bibliography did not address the demographic and socioeconomic characteristics of individual members within these initiatives. This gap has been recently addressed to some extent with the publication of the study by Varvarousis and Kallis (2021) with the examination of the demographic and socioeconomic characteristics of 404 members participating in 116 solidarity initiatives in various parts of Greece during the period 2016–2017. According to the empirical results of this study, the majority of participants are placed at the center of socioeconomic stratification and have attained a high educational level. We should keep in mind that these findings are based on members' self-perception. In addition, the same study reveals that despite the best of intentions, even radical initiatives do not seem to actively involve the migrant populations which they often serve in the management of the relevant initiatives. This finding is in alignment with the study on solidarity clinics (Adam & Teloni, 2015) where members of grassroots initiatives with radical political aspirations expressed their difficulty in transforming beneficiaries (native or foreigners) into active participants. In addition, in the rare cases where beneficiaries were engaged with the initiative, this had mostly to do with the execution of much-needed but routine tasks (i.e., cleaning, management of supplies) and not with the active participation in their governance and overall management.

All in all, we can state that grassroots radical initiatives in crisis-ridden Greece addressed the needs of social groups facing the risk of social exclusion. However, these social groups, which were mostly affected by the crisis and its neoliberal management, were not the founding members of the grassroots solidarity initiatives, and/or they were not actively engaged in their everyday operation.

Social Cooperatives for Social Inclusion: The Institutionalized Forerunners of Social Economy in Greece

We may now turn to the formal part of social and solidarity economy initiatives and explore their institutionalization process.

The first institutionalized work integration social enterprises in Greece emerged in association with the mental health reform unfolding in the 80s. In contrast with the experience of other Western European countries displaying an outburst of new social movements in the 1960s and 1970s, Greece was under a dictatorship during the same period, which was not conducive to similar social experimentation. After the admission of Greece to the EU (EEC at that time), psychiatrists exposed to new social movements abroad initiated a gradual psychiatric reform in Greece and opted for the cooperative form in order to promote the social rehabilitation of former psychiatric patients (Adam, 2014). The cooperative model fitted better with the community mental health approach, the need for targeted employment opportunities unavailable in the free market because of the psychiatric stigma, and the need for a more accommodative and empowering work environment. Therefore, the work and social integration of former psychiatric patients were assigned to the cooperative therapeutic units formed for that purpose. They were not legally registered as independent entities (they were using the legal entity and VAT of the associated psychiatric hospital) and were suffering from all the shortcomings related to their strong liaison with large public sector organizations (lack of entrepreneurial mindset, bureaucratic procedures, etc.). Thus, Article 12 of Law 2716/1999 instituted Social Cooperatives of Limited Liability (KOISPE in Greek) in order to address these shortcomings and as such institutionalized the first Work Integration Social Enterprises in Greece. KOISPE have managed to survive and multiply up to now. According to prior research (Adam, 2012), KOISPE created a safe work environment and employment opportunities for persons facing strong barriers in their entry into the labor market. However, their strong attachment to the public sector (main clientele) in conjunction with their operating in low-skill sectors (cleaning services) did not allow for secure financial sustainability. As a result, pay levels for employees coming from the target group could only sustain an existing livelihood in parallel with social welfare benefits. Moreover, despite the innovative aspects of the relevant law (i.e., participation of the target group in the Management Board of the cooperative), the meaningful participation of persons with mental health problems in the governance and management of these cooperatives was not achieved in practice (Adam, 2012).

In 2011, Law 4019/2011 provided the legal framework for the broader development of social enterprises in Greece. Three types of Social Cooperative Enterprises (SCEs) were envisaged in accordance with the principal goal pursued:

(a) Social inclusion with 40% of employees belonging to vulnerable social groups.
(b) Social welfare for the provision of social care services to specific target groups.
(c) General and/or productive purpose forming the broader category encompassing a multiplicity of goals and activities.

Law 4019/2011 was later followed by a Strategic Plan for the Development of the Social Entrepreneurship Sector in Greece (February 2013). The underlying hypothesis was the inherent link between social economy and social inclusion with a primary focus on social enterprises. In this framework, social enterprises were mainly seen as a tool for the (reintegration) into the labor market of frail social groups which were arbitrarily divided into two subcategories: (a) vulnerable and (b) special social groups.

Law 4019/2011 (Art. 1, para. 4) demarcates a distinction between vulnerable and special social groups which defies all advances in social policy regarding the structural causes of social exclusion. On the one hand, according to the relevant provisions, vulnerable social groups face barriers in their inclusion into social and economic life because of physical and mental causes or because of criminal conduct. This social group includes persons with disability[1] (physical or mental or developmental or sensory), persons with dependency problems and/or after rehabilitation, HIV positive, prisoners/ex-prisoners, and juvenile delinquents. On the other hand, special social groups are placed in a disadvantaged position in the labor market because of economic, social, and cultural factors. Indicatively, this social group includes persons such as young unemployed, unemployed women, unemployed above 50 years old, long-term unemployed, heads of single-parent households, members of large families, women/victims of abuse, illiterate persons, residents of detached mountainous and island areas, persons with cultural particularities, migrants and refugees.

According to these definitions, vulnerable social groups are excluded from socioeconomic life because of personal impairments, and not because of the existing socioeconomic organization. However, special social groups are excluded from the labor market because of social, economic, and cultural factors. What we gain in this second definition in terms of a more progressive framing of social exclusion, we lose by equating social exclusion with exclusion from the labor market. Therefore, the demarcation between vulnerable and special social groups denotes a poor understanding of the problem of social exclusion and an incoherent understanding of injustices based on both recognition and redistribution.

Contrary to policy expectations, the share of social inclusion to total SCEs was very small with the vast majority of SCEs falling under the general or productive purpose by the end of September of 2014 (Adam, 2016). By the end of 2015, the situation had not altered significantly as SCEs for Social Inclusion were still the minority of the total SCEs with a slightly greater concentration in Athens. However, 224 persons belonging to vulnerable social groups were registered as employees in SCEs out of a total of 813 employees irrespective of the type of SCE (not explicitly for Social Inclusion) (Greek Ministry of Labour & Social Affairs, 2017).

Law 4430/2016 "Social and Solidarity Economy and the development of its actors" constitutes an umbrella legal framework for legal entities registered as Social and Solidarity Economy Actors in Greece (Adam, 2019). The law unifies under Work Integration Social Enterprises, Social Cooperatives of Limited Liability described above and regulated by Article 12 of Law 2716/1999 and the Social Inclusion SCEs. The Law keeps rather intact the demarcation between vulnerable and special groups put forward by Law 4019/2011. However, it modifies SCEs for social inclusion in the following respects:

(a) It subdivides SCEs for Social Inclusion into those addressing vulnerable and special groups, respectively.

[1] When referring to the law, we use the terminology adopted by the law and not what we endorse when referring to the disabled according to the social model of disability.

(b) It imposes that each type of Social Inclusion SCE meets certain percentages from the two respective social groups in the composition of both members and employees, whereas the previous legal framework held certain percentages only for employees.
(c) A few changes are detected in the inclusion and exclusion of subgroups within each category. For example, HIV-positive persons are removed from the category of vulnerable social groups and are no longer explicitly referred to.

The category of special social groups explicitly specifies the young unemployed as persons who are up to 25 years old, whereas victims of abuse are now referred to as victims of domestic violence. The following subgroups are also included in the category of special social groups: victims of human trafficking, homeless, people living in conditions of poverty, and asylum seekers. Lastly, the following subgroups have been removed: unemployed women, illiterate persons, residents of detached mountainous and island areas, and persons in large families as they are supposed to be subsumed under the more general subgroup of persons living in poverty.

The introduction of Law 4430/2016 did not alter the development course of SCEs addressing social exclusion. The total number of Social Cooperatives of Limited Liability (KOISPE) and SCEs addressing both vulnerable and special social groups amounted to 4.3% of total entities registered as Social and Solidarity Economy Actors according to the new jargon of the relevant Law (Greek Ministry of Labour & Social Affairs, 2020). It is important to note that the SCEs addressing the social inclusion of special social groups were the fewest among them (10 out of 72 or 13.9%). In terms of employment, 292 persons of vulnerable social groups were registered as employees of SSE Actors out of a total of 1165 (around 25%) by 2018 (Greek Ministry of Labour & Social Affairs, 2020).

Hence, we could state that throughout the period of the crisis and the emergence of a new wave of co-operativism in Greece, it was not Social Cooperatives for the explicitly defined as vulnerable and/or special social groups that proliferated but rather cooperatives formed by mainly the general population.

A Working Hypothesis: Redistribution and Recognition Revisited

The relative under-representation of socially excluded groups in both grassroots solidarity initiatives and the institutionalized SCEs can be explained by three interrelated factors associated with the analytical framework of redistribution and recognition as a strategy against social exclusion.

The first factor relates to the peculiar development trajectory of the Greek welfare state which has historically suffered from a number of deficiencies. We will simply highlight the following structural aspects of social protection in Greece (Adam & Papathedorou, 2016):

(a) Statism-clientelism-familialism
(b) Predominance of pensions
(c) Quasi-public hospital care
(d) Rudimentary social assistance
(e) Ineffectiveness in reducing inequality and poverty
(f) Underdeveloped third sector welfare provision
(g) Lack of legitimacy

The inclusion of Greece to the EU (EEC at that time) effected changes in welfare state especially in the field of social exclusion. As such, the already fragmented character of the Greek social protection system was further exacerbated by the proliferation of EU funding priorities and opportunities. This patchwork is evident in the social exclusion discourse adopted by Law 4019/2011 and manifested in the demarcation of vulnerable and special social groups and the arbitrary reference to subgroups within each category. This policy direction and design has not been radically improved by Law 4430/2016 as the above demarcation line has been kept intact with a slight improvement in the definition of special social groups according to a discourse that related problems of social exclusion with poverty and income inequality.

Second, the associated underdevelopment of relevant social movements in the field of social policy in Greece did not allow for the opening up of recognition discourses for social groups such as persons with disability/ies, persons with mental health problems, and so on. Changes in the relevant discourses away from stigmatizing and toward empowering terms and practices are more often attributed to the initiative of progressive professionals in the relevant fields than to the autonomous development of movements on behalf of service users. As indicated above, the mental health reform was mainly organized and implemented by the initiative of progressive mental health professionals exposed to social movements in other countries (i.e., the movement of Democratic Psychiatry in Italy). Thus, we did not witness service users' movements claiming dignity, respect, and profound changes in the design and organization of social services in Greece as was the case in other European countries with vibrant social movements criticizing the modus operandi of the welfare state as reproducing the social exclusion of the alleged beneficiaries (Barnes, 2000; Beresford, 2001; Siebel, 2006). For example, with regard to disabled persons (Oliver, 1990; Shakespeare, 1993), the independent living movement criticized the dominant medical model of disability and proposed the social model that makes the distinction between individual impairment and disability as the inability of equal participation into socioeconomic life due to social and physical barriers (Barnes, 2000). In a similar vein, social movements in mental health adopted the term psychiatric survivors (Crossley, 1999, 2006) in order to denote that the basic problem that needs to be addressed is not the mental health problem itself but the experience of mental health care provision. These social movements have changed and constantly change the trajectory of social policy through new articulations of social needs and associated policy discourses. Needless to say, and without recourse to a chicken-egg game, this second factor of underdeveloped social movements in the field of social policy is strongly related to the development trajectory of the welfare state. In other words, there has to be a functional welfare state in order to exert criticism on it.

Third, redistributionist discourses and practices do not suffice by themselves to counterbalance the lack of recognition suffered from certain social groups within the current socioeconomic organization. This is often the case even within the framework of grassroots Solidarity Economy initiatives with radical values and orientations toward the accommodation of socially excluded constituencies. In other words, pleas to self-organization, horizontality, and direct democracy do not suffice to give voice and power to persons on the receiving end of the service provided. Differences in socioeconomic status, racial and national differentiation, gender identities, expressions, and sexual orientations may easily be transformed into power differentials. If this is the case, these power differentials need to be addressed explicitly by an effective articulation of redistribution and recognition leading eventually to new discourses and practices (i.e., facilitation of general assemblies, organization of specifically dedicated empowering sessions, etc.). Otherwise, the alleged supremacy of direct democracy may easily transform into the tyranny of the structurelessness as was critically expressed by the American feminist Jo Freeman (1972).

Concluding Remarks and Suggestions

This chapter intended to unfold the diverse premises and policy expectations behind the different discourses of social exclusion with a special focus on the role of third sector organizations. The previous discussion illustrated that social exclusion can be conceived in ways that differ significantly with regard to the necessity of collective intervention, the significance attributed to the problem of poverty, and inequality and the potential to surpass these problems within the existing socioeconomic organization.

This critical examination has helped us to formulate a working hypothesis behind the relative under-representation of those mostly in need in the organization of grassroots solidarity initiatives and SCEs in Greece. This hypothesis focuses on three interrelated factors: (a) the development trajectory of the Greek welfare state, (b) the associated underdevelopment of service users' movements, and (c) the lack of explicitly empowering mechanisms within informal and formal solidarity economy initiatives.

This line of argumentation can assist future research in fields such as service users' collective initiatives and movements, and empowering practices within formal and informal Social and Solidarity Economy initiatives. On the one hand, it would be helpful to systematically explore collective initiatives of the many facets of social exclusion in Greece (i.e., persons with mental health problems, disabled persons, migrants and refugees, and persons of the LGBTQ+ community) and examine any potential linkages with Social and Solidarity Economy initiatives. On the other hand, it would be interesting to systematically explore both informal and formal Social and Solidarity Economy initiatives in order to identify more or less accommodative practices for the effective inclusion and representation of those facing injustices of recognition and/or redistribution. What works best and for whom? How can we improve our everyday practices especially when we are directly responsible for their design as is often the case with grassroots and cooperative entities?

We can also address critical challenges at the policy level. First, we need to stress the need for theoretical coherence in the framing of social exclusion as a social problem. This is neither a quest for academic purism nor pedantic adherence to theoretical battles for their own merit. It is rather a firm understanding that there is nothing more practical than a good theory. A clear understanding of social exclusion guides policy-making in the design and delivery of social benefits and services. It practically helps to identify claimants and map stakeholders. It opens up the floor for the expression of unmet social needs. It exposes conflicting views and interests. It may even eventually allow for alliance and consensus building while acknowledging diverse claims and needs. And as such, it may actually address the quest for a universality which should after all be reflected in social welfare, state and citizen-driven alike.

In sum, we need to reconsider social exclusion as a problem of both redistribution and recognition and explore in greater detail the repertoire of available options in social policy and solidarity practice. We live in an era of systemic crises. If we want to address them collectively, we will need inclusive welfare states and solidarity practices.

References

Adam, S. (2012). *Social economy and active inclusion policies: Presentation of field work results on Work Integration Social Enterprises in Greece.* Observatory of Social & Economic Developments, Institute of Labor, General Confederation of Greek Labour. https://ineobservatory.gr/publication/kinoniki-ikonomia-ke-energitikes-politikes-entaxis/ (in Greek).

Adam, S. (2014). Social exclusion and work integration: Social cooperatives for people with mental health problems in Greece. *CIRIEC working paper series, WP14/08.* https://www.ciriec.uliege.be/wp-content/uploads/2015/08/WP14-08.pdf

Adam, S. (2016). Social enterprises, social and solidarity economy and youth: What role for policymaking? In M. Petmesidou, E. Delamonica, C. Papatheodorou, & A. Henry-Lee (Eds.), *Child poverty, youth (un)employment, and social inclusion* (pp. 223–242). CROP International Poverty Studies, University of Bergen (UiB), Ibidem, Verlag.

Adam, S. (2019). Legal provisions for Social and Solidarity Economy Actors. The case of Law 4430/2016 in Greece. *International Journal of Cooperative Law, 2*, 97–110.

Adam, S., & Kavoulakos, K. I. (2020). State and social solidarity economy: Friends or foes? The potential for co-construction of public policies for Social Solidarity Economy in Greece. *Greek Review of Social Research, 155*(Special Issue on Social Solidarity Economy), 121–150.

Adam, S., & Papathedorou, C. (2016). Dismantling the feeble social protection system of Greece: Crisis and austerity measures consequences. In K. Schumbert, P. de Villota, & J. Kuhlmann (Eds.), *Challenges to European welfare systems* (pp. 271–300). Springer.

Adam, S., & Teloni, D. (2015). *Solidarity clinics in crisis-ridden Greece. The experience of health care provision when the National Health System is on the retreat.* Observatory of Economic & Social Developments, Institute of Labor, General Confederation of Greek Labor. https://ineobservatory.gr/wp-content/uploads/2016/07/MELETH-441.pdf (in Greek).

Andritsos, T., & Velegrakis, G. (2014). Mapping and unifying the Greek geographies of resistance in times of crisis Introduction: Antinomies in times of crisis. In *64th annual international conference of political studies association.*
Arampatzi, A. (2017). The spatiality of counter-austerity politics in Athens, Greece: Emergent 'urban solidarity spaces'. *Urban Studies, 54*(9), 2155–2171.
Barnes, H. (2000). *Working for a Living? Employment, benefits and the living standards of disabled people*. The Policy Press.
Bekridaki, G., & Broumas, A. G. (2016). The Greek society in crisis and in motion – Bui*lding the material bases for an alternative society from the bottom up. *SSRN*. https://doi.org/10.2139/ssrn.2853050
Beresford, P. (2001). Service users, social policy and the future of welfare. *Critical Social Policy, 21*(4), 494–512.
Broumas, A., Ioakimoglou, E., & Charitakis, K. (2018). Greece: Grassroots labour struggles in a crisis-ridden country. *Historical Materialism Book Series, 150*, 56–81.
Butler, J. (1997). Merely cultural. *Social Text, Queer Transexions of Race, Nation, and Gender, 52*(*53*), 265–277.
Byrne, D. (2005). *Social exclusion* (2nd ed.). Open University Press.
Crossley, N. (1999). Working utopias and social movements: An investigation using case study materials from radical mental health movements in Britain. *Sage Publications, 33*(4), 809–830.
Crossley, N. (2006). *Contesting psychiatry. Social movements in mental health*. Routledge.
Daskalaki, M., Fotaki, M., & Sotiropoulou, I. (2018). Performing values practices and grassroots organizing: The case of solidarity economy initiatives in Greece. *Organization Studies*. https://doi.org/10.1177/0170840618800102
Daskalaki, M., & Kokkinidis, G. (2017). Organizing solidarity initiatives: A sociospatial conceptualization of resistance. *Organization Studies, 38*(9), 1303–1325.
Fraser, N. (1989). *Unruly practices: Power, discourse, and gender in contemporary social theory*. University of Minnesota Press. http://www.jstor.org/stable/10.5749/j.cttts7ps
Fraser, N. (1995). Recognition or redistribution? A critical reading of Iris young's justice and the politics of difference. *Journal of Political Philosophy, 3*(2), 166–180.
Fraser, N. (1997). Redistribution or recognition? Dilemmas of justice in a "Post-socialist" age. In K. Olson (Ed.), *Nancy Fraser debates her critiques*. Verso.
Freeman, J. (1972). The tyranny of structurelessness. *The Second Wave, 2*(*1*), 20.
Gough, J., Eisenschitz, A., & McCulloch, A. (2006). *Spaces of social exclusion*. Routledge.
Greek Ministry of Labour & Social Affairs. (2017). *National report 2017 & action plan for the development of the ecosystem of social solidarity economy 2017–2023*. https://kalo.gov.gr/etisia-ekthesi-2017-schedio-drasis-gia-tin-anaptyxi-toy-oikosystimatos-tis-koinonikis-kai-allileggyas-oikonomias-2017-2023/ (in Greek).
Greek Ministry of Labour & Social Affairs. (2020). *Report 2019–2020 of social solidarity economy*. https://kalo.gov.gr/k-al-o-ekthesi-eton-2019-2020/ (in Greek).
Kantzara, V. (2014). Solidarity in times of crisis: Emergent practices and potential for paradigmatic change. Notes from Greece. *Studi di Sociologia, Vita e Pensiero – Pubblicazioni dell'Università Cattolica del Sacro Cuore, 52*(*3*), 261–280.
Kavoulakos, K. I. (2018). Social solidarity economy, crisis and social movements. In N. Serdedakis & S. Tompazos (Eds.), *Aspects of the Greek crisis. Cycles of protest and institutional outcomes*. Gutenberg. (in Greek).
Levitas, R. (2005). *The inclusive society*. Palgrave Macmillan.
Loukakis, A. (2018). Not just solidarity providers investigating the political dimension of Alternative Action Organisations (AAOs) during the economic crisis in Greece. *Partecipazione E Conflitto, 11*(1, SI), 12–37.
Marlier, E., Atkinson, A. B., Cantillon, B., & Nolan, B. (2007). *The EU and social inclusion. Facing the challenges*. The Policy Press.
Oliver, M. (1990). *The politics of disablement*. Macmillan.
Papadaki, M., & Kalogeraki, S. (2018). Exploring Social and Solidarity Economy (SSE) during the Greek economic crisis. *Partecipazione E Conflitto, 11*(1), 38–69.

Petropoulou, C. (2013). Alternative networks of collectivities and solidarity-cooperative economy in Greek cities: Exploring their theoretical origins. *Journal of Regional & Socio-Economic Issues, 3*(2), 61–85.

Pierson, J. (2002). *Tackling social exclusion*. Routledge.

Rakopoulos, T. (2015). Solidarity economy in contemporary greece 'Movementality', economic democracy and social reproduction during crisis. In K. Hart (Ed.), *Economy for and against democracy* (pp. 161–181). Berghahn.

Shakespeare, T. (1993). Disabled people's self-organization: A new social movement? *Disability, Handicap and Society, 8*(*3*), 249–264.

Siebel, T. (2006). Disability studies and the future of identity politics. In L. M. Alcoff, M. Hames-García, S. P. Mohanty, & P. M. L. Moya (Eds.), *Identity politics reconsidered*. Palgrave MacMillan.

Varvarousis, A., & Kallis, G. (2021). *Routes out of the crisis. Solidarity and cooperative practices in Greece during the period 2016–2017*. Heinrich Boll Foundation. https://gr.boell.org/el/2021/04/06/diadromes-exodoy-apo-tin-krisi (in Greek)

Young, I. M. (1997). Unruly categories: A critique of Nancy Fraser's dual systems theory. In K. Olson (Ed.), *Nancy Fraser debates her critiques*. London & New York.

Digital Exclusion, Social Exclusion, the Workplace Digital Divide, Algorithmic Decision-Making, and the Digital Transformation of the Enterprise from a Legal-Social Perspective

Dimitrios I. Koukiadis

Abstract

The continuously evolving digitization of how we facilitate and disseminate information, educate ourselves, study, and how we do business presents a critical disruption of fundamental rights insofar as it manifestly increases the dependence of their application on digital technology and on a digital infrastructure of a networked world.

Access to the benefits of the Internet and the digital ecosystem enhances digital inclusion, which in turn improves social and economic inclusion. The right to access the Internet establishes a social right aiming at restraining social injustice and discrimination between the "haves" and the "haves not." Nevertheless, the level of access to the Internet and participation in the information society is not only volatile but very often also unequal and discriminatory. Inequality and discrimination applied in Internet access lead to the creation of a digital divide.

The digital organization of work based on the platform economy system, and the consequent bipolar division of labor into unskilled and high-tech labor are only some elements highlighting the new digital reality in the workplace environment. Given the immense footprint of the digital transformation on the organization of an enterprise, and the required skills it needs in order to thrive in the digital economy's ecosystem, it is imperative for national, supranational, and international authorities, as well as for employers and trade unions to promote policies that expand work opportunities, eliminate workforce's inequalities and the risk of being excluded from the benefits of the digital economy. Such a com-

D. I. Koukiadis (✉)
School of Law, University of Nicosia, Nicosia, Cyprus

D. Anagnostopoulou (ed.), *European Identities, Inclusion and Equality*, Diversity and Inclusion Research, https://doi.org/10.1007/978-3-031-90602-2_18

prehensive policy framework could be based on three pillars: lifelong learning, collective representation, and algorithmic decision-making control.

Introduction

The digital transformation of society is profoundly affecting the ways in which people communicate, live, and work. The most valuable "vehicle," serving this digitalization of our lives, has been the Internet. The French Conseil d'État, in its annual report in 2014, remarked that the Internet was, and always has been so far, a form of digital technology. Internet is defined as the representation and transmission of information, videos, images, sounds, e-games, texts, and data through a finite set of discrete values. It employs a transformative power based on its capacity to express disparate realities in a common universal language, enabling systematic processing and interrelation between them (Conseil d'État, 2014, p. 1). This dynamic framework results in a profound synthesis of technical, economic, and social transformations that permeate nearly every aspect of human conduct.

The Internet has initially emerged within a limited range of specialized sectors such as universities, telecommunications, software development, and computer services. Today, however, digital technology has expanded far beyond these origins and has already transformed almost all areas of our collective culture. It has reshaped cultural activities, communication, entertainment, information gathering, work, commerce, goods distribution, various services, transportation, medicine, and more.

> ...Digital technology is demonstrating its capacity to re-write the rules of the game and challenge the status quo in all these sectors. The business models of firms in the digital technology sector present specific characteristics: a focus on growth rather than short-term profitability, strategies to redefine the boundaries of the markets in which they operate, platform strategies that allow them to act as a gateway for consumers, and finally, intensive use of data, particularly personal data, to generate value... (Conseil d'État, 2014, p. 1)

In its 30 years of life,[1] the Internet has revolutionized not only our right and way to express ourselves but also our capacity to communicate with one another across all five continents in a flash of light. It has affected the way we facilitate and disseminate information locally and globally, the way we entertain and educate ourselves, the way we study and work, and the way we do business. In short, the Internet has

[1] Many different periods and birth years are attributed to Internet (1940s, 1962, 1983, 1993). For the purposes of this chapter, the birth of the modern version of Internet is considered to be the year 1993, when the development and widespread deployment of the World Wide Web brought with it a new online community, and when the Internet started to become massively accessible. If we went even further back in time, we would go in the 1940s, the first years of WWII, at Bletchley Park, England, where the concept of computation was born. A group of British, French, and Polish scientists was gathered by the British government in order to break the German Enigma Code. Apparently, after the end of the war, the real legacy of Bletchley Park has been something much more than anticipated: the birth of the computer era. For further analysis on the birth of the Internet, see the very comprehensive analysis of Leiner et al. (1997).

influenced immensely the whole function of our individual and collective culture and the way we live. The Internet provides an unprecedented platform for the exercise of almost all of our activities.

The aforementioned fields of human activity, beyond their social dimension, also have a profound normative significance. They embody fundamental rights such as freedom of speech, access to information, the right to work, the right to education, and the right to engage in economic activity. The ongoing digitization of these areas introduces a critical challenge to fundamental rights, as it significantly increases their reliance on digital technology, vast amounts of data generated online, and the infrastructure of a networked world. While the growing dominance of the Internet in our lives is not inherently negative, it raises important questions about the transformation of the content of specific fundamental rights,[2] the accessibility to them, and the way they are implemented. While the Internet increases the capacity of some individuals to enjoy the benefits of a digitalized world, such as social networking platforms, online working, or doing business online, at the same time, it excludes others who do not (or cannot) enjoy the benefits of Internet's ecosystem. Continuous digital innovation in communication, work, and economy, and the establishment of digital technology as a *sine qua non* aspect of human culture prompts the recognition of new fundamental rights and freedoms, changes the conditions under which they are exercised, and force us to reexamine how such rights could and should be protected.

The Concept of Digital Inclusion

In one of its recent highly influential judgments, the European Court of Human Rights (ECtHR, 2015, *Cengiz*, paras. 49, 52) remarked that "*...the Internet has now become one of the principal means by which individuals exercise their right to freedom to receive and impart information and ideas, providing as it does essential tools for participation in activities and discussions concerning political issues and issues of general interest. ... Moreover, as to the importance of Internet sites in the exercise of freedom of expression... in the light of its accessibility and its capacity to store and communicate vast amounts of information, the Internet plays an important role in enhancing the public's access to news and facilitating the dissemination of information in general...(and)...User-generated expressive activity on the Internet provides an unprecedented platform for the exercise of freedom of expression...*".[3]

Access to the Internet, as a derivative right of the right to freedom of expression, empowers individuals to engage in not only a typical participation but also in a

[2] Regarding the way digital technology has led to the birth of new fundamental rights out of traditional, well-established fundamental rights, see Conseil d'État (2014).

[3] The Court, in this case, refers also to two other relevant seminal rulings, that is, *Times Newspapers Ltd v. the United Kingdom* and *Delfi AS v. Estonia* (ECtHR, 2003, Times Newspaper Ltd; ECtHR, 2009, Delfi).

substantial involvement in the core functions of a liberal democratic society. It reinforces the notion that, in a democratic regime, citizens must have access to information in order to effectively govern themselves, making Internet access essential to this informational function. Intrinsically joined with this notion comes the perception that the free flow of ideas and critical thinking toward those in power serves as a "checks and balances" mechanism to guard against the abuse of governmental power.

Lastly, Internet access facilitates the active participation in the vast, online "marketplace of ideas,"[4] an activity providing that the best test of truth is the power of thought to get itself accepted in the competition of the open market of dialectic communication. This process increases the value of citizenship by promoting informed and active engagement in democratic life.

However, the right to Internet access, as a derivative right of freedom of expression (and, beyond that, the right to personality protection) compared to the right to freedom of expression, has not received judicially, so far, a universal recognition as an autonomous constitutional fundamental right. In the aforementioned case of ECtHR, *Cengiz v. Turkey* (*ECtHR,* Cengiz v. Turkey, 2015) the Court's ruling was founded on the violation of Article 10 of the European Convention on Human Rights (ECHR),[5] and not on an autonomous right to access the Internet. The Court held that there had been a violation of Article 10 of the Convention, finding that the

---

[4] The concept "marketplace of ideas" is one of the core doctrinal elements of freedom of speech protection under the First Amendment of the U.S. Constitution. According to this concept, any effort to repress this process would cause a "market distortion". The other rationales behind the freedom of speech protection are the self-governance, advancing autonomy, and promoting tolerance rationale. See relevantly Chemerinski (2013).

[5] The protection of the fundamental right to freedom of expression, under Article 10 of ECHR and Article 11 of the EU Charter of Fundamental Rights, is considered to be the "European First Amendment".

Article 10 of the European Convention on Human Rights:

1. Everyone has the right to freedom of expression. This right shall include freedom to hold opinions and to receive and impart information and ideas without interference by public authority and regardless of frontiers. This Article shall not prevent States from requiring the licensing of broadcasting, television or cinema enterprises.

2. The exercise of these freedoms, since it carries with it duties and responsibilities, may be subject to such formalities, conditions, restrictions or penalties as are prescribed by law and are necessary in a democratic society, in the interests of national security, territorial integrity or public safety, for the prevention of disorder or crime, for the protection of health or morals, for the protection of the reputation or rights of others, for preventing the disclosure of information received in confidence, or for maintaining the authority and impartiality of the judiciary.

Article 11 of the EU Charter of Fundamental Rights:

1. Everyone has the right to freedom of expression. This right shall include freedom to hold opinions and to receive and impart information and ideas without interference by public authority and regardless of frontiers.

2. The freedom and pluralism of the media shall be respected.

effects of the measure in question had been arbitrary and the judicial review of the blocking of access had been insufficient to prevent abuses. The Court accepted that this was not a blanket ban but rather a restriction on Internet access. However, the limited effect of the restriction did not lessen its significance, particularly as the Internet had now become one of the principal means of exercising the right to freedom of expression and information (ECtHR, Akdeniz v. Turkey, 2014, Conseil d'État, 2014, paras. 54 ff.).[6]

The Court, through this case, expanded the concept of "expression" and upheld the right not only of the one who imparts information but also of the recipients of information to have access to Internet websites. Moreover, it established that blocking an entire Internet domain, because some pages on that domain violate domestic law constituted a violation of the right to freedom of expression.

Being more radical and daring in its argumentation, in 2009, the French *Conseil Constitutionnel* decided with its 2009-580 "HADOPI" ruling that an administrative authority's decision to suspend access to the Internet due to intellectual property law infringement did violate the constitutionally protected right to freedom of speech, and that "*...the current state of the means of communication and given the generalized development of public online communication services and the importance of the latter for the participation in democracy and the expression of ideas and opinions, [the right to freedom of expression] implies freedom to access such services...*" (Constitutional Council's decision, 2009).

In the same spirit, the German Federal Court of Justice ruled, in 2013, that the Internet plays a very important role today and affects the private life of an individual in very decisive ways. Therefore, loss of Internet use is comparable to the loss of use of a car, in terms of its ability to disrupt lives (Bundesgerichtshof decision, 2013). Lastly, the United Nations General Assembly, in 2016, attributed the human right status to the right to Internet access, requesting all States to make efforts to bridge the many forms of digital divides (United Nations General Assembly, 2016).

In the Greek Constitution, after the constitutional revision in 2001, in Article 5A, the right to access the Internet is also autonomously protected: "1. *All persons have the right to information, as specified by law... 2. All persons have the right to participate in the Information Society.*[7] *Facilitation of access to electronically transmitted information, as well as of the production, exchange and diffusion thereof, constitutes an obligation of the State, always in observance of the guarantees of Articles 9, 9A and 19*". In both the above paragraphs, "information" is treated as an autonomous good, a good that goes beyond the traditional legal framework of the

[6] For further case law of the ECtHR on the access to Internet and freedom to receive and impart information and ideas, see also ECtHR, *Ahmet Yildirim*, 2012, *Akdeniz*, 2014, *Vladimir Kharitonov*, 2020, *Bulgakov* 2020, and *Engels*, 2020.

[7] The term "information society" is a much broader term than "Internet". Internet is one of the key, if not the most important, constituents of it. The information society is founded on both Internet's and telecommunications' infrastructure. What distinguishes information society from the prior industrial society is the predominance of the element of "information" as the chief driver of it, whereas in the earlier industrial society the steam power and steam engine were the driving forces behind it.

"freedom of speech", the "right to personality" and the "right to freedom of the Press". Two new rights are established, the right to information and the right to access the information society.

The key point of the above judicial and legislative confrontation of the right to access the Internet is the recognition of the Internet's public service value. Individuals, legal persons, online stakeholders, and communities, all form a multi-stakeholderism community.[8] Internet's fundamental role in fulfilling core activities establishes a legitimate claim for accessible, nondiscriminatory, affordable, and reliable online services. Therefore, no one should be subjected to an unlawful or disproportionate interference with the exercise of their human rights and fundamental freedoms when using the Internet.

The protection, under the umbrella of multilevel constitutionalism, national, supranational, or international—of the right to access the Internet and, therefore, the right to digital inclusion, primarily means abstention of both the public and private sectors from any action that might hinder or restrain access at the available online sources of information, and communication, as well as participation in the benefits and services of Information Society.

Any restrictions to this right should be prescribed by law, comply with the principles of proportionality and nondiscrimination, serve the public interest, and protect the fundamental rights of others. More specifically, considering the right to access the Internet as an extension of the right to freedom of expression, under international human rights standards,[9] any limitation to the right to Internet access should pass the following three-part test:

1. It shall be provided for by laws which, in turn, shall be clear and accessible.
2. It shall serve to protect a legitimate interest recognized under para. 3, of Article 19, of the International Covenant on Civil and Political Rights, that is, protect the rights or reputations of others or protect national security, order, health, and morals.
3. It shall prove necessary and the least restrictive to achieve its goal, taking into account the principles of necessity and proportionality.

According to the United Nations special rapporteur on the freedom of expression and the Internet, giving effect to the right to freedom of expression imposes an obligation on States to promote universal access to the Internet (International Mechanisms for Promoting Freedom of Expression, 2011). Cutting off access to the Internet, or parts of the Internet, or imposing slowdowns on the Internet or parts of

[8] For a general overview and analysis of "multistakeholderism" and its effect on the concepts of participation and governance, see Buxton (2019). More specifically, on the concept of multistakeholderism within the Internet ecosystem, see Internet Governance (2016).

[9] The three-part test comes from the International Covenant on Civil and Political Rights (ICCPR), Article 19, para. 3, and has been established by international doctrine and case law. The language of Article 19 of ICCPR is almost identical to the language employed in its counterpart Article 10, par. 2 of the ECHR. For the ICCPR text, see International Covenant on Civil and Political Rights (1966).

it, for whole populations or segments of the public can never be justified. Measures that limit access to the Internet, such as imposing registration or other requirements on service providers, are not legitimate unless they conform to the test for restrictions on freedom of expression under international law.

The Concept of "Net Neutrality" as a Constituent of the Digital Inclusion/Digital Exclusion Discourse

The aforementioned report of the United Nations Rapporteur on freedom of expression and access to the Internet makes a specific remark on the principle of net neutrality as an integral part of enhancing the protection of online freedom of expression and Internet access (International Mechanisms for Promoting Freedom of Expression, 2011, para. 5). According to it, there should be no discrimination in the treatment of the Internet data and traffic, based on the device, content, author, origin and/or destination of the content, service or application. In addition, the Internet intermediaries should be required to be transparent about any traffic or information management practices they employ, and relevant information on such practices should be made available in a form that is accessible to all stakeholders.

Net neutrality could be defined as the principle according to which data packets on the Internet should be moved impartially, without regard to content, destination, or source (Murray, 2019, p. 37), resulting in enhanced transparency and openness in the way Internet service providers operate. Net neutrality is the principle that someone cannot arbitrarily interfere in the dissemination of information and data in an unclear and discriminatory manner.

The most common cases of net neutrality breaches come with the blocking and filtering of specific online content, for example, the case with an online content-providing company interfering with the ability of their users to access specific online services and content. A user or an online consumer is entitled to access the lawful online content of his/her choice. This right is violated when the ability of users to access the content and online applications of their choice is severely disrupted. In 2012, a report by the Body of European Regulators for Electronic Communications (BEREC)[10] found that many traffic management practices, their implementation methods and policy justifications were leading to restrictions to the open Internet in Europe, and that violations of net neutrality affected at least one in five users in Europe. The report mentioned that blocked or slowed connections to services like VOIP, peer-to-peer technologies, gaming applications, and email were commonplace.

The principle of net neutrality,[11] although originally introduced as a mere structural, technical component of the Internet infrastructure, lies at the heart of the

[10] See also Sproul and Brown (2012); for a more versatile report on various forms of net neutrality breach, see Karr (2018).

[11] The first who popularized the term "net neutrality" was Professor Tim Wu. He examined the concept of network neutrality in telecommunications policy and its relationship to Darwinian theo-

access to Internet legal discourse, and has been, since the very beginning of the Internet, a game-changing factor in determining who has or has not access to the Internet. The legal aspect of a "neutral" Internet provides for equal dissemination and reception of information, leading to further enjoyment of the right to freedom of expression, and, furthermore, provides for an equal, nondiscriminatory exchange of information, services, and "peer to peer" files. In this context, the Council of Europe (CoE) adopted a Recommendation on the **protection and promotion of the right to freedom of expression and the right to Internet access in relation to network neutrality, demonstrating that "...***The principle of network neutrality underpins nondiscriminatory treatment of... users' right to receive and impart information... It reinforces the full exercise and enjoyment of the right to freedom of expression because Article 10 of the Convention applies not only to the content of information but also to the means of its dissemination. Also, the principle of network neutrality supports technological innovation and economic growth...*" (Council of Europe, 2016, para. 4).[12]

Furthermore, the European Union (EU), acknowledging the leading role of net neutrality to an open and widely accessible Internet, adopted the 2015/2120 Regulation, which declares that "... *This Regulation aims to establish common rules to safeguard equal and non-discriminatory treatment of traffic in the provision of internet access services and related end-users' rights. It aims to protect end-users and simultaneously to guarantee the continued functioning of the internet ecosystem as an engine of innovation...*" (Regulation 2015/2120, recital 1).[13] The Regulation grants Internet access providers the possibility to manage as they consider appropriate the trafficking of information as well as the Internet access itself by implementing reasonable traffic management measures.[14]

---

ries of innovation (Wu, 2003, pp. 141–179); See also Alissa Cooper and Ian Brown, who primarily address two central net neutrality questions, namely whether competition serves as a deterrent to the discriminatory treatment of Internet traffic, and whether discrimination creates barriers to application development and innovation (Cooper & Brown, 2015, pp. 1–21).

[12] **See also para. 2.1 declaring the need for equal and nondiscriminatory treatment of Internet traffic, and para. 3.2 providing for an exemption to the network neutrality principle if sufficient safeguards for users' ability to access, use, and impart information are in place. The Internet users must be informed about the impact that such different treatment might have on their ability to access, use, and impart information, diverse and pluralistic content that is publicly available, applications and services of their choice.**

[13] See also Regulation (EU) 2012/531.

[14] Regulation (EU) 2015/2120, Article 3, para. 33: "...*Providers of internet access services shall treat all traffic equally, when providing internet access services, without discrimination, restriction or interference, and irrespective of the sender and receiver, the content accessed or distributed, the applications or services used or provided, or the terminal equipment used...implementing reasonable traffic management measures. In order to be deemed to be reasonable, such measures shall be transparent, non-discriminatory and proportionate, and shall not be based on commercial considerations but on objectively different technical quality of service requirements of specific categories of traffic. Such measures shall not monitor the specific content and shall not be maintained for longer than necessary...*".

Net neutrality is firmly associated with the right to access the Internet and to be digitally active in all kinds of digital action, and the fundamentality of net neutrality is conjoined with the fundamentality of the right of access to the Internet. The aforementioned declaratory and legislative initiatives of the Council of Europe, the EU, and the United Nations highlight this very solid bond between the two concepts, and the need to preserve net neutrality as an integral part of the application of the right to be able to develop all dimensions of personality online. The right to Internet access is considered to be inherent in the principle of net neutrality, and encompasses the right to access information and communication as well as the right for each individual to participate in the information society.

Risks of Digital Exclusion: From Digital Inclusion to Social Exclusion

Internet access enhances digital inclusion, and digital inclusion improves social and economic inclusion. The right to access the Internet establishes a social right aiming at restraining social injustice and the discrimination between the "haves" and the "haves not", that is, the ones who do have the means, the equipment, the expertise to access the Internet, and the ones who, either due to factual barriers or due to external intervention do not have access at the benefits of the Internet.

Nevertheless, the level of Internet access and participation in the information society is not only volatile but often unequal and discriminatory. Inequality and discrimination in Internet access lead to the creation of a digital divide,[15] which stands for the chasm between people who are able to employ digital technologies, particularly the Internet, in a manner that ameliorates their lives and explores different levels of Internet use and skills sections, and people who do not possess the capacity, or are deprived of it, to fully, or partly, participate in the benefits of the information society.

The discourse on the digital divide has shifted from a pure connectivity and access to online resources issue in the 2000s decade to a holistic phenomenon encompassing not only the access to online information and communication technologies but also the skills and the overall utilitarian aspect of them. One successful attempt to conceptualize the social impact of the division in accessing and utilizing the digital ecosystem was introduced by Jan Van Dijk, in 2005, who has developed a framework for analyzing the concept of the digital divide, and a relevant theory trying to reconfigure the many faces of the digital divide leading to digital exclusion. According to his theory, the "resources and appropriation theory", digital divide, which might lead to digital exclusion, follows a sequential process of five stages (Van Dijk, 2017):

[15] The term first appeared in 1999, in a publication of the US Department of Commerce's National Telecommunications and Information Administration. For a more multidimensional approach to the various meanings of digital divide. See Sanders (2020).

1. Categorical inequalities in society produce an unequal distribution of resources.
2. Unequal distribution of resources causes unequal access to digital technologies.
3. Unequal access to digital technologies also depends on the characteristics of these technologies.
4. Unequal access to digital technologies brings about unequal participation in society.
5. Unequal participation in society reinforces categorical inequalities and unequal distributions of resources.

In order to further clarify and update the above process, Amit Schejter (Schejter et al., 2015) argued that contemporary digital media differ significantly from digital media of earlier generations in four dimensions:

(a) They offer an abundance of information resources and communication channels when compared to the relative paucity of both in the past.
(b) They offer mobility as opposed to the stationary nature of their predecessors.
(c) They are interactive in that they provide users with the capability to design their own media environments in contrast to the dictated environs of previous architectures.
(d) They allow users to communicate utilizing multiple forms of mediation, unlike the uniformity of sound or word that limited users in the past.

The key point here is that the changed architecture of contemporary digital resources immensely affects the way people shape their society, and demands an even more egalitarian access to all the above four dimensions of digital resources' function in society and economy. All four dimensions work in a cyclical way rather than in a sequential one. That means that the enhancement or reduction of social inequalities, as a result of digital divide, can be influenced by any of the above four steps.

As information society becomes more participatory, digital inequalities and digital and social exclusion get minimized.

A common theme in these theories is how the digital divide may lead to digital exclusion (or vice versa) and how digital exclusion may lead to social exclusion and social inequality. In the information society, the Roman axiom "*Beati possidentes*" finds a new application. Those with privilege are not only the ones who possess power, authority, and the weapons to impose it but also the ones who possess access to digital resources and information. The lack of access to these digital resources, and their unequal distribution leads to informational asymmetry, unequal participation in societal and economic life and, consequently to social exclusion.

Digital exclusion itself, does not, of course, suffice for social exclusion, but is a very influential channel that may lead to it.[16] The many faces of digital exclusion highlight how the broader conditions of people's lives—for example, the economic

[16] For a very thorough and detailed presentation of interrelationship between digital exclusion and social exclusion, see Elliot (2018, pp. 36–40).

and political paradigm, gender discrimination, racism, poverty, and digital illiteracy—create the living and working conditions people experience, the community resources they have access to, and eventually their behavioral responses.

The concept of social exclusion is a multidimensional one, transcends its linking with digital exclusion, and may involve lack of access to many forms of social, economic, and cultural resources, which are necessary for people to participate in the life of a community for the harmonious function of a social and economic system and, consequently, social cohesion itself. A definition of social exclusion building on its multidimensional nature and linking it with digital exclusion is given by Levitas et al.: "*Social exclusion is a complex and multi-dimensional process. It involves the lack or denial of resources, rights, goods and services, and the inability to participate in the normal relationships and activities, available to the majority of people in a society, whether in economic, social, cultural or political arenas. It affects both the quality of life of individuals and the equity and cohesion of society as a whole.*" (Levitas et al., 2007).

A Carnegie UK Trust report, in 2016, in its effort to reassess the relationship between digital exclusion—lacking access to online resources and services—and social exclusion—the inability of people to participate fully in social life to the detriment of themselves and society as a whole—set, in one of its chapters, the question of whether digital inclusion, or Internet access, can be a driver of different dimensions of social exclusions (Martin et al., 2016, p. 27 ff.).[17]

In short, the key findings of the report (Martin et al., 2016, p. 28) stated that

(a) The digital divide is based around social inequalities that drive low levels of access and skills to use the Internet.
(b) Those who are socially excluded are less likely to use the Internet and benefit from the Internet applications that may help them tackle their exclusion.
(c) Digital exclusion has the potential to exacerbate social exclusion, for example, in terms of poor educational attainment and some studies have shown a positive effect of digital participation on indicators of social exclusion.

A common denominator of the above analysis is that social exclusion strongly brings forward an interrelationship between the lack of access to resources, rights, goods, and services and the inability to participate in social, economic, cultural, and political life. The "nature" of the above resources can be either offline or digital. Digital inclusion can facilitate the alleviation of social exclusion by granting the digitally unprivileged groups access to the benefits of digital technology. Nevertheless, as long as offline social inequalities remain intact, these will always affect the online inequalities of those groups or individuals who lack digital literacy skills and are, thus, less likely to have access to the Internet.

[17] This report is strongly recommended to those who wish to go deeper in the couple of digital/social exclusion. It provides a very analytical and comprehensive presentation of the multifaceted role of digital exclusion on social exclusion. A plethora of statistics and tables backs the argumentation of the writers.

The EU Confrontation of Digital Divide

Due to the consequences of digital exclusion on the limited usage of digital technologies, and the inability of an individual to comprehensively participate in the social, economic, cultural, and political life, bridging the digital divide has been set as a cornerstone priority of the EU in the last decade as well as for the decade to come (European Commission, 2021a). Moreover, considering the COVID-19 pandemic, a time period in which digital technologies brought forward new ways of working, learning, communication, and entertainment, and new digital rights and principles have been introduced,[18] the challenges associated with the digitization of European society have been even more increased and strengthened. The need to confront the digital divide has been, for EU institutions, more urgent than ever. Throughout the last two decades, the EU's legislative[19] and policy-making endeavors regarding the digital divide issue have been based on the following three premises: firstly, the digital divide has been a continuously evolving concept;[20] secondly, the EU's progress on bridging the digital divide should target, among others, at an enhanced broadband connectivity[21] and Internet usage; and thirdly, support should be provided to multistakeholder partnerships and research projects to enhance digital inclusion and assistive technologies.

According to the European Parliament's survey in 2015, the number of EU citizens using mobile devices such as tablets and mobile phones to access the Internet has increased from 36% in 2012 to 51% in 2014 (European Parliament, December 2015, pp. 4–5), whereas according to a European Commission's survey in 2019,

[18] As far as digital rights are concerned, these include the traditional freedom of expression right's expansion to include the right to access the Internet and diverse, trustworthy, transparent information, the freedom to set up and conduct a digital enterprise, the right to personal data and privacy protection, and the protection of the intellectual creation of individuals online.

Regarding the new digital principles incorporated in the digitization of Europe, these include a secure and trusted online environment, universal digital education and skills, access to digital systems and devices that respect the environment, accessible and human-centered digital public services and administration, ethical principles for human-centered algorithms, protecting and empowering children in the online space, and access to digital health services. See European Commission (2021b).

[19] See as examples Directive 2014/61/EU (2014) on Measures to reduce the cost of deploying High-Speed Electronic Communications Networks, and Regulation 2015/2120 (2015) on Open Internet Access. European Commission (2013), "EU Guidelines for the application of State aid rules in relation to the rapid deployment of broadband networks"; European Commission Memo (2014), State aid: Commission adopts new General Block Exemption Regulation (GBER).

[20] The horizon of digital divide evolves and broadens as long as new technologies keep developing and new "smart" digital devices are being introduced. See relevantly also Graham and Dutton (2019). On the connection between the evolving digital divide and the digital inequality of digital skills, see Van Dijk (2012, pp. 1–19).

[21] The Digital Agenda for Europe launched in 2010, specifically on the issue of broadband connectivity, sets three targets: (1) to bring 'basic broadband' to all Europeans by 2013; (2) access to "fast broadband" speeds of above 30 Mbps (megabits per second) for all Europeans by 2020; (3) "ultra-fast broadband" speed connections above 100 Mbps for at least 50% of European households by 2020. See European Parliament (2015, p. 2, 2021a, 2021c).

43% of the adult population in Europe had limited digital skills, and 37% had no digital skills at all (European Commission, June 2019). Thus, as digital technologies continue developing, some users embrace them and enhance their online experiences, while others have limited Internet use or do not use the technology at all.

The decade 2020–2030 has been called, by the European Commission, "*the digital decade*". Within this time period, the EU's target is to establish a holistic digital environment which would empower both people and businesses to engage in digital technologies. To this end, the European Commission, on March 9, 2021, launched its project for the EU's digital transformation by the year 2030. This project focuses on four central areas: (a) Skills, (b) Government, (c) Infrastructures, and (d) Business. These four areas are part of EU's Digital Compass which will "*translate the EU's digital ambitions for 2030 in concrete terms via targets and key milestones, a robust joint governance structure including a traffic light monitoring system to identify successes and gaps, and multi-country projects combining investments from the EU, Member States and the private sector*" (European Commission, 2021b).

What has been a common ground in all EU initiatives, so far, to confront the digital divide within its territory, has been the strong belief that the digital divide can be tackled on two pillars of action: digital literacy and digital skills on the one hand, and inclusive digital services on the other, that is, the ability to become an active constituent of the benefits of the digital society which should be available for all, ordinary individuals, employees, senior people, persons with disabilities, and so on.[22] Therefore, the European Commission has been focusing its policy-making initiatives on the development of "*a high-performing digital education ecosystem, as well as on an effective policy to promote links with and attract talent from all over the globe*" (European Commission, 2021c, chapter 2).

The "Lydian stone" of the digital divide issue, not only within the EU area but globally, is the "*digital skills*" factor. This is the most essential ingredient "*to reinforce our collective resilience as a society*" and a key prerequisite for all citizens and workforce "*to participate actively in the (coming) Digital Decade*" (European Commission, 2021c, chapter 3).

The Digital Divide in the Workplace Environment

The analysis of the digital divide and digital/social exclusion phenomenon, which unveils new forms of dangers on the social, economic, and political relationships between the participants and nonparticipants in the merits of digital technology and economy, leads to the necessity of policies and methods to confront it for the sake of all participant stakeholders. Special issues emerge in legal/contractual relationships between Internet users and Internet/service providers creating mutual rights and obligations. These issues present themselves in greater intensity when one of the two contractual parties possesses asymmetrically large economic, political, and

[22] See the relevant analysis of Caradaica (2020). See also Hidalgoa et al. (2020, pp. 1–7) and Datta et al. (2019, pp. 78–81).

hierarchical power. One of the very representative examples of a power asymmetry is the subordinate working contract, in which, by definition, the one party is heavily dependent on the other.

Existing conditions highlight the new digital reality in the workplace environment: the digital organization of work based on the platform economy system, the weakening of “staff” as a unity, the dissolution of the traditional hierarchy in business, the transformation of closed businesses into digital networks of businesses, the bipolar division of labor into unskilled and high-tech labor, the transformation of bilateral labor relations into tripartite and multilateral relations—especially with the rise of the export of wage labor—the phenomenon of employers without employees, and employees without obvious employers, and the loss of working-time sovereignty.

Digital inclusion in the workplace means that employees can enjoy the benefits of digital technology at work, and have the opportunity and skills to make the best out of a work’s digital ecosystem in order to perform their work, develop, and thrive. Digital technology is one of the most important assets an employer has at his/her disposal in order to go through the digital organization of his/her business.

As in the wider society, so in the workplace, there are digitally excluded employees who lack skills, economic resources, digital literacy, confidence, and motivation, along with having limited or no access to equipment and connectivity to perform their work adequately, and come in grips with the challenges and transformations of the digital economy. A major paradigm of an employee’s digital exclusion is his/her inability to have access to the employer’s decision-making process using algorithmic data analysis without being controlled by anyone. This trend may lead to various employee evaluations of his/her working performance, his/her promotion, and even the grounds for his/her dismissal. This kind of evaluation might be abusive and arbitrary to the extent the employer sets the algorithms in a completely subjective way. The employee’s inability to check on the applied algorithms sets a new problem for his/her rights.

Issues of employee’s digital inclusion and digital divide have been created during the pandemic as well. The pandemic has launched a profound change in employers’ organization of their business. Teleworking and the so-called flexible working revolution brought a paradigm shift in how an enterprise can operate (Ghandi, 2020, p. ?). The pandemic has been a game-changer in accelerating the number of employees working from home and flexibility in work scheduling (Foxwell, 2022).

In the private sector, social class and race have also shaped this new reality to the extent that mainly the employees with higher education, job ranking, and income level had better chances to be part of digital work, work from home, and stay safe from COVID-19. But even those who belonged to the latter group did not all have equal access to digital technologies and resources or knew how to make the best of it.

Even before the pandemic, the transformation of the working relationship between employer and employee has been a game changer. Gradually and steadily the traditional subordinate working relationship has been substituted by freelance workers, creating a new category between subordinate workers and self-employed ones, the so-called para-subordinate workers. This is a new gray area of workers, whose digital inclusion and dependence have been often confronted in a similar way by the former groups of workers. Unisys Corporation in its 2021 global report identifies and describes six new groups of workers (UNISYS, 2021, pp. 14–16)[23] engaged in the digital working ecosystem, that is, the Knowledge worker, the Creative worker, the Shift worker, the Gig worker, the Field worker, and the Branch worker. These groups of workers set a new digital reality bringing forward new legal issues.

In this context, Dan Latendre remarks that there is a continuously mutating workforce mobility, a widening generation gap, an increasing use of personal devices and applications, as well as an escalating skills, talent, and expertise competition, which create a significant divide not only between employees but between employers and employees (Latendre, 2017). The key driving forces behind this fundamental shift in the nature of work are:

[23] These workers, equipped with different skills, attitudes, and tools, are employed across the researched sectors, in various roles from finance and creative, to shift and knowledge. (1) *The Knowledge worker*: He/she is typically a problem solver who works with information that is created, enhanced and shared among networks of peers, clients/customers, and employees. Common job roles include IT worker, consultant, customer service operative, and accountant. The Knowledge Worker pans sectors, however, are statistically most likely to be found in finance (13%), justice (11%), and social work (11%). They are also relatively unlikely to think they depend too much on technology (37%) and are not as worried that their job could be done by technology in the next 5 years (29%). (2) *The Creative worker:* He/she is a skilled professional, usually working in the arts, advertising, architecture or other creative industries. They use technology to draw, build, design, and manage, often working with visual data. The Creative Worker is likely to be full-time employed (74%), however, as is to be expected with this type of worker, could well be freelance. He/she is 6% more likely than others to use a tablet at work, which stands to reason with the advances made with tablet-based design programs. Their awareness of AI is high (76%), and they are reasonably likely to think they rely too much on tech (44%), perhaps missing the hands-on elements of design and creative work. (3) *The Shift worker*: He/she is a round-the-clock employee, responsible for the provision of service to clients. Either customer facing, or back office-oriented, the Shift worker is frequently supply-chain focused, either as a call center worker, midwife, or similar. They are most likely to work in health (14%), finance (13%), or justice (11%). He/she is the most likely to think their job could be done by technology in the next 5 years (38%), and the most likely to think they rely too much on tech (45%). (4) *The Gig worker*: He/she is a self-operated and reliant, flexible employee. Gig work is popular with students and people in urban areas, with the Gig worker likely to be in transport, childcare or hospitality. Inevitably, they are not full-time employed (0%). The Gig Worker is 10% more likely than others to work from a tablet and 7% more likely to work from an audio or wearable device. (5) *The Field worker*: He/she tends to work with colleagues and clients across a distributed and continually changing geography. He/she is likely to be in social work (23%), health (19%), or justice (17%), working as a district nurse or social worker; or in manual professions like plumbing and gas fitting. He/she is least likely to feel that their job is under threat to technology (30%) and second least likely to feel they rely too much on technology (38%). (6) *The Branch worker*: He/she is to be found at the end of the supply chain, is often branch-based, and almost always consumer-facing. He/she is the second least likely to be in full-time employment (63%) and tends to work in healthcare, banking, lifestyle, or hospitality. He/she demonstrates the lowest awareness of AI (5%), yet is the most likely to believe that their job could be done by tech in 5 years (41%).

1. *The workforce/work mobility*: Employees are working across geographies and time zones, a trend supported by mobile devices and policies that support flexible hours. According to Global Workplace Analytics, one-quarter of the global workforce engages in teleworking. Specifically, in the United States, 69% of US employees worked from home at the peak of the pandemic, and 5.7 million employees (4.1% of the US employee workforce) currently work-at-home half-time or more (Global Workplace Analytics, 2021). The effect of this kind of mobile workforce on employers' interest is not to be neglected. A typical employer can save an average of $11,000 per half-time telecommuter per year. The primary savings are the result of increased productivity, lower real estate costs, reduced absenteeism and turnover, and better disaster preparedness (Global Workplace Analytics, 2021).

   On top of that, mobility also has a very strong content connotation. It is not only the physical geography that is affected by digital technology but also the content of the provided work itself. Mobility of work content means a regular change in the substance of the work an employee provides. In one period, he/she may be required to offer his/her work in one specific field of action, and in a later stage in a different field of knowledge.
2. *The skills/talent competition:* The mobility of work content is one of the irritants that leads us to the digital skills and talent competition, the most dynamic force of all, a force that will shake the very essence of the concept of work. The backbone of the digitalized work and economy is the "skills" element of the employees. It is not so much the conventional knowledge that an employee acquires from a University or College once in his/her lifetime, but the continuously updated skills he/she acquires throughout his/her working life-time. Technology changes and develops constantly, and the 4th Industrial Revolution is founded on the best appropriation of digital "skills". Skills and capabilities are expected to extend from simple Internet applications to artificial intelligence, the Internet of Things, big data, and blockchain applications.

A sample of the minimum, basic digital skills needed as a framework for improvement and measurement of digital inclusion are (Sanders, 2020, pp. 13–14):

(a) *Managing information*: Using a search engine to look for information, finding a website visited before, or downloading or saving a photo found online.
(b) *Communicating*: Sending a personal message via email or online messaging service or carefully making comments and sharing information online.
(c) *Transacting*: Buying items or services from a website or buying and installing apps on a device.
(d) *Problem solving*: Verifying sources of information online or solving a problem with a device or digital service using online help.

The list of digital skills as well as the level of commanding them has no limit. The competition in skills and digital talent is (and will be) brutal. The enterprise or the organization that wins the "skills" war will have a significant advantage against its competitors. Thus, one of the top priorities of an enterprise will be to create a working environment supporting innovation and productivity, and create virtual spaces to attract the best talented and most highly skilled employees no matter their location, age, or preferred technologies.

3. *The generation gap:* Many different generations are met in contemporary global workforce: generation X, generation Y, generation Z, the Millenials, etc. Delegates of all these generations (and others) compose the greatest part of workforce. They all differ in their values, life experiences, digital literacy, ways of processing information, and ways of balancing the offline with the online reality. These differences can be a source of disruption and workforce integration, highlighting the need for digital workplace solutions that drive productivity no matter what attitudes and abilities are at play (Latendre, 2017).

The aforementioned thoughts create the danger of exclusion for specific groups of workers/employees leading to new inequalities. The new inequalities and workforce/work mobility lead to the necessity on the part of the State to introduce an updated social policy recognizing new specific workers' rights, and the restructuring of trade unions' strategy and priorities to diminish, as much as possible, the risk of being excluded.

The Three Pillars of a Digital Transformation of the Enterprise

Given the immense footprint the digital transformation leaves on work, the nature of work, the organization of an enterprise, and the required skills in order to survive and thrive in the digital economy's ecosystem, it is imperative for State's authority as well as for enterprises and trade unions to promote policies expanding work opportunities, eliminating, as much as possible, workforce's inequalities and the risk of being excluded from the benefits of the digital economy. Such a comprehensive policy framework could be based on three pillars: lifelong learning, collective representation, and algorithmic decision-making control.

Empowerment of Digital Skills and Lifelong Learning

As already argued above, digital skills and digital talents are the "Lydian stone" for surviving and succeeding in the digital working environment. All forms of workers/employees, that is, subordinate workers, self-employed, para-subordinate workers, and independent service providers, should be empowered with a mixture of skills. By a mixture of skills is meant pure digital skills, social skills, emotional skills, creative skills, job-specific skills, and problem-solving skills[24] and, above all, the

[24] Regarding the time framework of lifelong learning, the OECD report notes that initial education should focus on equipping young people with the knowledge, skills, and attitudes needed for the

key understanding of the constant change of the world of work and, hence, the constant change of the skills needed to perform a specific work (OECD, 2019, p. 1). The learning process of these skills is not for once and for all but a lifelong learning process.

Change is a constant feature of the world of modern work. Therefore, lifelong learning becomes a right and an obligation of the highest importance. Confronting digital exclusion and digital inequalities as well as leveraging the transformations underway to open new doors of success and create opportunities, would require that employees have an entitlement to lifelong learning (UN Declaration of Human Rights, Art. 26).[25] The goal is twofold in order to address two phenomena: the gradual disuse of traditional skills, and the rapid disuse of new skills. Lifelong learning encloses more than the typical skills needed to carry out a specific job. It is also about learning the skills needed to participate in a democratic society, and is linked to intergenerational social mobility, expanding the choices of future generations (Nybom, 2018, p. 13 ff).

To build an effective lifelong learning ecosystem, all stakeholders must participate in the endeavor: national or supranational authorities, enterprises, employers, employees, and educational institutions. Establishing a successful lifelong learning system is a multistakeholder task. National governments, besides creating and offering lifelong training programs, must also design a proper institutional framework and incentivize employers' and employees' organizations, as well as the business sector to have an autonomous, leading role in designing, offering, and delivering lifelong training.

Lifelong training outsourcing, that is, the facilitation of the private sector to engage actively in delivering lifelong training programs will save national governments significant amounts of organizing and training costs, and will provide for decentralized, flexible, updated training programs closer to the true needs of the market.

A major role in all stages of lifelong training is also to be played by educational institutions, that is, universities/colleges themselves. They have the human capital, the infrastructure, the research resources, and the budget to provide, for broad audiences,[26] for all kinds of training programs. They keep up with all the developments in the "new technology" sector, and they have established a tradition and a

---

new emerging opportunities in life and work while adult learning stands to play a crucial role in helping those already in the labor force acquire the skills needed in digitally enabled workplaces (OECD, 2019, p. 4). See also Grundke et al. (2018).

[25] Article 26 of the United Nations Declaration of Human Rights: "*Everyone has the right to education*… Technical and professional education shall be made generally available…".

[26] Considering the universality and the broad spectrum of lifelong learning, ILO, in its global report on the future of work, remarks that digital technologies address new opportunities for broad participation in lifelong training, as well as the opportunity to overcome time and resource constraints through flexible and shorter learning pathways. This must be in the context of access to universal quality education, delivered by well-trained teachers, whose skills, expertise, and mentorship cannot be replaced by technology (ILO/Global Commission on the Future of Work, 2019, p. 31).

"know-how", more than any other sector in society, to objectively deliver new knowledge.

The empowerment of digital skills through lifelong training programs should aim not only to technically bridge the gap between the digitally included and the digitally excluded but also to transform the "right to access the Internet" into the "ability to access the Internet". The ability to access the Internet and to make the best out of it means not only to be able to use the standard applications of the Internet but also to get familiar with all the developing and disrupting dimensions of it. Artificial intelligence, the Internet of Things, blockchain technology, and data analytics are all Internet applications. In the years to come, digital literacy will mean having a good grasp of knowledge on most of the above Internet applications.

Collective Representation

Collective representation, considering both employers' and trade unions' representation, by broadening and localizing decision-making, improves the content and legitimacy of decisions and fortifies commitment to its implementation. Within the realm of the digital economy, where geographic borders are overstepped, collective bargaining is not only a fundamental right but also a very powerful tool for social peace and economic success.

One central problem arising within the context of the digital transformation of work is the weakening role of trade unions' representativeness in promoting their interests (Brandl & Lehr 2016, p. 932).[27] What is needed is not only a new strategy for their demands but also the direct engagement of "new technologies" for their internal organization, as well as for the mobilization of workers within the networks of enterprises in the gig economy landscape.

Changes in national, supranational, and international legal frameworks, alongside changes in the organization of work and the persistence of informal employment, make it difficult for workers to organize, unite, plan, and represent their collective interests. Trade unions need to adjust to the innovative representation and organization standards, and make use of the "tools" provided by digital technology to organize themselves on a national, supranational, or global level. The successful paradigm of the first in the world collective agreement, within the gig economy spectrum, signed between the employer company "Hilfr.dk" and one of the biggest trade unions in Denmark is a very indicative one. In this case, the trade union of the

[27] Brandl and Lehr argue that the representativeness of employer and trade unions is declining, and set the question of whether employers' and employees' representation have become relics of a different era with no longer any purpose. Nevertheless, they point out that by adapting their organizational structure to the changing needs of business, employers and employees can be as "strong" and active as ever.

workers in the "cleaning services" sector made the best possible use of the platform economy in order to achieve their main goals.[28]

Resorting to the "tools" and "means" of digital technology will provide trade unions with the potential to connect with fellow workers from all over the world, and exchange new services, such as data mining and data sharing, in order to design effective strategies in the crowdworking and gig economy platforms. Workers in the informal economy have very often achieved the highest results through forging alliances with cooperatives and community-based organizations (Kabeer et al., 2013, p. 249 ff.).[29] For trade unions to achieve formalization and inclusion, they will have to adopt inclusive representation and organize strategies expanding membership to informal workers as well (Doellgast et al., 2018, p. 83 f.).[30]

The above remarks notwithstanding, collective representation does concern not only workers' representation but also employers' organizations. The above-mentioned paradigm of "Hilfr.dk" in Denmark is a successful example not only of workers' organization but of employers' organization, flexibility, and determination as well. Governments together with employers' and trade unions' organizations are parties in the "*tripartite negotiation*" model, responsible for the design and delivery of a social contract. Influential and powerful employers' organizations may provide for a balancing power deterring dominant market actors from determining economic policy on their own. As with trade unions above in the text, employers' organizations also need to adjust themselves to the advantages the platform economy offers and, thus, reinforce their capacity to represent a versatile set of business interests (Brandl & Lehr 2016, p. 932 ff.).

Through revitalizing collective representation, both workers' and employers', may turn out to be the most effective policy-makers in order to strengthen the merits of social dialogue and lead to a new social contract. The successful paradigms of the "tripartite" dialogue among all the involved stakeholders negotiating a social contract offer the parties the possibility to take into account the broader societal issues that digital transformation of works brings, and to reach a policy consensus.

Algorithmic Decision-Making Control and a "Human in Command" Approach to Technology

John MacCormick has defined the algorithm as a "*precise recipe that specifies the exact sequence of steps required to solve a problem*" (MacCormick, 2011, p. 3).[31]

[28] See the very successful case of the first, worldwide, collective agreement in digital platform economy, which was signed in Denmark by digital employer Hilfr.dk and one of the biggest and strongest trade unions in Denmark (Uni Global Union, 2018).

[29] The argument is for the importance of the "weapons of the organized" as opposed to the "weapons of the weak".

[30] See also Hayter and Lee (2018).

[31] For an excellent analysis on the relationship between algorithmic decision-making and the human factor, see also Christian and Griffith (2016). For further exposure to a critical and decon-

Since antiquity, algorithms have been originally designed and applied having as target the human behavior.[32] The initial motivation was the search for the best practices and most appropriate solutions against daily life's challenges. The mathematical and computational algorithms—applying inductive logic, and making decisions exhaustively analyzing all the possible choices before resorting to the right one regardless of time and effort—algorithmic predictive analytics, machine learning, and artificial intelligence, are all scientific conquests of the last 70 years.

By the term "decision" on the other hand, we mean any official or unofficial act of an authority, a private entity, or an individual that provides a determination or a ruling on an issue, and has a legal effect on those subjects targeted by this determination or ruling.[33] It further means that a particular attitude is taken toward a person or group of persons, and this attitude sets a degree of binding effect, which must be acted upon (Mendoza & Bygrave, 2017, p. 87). The automated decision-making is the process of making a decision exclusively by automated means without any human intervention. Such a decision is based exclusively on automated data processing without a person exercising any influence on the final outcome of the decision-making process. These kinds of decisions are allegedly based on factual data, as well as on digitally created profiles or inferred data.

The workplace environment has been one of the most susceptible environments to algorithmic decision-making. The cognitive limits of human processing power, as well as the inadequate human judgment and intuitive reasoning, have led enterprises to employ evaluative data analysis and predictive analytics for the employer to hire, evaluate, promote, degrade, or even dismiss an employee. Algorithmic decision-making can take place either in a fully automated form or complemented by human intervention.

A decision-making process is automated when the employer applies certain business rules, which have been generated and operated by business analytics. The key benefit of automated decision-making is that it can lead to quicker and more consistent decisions, particularly in cases where a very large volume of data needs to be analyzed and decisions made very quickly.[34] On the other hand, the drawbacks include decision-making processes that are invisible to individuals, uncontrolled processing of personal data,[35] no comprehension of how the process works, and the

structive analysis on the domination of automated decision-making on human life, see O'Neal (2016).

[32] Originally, the word "algorithm" comes from the name of the Persian mathematician Al-Khwarismi, who lived in the ninth century A.D. However, the first known mathematical algorithms go even further back in time, in the eighteenth century B.C. during the Sumerian civilization, near Babylon, where a clay tablet was found with algorithms used for factorization and finding square roots. See MacCormick (2011) and McFadden (2020).

[33] For an official definition of the term "decision", see EU Regulation 952/2013 laying down the Union Customs Code, Article 5(39).

[34] For a very concise and substantial overview of automated decision-making, see the relevant analysis of Information Commissioner's Office (ICO 2023).

[35] A very special, and one of the most challenging, section of the whole discourse on personal data protection deals with automated decision-making. Recitals 4, 24,38,60, 63, 71, 72, 73, and 91 and

cause of significant negative effects on the employees. The automated decision-making may also lead to discrimination to the extent it results from different types of biases arising from the training data, technical constraints, or societal or individual biases (European Parliament, 2019, p. 7 ff.).[36]

A "human in command" approach to algorithmic decision-making means that the decisions affecting the work and lives of employees within their workplace are taken not exclusively by sophisticated software programs but also by human involvement. Thus, an employee will be granted the possibility not to be subject to a decision, which may include recruiting, evaluation, promotion, degrading, or any other measure about his or her work performance, and which is founded exclusively on automated means, without any human intervention, and produces legal effects. An employee should have the right to demand human involvement, express his or her point of view, and assess the result of the algorithmic processing to which the decision relates. Furthermore, the application of algorithmic management and monitoring through cameras, smart devices, and motion detectors could be further scrutinized by an employee with the aim to protect his or her privacy, personal data, and dignity.

A "human in command" control of algorithmic decision-making also means the "understandability", "transparency", and "explainability" of the decision-making process, that is, the possibility of the employee to be familiar with the input and output of a decision-making process (European Parliament, 2019, pp. 25–26). The employee must have access to a visible, intelligible, and clearly legible version of the software algorithmic code already applied for an automated decision-process, or is intended to be applied for a future process. Only by having the full picture of how a specific decision has been taken concerning his/her working life will the employee be able to successfully challenge a decision before a court of law, take actions to get a decision, and confirm the employer's compliance with his/her contractual or legal obligations.

Article 22 of the General Data Protection Regulation (GDPR) are dedicated at the concept of automated decision-making and profiling in relation to personal data protection.

For a further explanation of these interrelated concepts, see Koukiadis (2019, p.127 ff.).

[36] However, these risks notwithstanding, the report of the EP also remarks that the risk of discrimination related to the use of automated decision-making should be compared with the risk of discrimination without the use of automated decision-making. Humans have their own sources of bias that can affect their decisions and, in some cases, these could be detected or avoided using automated decision-making (European Parliament, 2019, pp. 10–11).

One of the most recent, famous, biased automated algorithmic decision-making has been Amazon's recruitment algorithm. Amazon's hiring policy was based on an artificial intelligence program in order to give job candidates scores ranging from one to five stars. By the year 2015, the company realized that the employed automated decision-making system, when evaluating candidates for specific job positions, was biased against female candidates. That happened, because the applied algorithms were not gender neutral due to the fact that the patterns, with which the algorithm was working, came from men, reflecting thus the male dominance across the tech industry. Finally, the company abandoned this specific automated decision-making program.

In Lieu Of an Epilogue

Addressing the new dangers of evolving technologies on the dignity of the individual, and the new causes of exclusion from economic and social life should not be seen as questioning their enormous importance in increasing the individual's abilities and the well-being of the new society in general. On the contrary, we would argue that it is a necessary condition for maximizing its utilization for the benefit of society as a whole.

References

Brandl, B., & Lehr, A. (2016). The strange non-death of employer and business associations: An analysis of their representativeness and activities in Western European countries. *Economic and Industrial Democracy, 40*(4), 932–953. https://doi.org/10.1177/0143831X16669842

Bundesgerichtshof, decision III ZR 98/12, available at http://juris.bundesgerichtshof.de

Buxton, N. (Ed.). (2019). *Multistakeholderism: A critical look – Workshop report – Amsterdam* (pp. 1–16) https://www.tni.org/en/publication/multistakeholderism-a-critical-look

Caradaica, M. (2020). Digital divide in the European Union. In A. Taranu (Ed.), *Politics and knowledge: New trendsin social research, Proceedings of 7th ACADEMOS conference* (pp. 99–107) https://www.researchgate.net/publication/348365501_Digital_Divide_in_the_European_Union

Chemerinski, E. (2013). *Constitutional law* (4th ed.). Wolters Kluwer.

Christian, B., & Griffith, T. (2016). *Algorithms to live by: The computer science of human decisions*. Henry Holt & Co. https://kolegite.com/EE_library/books_and_lectures/%D0%9F%D1%80%D0%BE%D0%B3%D1%80%D0%B0%D0%BC%D0%B8%D1%80%D0%B0%D0%BD%D0%B5/algorithms-to-live-by-the-computer-science-of-tom--annas-archive--libgenrs-nf-3206012.pdf.

Conseil d'Etat, Annual report. (2014). *Fundamental rights in the Digital Age*. file:///C:/Users/User/Downloads/Fundamental%20rights%20in%20the%20Digital%20Age-1.pdf

Constitutional Council's decision no. 2009-580 DC of June 10th 2009. https://www.conseil-constitutionnel.fr/en/decision/2009/2009580DC.htm

Cooper, A., & Brown, I. (2015). Net neutrality: Discrimination, competition, and innovation in the UK and US. *AMC Transactions on Internet Technology (TOIT), 15*(2), 1–21. https://doi.org/10.1145/2700055

Council of Europe, Recommendation CM/Rec (2016)1 of the Committee of Ministers to member States on protecting and promoting the right to freedom of expression and the right to private life with regard to network neutrality. https://www.coe.int/en/web/freedom-expression/committee-of-ministers-adopted-texts/-/asset_publisher/aDXmrol0vvsU/content/recommendation-cm-rec-2016-1

Datta, A., Bhatia, V., Noll, J., & Dixit, S. (2019). Bridging the digital divide challenges in opening the digital world to the elderly, poor, and digitally illiterate. *IEEE Consumer Electronics Magazine, 8*(1), 78–81. https://doi.org/10.1109/MCE.2018.2867985. https://www.researchgate.net/publication/330061523_Bridging_the_Digital_Divide_Challenges_in_Opening_the_Digital_World_to_the_Elderly_Poor_and_Digitally_Illiterate

Decision No III ZR 98/12 of Bundesgerichtshof of 24 January 2013 (pp. 1–14). https://juris.bundesgerichtshof.de/cgi-bin/rechtsprechung/document.py?Gericht=bgh&Art=en&nr=63259&pos=0&anz=1

Directive 2014/61/EU of the European Parliament and of the Council of 15 May 2014 on Measures to reduce the cost of deploying High-Speed Electronic Communications Networks, OJ L 155/1 of 23 May 2014. https://eur-lex.europa.eu/eli/dir/2014/61/oj/eng/pdf

Doellgast, V., Lillie, N., & Pulignano, V. (Eds.). (2018). *Reconstructing solidarity: Labour unions, precarious work, and the politics of institutional change in Europe*. Oxford University Press.

Elliot, M. (2018). *Out of the maze: Building digitally inclusive communities*. The Workshop Wellington Publ.. https://internetnz.nz/assets/Archives/out-of-the-maze.pdf

European Commission. (2013). EU Guidelines for the application of State aid rules in relation to the rapid deployment of broadband networks, OJC 25/01 of 26 January 2013. https://eur-lex.europa.eu/LexUriServ/LexUriServ.do?uri=OJ:C:2013:025:0001:0026:EN:PDF

European Commission. (2016). *Communication from the commission to the European Parliament, The Council, The European Economic and Social Committee and the Committee of the Regions. A digital single market strategy for Europe*. https://eur-lex.europa.eu/legal-content/EN/TXT/?uri=celex%3A52015DC0192

European Commission. (2019). *Bridging the digital divide for a more inclusive Europe*. https://home-affairs.ec.europa.eu/publication/bridging-digital-divide-more-inclusive-europe_en

European Commission. (2021a). *Europe's digital decade: Digital targets for 2030*. https://commission.europa.eu/strategy-and-policy/priorities-2019-2024/europe-fit-digital-age/europes-digital-decade-digital-targets-2030_en

European Commission. (2021b). *Shaping Europe's digital future. The digital compass*. https://digital-strategy.ec.europa.eu

European Commission. (2021c). Communication from the Commission to the European Parliament, the Council, the European Economic and Social Committee and the Committee of the Regions. 2030 digital compass: The European way for the Digital Decade, Doc 118 final. https://eur-lex.europa.eu/legal-content/en/TXT/?uri=CELEX%3A52021DC0118

European Commission Memo, State aid: Commission adopts new General Block Exemption Regulation (GBER), 21 May 2014. https://ec.europa.eu/commission/presscorner/detail/en/MEMO_14_369

European Parliament. (2015). *Bridging the digital divide in EU*. https://www.europarl.europa.eu/RegData/etudes/BRIE/2015/573884/EPRS_BRI(2015)573884_EN.pdf

European Parliament. (2019). *Understanding algorithmic decision-making: Opportunities and challenges*. Study Panel for the Future of Science and Technology. https://www.europarl.europa.eu/RegData/etudes/STUD/2019/624261/EPRS_STU(2019)624261_EN.pdf

Foxwell, A. (2022). *The case for workplace digital inclusion for corporate social responsibility*. https://www.readspeaker.com/blog/impact-of-digital-inclusivity/

Ghandi, R. (2020). *Remote working and the digital divide*. https://www.datacenterdynamics.com/en/opinions/remote-working-and-digital-divide/

Global Workplace Analytics. (2021, June). *Latest work-at-home/telecommuting/mobile work/remote work statistics*. https://globalworkplaceanalytics.com/telecommuting-statistics

Graham, M., & Dutton, W. H. (Eds.). (2019). *Society and the Internet: How networks of information and communication are changing our lives* (2nd ed.). Oxford University Press.

Grundke, R., Marcolin, L., Bao, T.L., & Squicciaring, M. (2018). Which skills for the digital era?: Returns to skills analysis. *OECD science, technology and industry working papers*, no. 2018/09. https://www.oecd-ilibrary.org/docserver/9a9479b5-en.pdf?expires=1720098686&id=id&accname=guest&checksum=7C6BF768E5AE3965831EA2D3973095F6

Hayter, S., & Lee, C.-H. (Eds.). (2018). *Industrial relations in emerging economies: The quest for inclusive development*. Edward Elgar & ILO.

Hidalgoa, A., Gabalyb, S., Alonsoa, G. M., & Urueña, A. (2020). The digital divide in light of sustainable development: An approach through advanced machine learning techniques, 150. *Technological Forecasting and Social Change, 150*, 1–7. https://doi.org/10.1016/j.techfore.2019.119754. https://www.sciencedirect.com/science/article/abs/pii/S0040162519310637?via%3Dihub

ILO/Global Commission on the Future of Work. (2019). *Work for a brighter future*. file:///C:/Users/User/Downloads/wcms_662410.pdf

Information Commissioner's Office. (2023). *What is automated individual decision-making and profiling?* https://ico.org.uk/for-organisations/uk-gdpr-guidance-and-resources/

individual-rights/automated-decision-making-and-profiling/what-is-automated-individual-decision-making-and-profiling/

International Covenant on Civil and Political Rights. (1966). https://www.ohchr.org/en/instruments-mechanisms/instruments/international-covenant-civil-and-political-rights

International Mechanisms For Promoting Freedom Of Expression. (2011). JOINT DECLARATION ON FREEDOM OF EXPRESSION AND THE INTERNET by the United Nations (UN) Special Rapporteur on Freedom of Opinion and Expression, the OSCE Representative on Freedom of the Media, and the OAS Special Rapporteur on Freedom of Expression. https://www.osce.org/files/f/documents/8/f/39838.pdf

Internet Governance. (2016). *Internet governance – Why the multistakeholder approach works*. https://www.internetsociety.org/resources/doc/2016/internet-governance-why-the-multistakeholder-approach-works/

Kabeer, N., Milward, K., & Sudarshan, R. (2013). Organising women workers in the informal economy. *Gender and Development, 21*(2), 249–263. https://doi.org/10.1080/13552074.2013.802145

Karr, T. (2018). *Net neutrality violations: A brief history*. https://www.congress.gov/116/meeting/house/108845/documents/HHRG-116-IF16-20190207-SD002.pdf

Koukiadis, D. (2019). The employee as a subject of personal data according to the General Data Protection Regulation. *Sakkoulas Athina-Thessaloniki*. (in Greek).

Latendre, D. (2017). *How your digital workplace can help bridge the digital divide*. https://www.cmswire.com/digital-workplace/how-your-digital-workplace-can-help-bridge-the-digital-divide/

Leiner, B. M., Cerf, V. G., Clark, D. D., Kahn, R. E., Kleinrock, L., Lynch, D. C., Postel, J., Roberts, L. G., & Wolff, S. S. (1997). A brief history of internet, internet society. *Communications of the ACM, 40*(2), 102–108. https://doi.org/10.1145/253671.253741. https://www.researchgate.net/publication/234792183_The_Past_and_Future_History_of_the_Internet

Levitas, R., Pantazis, C., Fahmy, E., Gordon, D., Lloyd, E., & Patsios, D. (2007). *The multi-dimensional analysis of social exclusion, project report*. University of Bristol. https://www.researchgate.net/publication/267222796_The_Multi-Dimensional_Analysis_of_Social_Exclusion

MacCormick, J. (2011). *Nine algorithms that changed the future: The ingenious ideas that drive today's computers*. Princeton University Press.

Martin, C., Hope, S., & Zubairi, S. (2016). *The role of digital exclusion in social exclusion*. Ipsos MORI Scotland-Carnegie UK Trust. https://d1ssu070pg2v9i.cloudfront.net/pex/pex_carnegie2021/2016/09/06154120/LOW-2697-CUKT-Digital-Participation-Report-REVISE.pdf

McFadden, C. (2020). *The origin of algorithms we use every single day*. https://interestingengineering.com/innovation/origin-algorithms-use-every-day

Mendoza, I., & Bygrave, L.A. (2017). The right not to be subject to automated decisions based on profiling. *University of Oslo-faculty of law legal studies research paper series no. 2017–20*. https://doi.org/10.1007/978-3-319-64955-9_4

Murray, A. (2019). *Information technology law*. Oxford University Press.

Nybom, M. (2018). Intergenerational mobility: A dream deferred? *ILO research paper no. 7*. https://atlasoportunidades.fundacionfelipegonzalez.cotec.es/wp-content/uploads/2020/07/Intergenerational-mobility-a-dream-deferred.pdf

O'Neal, C. (2016). *Weapons of math destruction: How big data increases inequality and threatens democracy*. Crown Publishing.

OECD. (2019). Preparing for the changing nature of work in the digital era. *OECD going digital policy note*. https://policycommons.net/artifacts/3796533/preparing-for-the-changing-nature-of-work-in-the-digital-era/4602361/

Regulation (EU) 2015/2120 of the European Parliament and of the Council of 25 November 2015 laying down measures concerning open internet access and amending Directive 2002/22/EC on universal service and users' rights relating to electronic communications networks and services, OJ L 310, of 26.11.2015. https://eur-lex.europa.eu/legal-content/EN/TXT/PDF/?uri=CELEX:32015R2120

Regulation (EU) No 531/2012 of the European Parliament and of the Council of 13.06.2012 on roaming on public mobile communications networks within the Union, OJ L 172, of 30.06.2012. https://eur-lex.europa.eu/legal-content/EN/TXT/PDF/?uri=CELEX:32012R0531

Regulation (EU) No 952/2013 of the European Parliament and of the Council of 9 October 2013 laying down the Union Customs Code, OJ L 269, of 10.10.2013. https://eur-lex.europa.eu/legal-content/EN/TXT/PDF/?uri=CELEX:32013R0952

Sanders, R. (2020). Digital inclusion, exclusion and participation. *ESSS Outline*. https://www.iriss.org.uk/sites/default/files/2020-04/iriss_esss_outline_digital_inclusion_09042020_0.pdf

Schejter, A., Harush, O. B., & Tirosh, N. (2015). Re-theorizing the "digital divide": Identifying dimensions of social exclusion in contemporary media technologies. In *FACE conference: European media policy 2015: New contexts, new approaches*. https://eprints.qut.edu.au/86701/

Sproul, G., & Brown, M. (2012). *Net neutrality: Body of European regulators for electronic communications publishes final report and new consultations on net neutrality*. https://www.lexology.com/library/detail.aspx?g=08b9a3f5-b753-4ecb-b6eb-5ca8d1f89358

Uni Global Union. (2018). *World's first collective agreement between platform company and trade union in Denmark*. https://uniglobalunion.org/news/3f-reaches-groundbreaking-collective-agreement-with-platform-company-hilfr/

UNISYS. (2021). *The new digital workplace divide*. https://mma.prnewswire.com/media/711653/Unisys_Corporation.pdf

United Nations Declaration of Human Rights. https://www.un.org/sites/un2.un.org/files/2021/03/udhr.pdf

United Nations General Assembly – Oral Revisions of 30 June 2016. https://www.article19.org/data/files/Internet_Statement_Adopted.pdf

Van Dijk, J. A. G. M. (2012). The evolution of the digital divide the digital divide turns to inequality of skills and usage. In *Digital enlightenment yearbook 2012* (pp. 57–75). https://doi.org/10.3233/978-1-61499-057-4-57. https://www.utwente.nl/en/bms/vandijk/news/The%20Evolution%20of%20the%20Digital%20Divide/Evolution%20of%20the%20Digital%20Divide%20Digital%20Enlightment%20Yearbook%202012.pdf

Van Dijk, J. A. G. M. (2017). Digital divide: Impact of access. In P. Rössler et al. (Eds.), *The international encyclopedia of media effects* (pp. 1–11). John Wiley & Sons. https://www.utwente.nl/en/bms/vandijk/publications/digital_divide_impact_access.pdf

Wu, T. (2003). Network neutrality, broadband discrimination. *Journal of Telecommunications and High Technology Law, 2*, 141–179. https://papers.ssrn.com/sol3/papers.cfm?abstract_id=388863

European Court of Human Rights (ECtHR) Judgments

Ahmet Yildirim v. Turkey, judgment of 18 December 2012. https://hudoc.echr.coe.int/eng#{%22itemid%22:[%22001-115705%22]}

Akdeniz v. Turkey, judgment of 4 May 2021. https://hudoc.echr.coe.int/fre#{%22itemid%22:[%22002-13243%22]}

Cengiz and Others v. Turkey, judgment of 1 December 2015. https://hudoc.echr.coe.int/eng#{%22itemid%22:[%22001-159188%22]}

Delfi AS v. Estonia [GC], judgment of 10 October 2013. https://hudoc.echr.coe.int/fre#{%22itemid%22:[%22002-8960%22]}

Times Newspapers Ltd v. the United Kingdom, judgment of 10 March 2009. https://hudoc.echr.coe.int/eng#{%22itemid%22:[%22002-1623%22]}

Vladimir Kharitonov v. Russia, Flavus and Others v. Russia, Bulgakov v. Russia and Engels v. Russia, judgments of 23 June 2020. file:///C:/Users/User/Downloads/Judgment%20Kharitonov%20v.%20Russia%20and%20three%20other%20applications%20-%20official%20decisions%20to%20block%20websites.pdf

The manufacturer's authorised representative in the EU is Springer Nature Customer Service Centre GmbH, Europaplatz 3, 69115 Heidelberg, Germany. If you have any concerns regarding our products, please contact ProductSafety@springernature.com

Printed and bound by CPI Group (UK) Ltd, Croydon, CR0 4YY

30/09/2026

02225584-0010